7/16/15
$67.00

ISSN 1554-4397

ELECTRONIC AMERICA

Stephen Meyer

INFORMATION PLUS® REFERENCE SERIES
Formerly Published by Information Plus, Wylie, Texas

GALE
CENGAGE Learning·

Farmington Hills, Mich • San Francisco • New York • Waterville, Maine
Meriden, Conn • Mason, Ohio • Chicago

Electronic America

Stephen Meyer

Kepos Media, Inc.: Steven Long and
Janice Jorgensen, Series Editors

Project Editors: Tracie Moy, Laura Avery

Rights Acquisition and Management: Ashley M.
Maynard

Composition: Evi Abou-El-Seoud, Mary Beth
Trimper

Manufacturing: Rita Wimberley

For product information and technology assistance, contact us at
Gale Customer Support, 1-800-877-4253.
For permission to use material from this text or product,
submit all requests online at **www.cengage.com/permissions.**
Further permissions questions can be e-mailed to
permissionrequest@cengage.com

Cover photograph: © 2121fisher/Shutterstock.com.

While every effort has been made to ensure the reliability of the information presented
in this publication, Gale, a part of Cengage Learning, does not guarantee the accuracy of
the data contained herein. Gale accepts no payment for listing; and inclusion in the
publication of any organization, agency, institution, publication, service, or individual does
not imply endorsement of the editors or publisher. Errors brought to the attention of the
publisher and verified to the satisfaction of the publisher will be corrected in future
editions.

Gale
27500 Drake Rd.
Farmington Hills, MI 48331-3535

ISBN-13: 978-0-7876-5103-9 (set)
ISBN-13: 978-1-57302-638-3

ISSN 1554-4397

This title is also available as an e-book.
ISBN-13: 978-1-57302-676-5 (set)
Contact your Gale sales representative for ordering information.

Printed in the United States of America
1 2 3 4 5   19 18 17 16 15

TABLE OF CONTENTS

advances in online communication are examined, as are cyberbullying, augmented reality, and the gamification of everyday life. The integration of electronics and information technologies into American vehicles and household appliances and utilities is also studied, as are developments in robotics.

PREFACE

Electronic America is part of the *Information Plus Reference Series*. The purpose of each volume of the series is to present the latest facts on a topic of pressing concern in modern American life. These topics include the most controversial and studied social issues of the 21st century: abortion, capital punishment, crime, the environment, gambling, health care, immigration, national security, race and ethnicity, social welfare, women, youth, and many more. Even though this series is written especially for high school and undergraduate students, it is an excellent resource for anyone in need of factual information on current affairs.

By presenting the facts, it is the intention of Gale, Cengage Learning, to provide its readers with everything they need to reach an informed opinion on current issues. To that end, there is a particular emphasis in this series on the presentation of scientific studies, surveys, and statistics. These data are generally presented in the form of tables, charts, and other graphics placed within the text of each book. Every graphic is directly referred to and carefully explained in the text. The source of each graphic is presented within the graphic itself. The data used in these graphics are drawn from the most reputable and reliable sources, such as from the various branches of the U.S. government and from private organizations and associations. Every effort has been made to secure the most recent information available. Readers should bear in mind that many major studies take years to conduct and that additional years often pass before the data from these studies are made available to the public. Therefore, in many cases the most recent information available in 2015 is dated from 2012 or 2013. Older statistics are sometimes presented as well, if they are landmark studies or of particular interest and no more-recent information exists.

Although statistics are a major focus of the *Information Plus Reference Series*, they are by no means its only content. Each book also presents the widely held positions and important ideas that shape how the book's subject is discussed in the United States. These positions are explained in detail and, where possible, in the words of their proponents. Some of the other material to be found in these books includes historical background, descriptions of major events related to the subject, relevant laws and court cases, and examples of how these issues play out in American life. Some books also feature primary documents or have pro and con debate sections that provide the words and opinions of prominent Americans on both sides of a controversial topic. All material is presented in an evenhanded and unbiased manner; readers will never be encouraged to accept one view of an issue over another.

HOW TO USE THIS BOOK

During the late 20th and early 21st centuries the United States was transformed by the rapid development and adoption of new electronic devices, software programs, and other technologies. Computers, cell phones, CD-ROMs, cable television, e-mail, MP3s, DVDs, viruses, robots, spam, peer-to-peer networks, and massively multiplayer online role-playing games were in limited use in 1980, if they existed at all. By 2015 they had all become common, and many were ubiquitous. Their effect on the United States, and on the world, has been profound. New types of industries developed to produce and make use of these technologies. Existing businesses used them to become more efficient. New technologies also opened the door to new kinds of crime and criminals, and with them a need for changes in U.S. government and law enforcement. Last but not least, average Americans found that these technologies made it increasingly easy for them to communicate and find information, as well as to enjoy themselves, to be frustrated, or even to be victimized, in new and different ways.

Electronic America consists of nine chapters and three appendixes. Each chapter is devoted to a particular aspect of the changes in the United States brought about by high technology and its applications. For a summary of the information that is covered in each chapter, please see the synopses that are provided in the Table of Contents. Chapters generally begin with an overview of the basic facts and background information on the chapter's topic, then proceed to examine subtopics of particular interest. For example, Chapter 7: Information Technology and Government begins with an examination of the ways in which all levels of government have adopted Internet technologies since the 1990s. The chapter includes a discussion of federal laws and initiatives aimed at increasing the electronic capabilities of government agencies, both to improve operational efficiency and to cut down on waste, as with the Government Paperwork Elimination Act of 1998. Chapter 7 also considers the role of government in regulating the Internet, with a particular focus on the debate surrounding the issue of net neutrality. The chapter provides an overview of efforts by the National Security Agency, the Federal Bureau of Investigation, and other government agencies to monitor the transmission of electronic information in the interest of national security, and discusses opposition to these programs on the part of privacy advocates and other groups. Chapter 7 also investigates the ways in which information technology has transformed how Americans participate in the political process from expressing opinions online to high-tech voting procedures. The chapter concludes with a description of two government initiatives, the 511 Travel Information System and the National Do Not Call Registry, aimed at improving everyday life for Americans. Readers can find their way through a chapter by looking for the section and subsection headings, which are clearly set off from the text. They can also refer to the book's extensive Index, if they already know what they are looking for.

Statistical Information

The tables and figures featured throughout *Electronic America* will be of particular use to readers in learning about this topic. These tables and figures represent an extensive collection of the most recent and valuable statistics on new technology and its impact on the United States. For example, graphics cover how many Americans use the Internet, how they use it, and how usage differs depending on demographic characteristics; enrollment in distance learning programs by type of institution; and the number of Americans victimized by identity theft. Gale, Cengage Learning, believes that making this information available to readers is the most important way to fulfill the goal of this book: to help readers understand the issues and controversies surrounding new technologies in the United States and reach their own conclusions.

Each table or figure has a unique identifier appearing above it, for ease of identification and reference. Titles for the tables and figures explain their purpose. At the end of each table or figure, the original source of the data is provided.

To help readers understand these often complicated statistics, all tables and figures are explained in the text. References in the text direct readers to the relevant statistics. Furthermore, the contents of all tables and figures are fully indexed. Please see the opening section of the Index at the back of this volume for a description of how to find tables and figures within it.

Appendixes

Besides the main body text and images, *Electronic America* has three appendixes. The first is the Important Names and Addresses directory. Here, readers will find contact information for a number of government and private organizations that can provide further information on computers and high technology. The second appendix is the Resources section, which can also assist readers in conducting their own research. In this section, the author and editors of *Electronic America* describe some of the sources that were most useful during the compilation of this book. The final appendix is the Index. It has been greatly expanded from previous editions and should make it even easier to find specific topics in this book.

COMMENTS AND SUGGESTIONS

The editors of the *Information Plus Reference Series* welcome your feedback on *Electronic America*. Please direct all correspondence to:

Editors
Information Plus Reference Series
27500 Drake Rd.
Farmington Hills, MI 48331-3535

CHAPTER 1
THE INTERNET AND THE ELECTRONIC AGE

The Internet was a Cold War military project. It was designed for purposes of military communication in a United States devastated by a Soviet nuclear strike. . . . When I look at the Internet—that paragon of cyberspace today—I see something astounding and delightful. It's as if some grim fallout shelter had burst open and a full-scale Mardi Gras parade had come out.

—Bruce Sterling, in "Literary Freeware—Not for Commercial Use" (with William Gibson), *Speeches to the National Academy of Sciences Convocation on Technology and Education*, Washington, D.C., May 10, 1993

Since the 1980s electronics and communications technologies have become integrated into nearly every aspect of American life, transforming the ways in which people shop, work, learn, and communicate with one another. The speed with which these new technologies have proliferated through U.S. homes and offices is nothing short of astounding. Cell phones, which were once novelties occupying the front seat of a car, can now be found in the pockets of many 10-year-olds. Computers and the Internet, once accessible only to those who worked in government installations, large corporations, and academic institutions, are present in most American homes.

Jennifer Cheeseman Day, Alex Janus, and Jessica Davis report in *Computer and Internet Use in the United States: 2003* (October 2005, http://www.census.gov/prod/2005pubs/p23-208.pdf) that in 1984 only 8.2% of U.S. households had computers. By 2003 the number of homes with computers had increased to 61.8%. The Census Bureau (January 2014, http://www.census.gov/hhes/computer/files/2012/table4.xls) indicates that by 2012, 78.9% of American households (96.3 million out of 122 million) owned some form of personal computer (PC). Meanwhile, the number of Americans who used the Internet also grew sharply during this period. Figure 1.1 shows the steady increase in Internet use among adults between 1995 and 2013. Only 14% of American adults used the Internet in 1995; by September 2013 that figure

had risen to 86%. According to Internet Live Stats in "Internet Users by Country (2014)" (July 1, 2014, http://www.internetlivestats.com/internet-users-by-country), an estimated 279.8 million Americans had access to the Internet as of June 2014.

Since its inception, the Internet has reduced the time needed to complete dozens of mundane tasks, such as finding directions, writing personal correspondence, and conducting financial transactions. Because of these conveniences, online Americans continue to use the Internet more each year. Figure 1.2 indicates shifts in Internet usage between 2000 and 2013. The proportion of Internet users rose substantially during this period, from half of all adults in 2000 to 86% of all adults in 2013. The percentage of Internet users 65 years of age and older also rose dramatically over this span, from only 14% in 2000 to 59% in 2013.

Even though the development of technology has affected most people in a positive way, significant pitfalls have developed as well. Typically, underprivileged groups have been left at a bigger disadvantage because the most innovative technologies have been embraced faster by the well-educated and wealthy. The Internet and computer databases have also made fraud much easier. The number of cases of identity theft in the United States has skyrocketed. Each day thieves steal hundreds, if not thousands, of Social Security and credit card numbers by simply surfing the Internet or by sending out fraudulent e-mails. The Federal Trade Commission (FTC) reports in "FTC Announces Top National Consumer Complaints for 2013" (February 27, 2014, http://www.ftc.gov/news-events/press-releases/2014/02/ftc-announces-top-national-consumer-complaints-2013) that it received 290,056 identity theft complaints in 2013. This figure accounted for 14% of the roughly 2.1 million total consumer complaints the FTC received that year,

FIGURE 1.1

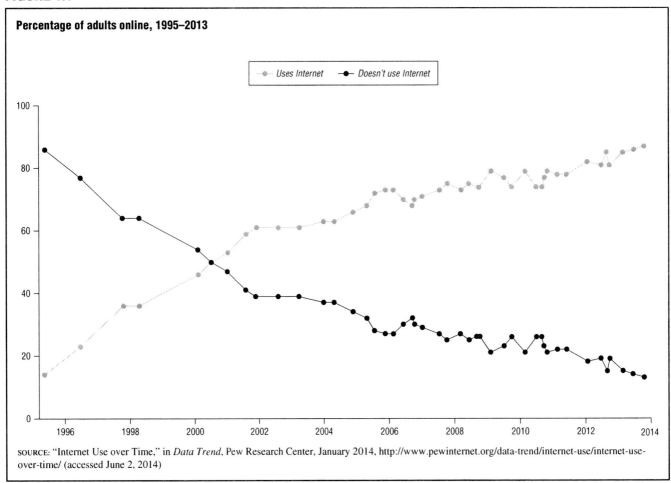

Percentage of adults online, 1995–2013

Uses Internet   Doesn't use Internet

SOURCE: "Internet Use over Time," in *Data Trend*, Pew Research Center, January 2014, http://www.pewinternet.org/data-trend/internet-use/internet-use-over-time/ (accessed June 2, 2014)

FIGURE 1.2

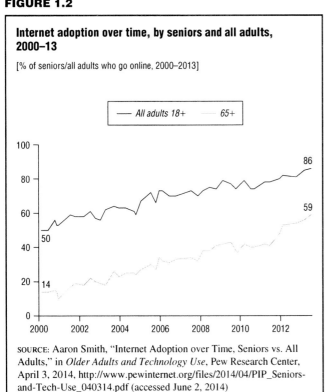

Internet adoption over time, by seniors and all adults, 2000–13

[% of seniors/all adults who go online, 2000–2013]

All adults 18+   65+

SOURCE: Aaron Smith, "Internet Adoption over Time, Seniors vs. All Adults," in *Older Adults and Technology Use*, Pew Research Center, April 3, 2014, http://www.pewinternet.org/files/2014/04/PIP_Seniors-and-Tech-Use_040314.pdf (accessed June 2, 2014)

the most of any type of complaint. (An extended discussion of technology and crime is presented in Chapter 4.)

Another problem that continues to confront owners of computers and mobile devices is the number of viruses, worms, botnets, and Trojan horses making their way around the Internet. Viruses are programs or codes that "infect" computers by secretly infiltrating systems and interfering with proper functioning; worms are destructive codes that copy themselves over and over on a computer or network; robot networks, or botnets, are groups of computers that have been invaded by a malignant software that is controlled by a hacker or other outside source, effectively transforming the infected computers into "zombies" or "drones"; and Trojan horses are software programs or files that seem legitimate yet act maliciously on the computer or secretly provide access to information contained on the computer to outsiders. Collectively, these invasive programs are often referred to as malicious software, or malware. Not only do viruses, worms, and hackers cost time and energy from their victims, but they also put valuable information at risk. Kaspersky Lab, a leading antivirus software firm, reports in "IT Threat Evolution: Q1 2014" (April 2014, https://www.securelist.com/en/downloads/vlpdfs/q1-it-threats-en.pdf) that it "detected and neutralized" 1.1 billion online security threats during the first quarter of 2014.

In addition, mobile phones are also susceptible to virus attacks. In October 2004 the first mobile phone virus was detected in Southeast Asia. The virus, known as Cabir, infected mobile phone software and could be used to steal information from mobile phone address books. Since that time other viruses have been identified that target mobile devices, particularly smartphones and those with enhanced web and data capabilities. In some cases the viruses caused mobile phones to send mass text messages using a service that charged the sender a high fee for each message. Others erased stored data, disabled functions, or automatically routed phone calls through high-priced communications providers.

Despite such difficulties, technological innovation showed no sign of slowing down. In 2014 more and more Americans were carrying powerful portable computers such as an Android, iPhone, BlackBerry, or other hand-held device. As Mark Walsh reports in "Android Ends 2013 as Top U.S. Smartphone Platform" (MediaPost .com, February 4, 2014), Android was the nation's leading smartphone platform in December 2013, accounting for just over half (51.5%) of the U.S. market, followed by Apple's iOS platform (41.8%), BlackBerry (3.4%), Microsoft's Windows Phone (3.1%), and Symbian (0.2%). Meanwhile, trends toward wireless fidelity (Wi-Fi) connectivity, touch-screen functioning, voice-recognition software, and alternative power sources continued. One development expected to become common-place is technology through which price tags at the grocery store will give off radio signals that automatically register the merchandise on a credit card when the buyer leaves the market. Meanwhile, robotic appliances are becoming available that automate some of the more tedious domestic chores, including lawn mowing, vacuuming, and cleaning gutters.

HISTORY OF THE INTERNET

At the center of the information technology and electronics revolution lies the Internet. Many believe the Internet had its origins on October 4, 1957, when the Soviet Union launched the *Sputnik 1* satellite into orbit with a military rocket. The news of *Sputnik 1*, a beeping steel sphere a little bigger in diameter than a basketball, sent the U.S. military into a frenzy. At the time, the United States and the Soviet Union were engaged in what became known as the Cold War (1947–1991), a period of sustained military buildup and ideological conflict. Americans were fearful that Soviet satellite technology could be used to spy on the United States or to launch missile attacks on U.S. targets. Technological superiority, the one advantage the United States thought it had over the Soviets, now seemed tenuous.

In response, the U.S. government formed the Advanced Research Projects Agency (ARPA) within the U.S. Department of Defense in 1958. The central mission of this new agency was to develop state-of-the-art technology to stay well ahead of the Soviet Union. One of the first projects on ARPA's agenda was to create a system by which ARPA operational bases could communicate with one another and their contractors via computer. The agency wanted the system to be resilient enough to survive a nuclear attack.

Joseph Carl Robnett Licklider (1915–1990), a scientist at the Massachusetts Institute of Technology (MIT), was appointed to oversee the computer research program at ARPA in 1962. He conferred with some of the leading researchers in networking technology at the time, including Leonard Kleinrock (1934–), then an MIT graduate student, and Lawrence Roberts (1937–). Their solution, first published in 1967, was a nationwide network of ARPA computers known as ARPANET. In this network a user on any computer terminal in the network would be able to send a message to multiple users at other computer terminals. If any one computer was knocked out in a nuclear attack, the remaining stations could still communicate with each other.

For this network to function properly, the researchers established that the computers would first have to break down information into discrete packets. These packets were then to be sent along high-speed phone lines and reassembled upon reaching their destination at another computer. At the time, telephone conversations traveled across dedicated telephone wires in one long stream of data from one user to another like a single train traveling along a track. Even though this was adequate for chatting with far-off relatives, it did not work well when one computer attempted to send data to several other computers on the network. By packetizing data, the information became more flexible. Much like cars on a highway, the packets could be routed easily to multiple computers. If one packet of information went bad during transmission, it did not disrupt the stream of data transmitting from one computer to another and could easily be resent. Packets could also carry information about themselves and where they were going, they could be compressed for speed, and they could be encrypted for security purposes.

After two years of engineering the parts needed for ARPANET, ARPA researchers set up the first four computer centers in the network. They were located at the University of California, Los Angeles (UCLA); Stanford Research Institute; the University of California, Santa Barbara; and the University of Utah. Between these nodes, AT&T had laid down telephone lines that were capable of transmitting data at 50 kilobytes per second. (Memory circuits are measured according to the base-two, or binary, number system. A kilobyte is equal to

2^{10} bytes, or 1,024 bytes.) The first test of the system commenced on October 29, 1969, when Charles S. Kline (1948–) at UCLA tried logging into the Stanford system. On encountering the letter *g* in the word *login*, the system crashed. Recalling the event 40 years later in the article "Internet a Teenager at 40" (SMH.com, October 26, 2009), Kleinrock noted, "So, the first message was 'Lo' as in 'Lo and behold.' ... We couldn't have a better, more succinct first message."

A Loose Affiliation of Networks

Eventually, the researchers at UCLA worked out the problems, and two years later ARPANET was fully functional and had 15 nodes linked to it. Figure 1.3 shows ARPANET in September 1971. Throughout the early and mid-1970s the development of networking technologies progressed slowly. Raymond Tomlinson (1941–) invented the first e-mail program in 1971 to send typed messages across the network, and a year later the first computer-to-computer chat took place at UCLA. In 1973 Robert Metcalfe (1946–) of Xerox Corporation developed Ethernet to connect computers and printers in a large organization. Three years later at AT&T Bell Labs, Michael E. Lesk (1945–) put together the program Unix-to-Unix-copy protocol (UUCP) that allowed Unix computers, which were typically used by academics, to communicate with one another over the phone lines.

Technological developments such as these allowed people and organizations that were not connected into ARPANET to set up networks of their own by the early 1980s. One of the largest of these was the Computer Science Network, which was established by a number of universities with help from the National Science Foundation (NSF). These universities recognized the advantages in resource sharing and communication that ARPANET provided the Ivy League and West Coast schools and

FIGURE 1.3

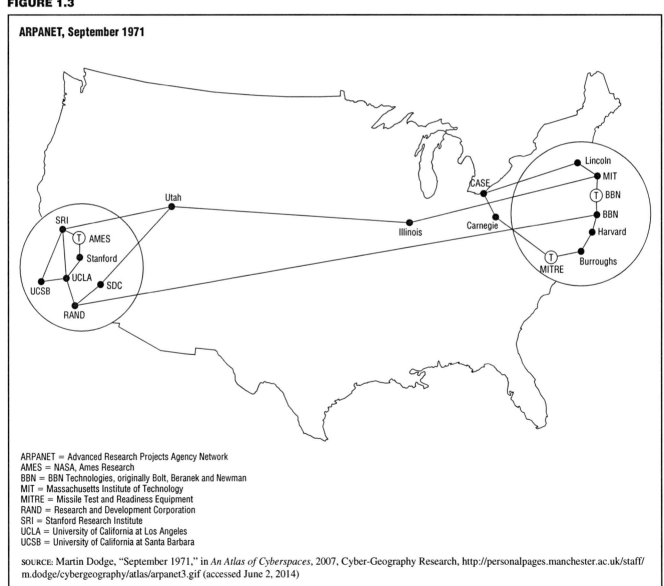

ARPANET, September 1971

ARPANET = Advanced Research Projects Agency Network
AMES = NASA, Ames Research
BBN = BBN Technologies, originally Bolt, Beranek and Newman
MIT = Massachusetts Institute of Technology
MITRE = Missile Test and Readiness Equipment
RAND = Research and Development Corporation
SRI = Stanford Research Institute
UCLA = University of California at Los Angeles
UCSB = University of California at Santa Barbara

SOURCE: Martin Dodge, "September 1971," in *An Atlas of Cyberspaces*, 2007, Cyber-Geography Research, http://personalpages.manchester.ac.uk/staff/m.dodge/cybergeography/atlas/arpanet3.gif (accessed June 2, 2014)

wanted to develop similar capabilities. Another network known as Usenet was initially established to connect researchers at Duke University and the University of North Carolina, and it eventually spread throughout the country. The Because It's Time Network (BITNET) was formed to connect computers in the City University of New York system. Most of these smaller networks used standard telephone lines to operate. They were set up primarily to transfer scientific data, share computing resources, post items on bulletin boards, and provide e-mail.

One major problem was that these different networks could not readily communicate with one another. Each network used different methods to identify the computers within the network. A computer in one network could not recognize the computers in different networks, and information packets sent out from one network could not navigate the other networks. The situation would be analogous to a state in the United States having its own unique postal address system that no mail carriers outside of that state could understand.

During the 1970s the engineers Vinton Gray Cerf (1943–) and Robert E. Kahn (1938–) devised the Transmission Control Program and the Internet Protocol (TCP/IP). This suite of programs created a universal address system that could be installed on any existing network. Once installed, the machines on the network could recognize and send information to a machine on any other network, provided they also had TCP/IP. In 1983 ARPANET was split into military and civilian sections, both of which adopted TCP/IP. Many consider the adoption of TCP/IP by ARPANET to be the event that gave birth to the Internet. To this day, each machine on the Internet has a unique IP address that identifies that machine on a network. Servers typically have permanent IP numbers assigned to them, whereas most PCs are given a different number by an Internet service provider (ISP) each time the user begins a new session.

In the year the Internet was born, home computing was still in its infancy. The Commodore 64 had just made its debut, sporting a 1 megahertz (or 1 million hertz, a unit used to measure computer processing speeds) microprocessor and 64 kilobytes of random access memory. Relatively few people owned home computers in 1983. Most of them used their machines for basic business applications, such as word processing and spreadsheets, and for playing games. Home users did not have direct access to the Internet. Low-speed modems were widely available by the mid- to late 1980s, and people could dial directly into servers that were owned by CompuServe, Quantum Computer Services (later to be renamed America Online and then simply AOL), and Prodigy. These services allowed people to post messages, go into chat rooms, play games, or send and receive e-mail. However, these services were not linked to the Internet, and e-mails could be sent only among people subscribing to the same service.

The only people who could surf the Internet freely were those who had access to powerful mainframe computers, most of which were owned by universities, the government, and large corporations. The Internet was an uninviting place during the early 1980s. Users connecting to the Internet had to know exactly what they were looking for to get it. To reach another computer or server on the Internet, users had to key in the IP address for that computer, which consisted of a string of up to 12 numbers, such as 69.32.146.63. To navigate a server, a computer operator had to type in computer code on a prompt line and sift through cryptic directories. There were no web browsers, colorful Internet pages, or search engines.

By 1984 the dedicated name server (DNS), developed by the University of Wisconsin, was introduced, making the Internet somewhat more user-friendly. A DNS is a computer server on the Internet with a database that pairs domain names with IP addresses, giving people the ability to type in a name instead of a multidigit number to reach an Internet destination. Modern Internet browsers contact one of many DNSs each time an address, such as http://www.google.com, is entered into the address bar. Most ISPs have a DNS that contains the names and IP address numbers of widely used sites. Once the browser makes the request from a DNS, the name server sends back the IP address number, which for Google is 209.85.225.105. The Internet browser then uses this IP address number to access the site (Google in this case).

Along with these name servers, a dedicated name system was also put into place so that no two names would be the same. Domain names with a minimum of two levels were established. The top level designated the country or economic sector a computer was in (e.g., .gov or .com), and a unique second-level domain name designated the organization itself (e.g., National Aeronautics and Space Administration [NASA] or Google). The Information Sciences Institute was put in charge of managing the root DNS in 1985 for all domains to make sure that no two were alike and to track who was registered for what name. Some of the first domain names to be registered were symbolics.com, mit.edu, think.com, and berkeley.edu.

A Major Expansion during the Mid-1980s

In 1986 Internet use expanded exponentially when the NSF installed new supercomputers and a new backbone for the U.S. Internet service, giving rise to the NSFNet. By 2008 ISPs and cable companies typically had their own backbones, which were all tied into one another. When a home user connects to the Internet via phone, digital subscriber line, satellite link, or cable, the signal is directed to a bank of modems called a point of presence (POP) that is owned by the service provider. (See Figure 1.4.) Each POP from each service provider,

FIGURE 1.4

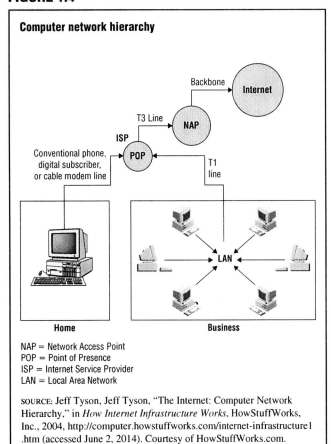

Computer network hierarchy

NAP = Network Access Point
POP = Point of Presence
ISP = Internet Service Provider
LAN = Local Area Network

SOURCE: Jeff Tyson, Jeff Tyson, "The Internet: Computer Network Hierarchy," in *How Internet Infrastructure Works*, HowStuffWorks, Inc., 2004, http://computer.howstuffworks.com/internet-infrastructure1 .htm (accessed June 2, 2014). Courtesy of HowStuffWorks.com.

be it AOL or Comcast or one of many others, feeds into a network access point (NAP). These NAPs are connected to one another via backbones that consist of bundles, or trunks, of fiber-optic cables that carry cross-country transmissions. The first NSF-funded backbone consisted of 56-kilobytes-per-second wire to connect the access points. The wire was laid down by AT&T. The NSF also provided five supercomputers to route traffic between the NAPs and bundles. In 1988 the NSF upgraded the NSFNet when it installed supercomputers that could handle 1.5 gigabytes of traffic per second and fiber-optic line that could transfer information at 1.5 megabytes per second. (Computers process the long lines of complex computer code in small quantities known as bytes. Each byte consists of a string of eight ones and zeros that can be used to represent binary numbers from 0 to 255. In binary, which is a base-two number system, 1 is 00000001, 2 is 00000010, 3 is 00000011, and so on up to 255, which is represented as 11111111. A thousand bytes equal a kilobyte, a million bytes equal a megabyte, and a billion bytes equal a gigabyte.)

The creation of the NSFNet ended the transmission bottlenecks that existed in the early Internet. The network also provided access for most major research institutions and universities. Academic departments and government agencies across the country jumped at the chance to set up servers and share information with their colleagues. Richard T. Griffiths notes in *History of the Internet, Internet for Historians* (October 11, 2002, http:// www.let.leidenuniv.nl/history/ivh/chap2.htm) that from 1986 to 1987 the number of hosts (machines with a distinct IP address) on the Internet jumped from 5,000 to 28,000.

The NSF strictly prohibited the use of its site for commercial purposes. Even though such a rule seemed harsh, it had the intended consequence of fostering the development of private Internet providers. In 1987 the UUNET became the first commercial Internet provider, offering service to Unix computers. Three years later, in 1990, The World (the first commercial provider of dial-up access) began operating, and computer scientists at McGill University in Montreal, Quebec, invented Archie, the first Internet search engine for finding computer files.

An Internet for Everyone

In 1991 Tim Berners-Lee (1955–) of the Conseil Européen pour la Recherche Nucléaire (CERN; European Organization for Nuclear Research), which is located in Switzerland, introduced the three technologies that would give rise to the World Wide Web. The first of Berners-Lee's technologies was the web browser, a program that allowed a user to jump from one server computer on the Internet to another. The second was the hypertext markup language (HTML), which was a programming language for creating web pages with links to other web pages and graphics. The third was the hypertext transfer protocol (HTTP), a command used by the browser to retrieve the HTML information contained on the server's website. In concert, these three innovations led to the World Wide Web as it became known during the early 21st century. On his server, Berners-Lee created the first website at CERN in 1990. Even though this site is no longer active, an early screen shot of Berners-Lee's web browser may be accessed at http://info.cern.ch/NextBrowser.html. As the technology spread, many more web servers and sites quickly came into being. As Internet Live Stats reports in "Total Number of Web Sites" (June 12, 2014, http:// www.internetlivestats.com/total-number-of-websites), by 2013 the total number of websites had grown to nearly 673 million.

With Berners-Lee's invention, people were no longer required to use complex computer codes or sift through cryptic directories to retrieve information from other computers on the Internet. To reach a server with a website, a user simply types in the name of a server along with the HTTP command (e.g., http://www.google.com) into the address bar of his or her browser. The browser then contacts a DNS server to get the IP address of the server. Once the browser connects with the website, the browser then sends out the HTTP command. The HTTP tells the server to send the browser the HTML code for the specified website. On receiving the HTML code, the browser deciphers the code and simply displays the web page on the user's computer (e.g., Google's home page).

At the same time that these strides were being made in establishing the Internet, the U.S. government took a more active role in its development. In 1991 Senator Albert Gore Jr. (1948–; D-TN) introduced the U.S. High Performance Computing Act into Congress. The act set aside more than $2 billion for further research into computing and to improve the infrastructure of the Internet. Even though most of it was earmarked for large agencies such as the NSF and NASA, some of the funds were placed into the hands of independent software developers.

Marc Andreessen (1971–) developed the Mosaic X web browser in 1993 using a federal grant received through this act. The browser was one of the first commercial browsers to employ the HTML program language and HTTP, and it became the first browser to be embraced by the general public. It was easy to set up, simple to use, and backed by a full customer support staff. It displayed images in an attractive way and contained many of the standard features used on present-day web browsers, such as the address prompt and Back and Forward buttons. Tens of thousands of copies of Mosaic X were sold.

Once Mosaic X became popular, more websites employing HTML and HTTP were posted. According to Robert H. Zakon in *Hobbes' Internet Timeline 10.2* (December 30, 2011, http://www.zakon.org/robert/internet/timeline), in June 1994 there were 2,738 web servers, by June 1995 there were an estimated 23,500 servers, and by June 1996 there were an estimated 252,000 servers. Zakon indicates that the growth in hosts, or computers with a unique IP address, during the same period reflected an increase from 3.2 million in July 1994, to 6.6 million in July 1995, to 12.9 million in July 1996.

The web was growing at such a rapid rate that the NSF created the Internet Network Information Center (InterNIC) as an agency to handle domain names. InterNIC contracted with Network Solutions to handle domain registration. By 1995 the companies that ran the older dial-up services for home users, such as CompuServe, AOL, and Prodigy, brought their clients to the Internet and offered Internet service for all. Internet network providers, such as MCI and Qwest, began laying fiber-optic cables and communications networks at a breakneck pace. Advertising appeared on the web for the first time (the first banner being for the alcoholic beverage Zima), e-shopping appeared on the Internet, and many companies such as Netscape went public. In the following years the Internet gained a firm foothold in American life. As of January 2014, the nonprofit Internet Systems Consortium (http://ftp.isc.org/www/survey/reports/current) estimated the number of Internet hosts at just over 1 billion.

DIGITAL DIVIDE

Even though the Internet swept into U.S. households at a faster rate than almost any other technology, many people were still not connected to the Internet well after the turn of the 21st century. Table 1.1 shows the demographic differences between those connected to the Internet and those who were not. The biggest discrepancies were in age, income, and educational attainment. For example, 97% of respondents aged 18 to 29 years were Internet users in January 2014; by comparison, only 57% of seniors aged 65 years and older went online. Table 1.1 also shows that those in typically disadvantaged demographics had the least exposure to the Internet. Seventy-seven percent of adults living in households earning less than $30,000 per year went online in 2014, compared with 99% of adults living in households earning $75,000 or more per year. Whereas 97% of college graduates used the Internet in 2014, only three-quarters (76%) of adults

TABLE 1.1

Demographics of Internet users, January 2014

[Among adults, the % who use the Internet, e-mail, or access the Internet via a mobile device]

	Use internet
All adults	**87%**
Sex	
a Men	87
b Women	86
Race/ethnicity*	
a White	85
b African-American	81
c Hispanic	83
Age group	
a 18–29	97[c, d]
b 30–49	93[d]
c 50–64	88[d]
d 65+	57
Education level	
a High school grad or less	76
b Some college	91[a]
c College+	97[a, b]
Household income	
a Less than $30,000/yr	77
b $30,000–$49,999	85
c $50,000–$74,999	93[a, b]
d $75,000+	99[a, b]
Community type	
a Urban	88
b Suburban	87
c Rural	83

Sample = 1,006 adults.
Note: Percentages marked with a superscript letter (e.g.,[a]) indicate a statistically significant difference between that row and the row designated by that superscript letter, among categories of each demographic characteristic (e.g., age).
*The results for race/ethnicity are based off a combined sample from two weekly omnibus surveys, January 9–12 and January 23–26, 2014. The combined total sample for these surveys was 2,008; sample = 1,421 for whites, sample = 197 for African-Americans, and sample = 236 for Hispanics.

SOURCE: "Internet Users in 2014," in *Data Trend: Internet User Demographics*, Pew Research Center, January 2014, http://www.pewinternet.org/data-trend/internet-use/latest-stats/ (accessed June 2, 2014)

who had earned only a high school diploma or had never finished high school were Internet users that year.

As Table 1.1 shows, variations in Internet usage between different races and ethnicities were marginal in 2014. Non-Hispanic whites (85%) were only slightly more likely than Hispanics (83%) and non-Hispanic African Americans (81%) to be Internet users that year. The type of community in which an individual lived also seemed to be an insignificant factor in determining Internet use during that time. In 2014 a comparable proportion of adults living in urban areas (88%) and adults living in suburban areas (87%) used the Internet, and more than four-fifths (83%) of rural Americans used the Internet that year. Roughly the same proportion of men (87%) and women (86%) were Internet users in 2014.

A more noticeable divide exists between those with faster, broadband connectivity and those with older equipment and slow connection speeds. For example, the overall number of Americans with access to broadband rose dramatically between 2000 and 2013. In 2000 only 3% of adults went online via broadband, compared with 34% who accessed the Internet with a dial-up connection. (See Figure 1.5.) By 2013 the percentage of adults with broadband access had risen to 70%, whereas those using dial-up had dropped to only 2%. Still, research indicates significant demographic differences among broadband users. As Table 1.2 shows, 81% of

adults aged 18 to 29 years accessed the Internet via broadband in 2013, compared with only 47% of adults aged 65 years and older.

Table 1.2 also shows a significant gap in broadband Internet use between low-income and high-income households. Slightly more than half (52%) of households earning less than $30,000 a year had broadband Internet access; by comparison, 91% of households with annual incomes of $75,000 or more used high-speed Internet connections. Table 1.2 also proves that education plays an important role in determining whether an adult is more or less likely to go online via a high-speed connection. For example, adults with a college degree (90%) were significantly more likely than those who had never finished high school (28%) to use a broadband Internet connection in 2013. Gaps in broadband use also existed between different races and ethnicities. That year, nearly three-quarters (74%) of non-Hispanic whites accessed the Internet via broadband, compared with slightly more than half (56%) of Hispanics.

Geography also seemed to play a considerable role in determining whether or not Americans had access to high-speed Internet, as suburban (74%) and urban (70%) Americans were considerably more likely than rural Americans (60%) to go online using a broadband connection in 2013. In *Broadband Internet Access and the Digital Divide: Federal Assistance Programs* (July 17, 2013, http://www.fas.org/sgp/crs/misc/RL30719.pdf),

FIGURE 1.5

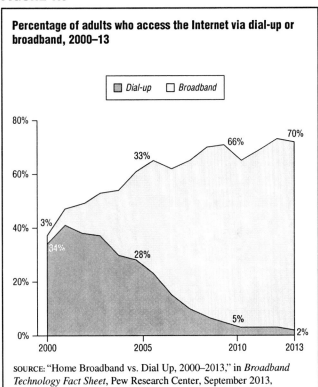

Percentage of adults who access the Internet via dial-up or broadband, 2000–13

SOURCE: "Home Broadband vs. Dial Up, 2000–2013," in *Broadband Technology Fact Sheet*, Pew Research Center, September 2013, http://www.pewinternet.org/fact-sheets/broadband-technology-fact-sheet/ (accessed June 2, 2014)

TABLE 1.2

Broadband users by selected characteristics, September 2013

	Broadband internet users
All adults	**70%**
a Men	70
b Women	70
a White, non-Hispanic	74
b Black, non-Hispanic	62
c Hispanic	56
a 18–29	81
b 30–49	77
c 50–64	68
d 65+	47
a No high school diploma	28
b High school grad	58
c Some college	80
d College+	90
a Less than $30,000/yr	52
b $30,000–$49,999	71
c $50,000–$74,999	85
d $75,000+	91
a Urban	70
b Suburban	74
c Rural	60

SOURCE: "Demographics of Broadband Internet Users," in *Broadband Technology Fact Sheet*, Pew Research Center, September 2013, http://www.pewinternet.org/fact-sheets/broadband-technology-fact-sheet/ (accessed June 2, 2014)

Lennard G. Kruger and Angele A. Gilroy of the Congressional Research Service provide a comprehensive breakdown of broadband access throughout the United States. Of the 19 million Americans without broadband access in August 2012, 14.5 million were from rural communities.

The researchers indicate that 6% of the U.S. population was unable to access broadband service in 2012. In urban and other nonrural areas, only 1.8% of Americans were unable to go online via a broadband connection; in stark contrast, 23.7% of rural Americans had no access to high-speed Internet. By a considerable margin, West Virginia had the highest proportion of residents without broadband access, at 45.9%; other states with a high percentage of residents without broadband were Montana (26.7%), South Dakota (21.1%), and Alaska (19.6%). On the opposite end of the spectrum, the most comprehensive broadband network in 2012 was in Rhode Island, where 99.8% of the population had access to high-speed Internet, followed by New Jersey (99.3%), Massachusetts (99%), and New York (98.7%).

THE FUTURE OF COMPUTING AND THE INTERNET

For many, the Internet has become an essential part of everyday life, and people increasingly want to be able to log on to the Internet from any location, in private or public spaces. It is therefore not surprising that more Americans are turning to wireless technologies. In *Generations and Their Gadgets* (February 3, 2011, http://www.pewinternet.org/~/media//Files/Reports/2011/PIP_Generations_and_Gadgets.pdf), Kathryn Zickuhr of the Pew Research Center reports that 52% of American adults owned laptop computers by 2010, compared with 59% who owned desktop computers. Younger adults were the most likely to use laptops rather than desktop computers. According to Zickuhr, 70% of adults between the ages of 18 and 34 years owned laptops in 2010, compared with 57% who owned desktops. As smartphones, tablet computers, and other mobile devices gain popularity, more and more adults are accessing the Internet using a wireless connection. As Zickuhr and Aaron Smith report in *Digital Differences* (April 13, 2012, http://www.pewinternet.org/files/old-media/Files/Reports/2012/PIP_Digital_differences_041312.pdf), 63% of adults were using either a laptop or cell phone to access the Internet in 2011. The highest numbers of wireless users were found among younger adults. Eighty-eight percent of adults aged 18 to 29 years went online with a laptop or cell phone in 2011, compared with 76% of adults aged 30 to 49 years, 53% of adults aged 50 to 64 years, and 21% of adults aged 65 years and older.

As with other technologies, wealth and educational attainment also play a role in determining wireless Internet use. Eighty-six percent of adults with annual household incomes of $75,000 or higher used wireless Internet, compared with 50% of adults with annual household incomes of less than $30,000. Adults with a college degree or higher (82%) were also more likely than adults who had never completed high school (36%) to go online with a wireless connection.

Improvements in cell phone technology were instrumental in the rapid growth of wireless Internet activity. Figure 1.6 shows the increase in cell phone Internet use between April 2009 and May 2013. During this period the proportion of cell phone owners who went online using their phones more than doubled, from 31% to 63%. Young adults were the most likely to use their phones to go online in 2013, with 85% of cell phone owners between the ages of 18 and 29 accessing the Internet with their mobile devices. (See Table 1.3.) Non-Hispanic African Americans (74%) were the most likely to use their cell phones to go online in 2013, followed by Hispanics (68%) and non-Hispanic whites (59%). Urban (66%) and suburban (65%) adults were considerably more likely than those living in rural areas (50%) to access the Internet with their phones, whereas a far higher percentage of adults with college degrees (74%) used their phones to go online than those who never completed high school (51%).

Tablet computers also played a key role in the rise of wireless computing during these years. As Zickuhr and Lee Rainie report in *E-Reading Rises as Device Ownership Jumps* (January 16, 2014, http://www.pewinternet.org/files/old-media/Files/Reports/2014/PIP_E-reading_011614.pdf), by January 2014 half (50%) of all adults owned either a tablet computer (such as an iPad) or an e-reading device (such as a Kindle). Zickuhr and Rainie note that wealth and education were key factors in determining whether or not someone owned a tablet computer. Among adults earning $75,000 or more per year, 65% owned tablet computers, and 59% of college graduates were tablet owners. By comparison, only 29% of adults without a high school diploma and 26% of adults who made less than $30,000 per year owned a tablet computer in 2014.

In "PC Is Dead. Cloud Computing, Mobile Devices Taking Over" (CSMonitor.com, June 8, 2011), Chad Brooks suggests that the popularity of tablet devices, combined with the proliferation of online data storage systems, or "cloud computing," might signal the end of the traditional desktop computer. "We don't need PCs anymore," Brooks quoted technology expert John Quain as saying. "They are dead." Indeed, as tablet ownership saw a dramatic increase, desktop computer sales declined in the United States. According to Gartner, Inc., in the press release "Gartner Says Worldwide PC Shipments Declined 6.9 Percent in Fourth Quarter of 2013" (January 9, 2014, http://www.gartner.com/newsroom/id/2647517), PC sales in the United States fell 7.5% between the fourth quarter of 2012 and the fourth quarter of 2013, from 17.1 million units to 15.8 million units.

FIGURE 1.6

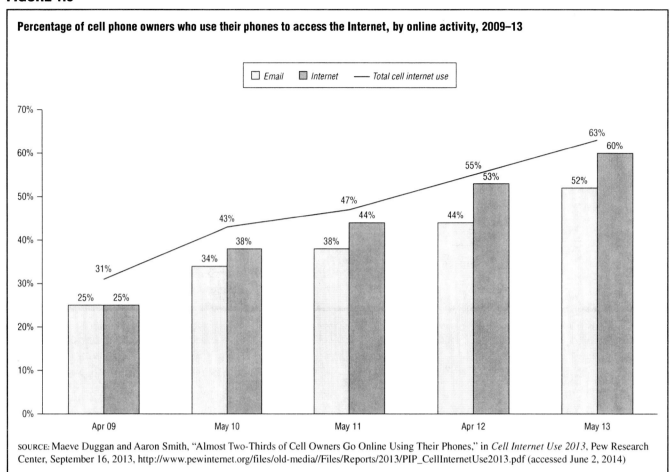

Percentage of cell phone owners who use their phones to access the Internet, by online activity, 2009–13

Legend: ☐ Email ▨ Internet —— Total cell internet use

SOURCE: Maeve Duggan and Aaron Smith, "Almost Two-Thirds of Cell Owners Go Online Using Their Phones," in *Cell Internet Use 2013*, Pew Research Center, September 16, 2013, http://www.pewinternet.org/files/old-media//Files/Reports/2013/PIP_CellInternetUse2013.pdf (accessed June 2, 2014)

The number of wireless hot spots has risen in response to increasing demand. The advertising network JiWire, which compiles an industry directory, indicates that the number of wireless Internet hot spots in the world surpassed the 100,000 mark in early 2006. According to JiWire (August 11, 2014, http://v4.jiwire.com/search-hot-spot-locations.htm), there were 890,422 wireless Internet locations in 145 countries in August 2014. The United States had the largest number of wireless hot spots in the world, with 199,125, followed by South Korea (186,758) and the United Kingdom (182,610). Within the United States, Philadelphia, Pennsylvania (3,063); Chicago, Illinois (2,374); San Francisco, California (2,240); New York City (1,705); Atlanta, Georgia (1,569); and Washington, D.C. (1,504) were the cities with the largest number of Wi-Fi hot spots in 2014.

Increasing Mobile Connectivity

As wireless devices grow in popularity, several emerging technologies allow people to access high-speed Internet on their laptops wherever they go. Worldwide interoperability for microwave access (WiMAX) uses base-station transmitters much like those in a mobile phone network. Any laptop computer that is equipped with a WiMAX receiver should be able to instantly log on to one of these stations and receive high-speed Internet access up to 30 miles (48 km) away.

One of the most popular technologies on the market during the first decade of the 21st century was high-speed third-generation (3G) cell phone service. First introduced in the United States in 2003, 3G service allows cell phones to receive and send signals that contain much more information than standard cellular phone signals, enabling 3G cell phone users to access the Internet at speeds approaching those of a cable modem. This high connection speed also enables 3G cell phone users to download various applications (commonly known as "apps") such as games, videos, online tools, and websites. As wireless technology advanced, 3G phones were capable of offering data transmission speeds of between 400 and 4,000 kilobytes per second (Kbps).

By 2010 most major cellular operators in the United States were offering 3G service to their customers, and devices such as the BlackBerry, the Apple 3G iPhone, and Samsung Instinct were making multifunction smartphones relatively affordable. Proving consumer demand for such products, the Apple 3G iPhone, which combined 3G phone, Internet, personal data, and music capabilities in one device, sold more than a million units in three days

TABLE 1.3

Percentage of cell phone owners who use their phones to access the Internet, by selected characteristics, 2012–13

	April 2012 (sample size = 1,954)	May 2013 (sample size = 2,076)	Change
All cell phone owners	55%	63%	+8 percentage points
Men	57	65	+8
Women	54	61	+7
Race/ethnicity			
White, non-Hispanic	52	59	+7
Black, non-Hispanic	64	74	+10
Hispanic	63	68	not sig.
Age			
18–29	75	85	+10
30–49	70	73	not sig.
50–64	36	51	+15
65+	16	22	+6
Education attainment			
No high school diploma	45	51	not sig.
High school grad	49	53	not sig.
Some college	57	67	+10
College+	64	74	+10
Household income			
Less than $30,000/yr	50	55	not sig.
$30,000–$49,999	52	60	not sig.
$50,000–$74,999	60	63	not sig.
$75,000+	69	79	+10
Urbanity			
Urban	62	66	not sig.
Suburban	56	65	+9
Rural	44	50	not sig.

SOURCE: Maeve Duggan and Aaron Smith, "Demographics of Cell Phone Internet Usage—Change over Time," in *Cell Internet Use 2013*, Pew Research Center, September 16, 2013, http://www.pewinternet.org/files/old-media//Files/Reports/2013/PIP_CellInternetUse2013.pdf (accessed June 2, 2014)

following its release in July 2008. Following the success of the iPhone, a number of other 3G portable wireless devices were introduced, including the iPod Touch and the iPad from Apple Inc., the Droid from Motorola Inc., and the Zune from Microsoft Corporation.

During this period a new wireless technology, known as long-term evolution (LTE), or fourth generation (4G) cell phone service, was beginning to emerge, with the promise of even faster connection speeds for consumers. Launched as an initiative by the International Telecommunications Union (ITU) in March 2008, the development of a new global 4G standard, offering connection speeds of between 100 megabytes and 1 gigabyte per second, became the top priority of telecommunications companies worldwide. With connection speeds that were expected to exceed those offered by 3G devices, 4G promised to enable cell phone users to stream much more advanced forms of data, such as live television broadcasts, interactive games, and other multimedia applications at a much faster rate. However, as companies became eager to sell 4G products to consumers, the ITU's efforts to establish universal 4G standards became a low

priority for cell phone carriers and the organization abandoned the initiative. As a result, several of the first phones to be marketed as 4G were actually no faster than their 3G predecessors. In "3G vs. 4G: What's the Difference?" (PCMag.com, February 24, 2012), Sascha Segan notes that by 2012 so many 4G technologies had emerged that the term had become "almost meaningless." Still, as 4G-LTE networks continued to expand throughout the United States, it was clear that 4G would eventually supersede 3G as the industry standard. In anticipation of this shift, Apple released its iPhone 5, the first iPhone to be compatible with 4G-LTE networks, in September 2012. By 2014 major telecommunications providers such as AT&T, Sprint, T-Mobile, and Verizon, had all built extensive 4G-LTE networks in the United States.

Internet2

In the long term, however, the future of the Internet will likely be the Internet2. Internet2 is not a new Internet, but a collaboration of dozens of academic institutions and corporations working together to develop technologies that will be integrated into the Internet. According to the organization's website (2014, http://www.internet2.edu/about-us), in 2014 the Internet2 community involved the cooperation of 252 U.S. universities and 82 corporations, in addition to 68 affiliates and 41 state and regional education networks. Globally, Internet2 also partnered with 65 research and education affiliates with sites in more than 100 countries worldwide. The group's guiding philosophy was based on a commitment to establishing a research climate conducive to the development and sharing of new technologies. "Innovation takes place when ideas are liberated to create practical, far-reaching solutions to the problems of society," the organization states. "Our community is laying the foundation for entirely new ideas: equipping the brightest people in the world with the most advanced technology in the world. If their previous track record is any indication, the future they create will be bold and brilliant."

One project the Internet2 consortium began testing in 2008 was version six of the Internet protocol (IPv6). By 2012 the number of computers, cell phones, and other devices using the Internet had grown exponentially. Each time one of these devices logs on to the Internet, it requires its own address. Until 2012 these devices all operated within version four of the Internet protocol (IPv4), which allowed for only a little more than 4 billion addresses. As the number of new IP addresses continued to rise, IPv4 would eventually prove insufficient to accommodate all users. IPv6 introduced a new Internet address system that would allow for trillions upon trillions of new addresses. With such a network, Americans would be able to watch high-definition television via the Internet, teleconference with associates and family at any time, and easily access entire libraries of music and books online.

In June 2011 a number of companies and institutions, including Google, Facebook, and the Department of Commerce, participated in World IPv6 Day, an event that was designed to test the functionality of the new IP. The experiment proved a success, and IPv6 was officially launched on June 6, 2012. Iljitsch van Beijnum reports in "IPv6 on Its Way to Conquer the World after World IPv6 Launch" (ArsTechnica.com, August 1, 2012) that 19 million IPv6 addresses saw activity during the launch, with 71% of the total traffic occurring in the United States. According to Fahmida Y. Rashid in "What to Expect for IPv6 Day" (PCMag.com, June 6, 2012), by the day of the launch 12% of existing Internet networks were compatible with the new protocol. By 2015, 28% of new Internet connections were expected to operate within the IPv6 system. While the existing IPv4 network continued to operate alongside IPv6, by 2014 it seemed clear that the new protocol represented the networking platform of the future. As Leon Spencer reports in "ICANN Urges IPv6 Adoption as Global Address Shortage Looms" (ZDNet.com, May 23, 2014), by May 2014 IPv6 accounted for 3.5% of all Internet traffic worldwide. Adoption was particularly high in Germany, where just over 8% of all web addresses used the IPv6 system, and the United States, where 7.4% of addresses were IPv6.

Future Incarnations of the Internet

As the Internet became integrated into society, many observers began raising questions about the ways an information-driven, interconnected world might transform human behavior. In *Digital Life in 2025* (May 14, 2014, http://www.pewinternet.org/files/2014/05/PIP _Internet-of-things_0514142.pdf), Janna Anderson and Lee Rainie surveyed more than 1,800 technology experts about how the Internet might evolve by 2025. By and large, the experts surveyed agreed that network technology would become increasingly interwoven into the physical world. This process would occur through the proliferation of digital tools designed to monitor and enhance everyday existence, creating what Anderson and Rainie describe as an "Internet of Things." Examples cited in the report include bodily devices that would measure the health, fitness and dietary activities of individuals, as well as remote-control sensors that could regulate appliances in the home. Respondents also surmised that network technology would have the capacity to measure changes to the earth's environment, allowing scientists to keep track of pollution levels and shifts in weather patterns in real time. For some respondents, these future developments represented a source of enormous opportunity for society. For example, harnessing network technology to monitor the flow of goods in the marketplace will help increase efficiency while reducing waste. Other experts expressed a more cautionary

perspective on the future of the Internet, notably in the ways that increased connectivity will erode, and ultimately destroy, any prospect for individual privacy.

At the same time, profound political ramifications are inherent in the expansion of network technologies. Indeed, questions concerning the free, open movement of information between individuals and societies are central to discussions of the Internet's future. In "Future Scenarios" (2014, http://www.internetsociety.org/internet/how-it%E2%80%99s-evolving/future-scenarios), the Internet Society, an advocacy group dedicated to ensuring that the World Wide Web remains accessible and open to all citizens, imagines several possible outcomes for the Internet. In one instance, the "Common Pool" scenario, the society envisions a future where barriers to online participation are eliminated, encouraging opportunity, innovation, and collaboration among all Internet users. By contrast, the "Moats and Drawbridges" scenario, in which the flow of information would be heavily controlled by government and corporate interests, would cripple innovation by forcing online participants to devote energy and resources to cultivating political connections in order to compete.

At the same time, by 2014 government control of online information had become a serious threat to Internet freedom in a number of countries throughout the world. As Eric E. Schmidt and Jared Cohen observe in "The Future of Internet Freedom" (NYTimes.com, March 11, 2014), however, emerging network technologies have enormous potential to undermine these censorship tactics. For example, citizens living under repressive regimes will increasingly be able to access secure connections through various "circumvention technologies" that link their computers to online networks overseas. Meanwhile, organizations dedicated to preserving a record of Internet activity as a countermeasure to online censorship have already begun to emerge. As Hannah Kuchler reports in "How to Preserve the Web's Past for the Future" (FT.com, April 11, 2014), the Internet Archive, a digital library based in San Francisco, has the capacity to capture and preserve threatened material before governments have the chance to take it off the Internet. At the same time, the archive is dedicated to preserving documentation relating to ordinary life, organizing and maintaining information ranging from school curricula to traditional recipes. Indeed, by expanding the availability of primary historical documents on such a massive scale, digital libraries are already transforming the ways that historians and others conduct their research. "The days of the lone scholar are gone," Ruth Page, a linguistics lecturer at the University of Leicester, told Kuchler. "In my personal opinion we really need to embrace creative ways to work collaboratively."

CHAPTER 2
DEVELOPMENTS IN TELECOMMUNICATIONS

Communication has undeniably been one of the central motivations behind the technical strides that have taken place since the beginning of the Cold War (1947–1991), a period of sustained military buildup and ideological conflict that pitted the United States and other capitalist powers against the Soviet Union and its communist allies. The Internet was first conceived as a way of connecting computers for the purpose of communication. By the 21st century, digital connectivity had become an indispensible aspect of everyday life in the United States, particularly among younger Americans. In 2012, 95% of individuals between the ages of 12 and 29 years were Internet users. (See Figure 2.1.) Among college-educated adults, this figure was even higher. As Table 2.1 shows, by 2014, 97% of people with college degrees used the Internet.

Electronic mail, or e-mail, was the first application to gain acceptance and widespread use on the Internet. In *Email Statistics Report, 2013–2017* (April 2013, http://www.radicati.com/wp/wp-content/uploads/2013/04/Email-Statistics-Report-2013-2017-Executive-Summary.pdf), Sarah Radicati and Justin Levenstein of the Radicati Group, Ltd., a technology marketing research firm, report that in 2013 there were approximately 3.9 billion e-mail accounts worldwide. Nearly 3 billion of these, or 76%, were consumer e-mail accounts.

E-mail is not the only communications system to flourish, however. Since the early 1980s a second phone system has sprung up across the United States. According to the *Proquest Statistical Abstract of the United States: 2014* (2014), the number of cell phone subscribers in the United States rose from 5.3 million in 1990 to 326.5 million in 2012. Meanwhile, the amount of revenue that was brought in by the cellular phone system rose from $4.5 billion to $185 billion over this 20-year period. At the same time, the average cost to the consumer declined significantly during this span. Whereas the average cell

phone bill was about $81 per month in 1990, it dropped to roughly $47 per month by 2011.

Meanwhile, as the 21st century progressed, more sophisticated modes of online communication continued to emerge. Instant messaging (IM) software allowed individuals to share text messages over the Internet almost instantly, while video phone platforms such as Skype enabled users to have face-to-face conversations over their computers. Furthermore, with the rapid rise in popularity of social media, online communication became increasingly varied and complex. Through such platforms as Facebook, Twitter, and Instagram, Internet users began to express themselves not only in writing, but also by posting photographs, sharing links to websites, and "liking" certain social media pages using some or all of these forms of communication.

In some ways these new forms of communication have made life easier. Most Americans no longer have to look for a pay phone and search for change when they need to make a phone call away from home. Nor do most travelers have to worry about being stranded on a deserted roadway miles from a phone. Using e-mail and instant messaging, online Americans can now easily stay in touch with anyone in any country around the world. Overall, Americans also feel that online communication helps to strengthen their relationships with friends and family. (See Figure 2.2.) At the same time, however, Americans now have to comb through spam daily, worry about unleashing e-mail viruses, and endure strangers' phone conversations and cell phone ring tones virtually everywhere they go.

E-MAIL

E-mail was the first of these new communications technologies to emerge. Not more than two years after the initial ARPANET test in 1969, Raymond Tomlinson (1941–) of ARPANET created the first e-mail program.

FIGURE 2.1

Internet use, by age, November 2004–September 2012

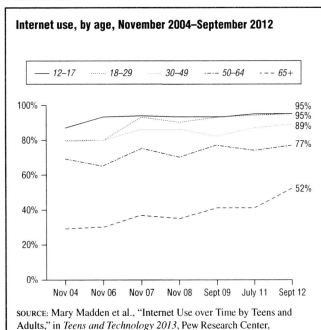

SOURCE: Mary Madden et al., "Internet Use over Time by Teens and Adults," in *Teens and Technology 2013*, Pew Research Center, March 13, 2013, http://www.pewinternet.org/files/old-media/Files/Reports/2013/PIP_TeensandTechnology2013.pdf (accessed June 3, 2014)

FIGURE 2.2

Impact of online communication on personal relationships, 2014

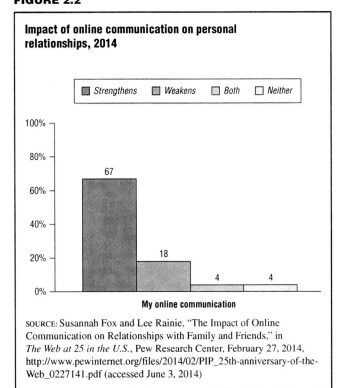

SOURCE: Susannah Fox and Lee Rainie, "The Impact of Online Communication on Relationships with Family and Friends," in *The Web at 25 in the U.S.*, Pew Research Center, February 27, 2014, http://www.pewinternet.org/files/2014/02/PIP_25th-anniversary-of-the-Web_0227141.pdf (accessed June 3, 2014)

TABLE 2.1

Internet user demographics, 2014

	Use internet
All adults	87%
Sex	
a Men	87
b Women	86
Race/ethnicity*	
a White	85
b African-American	81
c Hispanic	83
Age group	
a 18–29	97[c, d]
b 30–49	93[d]
c 50–64	88[d]
d 65+	57
Education level	
a High school grad or less	76
b Some college	91[a]
c College+	97[a, b]
Household income	
a Less than $30,000/yr	77
b $30,000–$49,999	85
c $50,000–$74,999	93[a, b]
d $75,000+	99[a, b]
Community type	
a Urban	88
b Suburban	87
c Rural	83

Note: Percentages marked with a superscript letter (e.g.,[a]) indicate a statistically significant difference between that row and the row designated by that superscript letter, among categories of each demographic characteristic (e.g., age).
*The results for race/ethnicity are based off a combined sample from two weekly omnibus surveys, January 9–12 and January 23–26, 2014. The combined total sample for these surveys was 2,008; sample = 1,421 for whites, sample = 197 for African-Americans, and sample = 236 for Hispanics.

SOURCE: Susannah Fox and Lee Rainie, "Internet Users in 2014," in *The Web at 25 in the U.S.*, Pew Research Center, February 27, 2014, http://www.pewinternet.org/files/2014/02/PIP_25th-anniversary-of-the-Web_0227141.pdf (accessed June 3, 2014)

The remote terminals, which were typically spread throughout the office building, were little more than a screen and a keyboard, and the office workers shared the resources of the central computer. Programs were written for these systems wherein people could leave messages for one another within the core computer. Tomlinson simply adapted one of these static internal mail programs into a program that could send messages to other computers on ARPANET. The first mass e-mail Tomlinson sent out with his program was a message to all ARPANET employees telling them that "electronic mail" was now available. He instructed them to address one another using the following convention: "user's log-in name@host computer name." This same convention is still being used.

The first e-mail program was not user-friendly. The e-mails did not have subject lines or date lines, they had to be opened in the order that they were received, and they read as strings of continuous text. Despite these inconveniences, the e-mail application caught on in the

Tomlinson developed the idea from a program that had been used on mainframe computers with time-share operating systems. These computers, which were prevalent during the early 1960s, consisted of a number of remote terminals that were all connected to a central host computer, where all the office files and programs were stored.

ARPANET community quickly, and the computer scientists in the organization worked out most of the kinks. Within several years users could list messages by subject and date, delete selected messages, and forward messages to other users. E-mail soon became the most popular application for the busy researchers working at ARPANET. When communicating by e-mail, they did not have to worry about the formalities or the long delays inherent in letter writing. Unlike a phone conversation, no time was wasted on small talk, and a copy of the communication could be retained. People could also send e-mails to one another at any time of day or night. By the late 1970s e-mail discussion groups had formed within the ARPANET community. Two of the more popular discussion groups were a science-fiction group and a group that discussed the potential future social impacts of e-mail.

During the late 1970s and early 1980s other networks began to develop, such as Usenet and Because It's Time Network (BITNET), which consisted of mainframe computers that were connected to one another over telephone lines. The central purpose of these networks was to connect universities and government agencies that were not on ARPANET. Some of these networks, such as Usenet, were set up for the express purpose of sending e-mail and posting messages on newsgroups. Usenet consisted of computers of various sizes all over the country. A relatively small number of large, powerful computers formed the backbone of the network, and many smaller computers logged on to the network through the larger ones. For example, to send an e-mail from Indiana to South Carolina a person on a small computer in Indiana would first dial into and post an e-mail onto the nearest large computer. The person operating the large computer in Indiana would then pass the e-mail via modem along with other messages from the region to all the other large computers in the network, including those in South Carolina. When the recipient of the e-mail in South Carolina logged into the network through the nearest large computer, the e-mail would then automatically be downloaded to his or her smaller computer.

By the late 1980s e-mail was commercially available for home users to a limited extent. Companies such as Quantum Computer Services (now known as AOL) and Prodigy set up chat rooms and e-mail services that could be enjoyed by people with home computers. Quantum Link, for example, was a service compatible with the Commodore 64 computer. Home users dialed into local Quantum Link mainframes, which were located in most major cities around the country. The mainframes were interconnected via open phone lines, so that anyone using the service could e-mail or chat with anyone else logged onto the service across the country. A member, however, could not contact someone on another commercial service or on the much larger Internet.

E-mail Becomes Widespread

The development of the National Science Foundation Internet and the standardization of Internet protocols during the mid-1980s brought most of the smaller academic networks such as BITNET together, allowing people throughout academia and government agencies to communicate with one another via e-mail. The invention of the World Wide Web, the Mosaic X web browser, and the widespread use of more powerful personal computers allowed home users access to Internet e-mail by the early 1990s. In 1994 AOL (known at the time as America Online) began offering people a limited service on the web with the ability to send and receive e-mail. Within a year, all the established dial-up services such as CompuServe and Prodigy moved their e-mail subscribers onto the larger Internet.

Since the mid-1990s e-mail has become the most used application on the Internet. In "Americans Going Online . . . Explosive Growth, Uncertain Destinations" (October 16, 1995, http://www.people-press.org/1995/10/16/americans-going-online-explosive-growth-uncertain-destinations), the Pew Research Center reports that 12 million adult Americans were regular users of e-mail in June 1995 (with "regular user" defined as one who checked e-mail at least once per week). Since that time e-mail use has skyrocketed. As Pew reports in "Usage over Time" (2014, http://www.pewinternet.org/files/2014/01/Usage-Over-Time-_May-2013.xlsx), e-mail use reached an all-time high in May 2010, when 94% of online adults were e-mail users and 62% sent and received e-mails daily. E-mail use actually dipped slightly in 2011 and 2012, largely due to the increasing popularity of other platforms for online communication, notably instant messaging and social networking sites such as Facebook. Still, with 89% of adults sending and receiving e-mails in 2012, e-mail remained the most prevalent form of online communication. Most people said e-mail helped them maintain relationships with friends, communicate better on their job, and interact more effectively with local governments. Indeed, by January 2014 a majority (57%) of Internet users reported that it would be either "very hard" or "somewhat hard" to stop using e-mail. (See Figure 2.3.)

Spam

By far one of the biggest problems facing e-mail in the early 21st century is spam, which is generally defined as unsolicited e-mail sent in bulk. Even though different organizations gauge the number of e-mails sent worldwide differently, most agree that the vast majority of them are spam. In "Spam Evolution 2013" (January 23, 2014, http://www.securelist.com/en/analysis/204792322/Kaspersky_Security_Bulletin_Spam_evolution_2013),

FIGURE 2.3

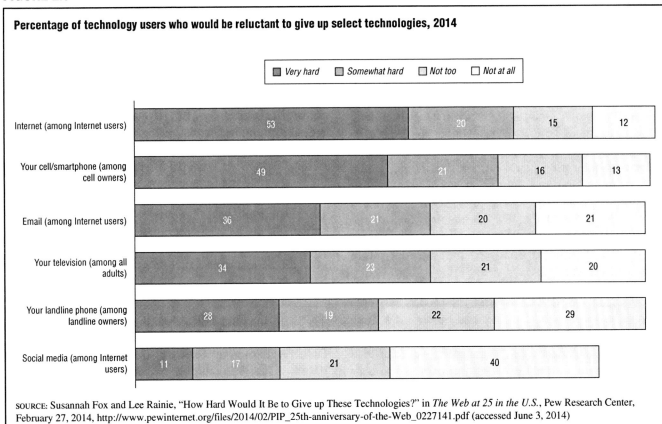

Percentage of technology users who would be reluctant to give up select technologies, 2014

Legend: ■ Very hard ▨ Somewhat hard ▢ Not too ▢ Not at all

Technology	Very hard	Somewhat hard	Not too	Not at all
Internet (among Internet users)	53	20	15	12
Your cell/smartphone (among cell owners)	49	21	16	13
Email (among Internet users)	36	21	20	21
Your television (among all adults)	34	23	21	20
Your landline phone (among landline owners)	28	19	22	29
Social media (among Internet users)	11	17	21	40

SOURCE: Susannah Fox and Lee Rainie, "How Hard Would It Be to Give up These Technologies?" in *The Web at 25 in the U.S.*, Pew Research Center, February 27, 2014, http://www.pewinternet.org/files/2014/02/PIP_25th-anniversary-of-the-Web_0227141.pdf (accessed June 3, 2014)

Kaspersky Lab, a leading antivirus software firm, indicates that 69.6% of all e-mail messages were spam in 2013. This figure actually represented a decline from 2012, when spam accounted for 72.1% of all e-mails. According to Kaspersky, China was responsible for nearly a quarter (23%) of all spam-generated e-mail in 2013, the most of any country; the United States was the second-largest distributor, accounting for 17.6% of all spam e-mails, followed by South Korea (12.7%) and Taiwan (11.5%). Overall, 55.5% of all spam originated in Asia in 2013.

The Spamhaus Project, an organization that tracks and works to eliminate spam, estimates in "The World's Worst Spammers" (June 14, 2014, http://www.spamhaus.org/statistics/spammers) that in 2014 approximately 80% of the world's spam was being generated by a group of roughly 100 spam operations known as "spam gangs." As Spamhaus reports in its "Register of Known Spam Operations" (June 14, 2014, http://www.spamhaus.org/rokso), or ROKSO, on average these gangs consisted of between one and five individual spammers; the total number of individual spammers involved in these operations was estimated to be between 300 and 400. In June 2014 one of the worst offenders was a long-running spam gang known as Canadian Pharmacy. Believed to be based in Ukraine, Canadian Pharmacy generated tens of millions of spam e-mail messages every day, primarily

through botnets. According to Spamhaus in "The World's Worst Spam Producing Countries" (August 19, 2014, http://www.spamhaus.org/statistics/countries), in August 2014 there were 2,598 high-volume spammers in the United States alone. Indeed, the United States was the country of origin for the largest number of spammers, about two and a half times the number of the second-ranked country, China (1,011). Other countries with major spam operations in August 2014 included the Russian Federation (678), Japan (488), Ukraine (349), Brazil (337), the United Kingdom (330), Germany (286), India (276), and France (273).

ANTISPAM LEGISLATION. As early as 2003 many people worried that spam was reaching epidemic proportions and was on the verge of making e-mail an impractical means of communication. In response to the growing concerns, the U.S. government attempted to limit spam, when, on January 1, 2004, the Controlling the Assault of Non-solicited Pornography and Marketing Act (CAN-SPAM Act) of 2003 went into effect. Enforced by the Federal Trade Commission (FTC) and the states' attorneys general, this act lays out a number of provisions that commercial e-mail senders must follow. One provision states that commercial e-mail senders must clearly identify unsolicited e-mail as solicitations or advertisements for products and services. Commercial e-mail senders must also provide a way for the recipient of the mail to opt out of receiving any more e-mails from them, and all e-mails must contain a legitimate address and use honest subject lines. Even though these provisions address the issue of spam in the United States, enforcement has been difficult. Creating a false identity on the Internet is easy, and once spammers know they are being tracked, they can easily relocate their operations to a different state or country. In "First Spam Felony Conviction Upheld: No Free Speech to Spam" (ArsTechnica.com, March 2, 2008), David Chartier reports that U.S. spammer Jeremy Jaynes of Raleigh, North Carolina, was the first person convicted in U.S. federal court of sending spam. Jaynes was sentenced to serve nine years in prison for sending an estimated 10 million spam messages during July and August of 2003.

In the face of this seemingly unstoppable nuisance, Internet Service Providers (ISPs), along with web security firms, developed new technologies that were aimed at reducing the volume of spam being dumped in people's in-boxes. In *Spam Summit: The Next Generation of Threats and Solutions* (November 2007, http://www.ftc.gov/os/2007/12/071220spamsummitreport.pdf), the FTC's Division of Marketing Practices reports that approximately two-thirds of e-mail users used some form of spam-filtering software. In a study published in the report, researchers found that two web-based ISPs were able to block the majority of spam e-mails through the use of filtering software; one ISP succeeded in blocking 92% of all spam e-mails, and the other managed to filter 68% of spam.

Still, in 2014 the problem of spam remained a fact of life among Internet users. Even though consumers typically object to spam, entrepreneurs recognize the potential profit in sending out unsolicited messages. Issuing spam costs next to nothing per message sent. Even if only 1% of people respond to a spam attack, be it for a legitimate digital cable filter or a fraudulent credit card scam, the spammer stands to make a lot of money or bring in a lot of credit card numbers. As long as a small percentage of the population responds to spam, it is potentially profitable. Bringing this number down to zero would likely be impossible. In the end, spam may just become another form of white noise that has to be endured in the modern world.

INSTANT MESSAGING

Instant messaging (IM) is a tool that allows people to communicate via text messages in near real time over the Internet and is typically available on personal computers and many cell phones. According to Gizmo's Freeware, a freeware review site, in "Best Free Instant Messaging Client" (TechSupportAlert.com, September 29, 2013), among the leading IM platforms in 2013 included Pidgin, Miranda IM, imo, Trillian, and Ebuddy. In *Email Statistics Report, 2013–2017*, the Radicati Group notes that the number of IM accounts worldwide exceeded 2.9 billion by 2013.

IM provides people some unique advantages that other communication devices do not. Most IM applications are compact in size and easy to access, making IM easy to use while taking part in other activities. In *How Americans Use Instant Messaging* (September 1, 2004, http://www.pewinternet.org/~/media//Files/Reports/2004/PIP_Instantmessage_Report.pdf.pdf), Eulynn Shiu and Amanda Lenhart report that in 2004, 32% of adult Americans said they were multitasking almost every time when they used IM. IM also has a clandestine aspect to it. A person can type a message without anyone knowing what he or she is doing. Nearly a quarter (24%) of all IM users said they used IM to converse with someone they were in close proximity to, typically because a class or meeting was in progress.

Like most forms of communication technology, IM evolved rapidly in the 21st century. According to the AOL–Associated Press survey "AP-AOL Instant Messaging Trends Survey Reveals Popularity of Mobile Instant Messaging" (BusinessWire.com, November 15, 2007), by 2007 roughly a quarter (24%) of IM users had begun to send and receive instant messages from their cell phones. Over the next five years the number of mobile IM users rose rapidly, driven largely by the increasing popularity of smartphone devices. Analysys Mason reports in the press release "IPhone Users Account for 80% of the Heaviest Smartphone Data Users" (May 30, 2012, http://www.analysysmason.com/About-Us/News/Press-releases1/consumer-smartphone-usage-May2012/?bp=%252fNews%252f/) that by 2012, 45% of smartphone owners used some form of IM service on their phone.

During this period IM began diversifying into new platforms. In April 2008 the popular social networking site Facebook introduced Facebook Chat, a communication tool that enabled users to initiate instant conversations with other people within their personal networks. In February 2010 Facebook reached an agreement with AOL to integrate their IM services, enabling users to communicate between the two IM platforms. Even as other messaging tools such as texting and Twitter were gaining popularity by decade's end, IM remained a vital form of rapid communication for many Internet users. As the Radicati Group reports in *Instant Messaging Market, 2013–2017* (September 2013, http://www.radicati.com/wp/wp-content/uploads/2013/09/Instant-Messaging-Market-2013-2017-Executive-Summary.pdf), by 2013 there were approximately 3.4 billion IM accounts worldwide.

SOCIAL NETWORKING

By 2014 social media had emerged as a popular way for people to maintain contact with friends and family

FIGURE 2.4

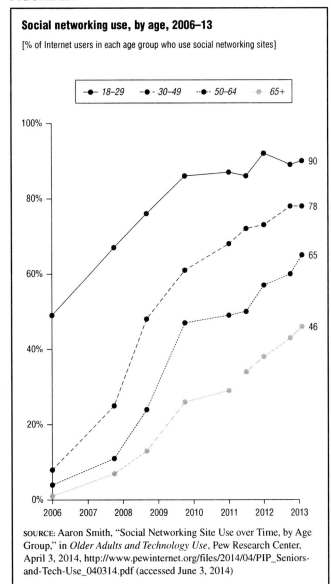

Social networking use, by age, 2006–13

[% of Internet users in each age group who use social networking sites]

— 18–29   — 30–49   — 50–64   — 65+

SOURCE: Aaron Smith, "Social Networking Site Use over Time, by Age Group," in *Older Adults and Technology Use*, Pew Research Center, April 3, 2014, http://www.pewinternet.org/files/2014/04/PIP_Seniors-and-Tech-Use_040314.pdf (accessed June 3, 2014)

FIGURE 2.5

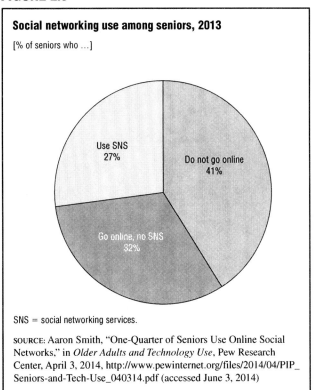

Social networking use among seniors, 2013

[% of seniors who ...]

Use SNS 27%

Do not go online 41%

Go online, no SNS 32%

SNS = social networking services.

SOURCE: Aaron Smith, "One-Quarter of Seniors Use Online Social Networks," in *Older Adults and Technology Use*, Pew Research Center, April 3, 2014, http://www.pewinternet.org/files/2014/04/PIP_Seniors-and-Tech-Use_040314.pdf (accessed June 3, 2014)

FIGURE 2.6

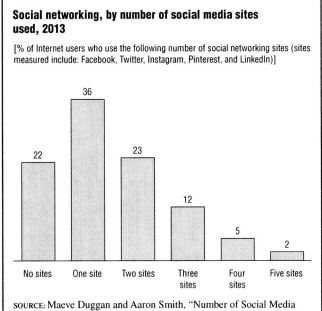

Social networking, by number of social media sites used, 2013

[% of Internet users who use the following number of social networking sites (sites measured include: Facebook, Twitter, Instagram, Pinterest, and LinkedIn)]

SOURCE: Maeve Duggan and Aaron Smith, "Number of Social Media Sites Used," in *Social Media Update 2013*, Pew Research Center, December 30, 2013, http://www.pewinternet.org/files/2013/12/PIP_Social-Networking-2013.pdf (accessed June 3, 2014)

members over the Internet. Indeed, social networking sites such as Facebook grew increasingly prevalent across all age demographics during this period. For example, in 2006 roughly half of all adults between the ages of 18 and 29 years used social media; by 2013 this figure had risen to 90%. (See Figure 2.4.) The increase in social media use among older Americans was even more dramatic during this span. As Figure 2.4 shows, use of social networking sites among online seniors was virtually non-existent in 2006, whereas by 2013 nearly half (46%) of all Internet users over the age of 65 were using social media. Among all seniors, more than one-quarter (27%) used social media in 2013, whereas roughly one-third (32%) went online without using social networking sites. (See Figure 2.5.) As Figure 2.6 shows, 78% of online adults used at least one of the following five social networking sites in 2013: Facebook, Instagram, LinkedIn, Pinterest, and Twitter. More than one-third (36%) of online adults maintained an account on only one of these

social networking sites; nearly one-quarter (23%) maintained two accounts, 12% had three accounts, 5% had four accounts, and 2% used all five sites.

Of the leading social networking sites, Facebook was far and away the most popular among adult Internet users

FIGURE 2.7

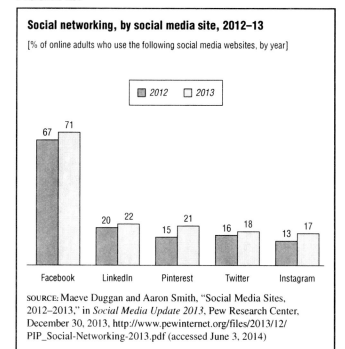

Social networking, by social media site, 2012–13

[% of online adults who use the following social media websites, by year]

Legend: ■ 2012   □ 2013

Facebook: 67, 71
LinkedIn: 20, 22
Pinterest: 15, 21
Twitter: 16, 18
Instagram: 13, 17

SOURCE: Maeve Duggan and Aaron Smith, "Social Media Sites, 2012–2013," in *Social Media Update 2013*, Pew Research Center, December 30, 2013, http://www.pewinternet.org/files/2013/12/PIP_Social-Networking-2013.pdf (accessed June 3, 2014)

FIGURE 2.8

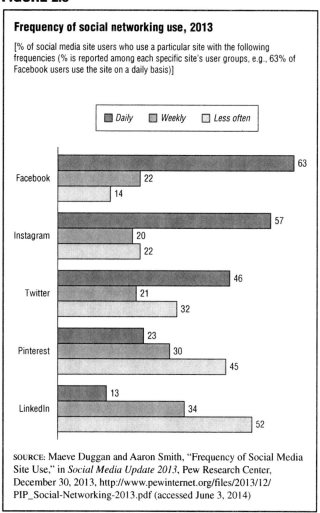

Frequency of social networking use, 2013

[% of social media site users who use a particular site with the following frequencies (% is reported among each specific site's user groups, e.g., 63% of Facebook users use the site on a daily basis)]

Legend: ■ Daily   ▨ Weekly   □ Less often

Facebook: 63, 22, 14
Instagram: 57, 20, 22
Twitter: 46, 21, 32
Pinterest: 23, 30, 45
LinkedIn: 13, 34, 52

SOURCE: Maeve Duggan and Aaron Smith, "Frequency of Social Media Site Use," in *Social Media Update 2013*, Pew Research Center, December 30, 2013, http://www.pewinternet.org/files/2013/12/PIP_Social-Networking-2013.pdf (accessed June 3, 2014)

in 2013. (See Figure 2.7.) That year, 71% of online adults used Facebook, up from 67% in 2012. By comparison, less than one-quarter (22%) of online adults used LinkedIn in 2013. Facebook users were also the most likely to check their social media page on a daily basis that year. As Figure 2.8 shows, 63% of Facebook users signed into their page every day, and another 22% checked their status at least once a week. Instagram and Twitter users also visited their pages frequently in 2013. That year, 57% of Instagram users checked their status daily, and 20% visited their page once a week; among Twitter users, nearly half (46%) checked their accounts daily, and 21% checked them at least once a week. (See Figure 2.8.)

Use of social networking sites is particularly prevalent among teen Internet users. As Figure 2.9 shows, 81% of online teens used social media in 2012, up from 55% in 2006. Teens were also 50% more likely than adults to use Twitter that year, with nearly one-quarter (24%) of online teens maintaining Twitter accounts in 2012, compared with 16% of online adults. Teen girls (84%) were more likely than teen boys (79%) to use social media in 2012; online teen girls were also significantly more likely than online teen boys to use Twitter, by a margin of 31% to 19%. (See Table 2.2.) As Table 2.3 shows, online teen girls (94%) were more likely than online teen boys (89%) to post photos of themselves on their social networking pages. By contrast, online teen boys were more likely than online teen girls to share contact information such as an e-mail address (57% vs. 49%, respectively) or cell phone number (26% vs. 14%, respectively) on social media sites.

Roughly one-quarter (27%) of teen Facebook users have 150 friends or fewer; another 27% have between 151 and 300 friends, and 24% have between 301 and 600 friends. (See Figure 2.10.) Only one in five (20%) teen Facebook users have more than 600 friends. Teens with large friend networks tend to check their Facebook status more frequently than those with fewer friends. Among teen Facebook users with more than 600 friends, 82% viewed their pages at least once a day (17%) or several times per day (65%) in 2012; by contrast, slightly more than half (51%) of teen Facebook users with 150 friends or fewer checked their status once per day (24%) or several times per day (27%) that year. (See Figure 2.11.)

In general, social networking is equally popular among white and African-American Internet users. Online African Americans between the ages of 18 and 29 years (96%) were somewhat more likely than online whites in that age group (90%) to use social media in 2013. (See Table 2.4.) Whereas college-educated African Americans (75%) were more likely than those with a high school diploma or less (68%) to visit social networking sites, African Americans who earned $75,000 a year or more in 2013 (68%) were less likely than those who

FIGURE 2.9

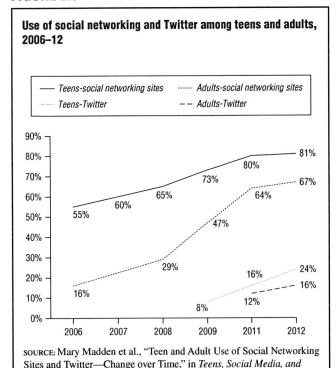

Use of social networking and Twitter among teens and adults, 2006–12

SOURCE: Mary Madden et al., "Teen and Adult Use of Social Networking Sites and Twitter—Change over Time," in *Teens, Social Media, and Privacy*, Pew Research Center, May 21, 2013, http://www.pewinternet.org/files/2013/05/PIP_TeensSocialMediaandPrivacy_PDF.pdf (accessed June 3, 2014)

TABLE 2.2

Social networking and Twitter use among teens, by age, gender, race and ethnicity, and household income, 2012

	Use a social networking site	Use Twitter
All teen Internet users (sample = 778)	**81%**	**24%**
Gender		
a Boys (sample = 395)	79	19
b Girls (sample = 383)	84	31[a]
Age		
a 12–13 (sample = 234)	65	13
b 14–17 (sample = 544)	89[a]	30[a]
Age/gender		
a Boys, 12–13 (sample = 118)	64	11
b Girls, 12–13 (sample = 116)	66	14[a]
c Boys, 14–17 (sample = 277)	85[a, b]	22[a]
d Girls, 14–17 (sample = 267)	93[a, b, c]	39[a, b, c]
Race/ethnicity		
a White, non-Hispanic (sample = 535)	81	23
b Black, non-Hispanic (sample = 115)	88	39[a, c]
c Hispanic (sample = 84)	77	19
Annual household income		
a Less than $50,000 (sample = 292)	83	24
b $50,000 or more (sample = 440)	78	24

Note: Columns marked with a superscript letter (a) indicate a statistically significant difference between that row and the row designated by that superscript letter. Statistical significance is determined inside the specific section covering each demographic trait.

SOURCE: Mary Madden et al., "Twitter and Social Networking Site Usage Demographics," in *Teens, Social Media, and Privacy*, Pew Research Center, May 21, 2013, http://www.pewinternet.org/files/2013/05/PIP_TeensSocialMediaandPrivacy_PDF.pdf (accessed June 3, 2014)

earned less than $30,000 annually (76%) to use social media. Online African Americans (22%) were more likely than online whites (16%) to use Twitter in 2013. (See Figure 2.12.)

VOICE OVER INTERNET PROTOCOL

Another type of Internet communications technology is voice over Internet protocol (VoIP). VoIP is an application that allows the user to make phone calls over the Internet. The user attaches the phone to an adapter that sits between the phone and the computer. When a call is in progress, the adapter breaks down the voice stream into data packets and sends them over the Internet just like e-mail to the user's destination. (Regular phone conversations typically travel as streams of continuous data over a dedicated phone line that connects two people directly.) If the person on the other end of the call is also equipped with VoIP, then the entire conversation is treated by the Internet as nothing more than an instant message or e-mail. If the person using VoIP dials to a traditional phone, then the call must be converted into a continuous voice stream by a telecommunications company before the call reaches its destination. Leading VoIP providers in 2014 included Skype, Vonage, BasicTalk, BroadVoice, and Phone.com.

During the early part of the 21st century VoIP began gaining widespread acceptance among consumers. According to the Pew Research Center and the New Millennium Research Council (June 30, 2004, http://www.newmillenniumresearch.org/news/pewvoip_coverage.html), by 2004, 34 million Americans (27% of Internet users) had heard of VoIP, and nearly 14 million (11%) had used VoIP at some point during their life. The marketing research firm TeleGeography indicates in the press release "US VoIP Gains Mean RBOC Pain" (May 19, 2008, http://www.telegeography.com/press/press-releases/2008/05/19/us-voip-gains-mean-rboc-pain/index.html) that "by the first quarter of 2008, 16.3 million consumer VoIP lines were in service, representing 13.8 percent of all U.S. households, and 27 percent of broadband households." This reflected growth of 758% since 2005, when 1.9 million households had subscribed to VoIP. In *Internet Phone Calling Is on the Rise* (August 1, 2013, http://www.pewinternet.org/2013/08/01/internet-phone-calling-is-on-the-rise), Pew reports that by December 2012 nearly one-third (30%) of Internet users had made a phone call online.

Meanwhile, the number of Americans using VoIP technology on their mobile devices also saw a substantial increase. As Christina Sterling reports in "Numbers Don't Lie: Impressive Stats on the VoIP Industry" (Virtual Phone Systems Review, October 17, 2013, http://virtualphonesystemreviews.com/numbers-dont-lie-impressive-stats-voip-industry), an estimated 228 million mobile phone owners were expected to use VoIP applications on their phones in

TABLE 2.3

Types of personal information posted to social media sites by teens, by age and gender, 2012

	Teen social media users	Boys[a]	Girls[b]	Teens 12–13[a]	Teens 14–17[b]
Your real name	92%	92%	92%	89%	93%
A photo of yourself	91	89	94	82	94[a]
Your interests, such as movies, music, or books you like	84	84	85	81	85
Your birthdate	82	81	83	79	83
Your school name	71	73	69	56	76[a]
The city or town where you live	71	73	69	67	72
Your relationship status	62	62	61	50	66[a]
Your email address	53	57	49	53	53
Videos of you	24	27	21	25	24
Your cell phone number	20	26[b]	14	11	23[a]

Notes: Rows marked with a superscript letter (a) indicate a statistically significant difference between that column and the column designated by that superscript letter. Statistical significance is determined inside the specific section covering each demographic trait.

SOURCE: Mary Madden et al., "Personal Info Posted to Social Media Profiles: Gender and Age," in *Teens, Social Media, and Privacy*, Pew Research Center, May 21, 2013, http://www.pewinternet.org/files/2013/05/PIP_TeensSocialMediaandPrivacy_PDF.pdf (accessed June 3, 2014)

FIGURE 2.10

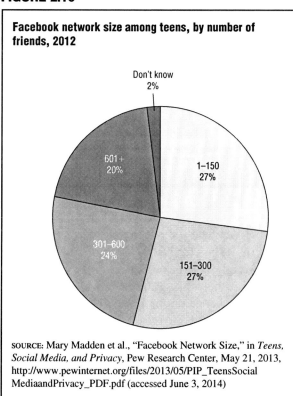

Facebook network size among teens, by number of friends, 2012

SOURCE: Mary Madden et al., "Facebook Network Size," in *Teens, Social Media, and Privacy*, Pew Research Center, May 21, 2013, http://www.pewinternet.org/files/2013/05/PIP_TeensSocial MediaandPrivacy_PDF.pdf (accessed June 3, 2014)

2013. VoIP technology also found massive growth potential in the business world by 2014, as providers such as Ring-Central, Nextiva, and Vonage Business Solutions offered cost-effective alternatives to traditional business telephony systems.

MOBILE PHONES

The cell phone is the only information technology adopted since the mid-1980s that has outpaced the Internet in terms of use. The development of the modern cell phone began during the mid-1940s, nearly 20 years before scientists even conceived of an Internet. In St. Louis, Missouri, the Bell System introduced the first commercial radio-telephone service that could connect to the national phone system. The radio-telephone, which was typically mounted under the front dashboard of a car or truck, received incoming telephone calls via radio waves that were transmitted from a large tower planted on a downtown building. A bell rang and a light went off on the radio-telephone to signify an incoming call. When the person using the radio-telephone answered, his or her side of the conversation was transmitted to one of several receiving stations around the city that were all open to the same frequencies. Both the incoming and outgoing signals were relayed through a switchboard and routed into the national phone system. From its inception in 1946, this system had a number of limitations. Calls had to be routed through a live switchboard operator, both parties involved in a conversation could not talk at once, and only three conversations could take place citywide at any given time because of bandwidth restrictions.

History and Development

D. H. Ring (1907–2000) at Bell Laboratories first posited the idea for the modern mobile cellular phone network in 1947 in an internal memorandum. The memo proposed a system that would overcome many of the flaws inherent in the Bell radio-telephone. The plan called for a network of low-powered cellular towers that could receive and transmit telephone calls via radio waves to and from mobile phones. Each tower would have a three-mile (4.8-km) broadcast radius. As the user of the mobile phone traveled across these cells, the call would be automatically routed from one tower to the next and the phone would switch frequencies. Because of a limited number of frequencies available in the spectrum, towers that were out of range of one another were to send and receive radio signals of the same frequency. That way two people who were three miles apart or more

FIGURE 2.11

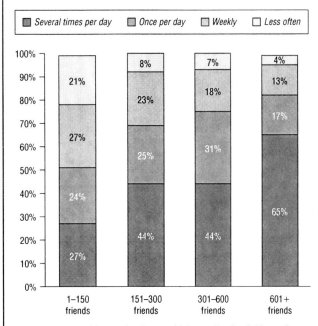

Frequency of social networking use among teens, by number of Facebook friends, 2012

Legend: Several times per day / Once per day / Weekly / Less often

	1–150 friends	151–300 friends	301–600 friends	601+ friends
Less often	21%	8%	7%	4%
Weekly	27%	23%	18%	13%
		25%	31%	17%
Once per day	24%			65%
Several times per day	27%	44%	44%	

SOURCE: Mary Madden et al., "Teens with Large Facebook Networks Visit Social Networking Sites with Greater Frequency Than Those with Smaller Networks," in *Teens, Social Media, and Privacy*, Pew Research Center, May 21, 2013, http://www.pewinternet.org/files/2013/05/PIP_TeensSocialMediaandPrivacy_PDF.pdf (accessed June 3, 2014)

TABLE 2.4

Social networking use among whites and African Americans, by select characteristics, 2013

	White	Black	Difference
Total for Internet users 18+	72%	73%	not sig
Gender			
Male	66	71	not sig
Female	77	74	not sig
Age*			
18–29	90	96	+6
30–49	79	75	not sig
50–64	65	61	not sig
Education			
High school grad or less	67	68	not sig
Some college	73	75	not sig
College+	74	75	not sig
Household income			
<$30,000	74	76	not sig
$30,000–$74,999	72	75	not sig
$75,000+	74	68	not sig
Other demographics			
Parents	78	80	not sig
Students	90	90	not sig

*Due to the small number of African American Internet users in the 65+ age group, this age group is not included in this table.
Notes: Population = 6,010 adults ages 18+. For results based on Internet users, sample size = 3,617 for whites and sample size = 532 for African Americans.

SOURCE: Aaron Smith, "Social Networking Site Use, among White vs. African American Internet Users," in *African Americans and Technology Use*, Pew Research Center, January 6, 2014, http://www.pewinternet.org/files/2014/01/African-Americans-and-Technology-Use.pdf (accessed June 3, 2014)

could carry on separate conversations using the same frequency without interfering with each other's reception.

To implement this vision on a large scale and make a profit, AT&T (the successor to Bell Labs) required more frequencies on the radio spectrum than the Federal Communications Commission (FCC) then allowed for two-way radio communications. The radio spectrum is essentially a long ribbon of frequencies that stretch from 3 kilohertz (kHz) to 300 gigahertz. Only one device in an area, be it a radio station or a television station, can use a particular part of this ribbon to broadcast or else interference will arise. The FCC regulates what type of devices can operate over various sections of the radio spectrum. Cell phones generally take up a large part of each spectrum because each cell phone requires two signals at two different frequencies (one signal for the incoming signal and one for the outgoing signal). With the limits the FCC imposed in 1947, only 23 cellular phone conversations could take place in a metropolitan area equipped with Bell Labs' proposed cellular system. When AT&T approached the FCC and asked for additional room on the radio spectrum, the FCC granted AT&T only a fraction of the space requested.

Over the next 20 years, mobile phone technology advanced slowly. In 1948 the Richmond Radiotelephone

Company implemented the first automated radio-telephone service that did not require a live switchboard operator. In 1964 the Bell System rolled out the Improved Mobile Telephone Service to replace its aging radio-telephone network. This system allowed for both people to talk at once during a call. The bandwidth that each phone occupied on the radio spectrum was narrowed, so more people in a city could use it.

Technological Developments after 1960

AT&T once again approached the FCC in 1958, this time asking for 75 megahertz (MHz) of spectrum located in the 800 MHz range of the radio spectrum. At the time, hardly anyone in the United States employed this part of the spectrum for broadcasting. The FCC did not review the proposal until 1968. It considered the request for two years and made a tentative decision to let AT&T use that part of the spectrum for two-way radio in 1970. Meanwhile, the Bell System, Motorola, and several other companies began engineering the technologies that were necessary for the cell phone network. In 1969 the Bell System installed the first working cell phone system aboard a train. The system consisted of a set of pay phones placed on the Metroliner trains that ran between New York City and

FIGURE 2.12

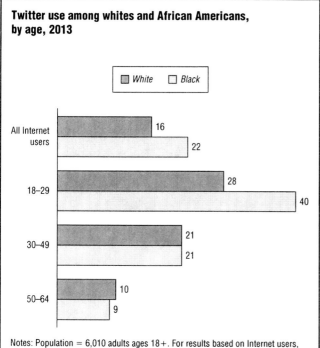

Twitter use among whites and African Americans, by age, 2013

White ☐ Black

All Internet users	White: 16 / Black: 22
18–29	White: 28 / Black: 40
30–49	White: 21 / Black: 21
50–64	White: 10 / Black: 9

Notes: Population = 6,010 adults ages 18+. For results based on Internet users, sample size = 3,617 for whites and sample size = 532 for African Americans.

SOURCE: Aaron Smith, "Young African Americans Have High Levels of Twitter Use," in *African Americans and Technology Use*, Pew Research Center, January 6, 2014, http://www.pewinternet.org/files/2014/01/African-Americans-and-Technology-Use.pdf (accessed June 3, 2014)

Washington, D.C. Cell phone towers were set up along the track. As the train sped along, telephone conversations were routed from tower to tower just as described in the 1947 Bell Labs proposal. Four years after this first cellular phone went into use, Martin Cooper (1928–) of Motorola Inc. developed the first personal, handheld cellular phone. Motorola erected a single prototype cellular tower in New York City to test the phone. Cooper made his first call to his rival at Bell Labs, who was attempting to create a similar device.

In 1978 the FCC allowed AT&T to test an analog cellular telephone service. AT&T chose Chicago, Illinois, as one of the trial cities and set up 10 cellular towers, which covered 21,000 square miles (54,000 sq km) of the Chicago metropolitan area. Customers who wanted to use the service leased large, car-mounted telephones. The trial run was a success, and Ameritech, the regional Bell in metropolitan Chicago, launched the first commercial cellular service in the United States in 1983. (Other cell phone services had already begun operating in Europe, Asia, and the Middle East.) Two months after Ameritech began service, Cellular One offered service in the Washington-Baltimore area. Most people had car-mounted phones that occupied the middle of the front seat of a car. The alternatives were large portable phones that were so big they had to be carried around in a suitcase. At first,

the cellular systems being put in place were not compatible with one another, and roaming outside of the calling area was not a possibility.

During the late 1980s the Telecommunications Industry Association established some basic standards for cell phone companies. The standards paved the way for a continuous, cross-country network that everyone could use regardless of which company was providing the service (oftentimes with extra charges for "roaming" outside one's home area). The first standard was for analog phones. Analog phones process signals in much the same way as car radios or traditional phones do. When a person speaks into the cell phone, the microphone turns the signal into a continuous stream of electrical impulses, which travels out from the phone's antennae and to the cellular tower. Both the outgoing signals and the incoming signals on modern analog phones were each allowed 30 kHz of space on the radio wave spectrum.

Modern Cell Phone Networks

The Census Bureau (2014, http://www.census.gov/compendia/statab/2012/tables/12s1149.pdf) indicates that by 1990 the number of people using cell phones increased dramatically to 5.3 million subscribers. With the analog standard and the frequency limitations imposed by the FCC, fewer than 60 people in each network were able to use one cellular tower at once. If the number of cell phone subscriptions continued to increase at its then-current rate, then cell phone companies would soon require new technologies that allowed more cell phone conversations to take place in a given area. The cell phone companies' solution was to adopt digital technology.

A digital signal is a signal that is broken down into impulses representing ones and zeros. When a digital cell phone receives a digital signal, a chip inside the phone known as a digital signal processor (DSP) reads these ones and zeros and then constructs an analog signal that travels to the phone's speaker. Conversely, the DSP also processes the analog signal coming from the phone's microphone, converting it into ones and zeros, before sending the signal to a cell tower. By breaking down the signal into ones and zeros, more telephone calls can be handled by one-frequency cell phone towers. The process is analogous to breaking down and cutting up boxes to allow more to fit inside a recycling bin. The first digital system widely used by the cell phone companies was the time division multiple access (TDMA) method. Figure 2.13 and Figure 2.14 show the difference between the older, frequency division multiple access (FDMA) used for analog phones and TDMA. FDMA requires each phone to use a different frequency. TDMA allows three cell phone conversations to be contained in the same 30-kHz-wide band

FIGURE 2.13

Use of radio frequencies for analog cell phone access

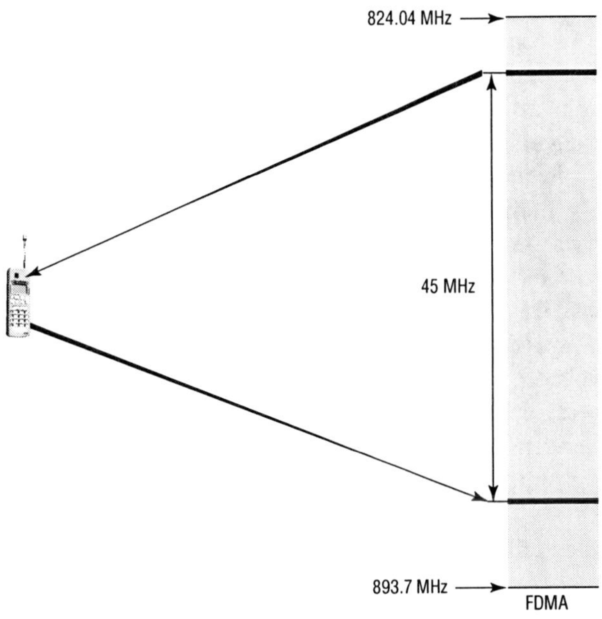

824.04 MHz →

45 MHz

893.7 MHz →

FDMA

FDMA = Frequency Division Multiple Access.

SOURCE: Marshall Brain, Jeff Tyson, and Julia Layton, "Cellular Access Technologies: FDMA," in *How Cell Phones Work*, HowStuffWorks, Inc., 2004, http://electronics.howstuffworks.com/cell-phone7.htm (accessed June 3, 2014). Courtesy of HowStuffWorks.com.

FIGURE 2.14

Use of radio frequencies for digital cell phone encoding and decoding

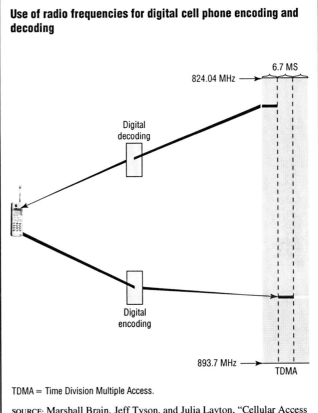

6.7 MS

824.04 MHz →

Digital decoding

Digital encoding

893.7 MHz →

TDMA

TDMA = Time Division Multiple Access.

SOURCE: Marshall Brain, Jeff Tyson, and Julia Layton, "Cellular Access Technologies: TDMA," in *How Cell Phones Work*, HowStuffWorks, Inc., 2004, http://electronics.howstuffworks.com/cell-phone7.htm (accessed September 25, 2012) Courtesy of HowStuffWorks.com.

that holds only one analog conversation. By the early 1990s cellular companies were erecting digital cellular towers enabled with TDMA across the country.

Meanwhile, the TDMA systems were looking as if they might hit capacity. In response, the FCC auctioned off more frequency bands in the radio wave spectrum between the 1850 MHz and 1900 MHz range. Services set up on these bands were known as personal communications services (PCS). PCS networks were designed for handheld mobile phones instead of car phones and had smaller cells than the original cellular network. The PCS networks also employed a newer technology known as code division multiple access (CDMA). CDMA could pack up to 10 calls into one frequency band. (See Figure 2.15.) With so many bands available, cell phone companies introduced a multitude of standard features into their phones, such as the ability to send instant messages, surf the web, play games, send e-mail, and check the identity of callers.

High-speed fourth-generation (4G) cell phone service, the newest generation of wireless technology, allows for even more integration of Internet technologies into cell phones. Because it is an advanced form of CDMA, 4G allows more people to share a broader bandwidth of frequencies on the current cell phone networks. Cell phone providers installed software known as high-speed

downlink packet access into cell phone base stations. This software increased the amount of data that could flow through cell phone networks and boosted Internet connection speeds to over 1 megabyte per second. With such high-speed access, more people began using their cell phones to download and play video files, watch newscasts, and shop online. By 2014 all major telecommunications companies had introduced 4G mobile wireless products, many of them offering connection speeds of up to 1 gigabyte per second. Continued development of smaller electronics and display screens will bring even higher quality cameras, video games systems, and web cameras to cell phones.

For both adults and teens, by the second decade of the 21st century cell phones had become an integral part of their daily lives. Between 2000 and 2014, the percentage of all adults who owned cell phones rose from 53% to 90%. (See Figure 2.16.) As Table 2.5 shows, younger adults were more likely than older adults to own cell phones. Among adults between the ages of 18 and 29 years, 98% owned cell phones in 2014; this figure remained roughly the same for adults between the ages of 30 and 49 years, 97% of whom owned cell phones that year. By comparison, cell phone ownership fell to 88% among adults between the ages of 50 and 64 years, and

FIGURE 2.15

Use of radio frequencies for code division multiple access

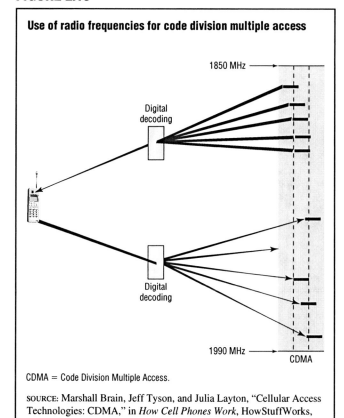

CDMA = Code Division Multiple Access.

SOURCE: Marshall Brain, Jeff Tyson, and Julia Layton, "Cellular Access Technologies: CDMA," in *How Cell Phones Work*, HowStuffWorks, Inc., 2004, http://electronics.howstuffworks.com/cell-phone7.htm (accessed June 3, 2014). Courtesy of HowStuffWorks.com.

FIGURE 2.16

Percentage of adults who own cell phones, 2000–14

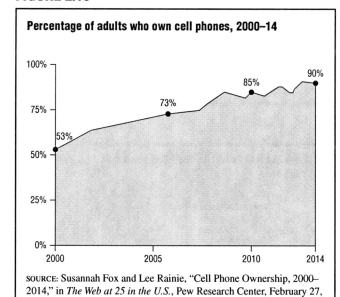

SOURCE: Susannah Fox and Lee Rainie, "Cell Phone Ownership, 2000–2014," in *The Web at 25 in the U.S.*, Pew Research Center, February 27, 2014, http://www.pewinternet.org/files/2014/02/PIP_25th-anniversary-of-the-Web_0227141.pdf (accessed June 3, 2014)

fewer than three-quarters (74%) of seniors aged 65 years and older owned cell phones in 2014. (See Table 2.5.) As Table 2.6 shows, wealth and educational attainment were significant factors in determining whether or not seniors

TABLE 2.5

Percentage of adults who own cell phones, by age, gender, and other select characteristics, 2014

	Have a cell phone
All adults	**90%**
Sex	
a Men	93
b Women	88
Race/ethnicity*	
a White	90
b African-American	90
c Hispanic	92
Age group	
a 18–29	98
b 30–49	97
c 50–64	88
d 65+	74
Education level	
a High school grad or less	87
b Some college	93
c College+	93
Household income	
a Less than $30,000/yr	84
b $30,000–$49,999	90
c $50,000–$74.999	99
d $75,000+	98
Community type	
a Urban	88
b Suburban	92
c Rural	88

*The results for race/ethnicity are based off a combined sample from two weekly omnibus surveys, January 9–12 and January 23–26, 2014. The combined total sample size for these surveys was 2,008; sample size = 1,421 for whites, sample size = 197 for African-Americans, and sample size = 236 for Hispanics.

SOURCE: "Cell Owners in 2014," in *Data Trend: Cell Phone and Smartphone Ownership Demographics*, Pew Research Center, January 2014, http://www.pewinternet.org/data-trend/mobile/cell-phone-and-smartphone-ownership-demographics/ (accessed June 3, 2014)

owned cell phones. Whereas 87% of college-educated adults over the age of 65 years owned cell phones in 2013, only 70% of seniors who either had only a high school diploma or else never finished high school owned cell phones that year. Among seniors with a household income of $75,000 a year or more, 92% owned cell phones in 2013; by contrast, only two-thirds (67%) of seniors who earned less than $30,000 annually had cell phones that year.

The proportion of American teenagers who owned cell phones during these years also rose considerably. As Table 2.7 shows, 78% of teens between the ages of 12 and 17 years owned cell phones in 2012. Children of college-educated parents (87%) were significantly more likely than children of parents who had either never finished high school or earned only a high school diploma (71%) to have cell phones that year. Among racial and ethnic groups, non-Hispanic white teens (81%) were the most likely to have cell phones in 2012, followed by non-Hispanic African American teens (72%) and Hispanics (64%). Teens growing up in suburban

TABLE 2.6

Percentage of seniors who own cell phones and smartphones, by select characteristics, 2013

[% of seniors (ages 65 and older) who own a...]

	Cell phone	Smartphone
Total for all 65+	77%	18%
Age		
65–69	84	29
70–74	84	21
75–79	72	10
80+	61	5
Education		
High school grad or less	70	10
Some college	80	19
College graduate	87	35
Household income		
<$30,000	67	8
$30,000–$49,999	83	15
$50,000–$74,999	88	28
$75,000+	92	42

SOURCE: Aaron Smith, "Cell Phone and Smartphone Adoption among Seniors," in *Older Adults and Technology Use*, Pew Research Center, April 3, 2014, http://www.pewinternet.org/files/2014/04/PIP_Seniors-and-Tech-Use_040314.pdf (accessed June 3, 2014)

areas (81%) were more likely to own cell phones than those living in urban (76%) or rural (73%) communities in 2012. (See Table 2.7.)

Texting and Other Nonvoice Applications

As Table 2.8 shows, more than four out of five cell phone owners (81%) sent or received text messages in 2013, making it the most popular nonvoice cell phone activity that year. Meanwhile, between 2011 and 2014 an increasing number of cell phone owners were using their mobile devices to access the Internet. In 2011, 35% of Americans owned smartphones; by 2014 this figure had risen to 58%. (See Figure 2.17.) As with traditional cell phones, smartphone ownership was more prevalent among younger adults. In 2014, 83% of adults between the ages of 18 and 29 years owned smartphones. (See Table 2.9.) The proportion of smartphone owners dropped slightly among adults between the ages of 30 and 49 years (74%), before dipping to 49% among adults aged 50 to 64 years. Smartphone ownership was lowest among seniors aged 65 years and older; among adults in this age demographic, only one in five (19%) owned smartphones in 2014. As Table 2.6 shows, seniors with annual household incomes of $75,000 or more (42%) were considerably more likely to own smartphones in 2013 than seniors with household incomes below $30,000 a year (8%).

Apps

As ownership of smartphones and other portable computing devices increased, a wide range of mobile applications, or apps, became available to consumers.

TABLE 2.7

Percentage of teens who own cell phones and smartphones, by age, gender, and other characteristics, 2012

	Own a cell phone (any kind)	Own a smartphone
All teens, ages 12–17 (sample = 802)	78%	37%
Teen gender		
a Boys (sample = 405)	77	36
b Girls (sample = 397)	78	38
Age of teen		
a 12–13 (sample = 246)	68	23
b 14–17 (sample = 556)	83[a]	44[a]
Teen gender and age		
a Boys, 12–13 (sample = 122)	65	20
b Boys, 14–17 (sample = 283)	83[a, c]	43[a, c]
c Girls, 12–13 (sample = 124)	71	26
d Girls, 14–17 (sample = 273)	82[a]	44[a, c]
Parent race/ethnicity		
a White, Non-Hispanic (sample = 542)	81[c]	35
b Black, Non-Hispanic (sample = 122)	72	40
c Hispanic (sample = 92)	64	43
Parent education		
a Less Than High School/High school grad (sample = 244)	71	35
b Some College (sample = 192)	79	35
c College+ (sample = 363)	87[a, b]	41
Parent household income		
a Less than $30,000/yr (sample = 154)	69	39[b]
b $30,000–$49,999 (sample = 155)	74	24
c $50,000–$74,999 (sample = 110)	81	38
d $75,000+ (sample = 335)	86[a, b]	43[b]
Urbanity		
a Urban (sample = 278)	76	42[c]
b Suburban (sample = 410)	81	39[c]
c Rural (sample = 101)	73	19

Note: Columns marked with a superscript letter (a) or another letter indicate a statistically significant difference between that row and the row designated by that superscript letter. Statistical significance is determined inside the specific section covering each demographic trait.

SOURCE: Mary Madden et al., "Teen Cell Phone and Smartphone Ownership Demographics," in *Teens and Technology 2013*, Pew Research Center, March 13, 2013, http://www.pewinternet.org/files/old-media/Files/Reports/2013/PIP_TeensandTechnology2013.pdf (accessed June 3, 2014)

TABLE 2.8

Percentage of adults who use their cell phones to perform various activities, 2013

81	Send or receive text messages
60	Access the Internet
52	Send or receive email
50	Download apps
49	Get directions, recommendations, or other location-based information
48	Listen to music
21	Participate in a video call or video chat
8	"Check in" or share your location

SOURCE: Maeve Duggan, "Cell Phone Activities," in *Cell Phone Activities 2013*, Pew Research Center, September 16, 2013, http://www.pewinternet.org/files/old-media/Files/Reports/2013/PIP_Cell%20Phone%20Activities%20May%202013.pdf (accessed June 3, 2014)

An app is a software program that enables smartphone users to perform certain functions on their mobile devices. Apps come in a variety of forms, from digital tools

FIGURE 2.17

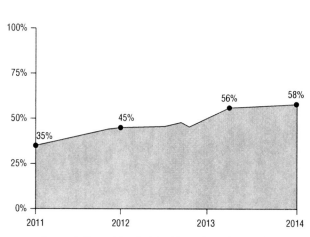

Percentage of adults who own smartphones, 2011–14

SOURCE: Susannah Fox and Lee Rainie, "Smartphone Ownership, over Time," in *The Web at 25 in the U.S.*, Pew Research Center, February 27, 2014, http://www.pewinternet.org/files/2014/02/PIP_25th-anniversary-of-the-Web_0227141.pdf (accessed June 3, 2014)

TABLE 2.9

Percentage of adults who own smartphones, by age, gender, and other select characteristics, 2014

[Among adults, the % who have a cell phone]

	Have a smartphone phone
All adults	**58%**
Sex	
a Men	61
b Women	57
Race/ethnicity*	
a White	53
b African-American	59
c Hispanic	61[a]
Age group	
a 18–29	83[b, c, d]
b 30–49	74[c, d]
c 50–64	49[d]
d 65+	19
Education level	
a High school grad or less	44
b Some college	67[a]
c College+	71[a]
Household income	
a Less than $30,000/yr	47
b $30,000–$49,999	53
c $50,000–$74,999	61[a]
d $75,000+	81[a, b, c]
Community type	
a Urban	64[c]
b Suburban	60[c]
c Rural	43

Note: Percentages marked with a superscript letter (e.g.[a]) indicate a statistically significant difference between that row and the row designated by that superscript letter, among categories of each demographic characteristic (e.g. age).
*The results for race/ethnicity are based off a combined sample from two weekly omnibus surveys. January 9–12 and January 23–26, 2014. The combined total in for these surveys was 2,008; sample size = 197 for African Americans, and sample size = 236 for Hispanics.

SOURCE: "Smartphone Owners in 2014," in *Data Trend: Cell Phone and Smartphone Ownership Demographics*, Pew Research Center, January 2014, http://www.pewinternet.org/data-trend/mobile/cell-phone-and-smartphone-ownership-demographics/ (accessed June 3, 2014)

(such as appointment calendars or navigation systems) to music players to interactive online games. As smartphone use became increasingly widespread, many companies, including banks, retailers, and streaming content providers such as Netflix and HBO Go, created apps to enable their customers to conduct transactions or access their accounts from their mobile devices. At the same time, social networking sites such as Facebook created apps that allowed users to update their status, upload photographs, and share their location from their phones. Half (50%) of all cell phone owners downloaded an app in 2013. (See Table 2.8.)

Leading app distributors in 2014 included the Apple Store, the Windows Phone Store, and Google Play. As Statista reports in "Most Popular Apple App Store Categories in June 2014, by Share of Available Apps" (June 2014, http://www.statista.com/statistics/270291/popular-categories-in-the-app-store), games accounted for nearly one in five (19.1%) of all apps downloaded from the Apple Store in June 2014; other popular app categories included education apps (10.6%), business apps (8.4%), and lifestyle apps (8.1%). Indeed, by 2014 smartphone owners were spending considerably more time using apps than web browsers. According to Sarah Perez in "Mobile App Usage Increases in 2014, as Mobile Web Surfing Declines" (TechCrunch.com, April 1 2014), smartphone users were spending an average of two hours and 42 minutes on their mobile devices in 2014. Of that time, two hours and 19 minutes, or 86%, was spent using mobile apps.

Issues and Concerns

DISTRACTED DRIVING. Even though cell phones have brought a great deal of convenience to modern society,

they have become a source of trouble as well. Cell phones contribute to automobile accidents because drivers cannot concentrate on the road appropriately while speaking or texting on a cell phone. As of 2014 Congress continued to debate whether or not to institute a nationwide ban on handheld cell phone use in automobiles, but many states already had laws in place. Table 2.10 indicates which states had adopted cell phone driving laws as of June 2014; at that time 12 states and the District of Columbia had statewide bans on the use of handheld devices while driving. In addition, 43 states and the District of Columbia banned drivers from text-messaging while behind the wheel; 37 states and the District of Columbia banned cell phones for drivers with learner permits or provisional licenses; and 20 states and the District of Columbia prohibited the use of cell phones by school bus drivers carrying passengers.

TABLE 2.10

State cell phone and texting laws, June 2014

State	Hand-held ban	All cell phone ban		Text messaging ban			Crash data
		School bus drivers	Novice drivers	All drivers	School bus drivers	Novice drivers	
Alabama			16, or 17 w/ intermediate license <6 months (primary)	Yes (primary)	Covered under all driver ban		Yes
Alaska				Yes (primary)	Covered under all driver ban		Yes
Arizona		Yes (primary)					Yes
Arkansas[a]	18–20 years old (primary)	Yes (primary)	<18 (secondary)	Yes (primary)	Covered under all driver ban		Yes
California	Yes (primary)	Yes (primary)	<18 (secondary)	Yes (primary)	Covered under all driver ban		Yes
Colorado			<18 (primary)	Yes (primary)	Covered under all driver ban		Yes
Connecticut	Yes (primary)	Yes (primary)	<18 (primary)	Yes (primary)	Covered under all driver ban		
Delaware	Yes (primary)	Yes (primary)	Learner or intermediate license (primary)	Yes (primary)	Covered under all driver ban		Yes
D.C.	Yes (primary)	Yes (primary)	Learners permit (primary)	Yes (primary)	Covered under all driver ban		Yes
Florida				Yes (secondary)	Covered under all driver ban		Yes
Georgia		Yes (primary)	<18 (primary)	Yes (primary)	Covered under all driver ban		Yes
Guam	Yes (primary)			Yes (primary)	Covered under all driver ban		
Hawaii	Yes (primary)		<18 (primary)	Yes (primary)	Covered under all driver ban		Yes
Idaho				Yes (primary)	Covered under all driver ban		Yes
Illinois	Yes (primary)	Yes (primary)	<19 (primary)	Yes (primary)	Covered under all driver ban		Yes
Indiana			<18 (primary)	Yes (primary)	Covered under all driver ban		Yes
Iowa			Restricted or intermediate license (primary)	Yes (secondary)	Covered under all driver ban		Yes
Kansas			Learner or intermediate license (primary)	Yes (primary)	Covered under all driver ban		Yes
Kentucky		Yes (primary)	<18 (primary)	Yes (primary)	Covered under all driver ban		Yes
Louisiana	Learner or intermediate license (regardless of age)	Yes (primary)	1st year of license (primary for <18)	Yes (primary)	Covered under all driver ban		Yes
Maine			<18 (primary)	Yes (primary)	Covered under all driver ban		Yes
Maryland	Yes (primary)		<18 w/Learner or provisional license (secondary)	Yes (primary)	Covered under all driver ban		Yes
Massachusetts		Yes (primary)	<18 (primary)	Yes (primary)	Covered under all driver ban		Yes
Michigan		Yes (primary)	Level 1 or 2 license (primary)	Yes (primary)	Covered under all driver ban		Yes
Minnesota		Yes (primary)	<18 w/Learner or provisional license (primary)	Yes (primary)	Covered under all driver ban		Yes
Mississippi		Yes (primary)			Yes (primary)	Learner or provisional license (primary)	Yes
Missouri						≤21 (primary)	Yes
Montana							Yes
Nebraska			<18 w/Learner or intermediate license (secondary)	Yes (secondary)	Covered under all driver ban		Yes
Nevada	Yes (primary)			Yes (primary)	Covered under all driver ban		Yes
New Hampshire[b]				Yes (primary)	Covered under all driver ban		
New Jersey	Yes (primary)	Yes (primary)	Permit or provisional license (primary)	Yes (primary)	Covered under all driver ban		Yes
New Mexico	In state vehicles		Learner or provisional license (primary)	Yes (primary) (eff. 7/2014)	Covered under all driver ban		Yes
New York	Yes (primary)			Yes (primary)	Covered under all driver ban		Yes
North Carolina		Yes (primary)	<18 (primary)	Yes (primary)	Covered under all driver ban		Yes
North Dakota			<18 (primary)	Yes (primary)	Covered under all driver ban		Yes
Ohio			<18 (primary)	Yes (secondary)	Covered under all driver ban		Yes
Oklahoma	Learner or intermediate license (primary)				Yes (primary)	Learner or intermediate license (primary)	Yes
Oregon	Yes (primary)		<18 (primary)	Yes (primary)	Covered under all driver ban		Yes

TABLE 2.10

State cell phone and texting laws, June 2014 [CONTINUED]

State	Hand-held ban	All cell phone ban		Text messaging ban			Crash data
		School bus drivers	Novice drivers	All drivers	School bus drivers	Novice drivers	
Pennsylvania				Yes (primary)	Covered under all driver ban		Yes
Puerto Rico	Yes (primary)			Yes (primary)	Covered under all driver ban		
Rhode Island		Yes (primary)	<18 (primary)	Yes (primary)	Covered under all driver ban		Yes
South Carolina							Yes
South Dakota			Learner or intermediate license (secondary)	Yes (secondary) (eff. 7/2014)	Covered under all driver ban		Yes
Tennessee		Yes (primary)	Learner or intermediate license (primary)	Yes (primary)	Covered under all driver ban		Yes
Texas[c]		Yes, w/passenger ≤17 (primary)	<18 (primary)		Yes, w/passenger ≤17 (primary)	<18 (primary)	Yes
Utah		Yes (primary)	<18 (primary)	Yes (primary)	Covered under all driver ban		Yes
Vermont	In work zones		<18 (primary)	Yes (primary)	Covered under all driver ban		Yes
Virgin Islands	Yes (primary)			Yes (primary)	Covered under all driver ban		Yes
Virginia		Yes (primary)	<18 secondary	Yes (primary)	Covered under all driver ban		Yes
Washington	Yes (primary)		Learner or intermediate licence (primary)	Yes (primary)	Covered under all driver ban		Yes
West Virginia	Yes (primary)		<18 w/Learner or intermediate licence (primary)	Yes (primary)	Covered under all driver ban		Yes
Wisconsin			Learner or intermediate licence (primary)	Yes (primary)	Covered under all driver ban		Yes
Wyoming			<18 primary	Yes (primary)	Covered under all driver ban		Yes
Total States	**12 + D.C. PR, Guam, Virgin Islands** All primary	**20 + D.C.** All primary	**37 + D.C.** primary (31 + D.C.) secondary (6)	**43 + D.C., PR, Guam, Virgin Islands** primary (38 + D.C., PR, Guam, Virgin Islands) secondary (5)	**3** All primary	**4** All primary	**48 + D.C., Virgin Islands**

[a]Arkansas also bans the use of hand-held cell phones while driving in a school zone or in a highway construction zone. This law is secondarily enforced.
[b]Dealt with as a distracted driving issue; New Hampshire enacted a comprehensive distracted driving law.
[c]Texas has banned the use of hand-held phones and texting in school zones.

SOURCE: "Distracted Driving Laws," in *State Laws & Funding,* Governors Highway Safety Association, June 2014, http://www.ghsa.org/html/stateinfo/laws/cellphone_laws.html (accessed June 3, 2014)

HEALTH RISKS. Health concerns associated with cell phone use have also been identified. In the landmark study "Nerve Cell Damage in Mammalian Brain after Exposure to Microwaves from GSM Mobile Phones" (*Environmental Health Perspectives*, vol. 111, no. 7, June 2003), Leif G. Salford et al. of Lund University found that cell phone radiation causes brain damage in rats. The researchers mounted a cell phone to the side of the rats' cage for two hours per day for 50 days to emulate the amount of exposure that is received by a habitual cell phone user. The rats' brains showed significant blood vessel leakage as well as areas of damaged neurons. Other studies followed but were inconclusive. However, the University of Pittsburgh Cancer Institute warns in "The Case for Precaution in the Use of Cell Phones" (July 22, 2008, http://www.upci.upmc.edu/news/pdf/The-Case-for-Precaution-in-Cell-Phone-Use.pdf) that:

> Electromagnetic fields generated by cell phones should be considered a potential human health risk. Sufficient time has not elapsed in order for us to have conclusive data on the biological effects of cell phones and other cordless phones—a technology that is now universal.

> Studies in humans do not indicate that cell phones are safe, nor do they yet clearly show that they are dangerous. But, growing evidence indicates that we should reduce exposures, while research continues on this important question.

The institute emphasizes that children are particularly at risk because their brains are still developing and suggests that children should not use mobile phones except in emergencies. Nevertheless, other studies find no evidence of human health risks related to cell phone use. In "Cell Phones: Current Research Results" (March 20, 2014, http://www.fda.gov/Radiation-EmittingProducts/RadiationEmittingProductsandProcedures/HomeBusinessandEntertainment/Cellphones/ucm116335.htm), the U.S. Food and Drug Administration (FDA), citing findings released by the World Health Organization, indicates that no specific health risks related to cell phone use have been identified. Nonetheless, the FDA also states that scientific research on the subject is still ongoing.

CHAPTER 3
INFORMATION TECHNOLOGY AND U.S. BUSINESS

The desire of U.S. corporations to make money fueled the proliferation of electronics and communications technologies during the 1980s and 1990s. High-technology (high-tech) companies such as Microsoft, Apple, and Intel strove to create affordable computers, Internet technologies, cell phones, and a variety of electronics-based products for use in the office, at home, and while on the go. A huge market segment, commonly referred to as the information technology (IT) industry, developed around the production of these new technologies and included the manufacture of computers and electronic products, software publishing, data processing services, advanced telecommunications, and computer systems design. As the technology research firm Gartner, Inc., reports in "Gartner Says Worldwide IT Spending on Pace to Reach $3.8 Trillion in 2014" (January 6, 2014, http://www.gartner.com/newsroom/id/2643919), global spending on information technology topped $3.7 trillion in 2013, and was expected to reach $3.8 trillion in 2014, an increase of 3.1%.

As information technologies spread through U.S. offices and corporations, they also transformed other industries outside of the IT sector. In the financial industries, innovations such as interconnected bank networks and electronic bill pay greatly reduced the number of paper checks in circulation daily. The retail industry discovered a new way to sell merchandise. The U.S. Census Bureau notes in *E-Stats* (May 22, 2014, http://www.census.gov/econ/estats/2012_e-stats_report.pdf) that by 2012, $227 billion in retail sales were conducted over the Internet annually. Furthermore, e-commerce manufacturing shipments in 2012 amounted to nearly $3 trillion. (See Table 3.1.) During the first quarter of 2013, e-commerce retail sales totaled $61.9 billion; during the first quarter of 2014 online retail sales reached $71.2 billion, an increase of 15% over the same period the previous year. (See Table 3.2.)

The economic impact of IT reverberated well beyond those industries that sold goods on the Internet, however. Every industry from trucking to real estate to health care to manufacturing incorporated new technologies that helped make doing business more efficient and affordable. Entire medical and law libraries were replaced by online databases that could be searched in minutes. Retail inventories, which used to be counted by hand, were linked directly to bar-code scans taken at cash registers, a process that ultimately made ordering stock more efficient and reduced expensive storage costs. Bookkeeping and accounting, which was once an arduous task completed in thick, paper ledgers, was done in a fraction of the time and at a fraction of the cost using computer accounting software.

Nevertheless, IT did not have a positive effect on all businesses. For example, travel agencies saw an enormous drop in revenue because many people began making their own travel arrangements using online reservations sites. The growth in online bookings led to a 40% drop in the number of travel agency jobs in the United States between 1999 and 2013. In *National Occupational Employment and Wage Estimates* (May 2013, http://www.bls.gov/oes/2013/may/oes_nat.htm), the U.S. Department of Labor's Bureau of Labor Statistics (BLS) states that 64,250 travel agents were employed in 2013, compared with 111,130 in 1999. The ease with which the typical consumer could make travel arrangements online was largely responsible for this decline.

IT INDUSTRY

Even though IT has been around since International Business Machines (IBM) began mass-producing computers in the early 1950s, it did not become a large part of the U.S. economy until the 1990s. A number of high-tech companies, such as Microsoft and Dell, had positioned themselves as the commercial leaders in Internet,

TABLE 3.1

Total and e-commerce shipments, sales, and revenues, 2011 and 2012

[Shipments, sales and revenues are in millions of dollars. Estimated measures of sampling variability for these estimates are provided in Measures of Sampling Variability—U.S. Shipments, Sales, Revenues and E-commerce: 2012 and 2011.]

| | Value of shipments, sales, or revenue | | | | Year to year percent change | | E-commerce as percent of total | |
| | 2012 | | 2011 | | | | | |
Description	Total	E-commerce	Revised total	Revised e-commerce	Total	E-commerce	2012	2011
Manufacturing	5,756,337	2,989,146	5,481,368	2,703,962	5.0	10.5	51.9	49.3
Merchant wholesale	6,771,454	1,789,095	6,451,323	1,695,826	5.0	5.5	26.4	26.3
Excluding MSBOs*	4,926,582	989,625	4,689,474	932,508	5.1	6.1	20.1	19.9
MSBOs	1,844,872	799,470	1,761,849	763,318	4.7	4.7	43.3	43.3
Retail	4,344,140	226,878	4,132,996	197,883	5.1	14.7	5.2	4.8
Selected services	12,004,067	366,277	11,544,042	337,913	4.0	8.4	3.1	2.9

*Manufacturers' Sales Branches and Offices.

SOURCE: "U.S. Shipments, Sales, Revenues and E-Commerce: 2012 and 2011, in *E-Stats: 2012 E-Commerce Multi-Sector Data Tables*," U.S. Department of Commerce, U.S. Census Bureau, May 22, 2014, http://www.census.gov/econ/estats/2012/2012summary.xls (accessed June 3, 2014)

TABLE 3.2

Estimated quarterly U.S. retail sales, total and e-commerce, 2013–14

[Estimates are based on data from the Monthly Retail Trade Survey and administrative records]

| | Retail sales (millions of dollars) | | E-commerce as a percent of total | Percent change from prior quarter | | Percent change from same quarter a year ago | |
Quarter	Total	E-commerce		Total	E-commerce	Total	E-commerce
Adjusted							
1st quarter 2014ᵃ	1,147,388	71,188	6.2	0.2	2.8	2.4	15.0
4th quarter 2013ᵇ	1,144,544	69,244	6.0	0.6	3.0	3.8	15.7
3rd quarter 2013	1,137,327	67,250	5.9	1.0	3.5	4.7	17.6
2nd quarter 2013	1,125,990	64,962	5.8	0.5	4.9	4.8	17.9
1st quarter 2013ᵇ	1,120,085	61,911	5.5	1.5	3.4	4.1	15.1
Not adjusted							
1st quarter 2014ᵃ	1,078,559	66,917	6.2	−9.9	−20.1	2.2	14.9
4th quarter 2013ᵇ	1,197,402	83,709	7.0	5.5	35.3	3.7	15.7
3rd quarter 2013	1,135,418	61,857	5.4	−0.4	2.2	5.4	17.5
2nd quarter 2013	1,140,006	60,498	5.3	8.0	3.9	4.7	18.0
1st quarter 2013	1,055,389	58,215	5.5	−8.6	−19.5	3.1	15.1

ᵃPreliminary estimate.
ᵇRevised estimate.
Notes: E-commerce sales are sales of goods and services where an order is placed by the buyer or price and terms of sale are negotiated over an Internet, extranet, Electronic Data Interchange (EDI) network, electronic mail, or other online system. Payment may or may not be made online.
Estimates are adjusted for seasonal variation, but not for price changes. Total sales estimates are also adjusted for trading-day differences and moving holidays.

SOURCE: Ian Thomas, William Davie, and Deanna Weidenhamer, "Table 1. Estimated Quarterly U.S. Retail Sales: Total and E-Commerce," in *Quarterly Retail E-Commerce Sales: 1st Quarter 2014*, U.S. Department of Commerce, U.S. Census Bureau, May 15, 2014, http://www.census.gov/retail/mrts/www/data/pdf/ec_current.pdf (accessed June 3, 2014)

---

personal computer, and cell phone technologies during the 1980s. When use of the World Wide Web became common in 1994 and the price of electronics began to drop, Americans flocked to these technologies. Revenues in the high-tech industry as a whole increased at a rate not seen in any industry since the postwar boom of the 1950s. Microsoft reported sales of $140 million in 1985. Ten years later its revenues had increased to $6 billion. Cisco Systems, the leading commercial maker of Internet routers and switches, grew at an even faster rate. Between 1990 and 2001 the company's revenues grew from $69 million to $22 billion. Dell, one of the top sellers of home computers in the U.S. market, saw

sales increase from $300 million in 1989 to $56.9 billion in fiscal year (FY) 2013.

The growth of these companies along with the rest of the IT-producing industries had a tremendous impact on the economy. Table 3.3 shows a list of the types of businesses that make up the IT-producing industries. According to the U.S. Department of Commerce in *Digital Economy 2003* (December 2003, http://www.esa.doc.gov/sites/default/files/reports/documents/dig_econ_2003.pdf), the IT industries made up roughly 8% to 9% of the U.S. domestic economy between 1996 and 2000. However, these industries were responsible for

TABLE 3.3

Information technology-producing industries

Hardware industries	Software/services industries
Computers and equipment	Computer programming
Wholesale trade of computers and equipment*	Prepackaged software
Retail trade of computers and equipment*	Wholesale trade of software*
Calculating and office machines	Retail trade of software*
Magnetic and optical recording media	Computer-integrated system design
Electron tubes	Computer processing, data preparation
Printed circuit boards	Information retrieval services
Semiconductors	Computer services management
Passive electronic components	Computer rental and leasing
Industrial instruments for measurement	Computer maintenance and repair
Instruments for measuring electricity	Computer related services, nec
Laboratory analytical instruments	**Communications services industries**
Communications equipment industries	Telephone and telegraph
Household audio and video equipment	communications
Telephone and telegraph equipment	Cable and other TV services
Radio and TV communications equipment	

*Wholesale and retail from computer manufacturer sales from branch offices.

SOURCE: David Henry and Donald Dalton, "Box 1.1. Information Technology Producing Industries," in "Information Technology Producing Industries—Hopeful Signs in 2003," *Digital Economy 2003*, U.S. Department of Commerce, Economics and Statistics Administration, December 2003, http://www.esa.doc.gov/sites/default/files/reports/documents/dig_econ_2003.pdf (accessed June 3, 2014)

1.4 percentage points of the nation's 4.6% annual average real gross domestic product (GDP) growth over these years. The GDP is one of the basic yardsticks used to measure the U.S. economy and is defined as the value, or sale price, of all goods that are produced in a country minus the cost of the materials that went into making those goods. In other words, the entire IT industry, which made up a little under one-tenth of the economy, accounted for over one-third of the economic growth. Between 1993 and 2000 employment in the IT industries expanded rapidly as well. IT companies hired people at twice the rate of all private industries and added more than 1.8 million jobs to the workforce in sectors such as software and computer services, computer hardware, and communication services.

End of the IT Boom

Toward the dawn of the 21st century many Americans thought the IT boom would continue indefinitely. They invested enormous sums of money in IT and IT-related stocks. From late 1998 to early 2000 the value of Microsoft stocks and Dell stocks doubled; Cisco Systems' stock value quadrupled. The National Association of Securities Dealers Automated Quotation System (NASDAQ), a stock index that tracks the value of many IT stocks, rose from 2,442 on August 10, 1999, to a peak value of 5,132 on Friday, March 10, 2000 (one of the largest increases of a major stock index in history). Many Americans invested not only in large, well-established corporations but also in small e-commerce companies such as Pets.com and eToys. Many of these dot-coms

were brand-new businesses that had yet to produce any profits. People invested in them in the hope that these dot-coms would enjoy the sort of huge rise in value that made early investors in Dell or Microsoft millionaires.

On Monday, March 13, 2000, the NASDAQ dropped roughly 300 points, from a high of 5,013 to a closing low of 4,706. The index dropped for a couple more days, rebounded to a point close to its all-time high, and then proceeded to fall intermittently for the next two-and-a-half years, finally hitting bottom on October 10, 2002, at 1,108. Other stock indexes, such as the Dow Jones Industrial Average and Standard and Poor's 500, followed this downward trend, ultimately returning to 1998 levels. The stock bubble burst because investors began to fear that many IT and IT-related companies were not living up to expectations and pulled their money out of the market.

The entire nation slipped into a recession. By 2001 numerous dot-coms were out of business, and many established IT companies were beginning to post losses. From 2001 to 2002 Cisco Systems' sales dropped more than $3.4 billion, and Dell's annual earnings dipped by roughly $700 million. The Department of Commerce explains in *Digital Economy 2003* that the main reason for the slowdown in the IT industries was that the private business sector stopped buying equipment. Throughout the 1990s just about every type of business (from law firms to paper producers to grocery stores to auto shops) was either buying or updating its computers, printers, and networks. Businesses that did not make such investments quickly became outdated and inefficient and did not survive. By the turn of the 21st century many companies outside of the IT industries had already made an initial investment in IT equipment and required only upgrades as hardware needed replacement or as software was updated. In addition, the components that make up the infrastructure for the Internet (fiber-optic cables, routers, and switches) had largely been laid down by the late 1990s, so the need for these components greatly diminished as well.

The industries that produced hardware components and communications equipment were the hardest hit. The overall GDP for these industries dropped 22% in 2000 and 18% in 2001. The Department of Commerce reports that among the most negatively affected industries, semiconductor manufacturing fell from $67.9 billion in 2000 to $44.1 billion in 2001, a 35% decrease. The industries that did reasonably well during this recessionary period were the software and services industries and the communications services industries. Prepackaged software, computer processing, information retrieval services, computer services management, computer maintenance and repair, and other computer-related services all showed modest gains. Even though U.S. businesses as a whole had bought much of their hardware, many still had the need for new software, Internet service, and computer maintenance.

Lost Jobs

To cut their losses in this down market, IT companies began laying off many of the workers they had hired during the 1990s. In *Digital Economy 2003*, the Department of Commerce reports that roughly 600,000 jobs were shed in the IT industries between 2000 and 2002. This job loss accounted for more than a quarter of all the jobs that were lost during the recession. The rate of job loss in the IT industries was six times that of all private industry. Not surprisingly, the industry that lost the most jobs was computer hardware, from a high of nearly 1.7 million jobs in 2000 to 1.4 million in 2002.

Even though many of the jobs that were lost simply ceased to exist, two additional trends combined to decrease the number of traditional employment positions. The term *outsourcing* refers to work that is contracted to nonemployees such as temporary workers; *offshoring* refers to situations in which the positions are assumed by workers located in another country where wages are cheaper. With the advent of e-mail, the Internet, and low-cost international phone calls, offices separated by continents could be linked through cyberspace. Geography was no longer a predominant concern for many companies. In India, for example, there were large numbers of highly educated people who spoke English, were knowledgeable about computer science, and were more than happy to work for a fraction of the typical U.S. hourly wage. Companies such as Dell moved high-paying technical assistance jobs, low-to midlevel computer programming jobs, and even technical documentation jobs to other countries.

IT Becomes a Mature Industry

According to the Department of Commerce in *Digital Economy 2003*, by 2003 the IT industries showed signs of recovery. The GDP in the IT-producing industries grew 4.8% to $871.9 billion in 2003 as business spending on IT equipment began to accelerate. In the first nine months of 2003 IT spending by the private sector as a whole rose an estimated 2.3% on average. Consumer and household spending on IT equipment, which did not abate as sharply during the recession, grew faster through 2002 and into 2003. In addition, the IT industries did not cut back on research and development during the recession. Consequently, many new products were being developed by the end of the recession. Nevertheless, employment numbers in the IT industries had not recovered significantly by 2003. The Department of Commerce considered these developments taken together to indicate that the IT industries had settled into maturity and predicted that future growth would likely be more modest and less volatile than it was during the 1980s and 1990s.

By 2013 the information and telecommunications industries reached a gross output of $1.4 trillion. (See Table 3.4; gross output equals the value of the industry's total sales and other operating income.) This figure represented growth of 4.3% over the $1.4 trillion in gross output experienced in 2012. Indeed, in spite of the general economic uncertainty of these years, many high-tech companies such as Google and Apple saw their revenues exceed expectations during this period.

Apple reported sales of $171 billion in 2013, an increase of 58% compared with the $108 billion in revenues the company generated in 2011. Google, which posted sales of $37.9 billion in FY 2011, saw revenues rise to $55.5 billion in 2013, an increase of 46%. Microsoft, which posted revenues of $69.9 billion in 2011, saw sales grow to $77.8 billion for FY 2013, an increase of 11%.

Trends in IT employment during this span also showed signs of the industry's economic rebound. In Table 3.5 the BLS charts a steep rise in IT layoffs between 2007 and 2009. (An extended mass layoff, as defined by the BLS, is one that affects at least 50 individuals from a single employer for a period of at least 31 days; the number of events and of workers affected in mass layoff statistics do not reflect totals for the industry, but are indicative of overall trends.) As Table 3.5 shows, extended mass layoffs in the IT sector swelled from 5,363 in 2007 to 8,259 in 2008, an increase of 54%. The industry's employment prospects declined even more sharply in 2009, when 11,824 extended mass layoffs were reported, an increase of 3,565 compared with the previous year. This trend was particularly notable in the computer hardware business, where extended mass layoff events rose from 91 in 2007 to 345 in 2009, an increase of 279%.

By decade's end, extended mass layoff events in the IT sector began to decline. After falling to 7,247 in 2010, extended mass layoffs for the IT sector dropped to 6,596 in 2011, before falling to 6,500 in 2012. Figures for the first part of 2013 revealed even stronger signs of recovery. Extended mass IT layoffs for the first quarter of 2013 fell to 914, which was nearly a 30% drop from the 1,294 extended mass layoffs the industry recorded for the first quarter of 2012.

EFFECT OF IT ON U.S. BUSINESSES

The rise of the IT industries, although dramatic, did not affect the U.S. economy nearly as much as the products that these industries produced. Nearly every task in a modern office, regardless of the business, employs some piece of technology that either was not present before the proliferation of IT or was present in only a limited way. These technologies have had a profound effect on both the productivity of businesses and individual employees.

TABLE 3.4

Gross output by industry, 2011–13

Code	Industry title	2011	2012	2013
GO	**All industries**	**27,526,888**	**28,693,461**	**29,667,167**
GO	Private industries	24,147,587	25,260,605	26,231,652
GO	Agriculture, forestry, fishing, and hunting	431,177	445,515	512,661
GO	Mining	550,371	572,307	634,416
GO	Utilities	398,796	378,146	400,990
GO	Construction	1,004,051	1,065,881	1,119,148
GO	Manufacturing	5,573,316	5,800,666	5,926,927
GO	Wholesale trade	1,354,370	1,413,058	1,477,355
GO	Retail trade	1,374,794	1,478,107	1,546,977
GO	Transportation and warehousing	925,933	965,254	1,004,414
GO	Information	1,305,828	1,377,784	1,437,684
GO	Publishing industries, except Internet (includes software)	297,337	303,094	—
GO	Motion picture and sound recording industries	134,689	140,237	—
GO	Broadcasting and telecommunications	717,464	757,361	—
GO	Data processing, internet publishing, and other information services	156,339	177,091	—
GO	Finance, insurance, real estate, rental, and leasing	4,624,774	4,831,798	5,016,548
GO	Real estate and rental and leasing	2,717,078	2,832,376	2,943,432
GO	Professional and business services	2,889,306	3,027,804	3,105,818
GO	Professional, scientific, and technical services	1,691,867	1,750,593	1,789,295
GO	Computer systems design and related services	310,035	326,986	—
GO	Management of companies and enterprises	483,679	531,148	568,791
GO	Administrative and waste management services	713,760	746,063	747,732
GO	Educational services, health care, and social assistance	2,147,576	2,249,311	2,339,372
GO	Educational services	291,662	311,727	324,318
GO	Health care and social assistance	1,855,913	1,937,584	2,015,054
GO	Arts, entertainment, recreation, accommodation, and food services	1,013,414	1,075,338	1,129,956
GO	Arts, entertainment, and recreation	254,674	268,584	277,329
GO	Accommodation and food services	758,741	806,754	852,627
GO	Other services, except government	553,882	579,634	579,385
GO	**Government**	**3,379,300**	**3,432,857**	**3,435,514**
GO	Federal	1,154,569	1,155,588	1,115,979
GO	State and local	2,224,731	2,277,269	2,319,535
	Addenda:			
GO	Private goods-producing industries[a]	7,558,914	7,884,369	8,193,152
GO	Private services-producing industries[b]	16,588,673	17,376,236	18,038,500
GO	Information-communications-technology-producing industries[c]	1,571,708	1,663,428	—

GO = Gross output (millions of dollars).

[a]Consists of agriculture, forestry, fishing, and hunting; mining; construction; and manufacturing.

[b]Consists of utilities; wholesale trade; retail trade; transportation and warehousing; information; finance, insurance, real estate, rental, and leasing; professional and business services; educational services, health care, and social assistance; arts, entertainment, recreation, accommodation, and food services; and other services, except government.

[c]Consists of computer and electronic product manufacturing (excluding navigational, measuring, electromedical, and control instruments manufacturing); software publishers; broadcasting and telecommunications; data processing, hosting and related services; internet publishing and broadcasting and web search portals; and computer systems design and related services.

SOURCE: Adapted from "GDP by Industry/VA, GO, II, EMP," in *Gross-Domestic-Product-(GDP)-by-Industry Data*, U.S. Department of Commerce, Bureau of Economic Analysis, May 15, 2014, http://www.bea.gov/industry/xls/GDPbyInd_VA_NAICS_1997-2013.xlsx (accessed June 3, 2014)

Figure 3.1 charts shifts in productivity in the private, nonfarm business sector between 1947 and 2013. Between 1979 and 1990 the productivity of workers in the United States increased at a rate of 1.5% per year. Between 1990 and 2000, the period in which the Internet became widespread, the productivity of workers rose significantly, to 2.2% growth per year. This upward trend continued for the next seven years, as annual productivity rates grew an average of 2.6% between 2000 and 2007, before dropping to 1.6% between 2007 and 2013.

In *Digital Economy 2003*, the Department of Commerce investigates some of the causes behind the sudden rise in worker productivity during the 1990s. To determine if this sudden acceleration in worker productivity was indeed because of the introduction of IT into the workplace, the Department of Commerce separates all private industry into those that were IT intensive, such as finance and retail, and those that were less IT intensive, such as construction. The department reports that IT-intensive industries, which already had a relatively high worker productivity growth per year, increased in productivity much faster than less IT-intensive industries in 1995. During the recessionary period in 2000 and 2001, the IT-intensive industries' worker productivity did not wane. Conversely, yearly growth in worker productivity in non-IT-intensive industries did not occur before 1995; it then rose 1% per year until 2000 before turning negative. Such results suggest that the introduction of IT into the workplace not only improved worker productivity for the long term but also increased the rate at which it improves.

TABLE 3.5

Extended mass layoffs in information-technology producing industries, 1996–2013

Year/quarter	Total extended mass layoffs		Computer hardware[a]		Software and computer services[b]		Communications equipment[c]		Communications services[d]	
	Layoff events	Separations	Layoff events	Separations	Layoff events	Separations	Layoff events	Separations	Layoff events	Separations
1996	4,760	948,122	121	20,598	14	6,982	36	5,857	33	6,612
1997	4,671	947,843	75	13,637	14	1,625	36	3,891	19	3,357
1998	4,859	991,245	178	40,350	16	3,160	38	7,444	28	4,512
1999	4,556	901,451	116	28,745	19	3,581	31	5,310	18	3,930
2000	4,591	915,962	76	19,991	40	6,514	36	7,250	27	4,375
2001	7,375	1,524,832	522	105,343	176	23,235	151	37,423	144	30,869
2002	6,337	1,272,331	318	63,284	127	17,687	121	24,537	180	32,445
2003	6,181	1,216,886	221	36,917	69	9,806	69	11,266	115	22,014
2004	5,010	993,909	94	13,974	44	6,184	21	3,011	82	17,446
2005	4,881	884,661	90	13,971	28	4,952	19	3,612	48	7,779
2006	4,885	935,969	66	16,662	19	1,965	28	5,334	37	5,275
2007	5,363	965,935	91	15,956	18	2,277	22	3,494	25	2,930
2008	8,259	1,516,978	156	31,448	57	7,720	21	3,456	65	10,836
2009	11,824	2,108,202	345	76,908	94	15,791	50	8,126	98	17,672
2010										
First quarter	1,870	314,512	35	6,248	15	1,570	5	1,089	25	6,023
Second quarter	2,008	381,622	24	3,714	14	1,614	9	912	13	1,924
Third quarter	1,370	222,357	24	2,851	7	2,217	6	498	12	1,825
Fourth quarter	1,999	338,643	7	1,019	9	1,345	3	451	15	3,255
Total	**7,247**	**1,257,134**	**90**	**13,832**	**45**	**6,746**	**23**	**2,950**	**65**	**13,027**
2011										
First quarter	1,490	225,456	14	2,027	14	1,930	4	558	14	2,124
Second quarter	1,810	317,546	11	1,691	18	2,432	7	930	10	7,322
Third quarter	1,393	235,325	12	2,247	12	1,764	3	238	10	3,015
Fourth quarter	1,903	334,383	21	3,857	14	1,635	4	694	6	1,381
Total	**6,596**	**1,112,710**	**58**	**9,822**	**58**	**7,761**	**18**	**2,420**	**40**	**13,842**
2012										
First quarter	1,294	246,956	13	1,989	18	3,331	4	467	8	1,387
Second quarter	1,959	385,983	21	5,020	23	3,203	e	e	15	3,196
Third quarter[f]	1,124	199,781	26	3,186	6	1,073	e	e	10	2,039
Fourth quarter[f]	2,123	424,492	20	3,140	9	1,310	4	492	9	972
Total[f]	**6,500**	**1,257,212**	**80**	**13,335**	**56**	**8,917**	**13**	**1,537**	**42**	**7,594**
2013										
First quarter[p]	914	154,374	11	1,338	6	858	3	262	6	930

[a]The industries included in this grouping, based on the 2012 NAICS, are: semiconductor machinery manufacturing; other commercial and service machinery mfg.; electronic computer manufacturing; computer storage device manufacturing; other computer peripheral equipment mfg.; bare printed circuit board manufacturing; semiconductors and related device mfg. capacitor, resistor, and inductor mfg.; electronic connector manufacturing; printed circuit assembly manufacturing; other electronic component manufacturing; industrial process variable instruments; electricity and signal testing instruments; analytical laboratory instrument mfg.; computer and software merchant wholesalers; and electronics stores.
[b]The industries included in this grouping, based on the 2012 NAICS, are: software publishers; data processing, hosting and related services; internet publishing and web search portals; office equipment rental and leasing; custom computer programming services; computer systems design services; computer facilities management services; other computer related services; and computer and office machine repair.
[c]The industries included in this grouping, based on the 2012 NAICS, are: telephone apparatus manufacturing; broadcast and wireless communications equip.; audio and video equipment manufacturing; blank magnetic and optical media mfg.; software and prerecorded media reproducing; and fiber optic cable manufacturing.
[d]The industries included in this grouping, based on the 2012 NAICS, are: wired telecommunications carriers; wireless telecommunications carriers; satellite telecommunications; telecommunications resellers; all other telecommunications; and communication equipment repair.
[e]Data do not meet BLS or state agency disclosure standards.
[p]Preliminary.
[f]Revised.
Notes: Information technology-producing industries are defined by the MLS program using the 2012 version of the North American Industrial Classification System (NAICS). MLS definitions closely follow definitions originally published in Digital Economy 2003, (U.S.Department of Commerce, Economics and Statistics Administration, 2003), which were based on NAICS 2002 industries.

SOURCE: "Information Technology-Producing Industries: Extended Mass Layoff Events and Separations, Private Nonfarm Sector, 1996–2013," in *Mass Layoff Statistics*, U.S. Department of Labor, Bureau of Labor Statistics, May 13, 2013, http://www.bls.gov/mls/miltprod.htm (accessed June 3, 2014)

How IT Has Increased Productivity

The ways in which IT increased productivity and made businesses more profitable are nearly endless. Word processors and desktop publishing software dramatically reduced the time necessary to complete many mundane office tasks, particularly in the communications industry. The reduction of paper filing systems in the workplace reduced corporate storage needs and made document retrieval more efficient. Computer systems in factories allowed manufacturers precise control over production lines, increasing efficiency and thus saving millions of dollars. Interoffice and Internet networks gave corporations daily access to sales numbers and profit margins, enabling them to make faster decisions to increase profitability. For example, if a line of clothing was not selling, a company could see the sales figures

FIGURE 3.1

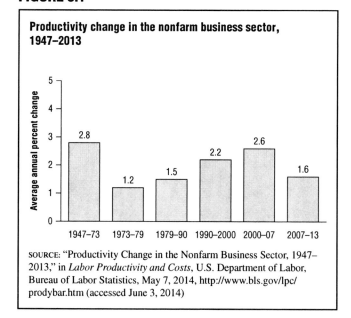

Productivity change in the nonfarm business sector, 1947–2013

SOURCE: "Productivity Change in the Nonfarm Business Sector, 1947–2013," in *Labor Productivity and Costs*, U.S. Department of Labor, Bureau of Labor Statistics, May 7, 2014, http://www.bls.gov/lpc/prodybar.htm (accessed June 3, 2014)

FIGURE 3.2

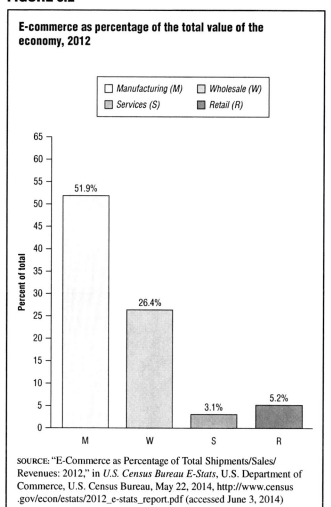

E-commerce as percentage of the total value of the economy, 2012

SOURCE: "E-Commerce as Percentage of Total Shipments/Sales/Revenues: 2012," in *U.S. Census Bureau E-Stats*, U.S. Department of Commerce, U.S. Census Bureau, May 22, 2014, http://www.census.gov/econ/estats/2012_e-stats_report.pdf (accessed June 3, 2014)

immediately and pull the line from the stores, rather than allow it to take up valuable retail space.

E-COMMERCE

E-commerce, which is simply the sale of goods and services over the Internet, has grown steadily every year since the debut of the World Wide Web in 1991. The Census Bureau provides a breakdown of e-commerce as a percentage of the value of sales in each industry that did business online in 2012. By far, most e-commerce that year occurred in manufacturing, where shipments ordered online accounted for 51.9% ($3 trillion) of the total value of all manufacturing shipments. (See Figure 3.2.) Merchant wholesalers conducted e-commerce sales representing 26.4% ($1.8 trillion) of business in 2012, and e-commerce accounted for 5.2% ($227 billion) of all retail sales. Selected services revenues were sales made by a number of sectors in the services industry and include businesses such as travel brokers and online publications. Some 3.1% ($366 billion) of the total revenues generated by the selected services industry came from e-commerce in 2012.

Manufacturers are companies that take raw materials and parts and manufacture products that are used by other businesses or individuals. For instance, a soft drink company typically buys its cans from a manufacturer that makes the cans from raw aluminum. Dell buys computer components from dozens of manufacturers around the world to assemble its computers. The reason so many manufacturers use the Internet to conduct business transactions is that the Internet cuts costs and streamlines the processes that are involved in buying and selling manufactured goods. E-commerce allows the buyer to compare competitors' prices, reduces the costs of writing up and sending paper purchase orders and invoices, maintains an

electronic copy of each sale, and decreases the time it takes for the goods to reach the buyer. The value of manufactured goods shipped through e-commerce rose 10.5% between 2011 and 2012, more than twice the growth rate of 5% for total manufacturing shipments. (See Table 3.6.) Leather and allied product manufacturing enjoyed the largest percentage boost in e-commerce sales, rising from $1.4 billion in 2011 to $1.8 billion in 2012, an increase of 26%. Only the textile mills and printing and related support activities manufacturing sectors saw a decline in e-commerce shipments during this span, falling 11.6% and 0.6%, respectively, between 2011 and 2012.

Merchant wholesale trade sales made up the second-largest block of e-commerce transactions in 2012. Wholesalers act as a mediator between manufacturers and retailers. Wholesalers typically buy large quantities of goods from a number of manufacturers and then resell these goods in bulk to retail outlets. The wholesalers save the retailers the trouble of contacting each manufacturer separately. Table 3.7 presents U.S. merchant wholesale trades in 2011 and 2012. Year-over-year wholesale e-commerce

TABLE 3.6

Total and e-commerce value of manufacturing shipments, 2011–12

[Data are based on the 2012 Economic Census—Manufacturing and 2011 Annual Survey of Manufactures. Value of shipments are shown in millions of dollars, consequently subsector estimates may not be additive. Estimated measures of sampling variability for these estimates are provided in the Measures of Sampling Variability for U.S. Manufacturing Shipments—Total and E-commerce Value: 2012 and 2011.]

| NAICS code | Description | Value of shipments | | | | Year to year percent change | | E-commerce as percent of total shipments | | Percent distribution of e-commerce shipments |
| | | 2012 | | 2011 | | | | | | |
		Total	E-commerce	Revised total	Revised e-commerce	Total shipments	E-commerce shipments	2012	2011	2012
	Total manufacturing	**5,756,337**	**2,989,146**	**5,481,368**	**2,703,962**	**5.0**	**10.5**	**51.9**	**49.3**	**100.0**
311	Food manufacturing	747,642	385,551	708,683	340,436	5.5	13.3	51.6	48.0	12.9
312	Beverage and tobacco product manufacturing	138,150	96,811	134,765	85,357	2.5	13.4	70.1	63.3	3.2
313	Textile mills	29,836	13,237	30,890	14,974	−3.4	−11.6	44.4	48.5	0.4
314	Textile product mills	21,841	11,033	22,368	10,805	−2.4	2.1	50.5	48.3	0.4
315	Apparel manufacturing	13,021	5,193	12,784	5,135	1.9	1.1	39.9	40.2	0.2
316	Leather and allied product manufacturing	5,593	1,771	5,665	1,405	−1.3	26.0	31.7	24.8	0.1
321	Wood product manufacturing	78,008	26,186	70,091	21,805	11.3	20.1	33.6	31.1	0.9
322	Paper manufacturing	181,692	98,267	175,552	86,897	3.5	13.1	54.1	49.5	3.3
323	Printing and related support activities	81,706	32,463	82,380	32,659	−0.8	−0.6	39.7	39.6	1.1
324	Petroleum and coal products manufacturing	844,042	444,034	838,083	441,837	0.7	0.5	52.6	52.7	14.9
325	Chemical manufacturing	802,933	402,481	773,080	365,155	3.9	10.2	50.1	47.2	13.5
326	Plastics and rubber products manufacturing	218,488	105,874	203,757	94,519	7.2	12.0	48.5	46.4	3.5
327	Nonmetallic mineral product manufacturing	98,426	36,221	92,585	30,988	6.3	16.9	36.8	33.5	1.2
331	Primary metal manufacturing	270,914	145,595	278,729	140,088	−2.8	3.9	53.7	50.3	4.9
332	Fabricated metal product manufacturing	340,425	136,771	323,664	125,931	5.2	8.6	40.2	38.9	4.6
333	Machinery manufacturing	407,669	217,626	365,010	177,872	11.7	22.3	53.4	48.7	7.3
334	Computer and electronic product manufacturing	337,362	171,906	338,047	169,484	−0.2	1.4	51.0	50.1	5.8
335	Electrical equipment, appliance, and components	123,978	63,668	118,500	55,544	4.6	14.6	51.4	46.9	2.1
336	Transportation equipment manufacturing	792,925	506,509	691,937	422,036	14.6	20.0	63.9	61.0	16.9
337	Furniture and related product manufacturing	67,685	30,404	62,285	27,006	8.7	12.6	44.9	43.4	1.0
339	Miscellaneous manufacturing	154,000	57,545	152,514	54,028	1.0	6.5	37.4	35.4	1.9

NAICS = North American Industry Classification System.

Note: Estimates are not adjusted for price changes. Establishments representing approximately 5 percent of the 2012 value of shipments did not have an opportunity to report e-commerce receipts. Estimates include data only for businesses with paid employees and are subject to revision.

SOURCE: "U.S. Manufacturing Shipments—Total and E-Commerce Value: 2012 and 2011," in *E-Stats: 2012 E-Commerce Multi-sector Data Tables*," U.S. Department of Commerce, U.S. Census Bureau, May 22, 2014, http://www.census.gov/econ/estats/2012/2012manufacturing.xls (accessed June 3, 2014)

TABLE 3.7

Total and e-commerce wholesale trade sales, 2011–12

[Estimates are based on data from the 2012 Annual Wholesale Trade Survey. Sales estimates are shown in millions of dollars, consequently industry group estimates may not be additive. Estimated measures of sampling variability for these estimates are provided in Measures of Sampling Variability for U.S. Merchant Wholesale Trade Sales, Including Manufacturers' Sales Branches and Offices—Total and E-commerce Sales: 2012 and 2011.]

NAICS code	Description	Value of sales				Year to year percent change		E-commerce as percent of total sales		Percent distribution of e-commerce sales
		2012		2011						
		Total	E-commerce	Revised total	Revised e-commerce	Total sales	E-commerce sales	2012	2011	2012
42	**Total merchant wholesale trade including MSBOs***	6,771,454	1,789,095	6,451,323	1,695,826	5.0	5.5	26.4	26.3	100.0
423	**Durable goods**	3,083,316	778,084	2,892,366	708,724	6.6	9.8	25.2	24.5	43.5
4231	Motor vehicles and automotive equipment	733,574	383,439	636,413	332,739	15.3	15.2	52.3	52.3	21.4
4232	Furniture and home furnishings	80,383	12,650	76,154	12,291	5.6	2.9	15.7	16.1	0.7
4233	Lumber and other construction material	140,542	12,190	130,623	S	7.6	S	8.7	S	0.7
4234	Professional and commercial equipment and supplies	517,929	119,351	515,433	123,060	0.5	-3.0	23.0	23.9	6.7
42343	Computer equipment and supplies	272,916	D	277,357	D	-1.6	D	D	D	D
4235	Metals and minerals, excluding petroleum	217,682	24,658	216,429	23,607	0.6	4.5	11.3	10.9	1.4
4236	Electrical goods	505,937	102,413	474,761	93,639	6.6	9.4	20.2	19.7	5.7
4237	Hardware, plumbing and heating equipment	126,698	16,973	117,605	15,319	7.7	10.8	13.4	13.0	0.9
4238	Machinery, equipment and supplies	516,272	79,469	466,030	68,983	10.8	15.2	15.4	14.8	4.4
4239	Miscellaneous durable goods	244,299	26,941	258,918	28,307	-5.6	-4.8	11.0	10.9	1.5
424	**Nondurable goods**	3,688,138	1,011,011	3,558,957	987,102	3.6	2.4	27.4	27.7	56.5
4241	Paper and paper products	136,546	46,634	134,873	44,326	1.2	5.2	34.2	32.9	2.6
4242	Drugs, drug proprietaries and druggists' sundries	630,012	440,346	621,661	437,495	1.3	0.7	69.9	70.4	24.6
4243	Apparel, piece goods, and notions	147,479	36,098	144,307	35,759	2.2	0.9	24.5	24.8	2.0
4244	Groceries and related products	783,214	195,521	749,582	186,360	4.5	4.9	25.0	24.9	10.9
4245	Farm-products raw materials	246,656	S	227,334	10,885	8.5	S	S	4.8	S
4246	Chemicals and allied products	214,744	28,659	206,898	26,111	3.8	9.8	13.3	12.6	1.6
4247	Petroleum and petroleum products	1,070,363	167,206	1,041,238	165,780	2.8	0.9	15.6	15.9	9.3
4248	Beer, wine, and distilled beverages	136,182	12,139	127,645	11,211	6.7	8.3	8.9	8.8	0.7
4249	Miscellaneous nondurable goods	322,942	74,416	305,419	69,175	5.7	7.6	23.0	22.6	4.2

S–Estimate does not meet publication standards because of high sampling variability or poor response quality (total quantity response rate is less than 50%), or other concerns about the estimate's quality. Unpublished estimates derived from this table by subtraction are subject to these same limitations and should not be attributed to the U.S. Census Bureau.

D–Denotes an estimate withheld to avoid disclosing data of individual companies; data are included in higher level totals.

NAICS = North American Industry Classification System.

*Manufacturers' Sales Branches and Offices.

Note: Estimates have not been adjusted for price changes. Measures of Sampling Variability—U.S. Merchant Wholesale Trade Sales, Including Manufacturers' Sales Branches and Offices—Total and E-commerce Sales: 2012 and 2011 provides estimated measures of sampling variability. Estimates include data only for businesses with paid employees and are subject to revision.

SOURCE: "U.S. Merchant Wholesale Trade Sales, Including Manufacturers' Sales Branches and Offices—Total and E-Commerce: 2012 and 2011," in *E-Stats: 2012 E-Commerce Multi-sector Data Tables*, U.S. Department of Commerce, U.S. Census Bureau, May 22, 2014, http://www.census.gov/econ/estats/2012/2012wholesale_total.xls (accessed June 3, 2014)

increased 5.5% between 2011 and 2012, which was slightly higher than the 5% growth generated by wholesale trades overall. Wholesale e-commerce growth outstripped overall merchant wholesale trades in several key businesses. For example, between 2011 and 2012 e-commerce sales of machinery, equipment, and supplies increased 15.2%, compared with a 10.8% growth rate in overall sales for that sector.

E-Commerce and Retail

Retail sales consist of any product that is sold to an individual customer or company for use. Since the late 1990s nearly every major retailer from AutoZone to Neiman Marcus to Wal-Mart has created a website. Many offer a greater variety of merchandise online than what is available in the store. The growth of such websites has allowed Americans to order just about anything and have it delivered to their front door within days.

The amount of money made from e-commerce in retail increased rapidly from the late 1990s. The Census Bureau explains in *E-Stats Archives* (2014, http://www.census.gov/econ/estats/archives.html) that e-commerce accounted for only 0.2% ($5 billion) of all retail sales in 1998. This percentage more than doubled to 0.5% ($15.6 billion) in 1999 and nearly doubled again to 0.9% ($28.8 billion) in 2000. In 2002 e-commerce represented 1.4%

($44.3 billion) of retail sales. E-commerce revenues more than quintupled by 2012, when online transactions accounted for 5.2% ($227 billion) of all retail sales. As Table 3.8 shows, well over half (59.5%, or $192 billion) of all sales revenues for electronic shopping and mail-order houses came from e-commerce transactions in 2012. By comparison, e-commerce accounted for just 0.1% of sales of food and beverage stores, which generated $900 million in revenues from online transactions.

Table 3.9 presents sales information on the electronic shopping and mail-order house segment of retail. Many of the businesses in this category, such as Dell, sell their products primarily online and through catalogs. Others are divisions of larger department stores, such as Nordstrom, and were created to sell the stores' products online. Online sales accounted for 59.5% of overall sales for electronic shopping and mail-order businesses in 2012, an increase of 14.5% from 2011. Regarding individual types of products, 90% of the revenues from the sale of music and videos came from online sales in 2012. This represented the highest percentage of online sales for any type of product in this retail segment, followed by books and magazines (87.7%) and electronics and appliances (84.7%). In terms of sheer sales volume, more clothing and accessories ($33 billion) were sold online than any other type of product.

TABLE 3.8

Total and e-commerce retail sales, 2011–12

[Estimates are based on data from the 2012 Annual Retail Trade Survey. Sales estimates are shown in millions of dollars, consequently industry group estimates may not be additive. Estimated measures of sampling variability for these estimates are provided in the Measures of Sampling Variability for U.S. Retail Trade Sales—Total and E-commerce: 2012 and 2011.]

NAICS code	Description	Value of sales 2012 Total sales	Value of sales 2012 E-commerce	Value of sales 2011 Revised total sales	Value of sales 2011 Revised e-commerce	Year to year percent change Total sales	Year to year percent change E-commerce sales	E-commerce as percent of total sales 2012	E-commerce as percent of total sales 2011	Percent distribution of e-commerce sales 2012
	Total retail trade	**4,344,140**	**226,878**	**4,132,996**	**197,883**	**5.1**	**14.7**	**5.2**	**4.8**	**100.0**
441	Motor vehicles and parts dealers	894,798	23,244	818,703	20,072	9.3	15.8	2.6	2.5	10.2
442	Furniture and home furnishings stores	94,898	488	90,124	401	5.3	21.7	0.5	0.4	0.2
443	Electronics and appliance stores	102,998	S	100,792	1,255	2.2	S	S	1.2	S
444	Building materials and garden equipment and supplies stores	294,656	S	279,402	S	5.5	S	S	S	S
445	Food and beverage stores	631,486	900	611,006	770	3.4	16.9	0.1	0.1	0.4
446	Health and personal care stores	275,645	S	272,555	S	1.1	S	S	S	S
447	Gasoline stations	551,888	Z	528,937	Z	4.3	Z	Z	Z	Z
448	Clothing and clothing accessories stores	241,386	2,843	229,327	2,316	5.3	22.8	1.2	1.0	1.3
451	Sporting goods, hobby, book, and music stores	85,190	1,851	82,466	1,787	3.3	3.6	2.2	2.2	0.8
452	General merchandise stores	649,754	S	630,557	S	3.0	S	Z	S	Z
453	Miscellaneous store retailers	112,966	2,179	111,256	1,810	1.5	20.4	1.9	1.6	1.0
454	Nonstore retailers	408,475	192,619	377,871	168,224	8.1	14.5	47.2	44.5	84.9
4541	Electronic shopping and mail-order houses	322,543	191,971	290,852	167,642	10.9	14.5	59.5	57.6	84.6

S–Estimate does not meet publication standards because of high sampling variability, poor response quality (total quantity response rate is less than 50%), or other concerns about the estimate's quality. Unpublished estimates derived from this table by subtraction are subject to these same limitations and should not be attributed to the U.S. Census Bureau.
Z–Estimate is less than five hundred thousand dollars or 0.05%.
NAICS = North American Industry Classification System.
Note: Retail total and other subsector totals may include data for kinds of business not shown. Estimates have not been adjusted for price changes. Estimates include data for businesses with or without paid employees and are subject to revision.

SOURCE: "U.S. Retail Trade Sales—Total and E-Commerce: 2012 and 2011," in *E-Stats: 2012 E-Commerce Multi-Sector Data Tables*, U.S. Department of Commerce, U.S. Census Bureau, May 22, 2014, http://www.census.gov/econ/estats/2012/2012retail.xls (accessed June 3, 2014)

TABLE 3.9

Total and e-commerce sales of electronic shopping and mail-order houses by merchandise line, 2011–12

[Estimates are based on data from the 2012 Annual Retail Trade Survey. Sales estimates are shown in millions of dollars, consequently merchandise line estimates may not be additive. Estimated measures of sampling variability for these estimates are provided in Measures of Sampling Variability for U.S. Electronic Shopping and Mail-Order Houses (NAICS 4541)—Total and E-commerce Sales by Merchandise Line: 2012 and 2011.]

| | Value of sales | | | | Year to year percent change | | E-commerce as percent of total sales | Percent distribution | |
| | 2012 | | 2011 | | | | | Total sales | E-commerce sales |
Description	Total sales	E-commerce	Revised total sales	Revised e-commerce	Total sales	E-commerce sales	2012	2012	2012
Total electronic shopping and mail-order houses (NAICS 4541)	322,543	191,971	290,852	167,642	10.9	14.5	59.5	100.0	100.0
Books and magazines	10,759	9,433	10,040	8,640	7.2	9.2	87.7	3.3	4.9
Clothing and clothing accessories (includes footwear)	39,904	33,023	34,805	27,998	14.7	17.9	82.8	12.4	17.2
Computer hardware	24,705	13,627	24,026	13,454	2.8	1.3	55.2	7.7	7.1
Computer software	7,169	4,647	6,701	4,370	7.0	6.3	64.8	2.2	2.4
Drugs, health aids, and beauty aids	88,883	14,684	80,975	11,731	9.8	25.2	16.5	27.6	7.6
Electronics and appliances	26,573	22,500	25,091	21,449	5.9	4.9	84.7	8.2	11.7
Food, beer, and wine	6,922	4,729	5,932	3,926	16.7	20.5	68.3	2.1	2.5
Furniture and home furnishings	19,210	15,881	16,886	13,700	13.8	15.9	82.7	6.0	8.3
Music and videos	10,317	9,290	8,313	7,294	24.1	27.4	90.0	3.2	4.8
Office equipment and supplies	8,416	6,634	8,038	6,295	4.7	5.4	78.8	2.6	3.5
Sporting goods	8,038	6,006	6,709	4,944	19.8	21.5	74.7	2.5	3.1
Toys, hobby goods, and games	7,241	5,853	6,501	5,133	11.4	14.0	80.8	2.2	3.0
Other merchandise[a]	44,093	29,734	39,308	25,213	12.2	17.9	67.4	13.7	15.5
Nonmerchandise receipts[b]	20,313	15,930	17,527	13,495	15.9	18.0	78.4	6.3	8.3

[a]Includes other merchandise such as collectibles, souvenirs, auto parts and accessories, hardware, lawn and garden equipment and supplies, and jewelry.
[b]Includes nonmerchandise receipts such as auction commissions, customer training, customer support, advertising, and shipping and handling.
NAICS = North American Industry Classification System.
Note: Estimates have not been adjusted for price changes. Estimates include data for businesses with or without paid employees, are grouped according to merchandise categories used in the Annual Retail Trade Survey, and are subject to revision.

SOURCE: "U.S. Electronic Shopping and Mail-Order Houses (NAICS 4541)—Total and E-Commerce Sales by Merchandise Line: 2012 and 2011," in *E-Stats: 2012 E-Commerce Multi-Sector Data Tables*, U.S. Department of Commerce, U.S. Census Bureau, May 22, 2014, http://www.census.gov/econ/estats/2012/2012electronic.xls (accessed June 3, 2014)

Online Auctions

When e-commerce developed during the mid-1990s, many small business owners created modest commercial websites, hoping to sell their wares. However, Internet fraud and the propagation of questionable websites made people reluctant to give personal information to unknown vendors on the web. Smaller vendors and buyers needed a common marketplace with rules and regulations to trade goods.

In 1998 Pierre Omidyar (1967–), Jeff Skoll (1965–), and Meg Whitman (1956–) went public with eBay. The company, which was at first an auction site for collectibles such as Beanie Babies, quickly attracted the attention of small business owners. For a modest insertion fee, people could list their products on eBay's website. Buyers then bid on the objects, and when a sale was final, the seller paid eBay a commission of 1.3% to 5% of the item's sale price. The website included payment options that did not require the purchaser to provide credit card information, and it even offered protections against fraud.

The eBay website and its imitators created a whole new economic outlet for small business owners and people who simply wanted to pawn off their used goods. No

longer was someone who wanted to sell embroidered pillows relegated to local flea markets. Individual vendors from crafters to high-end car salespeople could reach out to a nationwide audience. Even people with used stuff suddenly had more options than simply giving it to charity or holding a garage sale. As of August 2014, eBay (2014, http://www.ebayinc.com/who_we_are/one_company) had 149 million active users worldwide, with more than 700 million items listed for sale.

Virtual Goods and Currencies

One of the more unusual industries to develop, due in part to eBay, was the sale of virtual goods. Games such as *World of Warcraft* and *EverQuest* place players in virtual worlds with thousands of other people where they can buy virtual property, kill monsters, and collect gold and other valuable virtual artifacts. Some of these online games even provide the player with the option to marry and build houses in a virtual world. Progressing far in these games and obtaining a high level, however, requires hundreds of hours of playtime. As a result, an entire cottage industry developed around the sale of virtual gold and characters on auction sites such as eBay. Typically, a player would buy the game, build up a character and gold, and then sell his or her password to the game to a buyer on eBay, sometimes fetching hundreds of dollars. Such sales represented the first industry that was centered on completely virtual goods. Soon, other sites began trading in virtual currencies, as the online community bought and sold everything from virtual gaming weapons to virtual flowers. As Rip Empson reports in "Study: U.S. Consumer Spending on Virtual Goods Grew to $2.3 Billion in 2011" (TechCrunch.com, February 29, 2012), U.S. sales of virtual goods topped $2.3 billion in 2011, and was expected to reach $2.9 billion in 2012. According to Matt Bodimeade in "27 Million Virtual Goods Market Users Purchase through Facebook Payments" (Companies andMarkets.com, March 11, 2013), the worldwide market for virtual goods was $14.8 billion in 2012.

These years also saw a rise in the use of virtual currencies, a form of electronic money accepted as payment in certain online communities. To acquire a virtual currency, an individual visits an online exchange, where they can trade legal tender for some digital equivalent at a specified exchange rate. Virtual currencies appeal to Internet users who want to conduct business anonymously, or to vendors who want to avoid paying fees to banks. As of 2014, the most prominent virtual currency was Bitcoin. First introduced by its anonymous creator in 2009, Bitcoin quickly became the most prevalent form of exchange among online virtual currency users. After reaching a peak value of $1,151 per Bitcoin in December 2013, the digital currency's worth plunged precipitously in early 2014 amid ongoing uncertainties concerning its future legal status. By June 2014 the price of a single Bitcoin was hovering between $600 and $700. Although virtual currencies remained largely unregulated in 2014, the U.S. government was exploring ways to assert control over their use. In March 2014 the Internal Revenue Service ruled that Bitcoins were technically considered property, rather than currency, making them subject to capital gains tax. At the same time, Bitcoin and other electronic forms of money were increasingly being used to obtain controlled substances, weapons, and other illicit goods over the Internet, a source of growing concern among law enforcement officials worldwide. (For more on the relationship between virtual currency and online trafficking, see Chapter 4: Technology and Crime.)

E-Commerce in the Services Industries

The services industries in the United States are enormous and encompass everything from brokerage houses to real estate companies to travel agents to health care. Generally, any business that sells its services or some type of expertise belongs in this category. Of all the industries presented in Figure 3.2, e-commerce revenue made up the smallest percentage of total revenue for the services industries in 2012. In those areas of the services industry where e-commerce has broken through, however, it has created much change.

TRAVEL INDUSTRY. Probably no other type of business in the services sector was affected more by the Internet than travel reservations services. Before the Internet, travelers either combed through travel books and called airlines, hotels, restaurants, and other venues one by one, or hired a travel agent to do it for them. When the Internet became widely available, businesses such as Expedia set up websites where anyone could search for rates and make travel reservations with most airlines and hotels. Existing businesses, such as the airlines, developed websites of their own. These Internet innovations made it much easier for travelers to comparison shop and make travel plans on their own. E-commerce made up $12.9 billion (31.7%) of the total revenue ($40.5 billion) of travel arrangement and reservation services in 2012. (See Table 3.10.) In *Profile of U.S. Resident Travelers Visiting Overseas Destinations: 2012 Outbound* (November 2013, http://travel.trade.gov/outreachpages/ download_data_table/2012_Outbound_Profile.pdf), the International Trade Administration of the Department of Commerce notes that 38% of Americans traveling overseas for leisure purposes used the Internet to book their trips in 2012, compared with 23% who used travel agents.

FINANCIAL SERVICES. Another services industry that experienced a great deal of change because of IT was the financial brokerage business. Beginning in the early 1980s many of those who worked in the industry employed powerful computers and networking capabilities to track financial markets in real time and make financial transactions electronically. When the Internet became mainstream, large financial services organizations, such as Fidelity Investments and Charles Schwab, offered brokerage accounts to customers, allowing them to trade stocks online. Customers also had access to many of the research services that were available only to stockbrokers before the introduction of the World Wide Web. As Table 3.10 shows, of the $275.3 billion generated in securities and commodities trading in 2012, nearly $17 billion, or 6.2%, came from online transactions.

Dave Pettit and Rich Jaroslovsky indicate in *Wall Street Journal Online's Guide to Online Investing: How to Make the Most of the Internet in a Bull or Bear Market* (2002) that in 1996, 1.5 million brokerage accounts existed online; by 2001 this number had increased to 20 million. Even after the collapse of the global financial markets in 2008, competition among the top online brokerage firms remained fierce. Matt Krantz describes in "As Economy Heals, Online Brokerages Go after Investors" (USAToday.com, January 19, 2010) how several of the large online brokerage firms began slashing their commissions and fees as a way of attracting new investors. According to Krantz, much of the competition for clients was actually between Internet brokerages and

TABLE 3.10

Total and e-commerce revenue, selected services, 2011–12

[Except where indicated, estimates are based on data from the 2012 Service Annual Survey. Revenue estimates are shown in millions of dollars, consequently industry group estimates may not be additive. Estimated measures of sampling variability for these estimates are provided in Measures of Sampling Variability for U.S. Selected Services Revenue—Total and E-commerce: 2012 and 2011.]

NAICS code	Description	Value of revenue 2012 Total	Value of revenue 2012 E-commerce	Value of revenue 2011 Revised total	Value of revenue 2011 Revised e-commerce	Year to year percent change Total revenue	Year to year percent change E-commerce revenue	E-commerce as percent of total revenue 2012	E-commerce as percent of total revenue 2011	Percent distribution of e-commerce revenue 2012
	Total for selected service industries[a]	12,004,067	366,277	11,544,042	337,913	4.0	8.4	3.1	2.9	100.0
22	Utilities[b]	533,376	255	556,135	249	−4.1	2.4	0.0	0.0	0.1
2211	Electric power generation, transmission, and distribution	442,205	D	447,919	D	−1.3	D	D	D	D
4849y	Transportation and warehousing[c]	781,167	87,884	742,040	81,493	5.3	7.8	11.3	11.0	24.0
481	Air transportation	193,769	53,162	184,768	49,787	4.9	6.8	27.4	26.9	14.5
483	Water transportation	37,630	3,285	36,560	2,912	2.9	12.8	8.7	8.0	0.9
484	Truck transportation	230,632	16,879	215,884	15,211	6.8	11.0	7.3	7.0	4.6
485	Transit and ground passenger transportation	29,971	694	28,256	597	6.1	16.2	2.3	2.1	0.2
486	Pipeline transportation	36,396	2,830	35,948	3,002	1.2	−5.7	7.8	8.4	0.8
487	Scenic and sightseeing transportation	3,013	292	2,711	246	11.1	18.7	9.7	9.1	0.1
488	Support activities for transportation	140,275	S	133,747	9,033	4.9	S	S	6.8	S
492	Couriers and messengers	82,713	S	78,500	S	5.4	S	S	S	S
493	Warehousing and storage	26,768	420	25,666	472	4.3	−11.0	1.6	1.8	0.1
51	Information	1,213,291	69,744	1,160,558	65,559	4.5	6.4	5.7	5.6	19.0
511	Publishing industries (except Internet)	278,640	30,526	275,004	28,752	1.3	6.2	11.0	10.5	8.3
517	Telecommunications	561,193	10,082	539,554	9,514	4.0	6.0	1.8	1.8	2.8
518	Data processing, hosting, and related services	88,670	10,330	82,203	10,124	7.9	2.0	11.6	12.3	2.8
52	Finance and insurance[d]	3,404,710	71,832	3,293,641	67,427	3.4	6.5	2.1	2.0	19.6
5223	Activities related to credit intermediation	65,870	7,891	59,200	S	11.3	S	12.0	S	2.2
5231	Securities and commodity contracts intermediation and brokerage	275,254	16,972	267,590	16,493	2.9	2.9	6.2	6.2	4.6
53	Real estate and rental and leasing[e]	447,429	25,429	420,916	20,746	6.3	22.6	5.7	4.9	6.9
532	Rental and leasing services	123,834	21,592	117,938	17,691	5.0	22.1	17.4	15.0	5.9
54	Professional, scientific, and technical services[f]	1,419,174	26,476	1,363,303	24,730	4.1	7.1	1.9	1.8	7.2
5415	Computer systems design and related services	320,236	9,530	303,354	8,258	5.6	15.4	3.0	2.7	2.6
56	Administrative and support and waste management and remediation services	720,755	23,975	683,364	22,833	5.5	5.0	3.3	3.3	6.5
5615	Travel arrangement and reservation services	40,497	12,851	39,069	12,027	3.7	6.9	31.7	30.8	3.5
61	Educational services[g]	58,575	5,162	57,077	4,852	2.6	6.4	8.8	8.5	1.4
62	Health care and social assistance	2,096,734	992	2,001,318	928	4.8	6.9	0.0	0.0	0.3
71	Arts, entertainment, and recreation	208,669	6,759	199,404	5,964	4.6	13.3	3.2	3.0	1.8
72	Accommodation and food services[h]	702,809	36,601	666,825	33,188	5.4	10.3	5.2	5.0	10.0
81	Other services (except public administration)[i]	417,378	11,168	399,461	9,944	4.5	12.3	2.7	2.5	3.0
811	Repair and maintenance	146,474	2,458	141,099	2,333	3.8	5.4	1.7	1.7	0.7
812	Personal and laundry services	89,545	2,633	86,041	2,395	4.1	9.9	2.9	2.8	0.7
813	Religious, grantmaking, civic, professional, and similar organizations[i]	181,359	6,077	172,321	5,216	5.2	16.5	3.4	3.0	1.7

traditional full-service firms, as consumers were turning to online investing as a way of reducing their costs.

This trend toward discounted online trading eventually caught the attention of the larger investment houses. In July 2010 Merrill Lynch entered the virtual brokerage business with the creation of Merrill Edge, a new online investment account service. Theresa W. Carey reports in "The Best Online Brokers of 2014" (Barrons.com, March 15, 2014) that by 2014 many brokerage firms had introduced a wide range of technological tools to attract investors, including cell phone applications (apps) and social media features.

REAL ESTATE SERVICES. The real estate brokerage sector was another services industry that underwent many changes because of the Internet. Before the Internet became widely available, people could find real estate listings only in the newspaper or at a real estate agency. Many websites, such as Realtor.com, began listing thousands of houses for sale in every region of the country. These sites make it possible for people in Virginia, for example, to gain an understanding of real estate properties and prices in Alaska, Wyoming, or even their own neighborhood. The National Association of Realtors reports in "Realtor.com Traffic" (May 2014, http://www./sites/default/files/reports/2014/nar-website-traffic-stats-march-2014.pdf) that Internet traffic on its site

TABLE 3.10

Total and e-commerce revenue, selected services, 2011–12 [CONTINUED]

[Except where indicated, estimates are based on data from the 2012 Service Annual Survey. Revenue estimates are shown in millions of dollars, consequently industry group estimates may not be additive. Estimated measures of sampling variability for these estimates are provided in Measures of Sampling Variability for U.S. Selected Services Revenue—Total and E-commerce: 2012 and 2011.]

S—Estimate does not meet publication standards because of high sampling variability or poor response quality (total quantity response rate is less than 50%), or other concerns about the estimate's quality. Unpublished estimates derived from this table by subtraction are subject to these same limitations and should not be attributed to the U.S. Census Bureau.
D—Estimate in table is withheld to avoid disclosing data of individual companies; data are included in higher level totals.
NAICS = North American Industry Classification System.
[a]Includes NAICS 22 (Utilities), NAICS 4849y (Transportation and Warehousing), NAICS 51 (Information), NAICS 52 (Finance and Insurance), NAICS 53 (Real Estate and Rental and Leasing), NAICS 54 (Selected Professional, Scientific, and Technical Services), NAICS 56 (Administrative and Support and Waste Management and Remediation Services), NAICS 61 (Educational Services), NAICS 62 (Health Care and Social Assistance), NAICS 71 (Arts, Entertainment, and Recreation), NAICS 72 (Accommodation and Food Services), and NAICS 81 (Other Services (except Public Administration)).
[b]Excludes government owned utilities.
[c]Excludes NAICS 482 (Rail Transportation) and NAICS 491 (Postal Service).
[d]Excludes NAICS 525 (Funds, Trusts, and Other Financial Vehicles).
[e]NAICS published according to the 2007 NAICS definition, as is the 2007 Economic Census. The 2007 NAICS definition includes equity Real Estate Investment Trusts (REITs).
[f]Excludes NAICS 54112 (Offices of Notaries).
[g]Excludes NAICS 6111 (Elementary and Secondary Schools), NAICS 6112 (Junior Colleges), and NAICS 6113 (Colleges, Universities, and Professional Schools).
[h]Estimates are based on data from the 2012 Annual Retail Trade Survey.
[i]Excludes NAICS 81311 (Religious Organizations), NAICS 81393 (Labor Unions and Similar Labor Organizations), NAICS 81394 (Political Organizations), and NAICS814 (Private Households).
[j]Excludes NAICS 81311 (Religious Organizations), NAICS 81393 (Labor Unions and Similar Labor Organizations), and NAICS 81394 (Political Organizations).
Note: Estimates are not adjusted for price changes. Estimates are subject to revision and include data only for businesses with paid employees except for Accommodation and Food Services, which also includes businesses without paid employees.

SOURCE: "U.S. Selected Services Revenue—Total and E-Commerce: 2012 and 2011," in *E-Stats: 2012 E-Commerce Multi-sector Data Tables*, U.S. Department of Commerce, U.S. Census Bureau, May 22, 2014, http://www.census.gov/econ/estats/2012/2012services.xls (accessed June 3, 2014)

reached 22.4 million unique visitors in March 2014, up from 12.7 million unique visitors in March 2013.

The Internet has also become a valuable tool for real estate brokers and agents. According to J. Barlow Herget in "Internet Now an Indispensable Tool for Veteran Realtors Who Were Once Skeptical" (NewsObserver.com, July 14, 2012), e-mail and mobile phones enable realtors to maintain contact with a wider range of prospective homeowners, including those who live out of state or even overseas. Meanwhile, the Internet empowers consumers to identify desirable properties on their own, allowing real estate agents to streamline the home viewing process. Herget quotes Phyllis Brookshire of Allen Tate Realtors in Charlotte, North Carolina, as saying, "The Internet is an agent's best partner if they learn how to use it. You absolutely have to have it."

M-Commerce

As more Americans own handheld devices, retailers are beginning to explore ways to reach consumers through mobile wireless technology. This emerging trend, known as mobile commerce (m-commerce), has become a vital mode of communication between sellers and consumers in the 21st century. As the Internet Retailer reports in "The Internet Retailer 2014 Mobile 500" (InternetRetailer.com, 2014), in 2013 mobile commerce accounted for an estimated $34.2 billion in sales in the United States, compared with $21 billion in 2012. Overall, mobile transactions accounted for 13% of all e-commerce sales in 2013. The versatility and ease of mobile shopping also enabled consumers to perform a variety of tasks on their phone before making a purchase.

In "A Mobile Shopper's Journey: From the Couch to the Store (and Back Again)" (August 12, 2013, http://www.nielsen.com/us/en/newswire/2013/a-mobile-shoppers-journey--from-the-couch-to-the-store--and-back.html), the Nielsen Company reports that, in the first quarter of 2013, 56% of smartphone shoppers used their mobile devices to check the price of a product, and 54% researched product information on their phones. In addition, 70% of mobile shoppers used a store locator app to get directions to a retail outlet; of these, more than half (56%) used a store locator while in their vehicle. Overall, nearly one-quarter (24%) of mobile shoppers completed a transaction on their smartphone in the first quarter of 2013.

IT AND CURRENCY

IT has not only changed how people pay for merchandise but also how people make and receive payments in general. Credit cards, debit cards, electronic bank transfers, and online banking have eliminated much of the need to carry cash and personal checks. In "The Future of Banking in America: The Effect on U.S. Banking of Payment System Changes" (*FDIC Banking Review*, vol. 16, no. 2, 2004), Neil B. Murphy of Virginia Commonwealth University reports that 88% of households in the United States used some form of electronic payment in 2001. NACHA—The Electronic Payments Association (formerly the National Automated Clearing House Association) notes in "ACH Payment Volume Grows to Nearly 22 Billion in 2013" (April 7, 2014, https://www.nacha.org/news/ach-volume-grows-nearly-22-billion-payments-2013) that automated clearing houses (ACHs) processed nearly 22 billion electronic payment transactions in 2013, with an overall value of $38.7 trillion.

The advantages of a cashless system are undeniable. With credit and debit cards people always have buying power at their disposal, they can make purchases instantly, and they can access and transfer money online. Banks and businesses are no longer required to spend money moving paper bills and checks all over the country. Furthermore, store owners do not have to worry about the security risks that are inherent with keeping large amounts of cash on hand. At the same time, electronic financial transactions have a positive impact on the environment. According to PayItGreen in "Why PayIt-Green?" (2013, http://payitgreen.org/business/why-payit green), the average household could save up to 6 pounds (3 kg) of paper and 23 pounds (10 kg) of wood and reduce carbon emissions by 29 pounds (13 kg) annually by conducting all their financial activities online.

Credit and Debit Cards

In the 21st century credit and debit cards have become the predominant mode of payment for the majority of American consumers. By enabling individuals to make an array of purchases with a single piece of plastic, credit and debit cards bring unprecedented convenience to a range of financial transactions, from shopping at retail outlets to paying bills over the phone. Furthermore, credit and debit card accounts allow individuals to track their spending over the Internet, providing them with a range of new tools designed to help them manage their spending more easily and efficiently.

However, the ubiquity of credit and debit cards has also created unique risks for 21st-century consumers. For one, credit and debit cards provide potential thieves with relatively easy access to an individual's sensitive personal and financial information, leading to dramatic increases in the number of unauthorized purchases and identity theft cases. (See Chapter 4.) Also, credit card companies and banks charge transaction fees for credit and debit card purchases, which imposes additional expenses on merchants and retailers. David Lazarus reports in "Hidden from View, Credit Card 'Swipe Fees' May Still Raise Prices" (LATimes.com, July 17, 2012) that these additional costs are sometimes passed on to consumers, usually in the form of higher prices. "A lot of merchants will consider it a cost of doing business and will raise all their prices," the consumer advocate Linda Sherry told Lazarus. "Consumers won't know if this is for the processing fees or not." Furthermore, the ease of using credit and debit cards makes it challenging for some consumers to manage their money effectively. Daniel P. Ray and Yasmin Ghahremani report in "Credit Card Statistics, Industry Facts, Debt Statistics" (2014, http://www.creditcards.com/credit-card-news/credit-card-industry-facts-personal-debt-statistics-1276.php) that revolving debt (debt that changes from month to month,

based on consumer purchases and payments) in the United States reached $872.1 billion in May 2014.

CREDIT CARDS. The most firmly established of these electronic payment methods is the credit card. Diners Club issued the first general-purpose credit card in 1950. This credit card allowed restaurant patrons in Manhattan to charge a meal at any restaurant that participated in the program. Even though credit card use has increased almost every year since then, credit card transactions took place entirely on paper at first, which kept some people away. During the 1980s a computerized, networked credit card system was put into place using modems and other networking technologies. The result was that credit card use skyrocketed. Murphy estimates that in 2004 there were more than 1.2 billion credit cards in the United States. A little under half (551.9 million) of these cards were issued directly by retailers under a private label (e.g., Banana Republic or JC Penney). The rest were issued by banks or as travel and entertainment cards. Murphy reports that between 1997 and 2001 the number of credit card transactions grew from 12.9 billion to 17 billion. In *The 2013 Federal Reserve Payments Study: Recent and Long-Term Payment Trends in the United States: 2003–2012* (December 19, 2013, http://www.frbservices.org/files/communications/pdf/research/2013_payments_study_summary.pdf), the Federal Reserve System determines that 26.2 billion general-purpose credit card transactions, with a total value of $2.2 trillion, were processed in the United States in 2012. That year, the average general-purpose credit card transaction was $93.

DEBIT CARDS. Since their introduction to the U.S. market during the 1980s, debit cards have also become a popular method of payment for many Americans. Debit cards remove existing money from a money market or bank account when used, unlike credit cards, which are effectively making loans to their users. A debit card user does not owe money after the transaction, but must have sufficient funds in his or her account to cover the transaction.

Debit cards grew out of the automated teller machine (ATM) system that became widespread during the early 1980s. The first U.S. ATM was a Chemical Bank cash dispenser that went into operation in Long Island, New York, in 1969. Some ATM networks, which were originally constructed to allow bank cards access to ATMs at multiple banks, expanded their networks to grocery stores and select mainstream retail stores such as Wal-Mart. Customers could then use their ATM cards to buy groceries or merchandise at the register without first having to withdraw cash from a machine. When this debit card system appeared as if it might become widely used, Visa and MasterCard responded by opening their extensive networks to banks and debit card users. Since 1995 the use of debit cards has grown at a rapid pace. According to

Murphy, between 1995 and 2001 the percentage of American households using a debit card grew from 17.6% to 47%. In 1995 there were 1.4 billion debit card transactions, and by 2000 the number of transactions had increased to 8.3 billion. According to *2013 Federal Reserve Payments Study*, the total number of debit card transactions rose from 37.5 billion in 2009 to 47 billion in 2012, an increase of 7.7%. The total value of all debit card transactions exceeded $1.8 trillion in 2012, and debit cards accounted for more than one-third (38%) of all noncash payment transactions.

Electronic Transfer of Money

Another type of paperless monetary transaction that has grown in popularity is the electronic transfer of money, formally known as the ACH system. Electronic transfer is an electronic form of the checking system. When making an ACH transaction, the person or business with the checking account provides the account and routing number to another party along with the authorization to wire money directly into or out of an account. For the most part, large corporations employ this method of payment and receipt more extensively than individual households. Murphy notes that 97% of large corporations used the ACH system extensively in 2002, largely for business-to-business (B2B) transactions involving substantial amounts of money.

Individuals who use the ACH system typically do so to receive regular salary or Social Security payments and to make regular monthly payments. According to the Social Security Administration (August 2014, http://www.ssa.gov/deposit/GIS/data/Reports/T2StateSum.htm) in August 2014, 98.6% of Social Security recipients received their payments through direct deposit.

Many Americans also file their tax returns and receive refunds through an electronic payment method. The Internal Revenue Service (May 22, 2014, http://www.irs.gov/uac/Newsroom/Filing-Season-Statistics-for-Week-Ending-May-16,-2014) states that through May 2014, 117.8 million (86%) out of 136.9 million 2013 tax returns had been filed electronically. Meanwhile, the government paid $229.7 billion out of a total of $274.7 billion in tax refunds through direct deposit.

As electronic transfers have become more common, the number of paper checks written by Americans has steadily declined. According to the Federal Reserve in *2013 Federal Reserve Payments Study*, Americans wrote 18.3 billion checks in 2012, a 9.2% decrease from the 24.5 billion checks written in 2009. During this same period, the debit card surpassed the personal check as the most prevalent form of noncash payment in the United States. In 2012 the largest percentage of checks were those written by consumers to businesses (46%), followed by B2B check payments (28%) and business-to-consumer (B2C) checks (15%).

Because the cost of creating, mailing, and handling so many paper checks is enormous, the U.S. government has made efforts to reduce the number of paper checks in the system. Early in 2003 the Federal Reserve reduced what it charges banks for processing electronic transfers and raised the prices it charges banks for processing paper checks. Then in October 2003 Congress passed and President George W. Bush (1946–) signed the Check Truncation Act, which went into effect in October 2004. Under the Check Truncation Act banks are no longer required to hold onto the original paper checks they receive. Instead, when a payee deposits a check in a bank, the bank makes a digital copy of the check and shreds the original. The bank then simply wires the payer's bank for the money, avoiding the postage and processing involved in sending the actual check to the payer's bank. If the payer needs a copy of the check, the stored digital image can be printed. At the same time, more and more bank customers were using digital technology to deposit checks into their accounts remotely. As Susan Johnston writes in "How to Deposit Checks with Your Smartphone" (Money.USNews.com, October 9, 2012), by 2012 a number of banks had created mobile apps that enabled customers to take photographs of an endorsed check and then upload it to their accounts using their phones.

WILL AMERICANS ABANDON THE BANK?

Dennis Jacobe reports in *Banking Customers Still Love Bricks and Mortar* (June 10, 2003, http://www.gallup.com/poll/8593/Banking-Customers-Still-Love-Bricks-Mortar.aspx) that in 2003 Americans wanted both the option of banking electronically and of visiting their local bank branch. Because of the high costs of hiring tellers and leasing branch space, banks have encouraged the use of electronic banking among customers as a whole. The banks' efforts appear to be working. In March 2000 only 7% of Americans reported any experience with online banking, and by 2003, 29% of Americans said they banked online from home at least once a month. In *Usage over Time* (2014, http://www.pewinternet.org/files/2014/01/Usage-Over-Time-_May-2013.xlsx), the Pew Research Center reports that in March 2000, 17% of Internet users reported that they had banked online at some time. In January 2005 this percentage had increased to 44%. By May 2013 more than three-fifths (61%) of Internet users had used an online banking service at some point.

ANTITRUST LITIGATION

Throughout U.S. history, technological innovation has tended to give rise to the formation of monopolies. Those companies that create a widespread demand and a standard for new technologies often become the only producer of that technology, shutting down further competition in that industry. Since the passage of the Sherman Antitrust Act in 1890, companies in the private sector have been forbidden from blocking competitors from entering the market. If a company grows large enough and powerful enough to keep competitors out of the market and become a monopoly, then the U.S. Department of Justice (DOJ) typically intervenes and either reaches a settlement with the company or files an antitrust suit and takes the company to court. The U.S. government takes the stance that monopolies reduce competition, which impedes economic progress and innovation. Even though this law may appear easy to understand, the courts and the DOJ have to weigh a number of factors before breaking up a monopoly, including the negative effects the ruling may have on consumers.

In 1998 the DOJ and the attorneys general of 20 states filed an antitrust suit against Microsoft Corporation. Along with other charges, the government claimed that Microsoft violated antitrust law when it integrated its Internet Explorer web browser software with Windows. At the time, Windows was the only operating system widely available for the personal computer (PC). When Microsoft integrated Internet Explorer and Windows, other web browsers such as Netscape could not compete. The DOJ maintained that this act created unfair competition for those other companies that made browsers for PC systems. Microsoft officials claimed that Internet Explorer was now part of Windows and that separating the two would destroy the most current versions of the operating system and years of development on their part.

In November 1999 Judge Thomas Penfield Jackson (1937–2013) of the U.S. District Court presented a preliminary ruling, which asserted that Microsoft did have a monopoly with its PC operating system and that the monopoly prevented fair competition among companies that made software for personal computers. Five months later, in April 2000, Judge Jackson gave his final ruling, ordering that Microsoft should be split into two separate units: one that would produce the operating system and one that would produce other software components such as Internet Explorer.

Microsoft immediately appealed, and the case went to the federal appeals court under Judge Colleen Kollar-Kotelly (1943–). In the midst of the judicial review, the White House administration changed, and the DOJ, now led by John D. Ashcroft (1942–), came to an agreement with Microsoft that did not involve the breakup of the company. However, several of the states continued to battle the software giant in court. In November 2002 Judge Kollar-Kotelly ruled that the company should not be broken up and should follow the agreement laid down by the DOJ and accepted by the attorneys general of Illinois, Kentucky, Louisiana, Maryland, Michigan, New York, North Carolina, Ohio, and Wisconsin. Additional remedies proposed by California, Connecticut, the District of Columbia, Florida, Iowa, Kansas, Massachusetts, Minnesota, Utah, and West Virginia were dismissed. The agreement required Microsoft to take a number of steps that would allow competitors to once again compete in the market. Among these provisions, Microsoft was required to give computer makers the option of removing Internet Explorer and other Microsoft programs that run on top of the Windows operating system. Microsoft was also forced to reveal details about the Windows operating system that would allow makers of other software to better integrate software with Windows. The terms of the final judgment in the case required Microsoft to share technical documentation, provide feedback to software developers, promote data portability, and support interoperability among systems.

While the DOJ awaited a resolution of the Microsoft antitrust case, other high-profile tech companies came under scrutiny for allegedly monopolistic business practices. In "IBM Hits Back at 'Mainframe Monopoly' Accusations" (March 15, 2010, Information-age.com), Daniel Shane reports that in 2010 the Indian Council for Research on International Economic Relations filed a report claiming that IBM had attempted to assert monopoly control over India's computer mainframe business sector. Two years later, Google found itself the target of a European Union investigation, amid charges that the company had violated European antitrust law. Indeed, Susan P. Crawford notes in "Is Google a Monopoly? Wrong Question" (Bloombergview.com, July 8, 2012,) that in 2012 Google accounted for 80% of all search engine traffic on the European continent. Furthermore, as Tom Warren notes in "Ballmer Calls Google a 'Monopoly' that Authorities Should Control" (Verge.com, September 20, 2013), Google controlled more than two-thirds (67%) of all U.S. search engine traffic in 2013; by contrast, its nearest competitor, Bing, controlled only 17.9%. As both the IBM and Google cases illustrate, the era of economic globalization not only offered new opportunities for American tech companies to extend their reach into overseas markets but also introduced a range of potential new legal obstacles to overseas expansion.

CHAPTER 4
TECHNOLOGY AND CRIME

New technologies almost always introduce new problems into a society. The information technology that became widespread during the 1980s and 1990s is no exception. The advent of online shopping and the increased use of electronic currency have given rise to an identity theft epidemic. The digitization of music, movies, television, and the printed word has led to widespread intellectual property theft and losses of millions of dollars for the entertainment industry.

High-technology (high-tech) crime—also known as cybercrime, web crime, computer crime, netcrime, and electronic crime (e-crime)—has grown ever more common in the 21st century. The Federal Bureau of Investigation's (FBI's) Internet Crime Complaint Center (IC3) reports in its *2013 Internet Crime Report* (2014, http://www.ic3.gov/media/annualreport/2013_IC3Report.pdf) that 262,813 cybercrime incidents were reported to the IC3 in 2013. (See Figure 4.1.) Although this figure represented a 21.9% decline from 2009, when the center received a peak of 336,655 complaints, it was still 27% higher than the 206,884 complaints received in 2007. In addition, the Federal Trade Commission (FTC) estimates in "FTC Announces Top National Consumer Complaints for 2013" (February 27, 2014, http://www.ftc.gov/news-events/press-releases/2014/02/ftc-announces-top-national-consumer-complaints-2013) that Americans lost $1.6 billion to identity theft and other Internet scams in 2013. As more people become dependent on information technology, Internet crimes will likely continue to grow more common, in part because they do not require a face-to-face confrontation with the victim.

IDENTITY THEFT

The FTC has the responsibility of tracking identity theft and consumer fraud in the United States. Each year the FTC gathers consumer complaints of fraud and identity theft and logs them into its Consumer Sentinel database. In 2013 more reports of identity theft were cataloged in the Consumer Sentinel database than any other single type of fraud complaint. (See Table 4.1.) Simply put, identity theft is the theft of an individual's personal information such as a telephone number, address, credit card number, or Social Security number. Thieves use this information to buy things, set up false credit card and cell phone accounts, or perpetrate other crimes. With a victim's Social Security number, address, and phone number, a thief can apply for credit cards in the victim's name and proceed to run up the limits on these cards. Such a crime leaves the victim's credit history in shambles, making it difficult to apply for loans or additional cards in the future.

In some instances, identity theft is perpetrated on a massive scale by sophisticated criminal networks. One of the most extensive identity theft cases was broken in 2008, when federal prosecutors brought indictments against 11 individuals accused of operating an international identity theft ring. According to the press release "Retail Hacking Ring Charged for Stealing and Distributing Credit and Debit Card Numbers from Major U.S. Retailers" (August 5, 2008, http://www.usdoj.gov/opa/pr/2008/August/08-ag-689.html), between 2006 and 2008 the 11 defendants in the case stole an estimated 40 million credit and debit card numbers from patrons of retail chains throughout the United States. According to Department of Justice (DOJ) allegations, the accused defendants hacked into the wireless computer networks of TJX Companies, BJ's Wholesale Club, OfficeMax, Boston Market, Barnes & Noble, Sports Authority, Forever 21, and DSW to install "sniffer" programs that capture customers' account information. Once in possession of the credit and debit card numbers, the conspirators used them to encode the magnetic strips of blank cards, or else sold them to other criminals. As the DOJ reports in "Leader of Hacking Ring Sentenced for Massive Identity

FIGURE 4.1

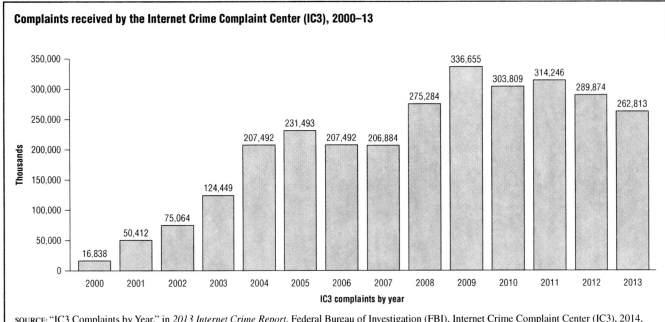

Complaints received by the Internet Crime Complaint Center (IC3), 2000–13

SOURCE: "IC3 Complaints by Year," in *2013 Internet Crime Report*, Federal Bureau of Investigation (FBI), Internet Crime Complaint Center (IC3), 2014, http://www.ic3.gov/media/annualreport/2013_IC3Report.pdf (accessed June 7, 2014)

Thefts from Payment Processor and U.S. Retail Networks" (March 26, 2010, http://www.justice.gov/opa/pr/2010/March/10-crm-329.html), the ringleader of the scam, Albert Gonzalez, was eventually convicted on multiple charges, including aggravated identity theft, and sentenced to 20 years in prison.

Another high-profile case, dubbed Operation Swiper, was exposed in October 2011. As Julia Greenberg reports in "111 Indicted in One of Largest Identity-Theft Cases in the U.S." (October 7, 2011, IBTimes.com), the ringleaders of the scam recruited bank tellers, restaurant employees, and retail associates throughout the New York City borough of Queens to steal credit card information from customers. One of the four principal organizers of the operation, Amar Singh, was eventually sentenced to up to 10⅔ years in prison for his role in the scam, according to Allie Compton, in "Largest ID Theft Case in U.S. History: Amar Singh and Wife, Neha Punjani-Singh, Plead Guilty to Massive Fraud" (August 7, 2012, Huffington Post.com).

Since the 1980s credit card companies and other financial institutions have made obtaining a credit card or setting up a financial account much easier. Because of the convenience of debit and credit cards, nearly every brick-and-mortar store, website, and catalog now accepts them, often with no proof of identification. Consequently, identity theft is not difficult, and it continues to grow. In its *Consumer Sentinel Network Data Book for January–December 2013* (February 2014, http://www.ftc.gov/system/files/documents/reports/consumer-sentinel-network-data-book-january-december-2013/sentinel-cy2013.pdf),

the FTC reports that in 2013 it received roughly 2.1 million fraud complaints. Of these, 14% were related to identity theft. (See Figure 4.2.)

Table 4.2 displays reported incidents of identity theft by state. California had the highest number of complaints in the country in 2013, with 40,404. Florida topped the list with the highest rate of reported cases of identity theft per capita, registering 192.9 complaints per 100,000 population. The FTC notes that if the District of Columbia were included among the states listed in Table 4.2, then it would be second with a rate of 147.9 identity theft victimization reports per 100,000 population. Georgia (134.1 per 100,000 population) and California (105.4) also experienced rates higher than 100 complaints per 100,000 population. North Dakota (32.1) and South Dakota (33.4) had the lowest number of reported victims of identity theft per 100,000 population in 2013.

The FBI monitors U.S. and global cybercrime incidents through its IC3, which publishes its findings annually. According to the *2013 Internet Crime Report*, the IC3 received 238,189 cybercrime complaints from the United States in 2013; this figure accounted for more than 90% of all complaints received worldwide that year. (See Table 4.3.) As Table 4.4 shows, the highest number of complaints came from California, with a total of 28,888 complaints, or 12.1% of all complaints originating in the United States in 2013. California was also the leading state in terms of financial losses linked to cybercrime that year, with a total of $105.1 million reported lost; this figure represented nearly one-fifth (18.3%) of all financial losses reported to the IC3 in 2013. (See

TABLE 4.1

Top consumer fraud complaints reported to the Consumer Sentinel Network, 2013

Rank	Category	No. of complaints	Percentages*
1	Identity theft	290,056	14%
2	Debt collection	204,644	10%
3	Banks and lenders	152,707	7%
4	Impostor scams	121,720	6%
5	Telephone and mobile services	116,261	6%
6	Prizes, sweepstakes and lotteries	89,944	4%
7	Auto-related complaints	82,701	4%
8	Shop-at-home and catalog sales	66,024	3%
9	Television and electronic media	53,087	3%
10	Advance payments for credit services	50,422	2%
11	Internet services	50,311	2%
12	Health care	39,452	2%
13	Credit cards	35,086	2%
14	Business and job opportunities	32,939	2%
15	Credit bureaus, information furnishers and report users	31,810	2%
16	Travel, vacations and timeshare plans	30,094	1%
17	Foreign money offers and counterfeit check scams	24,752	1%
18	Internet auction	21,026	1%
19	Mortgage foreclosure relief and debt management	20,540	1%
20	Office supplies and services	19,584	1%
21	Real estate	17,798	1%
22	Magazines and books	14,471	1%
23	Computer equipment and software	14,028	1%
24	Home repair, improvement and products	9,543	<1%
25	Grants	7,969	<1%
26	Investment-related complaints	5,645	<1%
27	Education	3,569	<1%
28	Charitable solicitations	2,477	<1%
29	Buyers' clubs	1,847	<1%
30	Clothing, textiles and jewelry	1,720	<1%

*Percentages are based on the total number of Consumer Sentinel Network CSN complaints (2,101,780) received by the Federal Trade Commission (FTC) between January 1 and December 31, 2013.

SOURCE: "Consumer Sentinel Network Complaint Categories, January 1–December 31, 2013," in *Consumer Sentinel Network Data Book for January–December 2013*, Federal Trade Commission, February 2014, http://www.ftc.gov/system/files/documents/reports/consumer-sentinel-network-data-book-january-december-2013/sentinel-cy2013.pdf (accessed June 3, 2014)

FIGURE 4.2

Percentage of identity theft and other fraud complaints received by the Consumer Sentinel Network, 2011–13

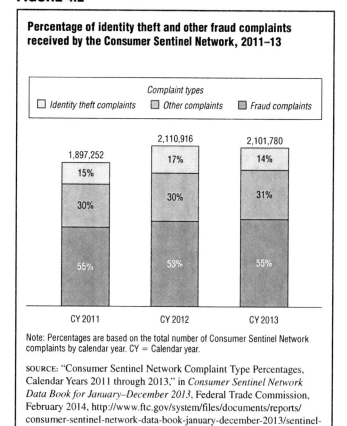

Note: Percentages are based on the total number of Consumer Sentinel Network complaints by calendar year. CY = Calendar year.

SOURCE: "Consumer Sentinel Network Complaint Type Percentages, Calendar Years 2011 through 2013," in *Consumer Sentinel Network Data Book for January–December 2013*, Federal Trade Commission, February 2014, http://www.ftc.gov/system/files/documents/reports/consumer-sentinel-network-data-book-january-december-2013/sentinel-cy2013.pdf (accessed June 3, 2014)

Table 4.5.) Overall, the United States accounted for $574.3 million in total losses, or nearly three-quarters (73.5%) of all financial losses reported to the IC3 worldwide in 2013. (See Table 4.6.)

According to the *Consumer Sentinel Network Data Book for January–December 2013*, more than half of those reporting identity theft in calendar years 2012 and 2013 were over the age of 40. (See Table 4.7; note that total numbers do not coincide with those in Table 4.1 because not all victims reported their age.) In 2013, 18% of complaints came from those between the ages of 40 and 49, and 17% were received from those aged 50 to 59. Between 2012 and 2013, the number of identity theft complaints received from those 19 years old and younger declined by more than 25%, from 16,072 to 11,967. Complaints from those 70 years old and older rose considerably between 2011 and 2012, from 15,786 to 21,909,

before falling to 16,993 in 2013. (See Table 4.7.) On the whole, men registered more complaints than women with the IC3 in 2013; the one exception was among adults between the ages of 40 and 49, where women (29,170) registered more complaints than men (26,668) that year. (See Table 4.8.)

The FTC also provides information on how identity theft victims' information was misused. Overall, one-third (33.9%) of victims reported that someone had used their identity to obtain government benefits or documents, including tax- or wage-related fraud (30%), benefits fraud (2.3%), and driver's license fraud (0.6%). (See Table 4.9.) Another 16.9% of victims suffered credit card fraud in 2013, with 11.2% reporting that new accounts were set up in their name, and 5.7% reporting bogus charges made to their existing accounts. These figures represented an increase from 2012, when 13.5% of victims experienced credit card fraud. Phone and utilities fraud was reported by 13.5% of victims in 2013, with 3.5% indicating that imposters set up wireless accounts in their name, and another 0.6% claiming that bogus telephone accounts had been established under their personal information. Bank fraud, which was reported by 6.4% of identity theft victims in 2012, rose to 7.7% in 2013. Bank fraud complaints included unauthorized electronic fund transfers (3.7%), fraudulent new accounts (2.2%), and

TABLE 4.2

Fraud, identity theft, and other complaints received by the Consumer Sentinel Network, by state, 2013

	Fraud & other complaints				Identity theft complaints		
Rank	Consumer state	Complaints per 100,000 population*	Complaints	Rank	Victim state	Complaints per 100,000 population*	Complaints
1	Florida	804.9	157,383	1	Florida	192.9	37,720
2	Nevada	622.0	17,354	2	Georgia	134.1	13,402
3	Georgia	621.7	62,121	3	California	105.4	40,404
4	Delaware	592.3	5,483	4	Michigan	97.1	9,606
5	Michigan	579.6	57,358	4	Nevada	97.1	2,708
6	Maryland	572.2	33,922	6	Maryland	95.5	5,660
7	California	524.0	200,870	7	Arizona	91.2	6,043
8	New Jersey	514.7	45,801	8	Texas	88.0	23,266
9	Arizona	508.8	33,714	9	New York	86.9	17,072
10	Texas	504.2	133,345	10	Illinois	85.9	11,069
11	Virginia	497.5	41,093	11	Delaware	81.1	751
12	Colorado	494.3	26,039	12	New Jersey	80.6	7,176
13	New Hampshire	475.8	6,297	13	Colorado	79.6	4,195
14	Washington	464.5	32,381	14	Alabama	74.7	3,610
15	Massachusetts	448.7	30,029	14	Mississippi	74.7	2,233
16	New York	441.1	86,673	16	Virginia	73.1	6,037
17	Pennsylvania	439.8	56,185	17	South Carolina	70.7	3,374
18	Ohio	438.7	50,765	18	Pennsylvania	70.0	8,943
19	Connecticut	437.3	15,724	19	New Mexico	69.4	1,448
20	Missouri	435.5	26,320	19	Connecticut	69.4	2,496
21	Tennessee	433.5	28,163	21	Louisiana	69.3	3,204
22	Oregon	428.2	16,827	22	Tennessee	68.8	4,468
23	North Carolina	423.0	41,654	23	Washington	68.0	4,739
24	Rhode Island	422.1	4,438	24	North Carolina	67.8	6,679
25	South Carolina	419.0	20,005	25	Missouri	67.0	4,052
26	Louisiana	412.3	19,070	26	Ohio	64.8	7,502
27	Alabama	402.3	19,447	27	Massachusetts	63.3	4,237
28	New Mexico	397.6	8,292	27	Wisconsin	63.3	3,635
29	Idaho	397.4	6,407	29	Arkansas	62.1	1,839
30	Illinois	388.8	50,080	30	Kansas	61.6	1,783
31	Alaska	384.4	2,826	31	West Virginia	60.6	1,124
32	Wisconsin	380.8	21,869	31	Rhode Island	60.6	637
33	Minnesota	380.2	20,610	33	Oregon	60.3	2,370
34	Hawaii	377.9	5,306	34	Oklahoma	60.0	2,309
35	West Virginia	377.1	6,993	35	Indiana	58.5	3,845
35	Indiana	377.1	24,777	36	Minnesota	53.8	2,917
37	Kentucky	368.6	16,203	37	Alaska	52.2	384
38	Wyoming	360.4	2,100	38	New Hampshire	51.9	687
39	Kansas	359.0	10,390	39	Nebraska	51.6	965
40	Nebraska	355.3	6,638	40	Montana	50.1	509
41	Montana	352.2	3,575	40	Kentucky	50.1	2,201
42	Maine	351.4	4,668	42	Wyoming	49.6	289
43	Mississippi	350.6	10,486	43	Idaho	49.5	798
44	Utah	345.4	10,020	44	Utah	49.3	1,429
45	Vermont	344.5	2,159	45	Vermont	43.7	274
46	Arkansas	344.4	10,193	46	Iowa	40.4	1,248
47	Oklahoma	343.0	13,206	47	Maine	38.5	511
48	Iowa	314.4	9,717	48	Hawaii	37.8	531
49	South Dakota	282.4	2,386	49	South Dakota	33.4	282
50	North Dakota	270.9	1,960	50	North Dakota	32.1	232

*Per 100,000 unit of population estimates are based on the 2013 U.S. Numbers for the District of Columbia are: Fraud and Others = 4,996 complaints and 772.8 complaints per 100,000 population; Identity theft = 956 victims and 147.9 victims per 100,000 population.
Note: In calculating the State and Metropolitan Areas rankings, we excluded 16 state-specific data contributors' complaints (the Montana, North Carolina and Oregon Departments of Justice, the South Carolina Department of Consumer Affairs, the Tennessee Division of Consumer Affairs, and the Offices of the Attorneys General for California, Colorado, Idaho, Indiana, Iowa, Louisiana, Maine, Michigan, Mississippi, Ohio, and Washington).

SOURCE: "Consumer Sentinel Network State Complaint Rates, January 1–December 31, 2013," in *Consumer Sentinel Network Data Book for January–December 2013*, Federal Trade Commission, February 2014, http://www.ftc.gov/system/files/documents/reports/consumer-sentinel-network-data-book-january-december-2013/sentinel-cy2013.pdf (accessed June 3, 2014)

misuse of existing accounts (1.8%). Loan fraud was reported by 3.9% of identity theft victims in 2013. Those reporting identity theft crimes to the FTC in 2013 experienced many other types of fraud, including everything from phony child-support claims to property rental fraud. In addition, 16% of identity theft complaints in 2013 included more than one type of fraud.

Identity Theft and the Internet

Identity thieves can operate alone or as part of a large crime organization. They can be someone the victim knows or a complete stranger. They gather personal information in various ways, stealing wallets and checkbooks or going through trash bins outside of homes and businesses to dig out credit card statements, old checkbooks,

TABLE 4.3

Complaints filed with the Internet Crime Complaint Center (IC3), by country, 2013

Rank	Country	Complaint count	Percentage of complaints	Rank	Country	Complaint count	Percentage of complaints
1	United States	238,189	90.63%	25	Malaysia	207	0.08%
2	Canada	3,621	1.38%	27	United Arab Emirates	201	0.08%
3	United Kingdom	2,225	0.85%	28	Colombia	179	0.07%
4	India	1,867	0.71%	29	Argentina	167	0.06%
5	Australia	1,810	0.69%	29	Belgium	167	0.06%
6	Macedonia, The Former Yugoslav Republic of	1,670	0.64%	31	Romania	164	0.06%
7	Mexico	711	0.27%	32	Portugal	163	0.06%
8	Puerto Rico	550	0.21%	33	Saudi Arabia	161	0.06%
9	Brazil	505	0.19%	34	Ireland	156	0.06%
10	South Africa	502	0.19%	34	Afghanistan	156	0.06%
11	France	463	0.18%	34	Hong Kong	156	0.06%
12	Germany	438	0.17%	37	Greece	154	0.06%
13	Philippines	434	0.17%	38	Indonesia	147	0.06%
14	Pakistan	391	0.15%	39	Switzerland	140	0.05%
15	Netherlands	348	0.13%	40	Denmark	136	0.05%
16	Russian Federation	306	0.12%	41	Norway	134	0.05%
17	Spain	293	0.11%	42	Turkey	129	0.05%
18	Sweden	258	0.10%	43	Ukraine	123	0.05%
19	New Zealand	252	0.10%	44	Bulgaria	122	0.05%
20	Italy	244	0.09%	45	Egypt	121	0.05%
21	China	236	0.09%	46	Thailand	113	0.04%
22	Israel	230	0.09%	47	Poland	103	0.04%
23	Nigeria	219	0.08%	47	Venezuela	103	0.04%
24	Singapore	208	0.08%	49	Chile	90	0.03%
25	Japan	207	0.08%	50	Hungary	88	0.03%

Note: This represents a ranking of the top 50 countries that reported complaints to the IC3 and is based upon the total number of victim originated complaints received by IC3 in 2013 and their countries of residence. As demonstrated by the chart, the majority of victims reside in the United States. Figures were rounded to the nearest hundredth and do not total 100 percent.

SOURCE: "Victim Countries by Complaint Count 2013," in *2013 Internet Crime Report*, Federal Bureau of Investigation (FBI), Internet Crime Complaint Center (IC3), 2014, http://www.ic3.gov/media/annualreport/2013_IC3Report.pdf (accessed June 7, 2014)

TABLE 4.4

Complaints filed with the Internet Crime Complaint Center (IC3), by state, 2013

Rank	State	Complaint count	Percentage of complaints	Rank	State	Complaint count	Percentage of complaints
1	California	28,888	12.13%	27	Alaska	2,662	1.12%
2	Florida	17,739	7.45%	28	Kentucky	2,385	1.00%
3	Texas	16,056	6.74%	29	Connecticut	2,197	0.92%
4	New York	12,612	5.29%	30	Louisiana	2,112	0.89%
5	Pennsylvania	7,914	3.32%	31	Oklahoma	1,862	0.78%
6	New Jersey	7,647	3.21%	32	Utah	1,775	0.75%
7	Illinois	7,024	2.95%	33	Kansas	1,621	0.68%
8	Virginia	6,764	2.84%	34	Arkansas	1,583	0.66%
9	Ohio	6,541	2.75%	35	Iowa	1,580	0.66%
10	Georgia	6,151	2.58%	36	New Mexico	1,404	0.59%
11	Washington	6,009	2.52%	37	Mississippi	1,314	0.55%
12	North Carolina	5,981	2.51%	38	West Virginia	1,244	0.52%
13	Michigan	5,493	2.31%	39	Idaho	1,019	0.43%
14	Arizona	5,310	2.23%	40	Hawaii	993	0.42%
15	Maryland	5,268	2.21%	41	New Hampshire	918	0.39%
16	Colorado	4,613	1.94%	42	Nebraska	845	0.35%
17	Massachusetts	4,085	1.72%	43	Montana	730	0.31%
18	Tennessee	3,969	1.67%	44	Maine	704	0.30%
19	Indiana	3,695	1.55%	45	District of Columbia	702	0.29%
20	Nevada	3,497	1.47%	46	Delaware	684	0.29%
21	Missouri	3,352	1.41%	47	Rhode Island	588	0.25%
22	Wisconsin	3,335	1.40%	48	Wyoming	454	0.19%
23	Alabama	3,105	1.30%	49	North Dakota	416	0.17%
24	Oregon	2,956	1.24%	50	Vermont	414	0.17%
25	South Carolina	2,868	1.20%	51	South Dakota	364	0.15%
26	Minnesota	2,719	1.14%				

Note: This represents a ranking of states and the District of Columbia and is based upon the number of victim originated complaints reported to the IC3 in 2013 and their states of residence. Also, 10.09 percent (24,028) of the complaints did not provide location information. Figures were rounded to the nearest hundredth and do not total 100 percent.

SOURCE: "Victim States by Complaint Count 2013," in *2013 Internet Crime Report*, Federal Bureau of Investigation (FBI), Internet Crime Complaint Center (IC3), 2014, http://www.ic3.gov/media/annualreport/2013_IC3Report.pdf (accessed June 7, 2014)

TABLE 4.5

Financial losses reported to the Internet Crime Complaint Center (IC3), by state, 2013

Rank	State	Complaint total loss	Percentage of complaints	Rank	State	Complaint total loss	Percentage of complaints
1	California	$105,118,346	18.30%	27	Oklahoma	$5,199,764	0.91%
2	Texas	$56,534,880	9.84%	28	South Carolina	$4,839,453	0.84%
3	Florida	$48,778,217	8.49%	29	Louisiana	$4,627,893	0.81%
4	New York	$38,027,647	6.62%	30	Maine	$4,137,228	0.72%
5	Virginia	$20,319,530	3.54%	31	Kentucky	$4,117,820	0.72%
6	Georgia	$18,693,316	3.26%	32	Connecticut	$3,909,247	0.68%
7	Illinois	$15,907,173	2.77%	33	Iowa	$3,671,707	0.64%
8	Pennsylvania	$14,398,601	2.51%	34	Mississippi	$3,084,199	0.54%
9	Washington	$14,138,154	2.46%	35	New Mexico	$2,888,398	0.50%
10	New Jersey	$13,402,721	2.33%	36	Idaho	$2,748,012	0.48%
11	Arizona	$12,518,439	2.18%	37	Arkansas	$2,628,423	0.46%
12	Ohio	$12,351,755	2.15%	38	Kansas	$2,572,215	0.45%
13	Michigan	$10,697,615	1.86%	39	Hawaii	$2,415,892	0.42%
14	Colorado	$10,611,521	1.85%	40	Nebraska	$2,353,819	0.41%
15	Massachusetts	$10,570,678	1.84%	41	Delaware	$2,180,846	0.38%
16	North Carolina	$10,416,194	1.81%	42	New Hampshire	$1,683,034	0.29%
17	Nevada	$10,171,633	1.77%	43	Rhode Island	$1,620,972	0.28%
18	Maryland	$9,522,259	1.66%	44	West Virginia	$1,582,525	0.28%
19	Indiana	$8,142,650	1.42%	45	North Dakota	$1,446,979	0.25%
20	Tennessee	$7,091,950	1.23%	46	Alaska	$1,134,677	0.20%
21	Minnesota	$6,731,363	1.11%	47	District of Columbia	$918,293	0.16%
22	Oregon	$6,398,079	1.11%	48	Montana	$901,950	0.16%
23	Wisconsin	$6,382,394	1.11%	49	Vermont	$901,275	0.16%
24	Alabama	$6,097,466	1.06%	50	South Dakota	$768,105	0.13%
25	Utah	$5,941,062	1.03%	51	Wyoming	$751,337	0.13%
26	Missouri	$5,845,699	1.02%				

Note: This is the total dollar losses for complaints from each state and the District of Columbia. Also, 4.59 percent (or $26,383,019.60 in losses) of the complainants did not provide location information. Figures were rounded to the nearest hundredth and do not total 100 percent.

SOURCE: "Victim States by Complaint Total Loss 2013," in *2013 Internet Crime Report*, Federal Bureau of Investigation (FBI), Internet Crime Complaint Center (IC3), 2014, http://www.ic3.gov/media/annualreport/2013_IC3Report.pdf (accessed June 7, 2014)

TABLE 4.6

Financial losses reported to the Internet Crime Complaint Center (IC3), by country, 2013

Rank	Country	Complaint total loss	Percentage of complaints	Rank	Country	Complaint total loss	Percentage of complaints
1	United States	$574,276,422	73.45%	26	Indonesia	$1,011,606	0.13%
2	Pakistan	$100,921,345	12.91%	27	Taiwan, Province of China	$958,833	0.12%
3	Canada	$14,414,723	1.84%	28	Nigeria	$900,164	0.12%
4	United Kingdom	$13,005,869	1.66%	29	France	$898,228	0.11%
5	Australia	$8,940,931	1.14%	30	Finland	$856,030	0.11%
6	India	$4,399,440	0.56%	31	Malaysia	$754,561	0.10%
7	Singapore	$3,679,687	0.47%	32	Thailand	$737,190	0.09%
8	Bangladesh	$3,113,128	0.40%	33	Belgium	$736,042	0.09%
9	Sweden	$2,775,697	0.36%	34	Korea, Republic of	$717,675	0.09%
10	China	$2,697,852	0.35%	35	Norway	$655,262	0.08%
11	South Africa	$2,295,347	0.29%	36	New Zealand	$643,357	0.08%
12	Italy	$2,178,850	0.28%	37	Portugal	$637,159	0.08%
13	Brazil	$2,122,253	0.27%	38	Saudi Arabia	$617,171	0.08%
14	Germany	$2,060,673	0.26%	39	Poland	$610,691	0.08%
15	Mexico	$2,021,526	0.26%	40	Switzerland	$598,970	0.08%
16	Philippines	$1,817,830	0.23%	41	Greece	$592,648	0.08%
17	Kyrgyz Republic	$1,796,751	0.23%	42	Bahrain	$582,661	0.07%
18	Russian Federation	$1,749,575	0.22%	43	Denmark	$563,521	0.07%
19	Spain	$1,721,446	0.22%	44	Kuwait	$547,532	0.07%
20	Hong Kong	$1,577,618	0.20%	45	Trinidad and Tobago	$513,160	0.07%
21	Netherlands	$1,316,352	0.17%	46	Turkey	$511,340	0.07%
22	Japan	$1,180,511	0.15%	47	Venezuela	$497,926	0.06%
23	United Arab Emirates	$1,081,393	0.14%	48	Israel	$483,414	0.06%
24	Puerto Rico	$1,052,505	0.13%	49	Ghana	$458,479	0.06%
25	Lebanon	$1,035,760	0.13%	50	Afghanistan	$453,874	0.06%

Note: This represents a ranking of the top 50 countries that reported complaints to the IC3 in 2013 and is based upon the reported total dollar losses victims reported in their complaints. Figures were rounded to the nearest hundredth and do not total 100.

SOURCE: "Victim Countries by Complaint Total Loss 2013," in *2013 Internet Crime Report*, Federal Bureau of Investigation (FBI), Internet Crime Complaint Center (IC3), 2014, http://www.ic3.gov/media/annualreport/2013_IC3Report.pdf (accessed June 7, 2014)

TABLE 4.7

Identity theft complaints received by the Consumer Sentinel Network, by victims' age, 2011–13

Consumer age	CY-2011		CY-2012		CY-2013	
	Complaints	Percentages*	Complaints	Percentages*	Complaints	Percentages*
19 and under	19,597	8%	16,072	6%	11,967	6%
20–29	56,653	23%	57,258	21%	39,335	20%
30–39	49,774	20%	52,408	19%	38,097	19%
40–49	45,035	18%	49,110	18%	35,517	18%
50–59	37,985	15%	45,209	17%	34,122	17%
60–69	23,066	9%	30,356	11%	24,362	12%
70 and over	15,786	6%	21,909	8%	16,993	8%
Total reporting age	**247,896**		**272,322**		**200,393**	

*Percentages are based on the total number of victims reporting their age in CSN identity theft complaints for each calendar year: CY-2011 = 247,896; CY-2012 = 272,322; and CY-2013 = 200,393. Of the consumers who contacted the FTC, 69% reported their age in CY-2013, 74% in CY-2012 and 89% in CY-2011.
CSN = Consumer Sentinel Network. CY = Calendar year. FTC = Federal Trade Commission.

SOURCE: "Consumer Sentinel Network Identity Theft Complaints by Victims' Age, Calendar Years 2011 through 2013," in *Consumer Sentinel Network Data Book for January–December 2013*, Federal Trade Commission, February 2014, http://www.ftc.gov/system/files/documents/reports/consumer-sentinel-network-data-book-january-december-2013/sentinel-cy2013.pdf (accessed June 4, 2014)

TABLE 4.8

Complaints received by the Internet Crime Complaint Center (IC3), by sex, age, and amount of financial loss, 2013

Age range	Male count	Male loss	Female count	Female loss	Total complaints	Total combined losses
Under 20	5,194	$103,298,649	3,602	$2,364,515	8,796	$105,663,164
20–29	24,549	$42,144,452	23,483	$23,619,502	48,032	$65,763,954
30–39	28,391	$71,022,425	26,389	$41,784,048	54,780	$112,806,473
40–49	26,668	$89,559,205	29,170	$70,355,407	55,838	$159,914,612
50–59	29,220	$93,705,383	26,239	$83,858,340	55,459	$177,563,723
Over 60	23,074	$87,244,816	16,834	$72,884,870	39,908	$160,129,686
Totals	**137,096**	**$486,974,929**	**125,717**	**$294,866,681**	**262,813**	**$781,841,611**

SOURCE: "Overall Age Gender 2013 Statistics," in *2013 Internet Crime Report*, Federal Bureau of Investigation (FBI), Internet Crime Complaint Center (IC3), 2014, http://www.ic3.gov/media/annualreport/2013_IC3Report.pdf (accessed June 7, 2014)

and receipts. Some pilfer financial statements and other private information from open mailboxes. Since the mid-1990s many thieves have turned to the Internet to steal information.

There are a number of ways in which thieves employ the Internet to retrieve personal information. Tech-savvy crooks will often take the direct method and hack into business and bank servers and make off with hundreds of credit card numbers. Most identity thieves, however, do not deal in such sophisticated methods. According to Duncan Graham-Rowe in "Internet Fuels Boom in ID Theft" (NewScientist.com, March 13, 2004), one of the easiest ways to steal identities is simply to use a search engine such as Google. Many people naively post all manner of personal information on home and even office websites, including their Social Security number, date of birth, mother's maiden name, current address, and phone number. Simply typing "driver's license" or "passport" into a search engine yields hundreds of photos of driver's licenses and passports from around the country and the world.

Businesses or institutions that keep lists of Social Security and credit card numbers sometimes inadvertently place the information in an insecure location. In "Foreign Hacker Steals 3.6 Million Social Security Numbers from State Department of Revenue" (October 26, 2012, GreenvilleOnline.com), Tim Smith reports that between August and October 2012 a hacker exploited a vulnerability in the South Carolina Revenue Department's database, stealing millions of Social Security and credit card numbers of state residents.

In other cases hackers have conspired to perpetrate cybercrimes on a global scale. One notable plot was uncovered in July 2013, when four Russians and a Ukrainian were indicted for breaking into the computer records of several retailers, payment processing firms, and banks, stealing more than 160 million credit card numbers and selling the information on the black market. Targets of the scheme included the convenience store chain 7-Eleven, the banking giant Citigroup, and the French retailer Carrefour. As David Voreacos reports in "5 Hackers Charged in Latest Data-Breach Scheme in the U.S." (July 26, 2013,

TABLE 4.9

How identity theft victims' information was misused, 2011–13

Theft subtype	Percentages		
	CY-2011	CY-2012	CY-2013
Government documents or benefits fraud			
Tax-or wage-related fraud	24.3%	43.4%	30.0%
Government benefits applied for/received	1.5%	1.6%	2.3%
Other government documents issued/forged	0.8%	0.8%	1.0%
Driver's license issued/forged	0.8%	0.6%	0.6%
Total	**27.4%**	**46.4%**	**33.9%**
Credit card fraud			
New accounts	8.5%	8.9%	11.2%
Existing account	5.8%	4.6%	5.7%
Total	**14.3%**	**13.5%**	**16.9%**
Phone or utilities fraud			
Utilities—new accounts	8.8%	6.2%	8.8%
Wireless—new accounts	3.1%	2.5%	3.5%
Telephone—new accounts	1.0%	0.6%	0.6%
Unauthorized charges to existing accounts	0.5%	0.4%	0.6%
Total	**13.4%**	**9.7%**	**13.5%**
Bank fraud			
Electronic fund transfer	3.8%	3.0%	3.7%
New accounts	2.6%	1.9%	2.2%
Existing accounts	2.3%	1.5%	1.8%
Total	**8.7%**	**6.4%**	**7.7%**
Employment-related fraud			
Employment-related fraud	8.4%	5.4%	5.6%
Loan fraud			
Business/personal/student loan	1.4%	1.3%	2.0%
Auto loan/lease	0.9%	0.6%	1.1%
Real estate loan	0.8%	0.5%	0.8%
Total	**3.1%**	**2.4%**	**3.9%**
Other identity theft			
Miscellaneous	8.5%	7.5%	8.7%
Uncertain	8.2%	6.1%	8.5%
Internet/email	1.6%	1.2%	1.7%
Data breach	1.7%	1.1%	1.3%
Evading the law	1.2%	0.8%	1.0%
Medical	1.0%	0.7%	0.9%
Apartment or house rented	0.7%	0.4%	0.5%
Insurance	0.3%	0.2%	0.3%
Securities/other investments	0.1%	0.1%	0.2%
Bankruptcy	0.1%	0.1%	0.1%
Property rental fraud	0.1%	0.1%	0.1%
Child support	0.1%	0.1%	0.1%
Magazines	0.1%	0.1%	0.1%
Total	**23.7%**	**18.5%**	**23.5%**
Attempted identity theft			
Attempted identity theft	6.8%	6.6%	7.2%

Notes: CY = Calendar year. Percentages are based on the total number of Consumer Sentinel Network (CSN) identity theft complaints for each calendar year: CY-2011 = 279,216; CY-2012 = 369,145; and CY-2013 = 290,056. Note that 16% of identity theft complaints include more than one type of identity theft in CY-2013, 11% in CY-2012; and 13% in CY-2011.

SOURCE: "Consumer Sentinel Network Identity Theft Complaints: How Victims' Information Is Misused, Calendar Years 2011 through 2013," in *Consumer Sentinel Network Data Book for January–December 2013*, Federal Trade Commission, February 2014, http://www.ftc.gov/system/files/documents/reports/consumer-sentinel-network-data-book-january-december-2013/sentinelcy2013.pdf (accessed June 4, 2014)

compromised the credit card records of 40 million customers, as well as the contact information of another 70 million customers.

Another technique thieves use to acquire personal information is known as phishing. Thieves will often send out bogus e-mails to scores of people. Typically, these e-mails will look like authentic e-mails from a prominent Internet service provider or bank. The e-mail will inform the receivers that there is something wrong with their account and that the problem can be fixed by clicking on a hyperlink. When victims click on the link, they are then taken to an official-looking site, where they are asked to provide passwords, Social Security information, and even credit card information. The moment the victims type in their personal information, the thieves have them. Once crooks have a credit card in another person's name, the Internet makes it easy to purchase items. No longer do criminals have to risk being caught using someone else's account in a shopping mall or grocery store.

Efforts to Combat Identity Theft

In response to these threats, federal law enforcement agencies have established unique task forces and initiatives aimed at countering identity theft. As part of its counteroffensive, the government has also placed a high priority on keeping citizens informed about potential risks. The FBI provides information about cybercrime on its Identity Theft page (2014, http://www.fbi.gov/about-us/investigate/cyber/identity_theft), which contains an overview of law enforcement initiatives targeting Internet fraud, as well as valuable advice on how consumers can identify and avoid online threats. Along these lines, IC3 has created a comprehensive list of "Internet Crime Schemes" (2014, http://www.ic3.gov/crimeschemes.aspx), which contains detailed descriptions of some of the most common online scams. The federal government also maintains an Internet Fraud site (2014, http://www.usa.gov/Citizen/Topics/Internet-Fraud.shtml), which provides a list of resources aimed at helping citizens understand potential Internet threats, while providing information on how to report incidences of identity theft and other online crimes. In addition, the Department of Homeland Security (DHS) oversees a Cyber Crimes Center (C3; 2014, http://www.ice.gov/cyber-crimes), dedicated to fighting identity theft and other cybercrimes both at home and abroad. The center comprises three units: the Cyber Crimes Unit, which investigates various forms of Internet fraud, as well as the use of technology in such activities as drug trafficking and money laundering; the Child Exploitation Investigations Unit, which monitors the online operations of sexual predators and child pornographers; and the Computer Forensics Unit, which provides support in decoding and analyzing encrypted data.

Bloomberg.com), it was the largest data breach in U.S. history. Between November and December 2013, retail giant Target was affected by a massive data breach that

U.S. government agencies have also become increasingly active in combating cybercrime by cooperating with law enforcement allies overseas. One major investigation came to a close in December 2012, when Australian police arrested fugitive hacker Tobechi Onwuhara. As the FBI reports in "Scam on the Run" (January 22, 2014, http://www.fbi.gov/news/stories/2014/january/fugitive-identity-thief-led-global-criminal-enterprise/fugitive-identity-thief-led-global-criminal-enterprise), Onwuhara and his criminal associates operated a home equity line-of-credit scam, using the financial information of hundreds of U.S. home-owners to steal approximately $13 million. His arrest was the culmination of an international manhunt that lasted nearly five years.

In another high-profile case with international scope, in 2014 the FBI, working with the Criminal Investigations division of the Internal Revenue Service, uncovered an identity theft operation that had stolen $10 million from 2,400 victims over a nearly 10-year span. As Rich Lord writes in "5 Indicted in Massive Identity-Fraud Scheme" (April 23, 2014, Post-Gazette.com), the stolen funds eventually found their way to criminal organizations in Nigeria.

INTERNET FRAUD

Internet fraud takes other forms than identity theft, including auction fraud, phishing schemes, and fund-transfer scams. The FTC notes in *Consumer Sentinel Network Data Book for January–December 2013* that 48% of fraud complainants reported the method used by companies to contact them: 40% were contacted by phone, 33% were solicited through e-mail, and 15% had initial contact via a website. In comparison, 5% were contacted through surface mail.

In a typical Internet auction scheme, a con artist advertises merchandise on an auction site until a buyer is found. The buyer then sends a payment but receives no merchandise. In 2013 the FTC received 21,026 complaints of Internet auction fraud. (See Table 4.1.) Another type of scheme involves the wire transfer of funds drawn on what turns out to be a bogus check. Typically, a victim receives overpayment for a product or service that they have sold and is instructed to immediately deposit the money and wire a portion to a third party; however, the initial check payment turns out to be false, leaving the victim at a loss.

Even though identity theft and auction fraud make up a sizable proportion of crimes on the Internet, countless other frauds have been perpetrated over the years. These ranged from false merchandise advertised on a phony web page to work-at-home e-mail schemes in which the victim is told to send in money as an initial investment.

One of the more famous e-mail scams is the Nigerian letter fraud scam, which has been circulating via traditional mail since the early 1980s. In its electronic form, an e-mail purportedly from a "Nigerian dignitary" informs the victim that he or she has the opportunity to receive vast sums of money currently being held in Nigeria. When the victim responds to the message, he or she is then told that the Nigerian dignitary requires money in advance, usually to bribe government officials, so that the funds can be released and deposited in the victim's account. According to the FTC in the *Consumer Sentinel Network Data Book for January–December 2013*, Nigeria was home to the fourth-highest percentage (1%) of Internet fraud perpetrators in 2013, behind the United States (88%), Canada (4%), and the United Kingdom (1%).

Still other, more elaborate scams were designed to manipulate the stock market. Such scams were particularly effective in the late 1990s during the stock market bubble. The best known of these is the pump-and-dump scam. The criminals invest in a stock that is lightly traded and then trick online investors into buying it. Typically, this involves posting fake documents and press releases on financial websites or sending fake e-mail announcements, telling investors that the company is either about to be bought out or has developed a new, moneymaking product. In other instances scam artists bribe lesser-known stock pundits to tout the lifeless stock. After the stock takes off, the criminals simply sell their holdings, leaving other investors holding the bag as the stock goes back down to sustainable levels.

Each year the IC3 profiles in its annual report several cases that it has helped solve. In the *2013 Internet Crime Report*, the IC3 reports that beginning in July 2007 it began receiving complaints about an international scam targeting law firms and involving third-party debt collection. In this type of fraud, criminals approach U.S. law firms via e-mail seeking legal assistance with the wire transfer of a large sum of money. The perpetrators then send the law firms counterfeit checks, requesting that the firms subsequently wire the money in question (minus legal fees) to a third party; in some instances, fake checks were issued for amounts exceeding $100,000. In one high-profile case of this type, a Nigerian man named Emmanuel Ekhator operated a third-party debt collection scam that ultimately defrauded U.S. law firms out of more than $29 million. In August 2011 a Nigerian court ruled to allow Ekhator's extradition to the United States, where he was to stand trial on fraud charges in a U.S. District Court in Pennsylvania. In 2013 Ekhator was sentenced to 100 months in prison, and ordered to pay restitution of nearly $11.1 million.

VIRUSES

The term *computer virus* is often used to refer to all malware (*mal*icious soft*ware*)—that is, programs such as viruses, worms, and Trojan horses that infect and destroy computer files. Technically speaking, viruses are self-replicating programs that insert themselves into other computer files. The virus is spread when the file is transferred to another computer via the Internet or portable media such as a CD-ROM. The first computer virus was created in 1982, when 15-year-old Rich Skrenta (1967–) wrote Elk Cloner, a virus that attached itself to an Apple DOS 3.3 operating system and spread to other computers by floppy disk.

People have all sorts of reasons for creating and sending viruses. Some viruses are written as pranks. Others are written by political activists or terrorists. Still other viruses are intended to injure specific corporations. Regardless of the virus creators' intentions, the number of viruses infecting the world's computers continues to grow. The first computer worm to attract attention appeared in 1988 and was written by Robert T. Morris (1965–), a graduate student at Cornell University. Worms are self-contained, self-replicating computer programs that spread through the Internet from computer to computer. Unlike viruses, they spread via the Internet under their own power and do not rely on people's actions or files to move from one machine to another. Like viruses, worms can destroy files and take advantage of vulnerabilities in computer programs or operating systems.

A Trojan horse does not self-replicate and is typically disguised as something more innocent, such as an e-mail attachment. When the user opens the e-mail, malicious code is unleashed on the computer. As malware has become more advanced, the distinctions between types of malware have become less obvious. For example, Trojan horses often contain viruses that replicate through computer files. For this reason the term *virus* will be used in this chapter to designate any type of malware, unless otherwise specified.

Viruses behave in a number of different ways. For example, the Netsky virus is typically hidden in an e-mail attachment and is launched when the user opens the attachment. Once active, Netsky sets up its own e-mail protocol, looks for e-mail accounts on the hard drive, and mass-mails itself to these accounts. Another virus named MSBlaster appeared on August 13, 2003, and quickly wormed its way through the Internet, infecting hundreds of thousands of computers in a day through vulnerability in the Windows operating system. Once on a personal computer, the virus instructed the computer to take part in a distributed denial-of-service (DDoS) attack on the Windowsupdate.com website. (A DDoS attack occurs when thousands of computers are used to access a single website, thus making it inaccessible.) Other viruses

known as "bombs" lie dormant in a computer until a specific date is registered on the computer's clock. Still other viruses disable any virus removal program on the computer, making the virus difficult to remove.

Computer Emergency Response Team

Two weeks after the Morris worm was let loose on the Internet in November 1988, the Defense Advanced Research Projects Agency formed the Computer Emergency Response Team (CERT) with headquarters at Carnegie Mellon University in Pittsburgh, Pennsylvania. The purpose of the organization is to identify threats to the Internet as a whole. CERT coordinates the actions of the private and public sectors when major Internet incidents occur. Even though CERT issues alerts on individual viruses that affect home users, it is more concerned with the big picture. The organization provides emergency incident response for network access ports, root dedicated name servers, and other components that make up the Internet's infrastructure. It analyzes virus code to develop solutions that thwart viruses. CERT also coordinates responses to large automated attacks against the Internet, and monitors threats to U.S. government computers in coordination with the U.S. Computer Emergency Readiness Team, which was formed in 2003 by the DHS.

In 2008 the Internet security researcher Dan Kaminsky (1978?–) discovered a vulnerability in the design of the domain name system (DNS). The security breach allowed criminals to attack the system and reroute Internet traffic to imposter websites, with users completely unaware that they had been directed to fraudulent sites. How it worked was fairly simple. Each time an address such as http://www.google.com is entered into the address bar of an Internet browser, the browser contacts one of many domain name servers distributed on the Internet. Once the browser makes the request from the DNS, the name server sends back the corresponding address number, which for Google is 209.85.225.147. The Internet browser then uses this numeric address to access the site (Google in this case). Each domain name server has a cache that stores widely used sites' names and numeric addresses for a limited time. The vulnerability, known as "cache poisoning," worked by substituting a vandal-controlled Internet address for the one normally linked with a well-known domain name. For a name not stored in its cache, a name server forwards the request to other name servers on the network until it finds the address or one very similar. The attack allowed criminals to flood the DNS with requests that would ensure that their site addresses were stored and distributed rather than the legitimate ones.

In March 2008 experts in Internet security met secretly at Microsoft Corporation headquarters in Redmond,

Washington, to discuss the problem and determine a plan of action. They did not reveal the vulnerability to the public until patches were available to fix the situation in July 2008. As reported by Stuart Corner in "Major DNS Flaw: Details Likely to Be Revealed at Black Hat" (August 5, 2008, iTWire.com), Kaminsky explained the effectiveness of the patch in his blog at DoxPara Research:

> After the attack: A bad guy has a one in 65,000 chance of stealing your Internet connection, and he can try a couple thousand times a second.
>
> After the patch: A bad guy has a one in a couple hundred million, or even a couple billion chance of stealing your Internet connection. He can still try to do so a couple thousand times a second, but it's going to make *a lot* of noise.

In spite of the proven success of the DNS patch, computer security breaches remain a constant threat in the second decade of the 21st century. As Internet Security firm Sophos reports in "Trends to Watch in 2014" (2014, http://www.sophos.com/en-us/security-news-trends/security-trends/network-security-top-trends.aspx), the growth of mobile data, social networking platforms, and cloud computing provided hackers and other criminals with new ways to exploit the online vulnerabilities of both businesses and individuals. Indeed, 2013 saw a sharp rise in the volume of malware attacks on Android phone platforms, and the proliferation of personal data stored on mobile devices and social networking accounts provided potential hackers with a host of new ways to access and exploit sensitive information. At the same time, corporations who used cloud computing services to manage financial data were increasingly at risk of attack.

At times, threats to Internet security originated not from criminals or hackers but from routine programming errors. The potential for system flaws to generate massive security breaches became evident in April 2014, when reports emerged that OpenSSL, an open source encryption software used to transmit data over the Internet, contained a coding defect that enabled servers to expose sensitive user information online. As Lisa Eadicicco reports in "How the Heartbleed Bug Slipped under the Radar More than Two Years Ago" (BusinessInsider.com, April 10, 2014), the security flaw, known as the Heartbleed bug, was inadvertently introduced by German programmer Robin Seggelman in 2011 and went undetected for over two years. Further controversy arose when it was discovered that the U.S. National Security Agency (NSA) had actually discovered the bug shortly after it first emerged but had declined to reveal the fact to the public. As Michael Riley notes in "NSA Said to Exploit Heartbleed Bug for Intelligence for Years" (Bloomberg.com, April 12, 2014), the agency had been using the vulnerability to gather information with the potential to pose security threats to the United States. Although programmers quickly devised patches for Heartbleed, it was estimated that the bug had compromised up to two-thirds of all Internet sites in the period before its exposure.

E-CRIME AND ORGANIZATIONS

Except for computer viruses, e-crimes that affect individuals, such as auction fraud or identity theft, are usually different from the e-crimes that affect businesses. Most large organizations are concerned about hackers entering into their servers or dissatisfied employees sabotaging their computer network. One of the most common external threats to corporations are zombie computers, or zombie bots, a type of malware that enables outsiders to gain control over a computer or system without being detected. In *2013 U.S. State of Cybercrime Survey: How Bad Is the Insider Threat* (2013, http://_resources.sei.cmu.edu/asset_files/Presentation/2013_017 101_58739.pdf), CERT provides a detailed picture of how e-crimes affect companies in the United States. The survey polled more than 500 organizations of all sizes and asked them about the problems they faced with regard to computer crimes in 2012. According to the survey, more than half (56%) of electronic crime incidents that year were initiated by individuals or entities outside the company, whereas just under one-quarter (23%) were caused by individuals within the organization; 21% of all e-crime incidents were of unknown origin. At the same time, more respondents reported that the damage caused by insiders (34%) was ultimately more serious than that caused by outsiders (31%).

In *Key Findings from the 2013 U.S. State of Cybercrime Survey* (2013, http://www.pwc.com/en_US/us/increasing-it-effectiveness/publications/assets/us-state-of-cybercrime.pdf), professional services firm Pricewaterhouse Coopers reports on the biggest cyberthreats confronting businesses in 2013. According to the report, roughly one in five (22%) companies surveyed believed that hackers posed the gravest threat to their organization in 2013; a comparable proportion of respondents (21%) reported that current and former employees represented the most significant risk to their cybersecurity. Another 11% of companies believed that foreign countries posed the biggest threat, whereas 5% were most concerned about activists or other politically motivated groups or individuals. Of the organizations surveyed, one-third (33%) reported that incidents of cybercrime targeting their company had increased in the previous 12 months; one-quarter (25%) reported that cybercrime incidents had declined, and 42% reported that they had remained roughly the same.

INTELLECTUAL PROPERTY THEFT

Intellectual property, which includes copyrighted material such as games, software, and movies, is a huge part of the U.S. economy. These industries are important to the economy and to the people employed in them, and financial profit is critical for those who create music, video games, books, or software. As such, the issue of intellectual property theft is of vital importance to the federal government.

Intellectual property theft has posed perhaps the greatest single threat to the copyright industries since the 1990s. In the mid-1980s pirating software and entertainment media on a large enough scale to make a profit demanded a large initial investment and a huge time commitment. For example, pirating movies required large banks of videocassette recorders (VCRs) along with hundreds of blank tapes. Copies of the movie were typically of much lower quality than the original, and national copyright laws made storing, selling, and distributing the bulky tapes difficult. As a result, most pirated copies of movies, music, games, or software were copied and distributed overseas in countries where copyright law was nonexistent or not enforced.

Technological advances during the 1990s put an end to many of the hassles faced by intellectual property thieves. The Internet, along with powerful computers and the conversion of nearly every type of media into digital form, made copying and distributing intellectual property easy even within the United States. Once a thief finds a way around the copyright protection that exists on the digitized copyrighted material, the computer provides an easy way to store the material. Because digital media do not degrade when copied, the thief can produce perfect duplicates. Distribution of the media to any country in the world is easily accomplished over the Internet using peer-to-peer (P2P) networks or file transfer protocol (FTP) sites, which employ standard file copying protocols to upload and download files on a server.

Creative Industries Fight Copyright Violators

Indeed, one of the biggest threats to music industry profitability has been peer-to-peer networks. In the late 1990s peer-to-peer networks were created to connect music lovers around the world. Napster was the largest of these, with tens of millions of users at its peak. Napster, like all peer-to-peer networks, did not contain any music on its own website. Instead, Napster tracked the songs and albums its members had on their individual computers. By logging into the central server of the network owned by Napster, members could first locate what music files were available on the network and then proceed to download the music from another member's computer. From the industry point of view, the problem with peer-to-peer networks was that once an album made it on to the network, millions of people suddenly had access to it for free.

Less than a year after the Napster website opened, the RIAA filed a case against Napster in U.S. federal court on December 6, 1999. The RIAA represented most major recording labels and claimed that Napster infringed on the companies' copyrights. The court sided with the RIAA. Napster appealed the ruling, but in September 2001 it settled with the RIAA by paying $26 million for copyright infringement. Before the case was settled, the Napster creator Shawn Fanning (1980–) sold Napster to Bertelsmann, a huge German media conglomerate. Bertelsmann dismantled the file-sharing network and constructed a database of songs that could be downloaded for a fee, part of which goes to pay the record company royalties.

The court's ruling against the practice of open music file-sharing meant that the RIAA and other organizations could continue to sue peer-to-peer networks that allowed the sharing of copyrighted material for free. However, while the RIAA was suing Napster, a new problem arose. Networks began popping up that did not have a clearly defined center of operations. For example, the Kazaa and Gnutella networks had no central server to let members know who on the network had which songs. Instead, each member of the network installed a program that allowed him or her to see the individual music libraries of others on the network. Michael Desmond estimates in "Sneaky Sharing" (PCWorld.com, September 2, 2004) that despite music industry attempts to curb illegal file sharing, users were developing new techniques for acquiring music as sales dropped from an all-time high of $14.6 billion in 2000 to $11.9 billion in 2003, which was well after the original Napster was shut down.

In late 2003 the RIAA began to go after individual file swappers. Lee Rainie et al. of the Pew Research Center report in *Data Memo: The Impact of Recording Industry Suits against Music File Swappers* (January 2004, http://www.pewinternet.org/~/media/Files/Reports/2004/PIP_File_Swapping_Memo_0104.pdf.pdf) that the RIAA filed 382 lawsuits in 2003 against individual illegal music file swappers, most of whom quickly settled their cases for between $2,500 and $10,000.

On January 27, 2005, the RIAA announced 717 new lawsuits against individual file swappers. Six months later, the U.S. Supreme Court made a landmark decision in favor of the movie and music industries. In *Metro-Goldwyn-Mayer Studios v. Grokster* (545 U.S. 913 [2005]), the court unanimously ruled that businesses that encourage others to steal intellectual property are liable for their customers' illegal actions. Because companies such as Grokster developed their technology almost solely for the purpose of swapping music and video files illegally, they likely were in violation of the ruling.

Inspired by the music industry's success, the MPAA also took steps to prevent piracy. Usually, the most damaging instances of piracy in the motion picture business occur when bootleggers digitally record movies in theaters as they watch the films. The bootleggers then transfer the recorded movies via the Internet to buyers, who then offer the movies on the Internet or make copies on a digital video disc (DVD) and sell them in foreign countries. In "It's Curtains for Video Pirates" (NewScientist.com, August 14, 2004), Barry Fox explains that the Warner cinema chain began handing out night-vision goggles to some employees in California to look for these bootleggers during premieres. In 2004 the MPAA began working with the high-tech engineering firm Cinea in Reston, Virginia, to develop imaging techniques that would prevent digital camcorders from recording movies in theaters. One technique involved altering the frame rate in movies so that the film would move out of synchronization with most digital camcorders' refresh rate, resulting in a copy of the movie that shudders when played. Finally, in November 2004 the MPAA announced that it, too, would be prosecuting individuals who used peer-to-peer networks to view movies. The organization filed 250 lawsuits in 2005 against individuals who downloaded movies. The MPAA also prosecuted websites such as isoHunt.com (http://isohunt.com) and Torrentspy.com (http://www.torrentspy.com) that directed visitors to places on the web where movies could be downloaded free of charge. As a result of these lawsuits, by 2014 both Torrentspy.com and isoHunt.com had been permanently shut down.

Even with the success of these measures, however, online piracy remained a persistent problem for the entertainment industry. In response, the MPAA urged members of Congress to pass a new law, the Stop Online Piracy Act (SOPA), as a means of cracking down on copyright infringement. Introduced in Congress in October 2011 by Representative Lamar Smith (1947–; R-TX), SOPA was referred to the House Subcommittee on Intellectual Property, Competition, and the Internet in December 2011. No further action had been taken as of August 2014.

DOJ Begins to Crack Down

Most litigation over copyright law is conducted in civil courts where individual citizens and organizations sue one another. If the defendant is found guilty, such as in the *RIAA v. Napster* case, then the defendant typically has to pay money to the plaintiff. In a criminal case the defendant serves jail or probationary time if found guilty. The DOJ is in charge of prosecuting criminal cases against people and organizations that violate national copyright laws. The DOJ also has specialized units based in cities where high-tech theft is common. These units are known as the Computer Hacking and Intellectual Property (CHIP) units, and they identify and help prosecute intellectual-property suspects. Most of these investigations involve international copyright crime organizations

or individuals who make tens of thousands of dollars stealing intellectual property.

Responding to the increased threats to intellectual property brought on by new media, the U.S. attorney general, John D. Ashcroft (1942–), created the DOJ's Task Force on Intellectual Property in March 2004. The task force was assigned to examine the entire range of intellectual property theft from counterfeit automotive parts to the theft of trade secrets to copyright infractions in the entertainment industry. In October 2004 the task force published *Report of the Department of Justice's Task Force on Intellectual Property* (http://www.justice.gov/olp/ip_task_force_report.pdf), which included its recommendations on how to address the rise in intellectual property theft. The task force recommended that five additional specialized CHIP units be placed in areas rife with intellectual property theft and that more FBI agents be put on intellectual property theft cases. In addition, the task force suggested that Congress pass an act making it illegal for people to post copyrighted material they do not own on the Internet.

In 2005 President George W. Bush (1946–) signed the Family Entertainment Copyright Act into law. Under this act any attempt to record a movie in a theater can result in federal prosecution, fines, and up to three years in prison. A similar sentence can be given to anyone who distributes a creative work that is intended for commercial distribution but has not been released, such as a video game or movie that is still in production. Since the passing of the act, a number of people have been prosecuted by the DOJ for violating the law (although most litigation still takes place in civil courts). Manuel Sandoval, a 70-year-old retired painter from Los Angeles, was the first person to be convicted under the new act in April 2006. He was caught recording the matinee showing of *The Legend of Zorro* in Los Angeles in October 2005.

Table 4.10 shows the number of intellectual property crimes investigated and prosecuted by the U.S. Attorney General's Office between fiscal years 2008 and 2012. These figures represent crimes such as trafficking in counterfeit labels for audio recordings and copies of motion pictures; criminal infringement of copyright, including unlawful reproduction or distribution of copyrighted works; producing and distributing sounds and images of live musical performances without the consent of the performers; and trafficking in counterfeit goods or services. As Table 4.10 shows, the number of filed intellectual property theft cases peaked at 179 in 2008, before dropping to 150 in 2009, 158 in 2010 and 2011, and 152 in 2012.

Meanwhile, the prosecution of intellectual property crimes reached global proportions, requiring the collaboration of law enforcement agencies from throughout the world. One high-profile case emerged in January 2012,

TABLE 4.10

Intellectual property crimes investigated and prosecuted by the U.S. Department of Justice, fiscal years (FY) 2008–12

	All districts—all statutes				
	FY 08	FY 09	FY 10	FY 11	FY 12
Referrals and cases					
Number of investigative matters received	303	243	343	330	314
Number of defendants	467	404	543	481	496
Number of cases filed	179	150	158	158	152
Number of defendants	239	203	239	203	218
Number of cases resolved/terminated	174	175	152	135	144
Number of defendants	270	230	212	206	205
Disposition of defendants in concluded cases					
Number of defendants who pleaded guilty	220	198	185	178	183
Number of defendants who were tried and found guilty	8	5	7	13	4
Number of defendants against whom charges were dismissed	26	21	14	11	11
Number of defendants acquitted	8	2	2	1	2
Other terminated defendants	8	4	4	3	5
Prison sentencing for convicted defendants (# represents defendants)					
No imprisonment	101	114	114	92	88
1 to 12 months imprisonment	46	31	33	26	43
13 to 24 months	39	27	25	31	25
25 to 36 months	20	6	9	15	15
37 to 60 months	19	17	7	21	15
61+ months	3	8	4	6	1

SOURCE: "Title 18, United States Code, Sections 2318, 2319, 2319A, 2320 or Title 17, United States Code, Section 506," in *FY 2012 Performance and Accountability Report*, U.S. Department of Justice, November 2012, http://www.justice.gov/ag/annualreports/pr2012/par2012.pdf (accessed June 4, 2014)

when authorities in New Zealand, working with the U.S. Department of Justice, arrested Kim Schmitz (1974–; alias Kim Dotcom), founder of the popular file-sharing site Megaupload, on charges of copyright infringement. In "Feds Shutter Megaupload, Arrest Executives" (Wired.com, January 19, 2012), David Kravets reports that at the time Megaupload accounted for 4% of all traffic on the Internet, receiving roughly 50 million visits per day. In December 2012 authorities in Cambodia arrested Gottfrid Svartholm Warg (1984–), cofounder of Pirate Bay, the largest file-swapping site on the Internet. Warg had fled Sweden earlier that year in order to avoid serving prison time for his role in a copyright infringement case dating to 2009. Another cofounder of Pirate Bay, Peter Sunde (1978–), was arrested in Sweden in May 2014.

Still, some experts questioned whether lawsuits or prosecutions were having any real impact on deterring intellectual property theft. As Nolan Feeney reports in "Pirate Bay Co-founder Arrested in Sweden" (Time .com, June 1, 2014), Pirate Bay continued to operate even after its owners were detained by authorities. Meanwhile, the proportion of Internet users seeking free copyrighted material online continued to grow steadily. As Figure 4.3 shows, the number of people who visited sites offering copyright infringing content grew by nearly 10% between 2012 and 2013, increasing from 297.6 million to 327 million. The total number of page views on these sites grew at a comparable rate, rising from 12.7 billion views to 13.9 billion views, an increase of 9.8%.

FIGURE 4.3

Number of Internet users seeking copyright infringing content online, with total page views of piracy websites, November 2011 and January 2013

[North American, Europe, and Asia-Pacific regions]

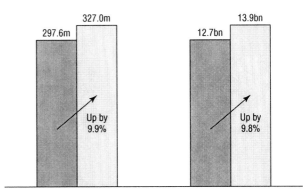

SOURCE: David Price, "Growth in Infringement, November 2011–January 2013 (North America, Europe, and Asia-Pacific Regions)," *Sizing the Piracy Universe*, NetNames Piracy Analysis, September 2013, http://copyrightalliance.org/sites/default/files/2013-netnames-piracy.pdf (accessed June 7, 2014)

By far, the largest number of bittorrent (a popular peer-to-peer file distribution system) users in 2013 lived in Europe. As Figure 4.4 shows, nearly half (47.1%) of all visitors to bittorrent portals came from Europe that year. Asians accounted for nearly one-quarter (24.7%) of bittorrent users in 2013, and 15.5% lived in North America.

FIGURE 4.4

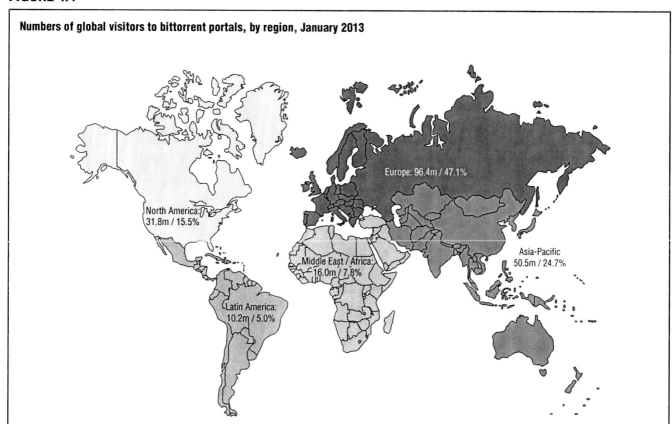

Numbers of global visitors to bittorrent portals, by region, January 2013

SOURCE: David Price, "Chart 3.2.2.1. Regional Breakdown of Visitors to Bittorrent Portals (comScore / NetNames)," *Sizing the Piracy Universe*, NetNames Piracy Analysis, September 2013, http://copyrightalliance.org/sites/default/files/2013-netnames-piracy.pdf (accessed June 7, 2014)

CHILD PORNOGRAPHY AND OTHER INTERNET-RELATED CRIMES

Unlike any other technology in human history, the Internet has enabled individuals to communicate with unprecedented speed and frequency. One of the downsides of the Internet's ability to help people share information more easily, however, is that it also provides criminals and other predators with a powerful weapon to use against potential victims. One area of major concern to law enforcement officials is the proliferation of child pornography on the Internet. The National Center for Missing & Exploited Children (NCMEC) monitors reports of child pornography and other forms of sexual exploitation through its CyberTipline (http://www.missingkids.com/CyberTipline), an online reporting system. Between 1998 and 2014 the CyberTipline received more than 2.3 million reports of child exploitation. As the NCMEC reports in "Key Facts" (2014, http://www.missingkids.com/KeyFacts), the agency received 3.9 million calls related to missing or exploited children between 1984 and 2014. During this span, the NCMEC assisted in the recovery of 199,575 missing children, and its recovery rate rose from 62% in 1990 to 97% in 2014.

Technological innovations have also created avenues for new forms of online criminal behavior. One disturbing new trend that emerged with the increasingly widespread popularity of wireless handheld devices was called sexting. Sexting is defined as the practice through which individuals share sexually suggestive images of each other via text message. As Amanda Lenhart reports in *Teens and Sexting* (December 15, 2009, http://pewresearch.org/assets/pdf/teens-and-sexting.pdf), among teens aged 12 to 17 who own cell phones, 15% have received nude or seminude images from someone they know in a text message, and 4% admit to having sent sexually suggestive images of themselves.

One website that has come under increasing criticism for abetting criminal behavior in recent years is Craigslist (https://www.craigslist.org/about/sites). In addition to providing online classified ads for such things as apartment rentals and sales of goods, Craigslist also allows users to post listings for services. While most of these listings are legitimate, they can also make it easier for online predators to attract victims. In one notable case, Boston University Medical School student Philip Markoff (1986–2010) was arrested in April 2009 for the murder of Julissa Brisman (1983–2009), a masseuse whom Markoff had contacted through the website's adult services section. Dubbed the "Craigslist Killer," Markoff killed himself in his jail cell in August 2010 before standing trial for the murder. In the wake of these and other incidents, law enforcement officials urged Craigslist to shut down its adult services listings altogether. As Evan Hansen reports in "Censored! Craigslist Adult Services Banned in U.S." (Wired.com, September 4, 2010), the website's adult services listings often served as a cover for prostitution and other forms of illegal sex-trafficking. Craigslist resisted opposition to its policy on adult listings for years, largely for financial reasons. As Hansen reports, the adult services section accounted for roughly 30% of the company's total revenue in 2010. Still, negative publicity and increased pressure from state attorneys continued to plague the online classifieds site, and in September 2010 Craigslist abruptly discontinued its adult services listings, replacing it with a black bar reading "Censored." In spite of these measures, other sites, notably Backpage.com, soon replaced Craigslist as popular sources of adult services listings.

DARKNET AND THE DEEP WEB

One area of growing concern to law enforcement in 2014 was the potential for criminals to conduct illegal activity on the Deep Web. Generally speaking, the Deep Web refers to anonymous Internet activity that is inaccessible on conventional web browsers, making it undetectable by search engines. Although a significant portion of the Deep Web is composed of databases, academic journals, and other web pages that do not come up in searches, a substantial amount of Deep Web activity occurs on secret websites hosted by anonymous networks. As Jose Pagliery reports in "The Deep Web You Don't Know About" (Money.CNN.com, March 10, 2014), in 2014 the Deep Web accounted for over 99% of all web activity.

One of the most prominent secret networks on the Deep Web is Tor. The idea of Tor was first proposed in 1996, by a small team of scientists at the U.S. Naval Research Laboratory. Originally known as the Onion Router, Tor encrypted Internet traffic to the point of making it thoroughly untraceable. The first Tor network was launched in 2003. In its conception, Tor was designed to enable government agencies to engage in a range of secret activities, from conducting criminal investigations anonymously to exchanging classified documents. However, Tor soon attracted a range of other users, who were drawn to the possibility of using the Internet with complete anonymity.

The prospect of using the Internet in total secrecy had obvious appeal to criminals, and an area of the Deep Web commonly known as the Darknet emerged. Tor quickly became a haven for illegal activity on the Darknet, ranging from terrorist communications to the exchange of malware programs among computer hackers; it also gave rise to an illicit economy, where Internet users could acquire controlled substances, weapons,

and child pornography outside the scrutiny of law enforcement. For some politically minded individuals, Tor represented an opportunity to exist outside of the control of government. These libertarian tendencies were at the heart of Silk Road, an online marketplace where users could buy and sell illegal drugs. As Lev Grossman and Jay Newton-Small report in "The Secret Web: Where Drugs, Porn and Murder Live Online" (Time.com, November 11, 2013), the site was first launched in January 2011 by Ross Ulbricht (1985–; alias Dread Pirate Roberts, or DPR), who quickly became an "antiestablishment hero" in the eyes of many Silk Road users. Although most visitors used the site to acquire drugs, Silk Road also provided access to books, erotica, and a range of digital goods. As Grossman and Newton-Small note, Silk Road was considered especially secure because all of its transactions were conducted with Bitcoin, a virtual currency that cannot be traced to its users.

In spite of this extraordinary level of secrecy, law enforcement eventually discovered clues linking Dread Pirate Roberts to Ulbricht, and he was arrested in October 2013 while accessing Silk Road at a public library in San Francisco. Among the charges leveled against Ulbricht included drug trafficking, money laundering, and conspiracy to commit murder. In two and a half years, roughly 1 million customers spent $1.2 billion on Silk Road transactions, while Ulbricht collected an estimated $80 million in transaction fees. Following Silk Road's closure, the FBI posted a notification on the site announcing that it had been seized. (See Figure 4.5.) Despite the site's closure, new Darknet pages appeared to take its place. Notable among these was Silk Road's successor, Silk Road 2.0, which became the leading online marketplace for illegal drugs in 2014.

HIGH-TECH LAW ENFORCEMENT

Criminals have not been the only ones taking advantage of high tech. Since the 1980s new technologies have provided law enforcement with myriad resources to combat crime and protect citizens. Video cameras have helped tremendously in identifying thieves who rob automated teller machines, banks, and convenience stores. Wiretaps and surveillance equipment have allowed law enforcement officials to catch criminals without putting themselves in harm's way. However, the biggest boon to law enforcement by far has been the increased access law enforcement officers have had to information. During the 1970s, for example, if a law enforcement officer in New York wanted the records of a criminal in California, he or she would have to call a police station in California and have the information read over the phone. Computer databases and communications technologies have connected law enforcement offices and provided them easy access to criminal records across the country.

FIGURE 4.5

Notification posted by Federal Bureau of Investigation (FBI) on Silk Road website following its closure on October 2, 2013

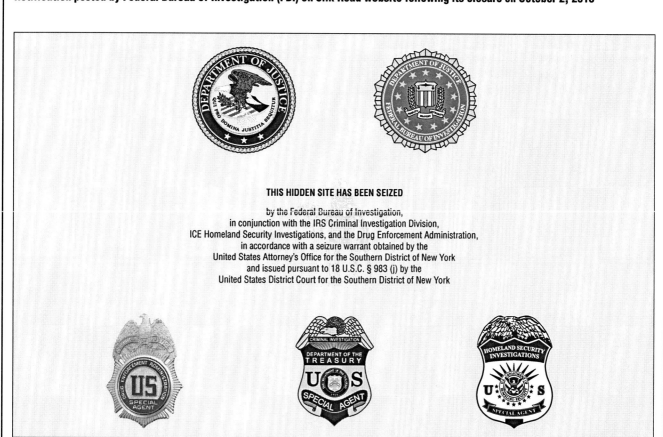

SOURCE: "File:Silk Road Seized.jpg," in Federal Bureau of Investigation (FBI; via Wikimedia Commons), 2014, http://commons.wikimedia.org/wiki/File%3ASilk_Road_Seized.jpg (accessed June 7, 2014)

In 1995 the FBI launched Law Enforcement Online (LEO; http://www.fbi.gov/about-us/cjis/leo), an online communication and data system that enables law enforcement agencies from around the world to exchange information about criminal investigations. Originally comprising just 20 members using a dial-up network, by 2014 LEO had more than 100,000 participants worldwide. At the same time, phone networks and portable computers have also given the police the ability to access criminal records and information on vehicle registrations and license holders from within the patrol car. Electronic credit and debit card networks, bank machines, and rental car records have all provided law enforcement with easily accessible, real-time information on where criminals have been and where they are going.

Communications technologies have also allowed law enforcement agencies to inform communities of terrorism, kidnapping, or other criminal activity to bring the perpetrators to justice. America's Missing: Broadcast Emergency Response (AMBER) Plan is named after nine-year-old Amber Hagerman (1986–1996), who was kidnapped and murdered in Arlington, Texas, in 1996.

After her murder Texas instituted the first statewide AMBER Plan in 1999. Since that time the program has been introduced by the DOJ into the 49 other states. When an AMBER Alert is issued, the regional Emergency Alert System is used to tell the public about the missing child. Programs on television and radio stations are interrupted and followed by pertinent information about the abduction. All law enforcement officers are put on alert, and digital emergency signs above the highways tell people on the freeway where to receive more information about the abduction. The DOJ's AMBER Alert statistics (2014, http://www.amberalert.gov/statistics.htm) indicate that as of June 2014, 685 children had been recovered as a result of the plan. In the *National Center for Missing and Exploited Children 2012 AMBER Alert Report* (2013, http://www.missingkids.com/en_US/documents/2012AMBERAlertReport.pdf), the NCMEC analyzes the effectiveness of AMBER Alert broadcasts. In more than half (57%) of cases in which children were safely recovered in 2012, either a law enforcement official or another individual recognized the vehicle described in an AMBER Alert (38%), or else an individual contacted authorities after recognizing either the child or the abductor after hearing an AMBER Alert broadcast (19%). In 19% of cases, the abductor released the victim after hearing the Amber Alert.

In the meantime, the continually evolving nature of online threats posed arguably the biggest challenge to law enforcement agencies in the 21st century. As Tony Bradley reports in "The Top 5 Security Threats to Watch for in 2014" (PCWorld.com, January 30, 2014), criminals had begun to embrace virtual currencies as a way of conducting illegal transactions while evading detection by law enforcement. In addition, Bradley notes, the increasingly interconnectedness of digital technology (for example, the ability of individuals to monitor home security systems through their mobile devices) offered a wider range of potential targets for hackers and other online criminals to attack.

CHAPTER 5
ELECTRONICS, THE INTERNET, AND ENTERTAINMENT MEDIA

For many Americans, new technologies simply mean new toys. Almost every advancement in consumer technology since the 1980s has in some way been tied to entertainment. The *Proquest Statistical Abstract of the United States: 2014* (2014) examines media usage among Americans in 2012. According to the report's findings, more adults watched television (91.6%) than any other entertainment medium in 2012; 82.1% listened to the radio, and 79.5% surfed the Internet. When broken down into age demographics, however, these figures shift considerably. For example, the Internet was the most popular source of media for adults between the ages of 18 and 24 (92.5%) and between the ages of 25 and 34 (91.2%); by comparison, fewer than half (47.5%) of seniors 65 years of age and older used the Internet in 2012. On the other hand, adults 65 years of age and older were the biggest consumers of television that year, with 96.5% of seniors in that age demographic reporting they watched TV in 2012, 10 percentage points higher than adults between the ages of 18 and 24 (86.5%) and between the ages of 25 and 34 (86.9%).

Indeed, even though television remained the dominant media outlet in 2014, Americans were rapidly turning to new forms of entertainment made available by the Internet and other technologies. Figure 5.1 shows changes in electronic device ownership among adults between 2000 and 2014. In 2000 just over 50% of adults owned cell phones; by 2013 this figure exceeded 75%. Whereas less than one-quarter of adults had MP3 players in 2006, by 2010 nearly half of adults owned MP3 players; this number subsequently dipped between 2010 and 2013, in large part due to the increasing popularity of smartphones. As Figure 5.1 shows, the technologies that saw the most substantial increases in popularity between 2009 and 2014 included electronic readers (e-readers or eBook readers), tablet computers, and smartphones.

Table 5.1 offers a more detailed breakdown of changes in device ownership between 2005 and 2013.

Whereas smartphone ownership was negligible in 2005, by 2013 it had been adopted by nearly two-thirds (62%) of American adults. At the same time, ownership of regular cell phones dropped considerably during this span, from 78% in 2005 to only 45% in 2013. Other technologies that saw dramatic rises in use between 2005 and 2013 included laptop computers, which rose from 30% to 64% during this period; tablet computers, which had been adopted by 38% of adults in 2013; and Internet streaming services such as Roku and Netflix, which were being used by 39% of adults that year. By contrast, ownership of videocassette recorders (VCRs) fell 30 percentage points between 2005 and 2013, and the percentage of adults who owned desktop computers fell from 65% to 57%.

Device ownership varied considerably among adults in different age groups. As Table 5.2 shows, adults between the ages of 18 and 29 were more likely than seniors 65 years of age and older to own smartphones (88% compared to 25%, respectively), video game systems (64% and 10%, respectively), and laptop computers (79% and 41%, respectively). By contrast, seniors (61%) were far more likely than young adults (24%) to own regular cell phones, VCRs (74% and 41%, respectively), and desktop computers (58% and 41%, respectively).

ELECTRONIC GAMING

Once considered the pastime of children and socially challenged adults, video and computer games now represent a major form of entertainment in the United States. Video games, also known as console and arcade games, are played using a computer that is specifically designed to play games. By contrast, computer games are just one type of program that can be run on standard personal computers. The difference between the two types of games is in how they are accessed, not necessarily in their content. Many games can be played using either a video game system or a computer. Thus, the terms *video*

FIGURE 5.1

Electronic device ownership among adults, by type of device, 2000–14

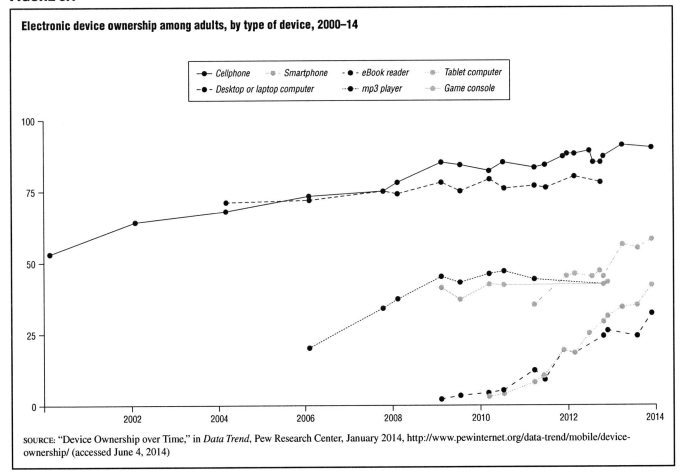

SOURCE: "Device Ownership over Time," in *Data Trend*, Pew Research Center, January 2014, http://www.pewinternet.org/data-trend/mobile/device-ownership/ (accessed June 4, 2014).

TABLE 5.1

Percentage change in device ownership, by type of device, 2005 and 2013

[Sorted by Yes, have (2013)]

	Yes, have (2005)	Yes, have (2013)	Change from 2005
	%	%	pct. pts.
A DVD player or Blu-ray player	83	80	−3
Wireless Internet access, or Wi-Fi, in your home	—	73	n/a
Cable TV	68	68	0
A laptop computer	30	64	+34
A smartphone, that is, a cellular phone that has built-in applications and Internet access, such as an iPhone or Android	—	62	n/a
A VCR	88	58	−30
A desktop computer	65	57	−8
A basic cellular phone that is not a smartphone	78	45	−33
An iPod or MP3 music player	19	45	+26
A video game system, such as Xbox or PlayStation	36	41	+5
An Internet streaming service like Hulu, Netflix, or Roku	—	39	n/a
A tablet computer such as an iPad or Kindle Fire	—	38	n/a
Satellite TV	30	34	+4
An E-reader, such as a Kindle or Nook	—	26	n/a

n/a = Not applicable.

SOURCE: Andrew Dugan, "Possession of Electronic Devices in the U.S.," in *Americans' Tech Tastes Change with Times*, The Gallup Organization, January 6, 2014, http://www.gallup.com/poll/166745/americans-tech-tastes-change-times.aspx (accessed June 4, 2014). Copyright © 2014 Gallup, Inc. All rights reserved. The content is used with permission; however, Gallup retains all rights of republication.

game and *computer game* are sometimes used interchangeably. According to Kathryn Zickuhr of the Pew Research Center (February 3, 2011, http://www.pewin ternet.org/~/media//Files/Reports/2011/PIP_Generations _and_Gadgets.pdf), 63% of adults between the ages of 18 and 46 owned gaming consoles in 2010. In *Essential*

TABLE 5.2

Age gap in device ownership among adults aged 18–29 and adults older than 65, by age group and type of device, December 2013

	18 to 29 % Yes, have	65+ % Yes, have	Gap in ownership, 18 to 29 minus 65+ pct. pts.
Skew youngest			
Smartphone	88	25	+63
Video game system	64	10	+54
Internet streaming service	62	15	+47
IPod/MP3 player	63	16	+47
Laptop computer	79	41	+38
Skew oldest			
Satellite TV	32	41	−9
Cable TV	62	74	−12
Desktop computer	41	58	−17
VCR	41	74	−33
Basic cell phone	24	61	−37

SOURCE: Andrew Dugan, "Technology Use and Age Skew," in *Americans' Tech Tastes Change with Times*, The Gallup Organization, January 6, 2014, http://www.gallup.com/poll/166745/americans-tech-tastes-change-times.aspx (accessed June 4, 2014). Copyright © 2014 Gallup, Inc. All rights reserved. The content is used with permission; however, Gallup retains all rights of republication.

Facts about the Video Gaming Industry (2014, http://www.theesa.com/facts/pdfs/esa_ef_2014.pdf), the Entertainment Software Association (ESA) reports that 59% of Americans played video games in 2013. Of households that owned consoles, smartphones, or wireless gaming devices, 68% played games on their consoles, 53% played on their smartphones, and 41% played on wireless gaming devices. Nearly four out of 10 (39%) Americans who played video games in 2013 were over the age of 35; three out of 10 (29%) video game players were under the age of 18 that year. As the ESA reports, the most popular types of online games in 2013 were categorized as casual or social games, which were enjoyed by 30% of video game players; 28% of game players enjoyed puzzles, trivia, card games, board games, or game show games, whereas nearly one-quarter (24%) preferred action, sports, or role-playing games. Among mobile game players, casual or social games (46%) were the most popular in 2013.

On the whole, parents view video games as having a positive impact on the lives of their children. According to the ESA in *Essential Facts about the Video Gaming Industry*, more than half (52%) of parents considered video games "a positive part of their children's lives" in 2013. Of these, 56% believed that video games had a positive effect on their children. Among parents who played video games with their children, 88% did so because it provided a way for them to enjoy themselves as a family, and 75% reported that it provided a good way to spend time with their children; fewer than half (47%) of parents reported that they enjoyed playing video games as much as their children.

Rise of Video and Computer Games

Computer and video games are almost as old as computers. Many credit Alexander Shafto Douglas (1921–2010) with creating the first graphics-based computer game at Cambridge University in England in 1952. Part of his doctoral research on human-computer interaction, the game was played on an enormous Electronic Delay Storage Automatic Calculator (EDSAC) computer, which was one of the first computers in existence and was made primarily from rows and rows of vacuum tubes. The EDSAC display screen was a 35 x 16 array of monochromatic dots. The name of Douglas's game was *OXO*, or *Noughts and Crosses*, a human-versus-machine version of tic-tac-toe in which the human player chose the first square. Ten years later, computer games were developed on mainframe computers and eventually on ARPANET, the nationwide network of military defense computers that preceded the Internet.

One of the more popular games that spread to computer mainframes across the United States during the 1960s was *Spacewar!* The game was created in 1961 by Steve Russell (1937–), Martin Graetz (1935–), and Wayne Wiitanen (1935–) at the Massachusetts Institute of Technology to test the capabilities of the $120,000 Digital Equipment Corporation PDP-1 computer. The game consisted of two low-resolution ships, one shaped like a needle and the other like a wedge, flying around a dot that represented a sun in the middle of the screen. The object was to destroy the other player's ship while maneuvering through the sun's gravitational pull.

In 1971 Nutting Associates released *Computer Space*, the first video game for the general public. *Computer Space*, a direct imitator of *Spacewar!*, was set in a futuristic arcade-style cabinet. Most people considered the game too complicated at the time, so Nutting made only 1,500 units and then stopped production. The next year, however, Atari released *Pong*. In this monochromatic game, a small cube was bounced back and forth between two slightly larger rods controlled by the player(s). The video game was a smash hit, and Atari sold more than 800,000 arcade cabinets. A month earlier, Magnavox released the Odyssey, which was the first home-console video game system that ran on a television set. The Odyssey, which sold for $100 (about $565 in 2014 dollars), had several different games installed on it, all of which involved hitting a pixilated square (or squares) on the screen with rectangles. According to the Atari Museum (2014, http://www.atarimuseum.com/videogames/dedicated/homepong.html), the Atari home version of *Pong* was released in 1975 and sold over 150,000 units during the holiday season alone.

Golden Age of Video Games

Within a year after these initial offerings, video games quickly gained a foothold in the United States. A steady stream of unremarkable cabinet games was released throughout the 1970s. For most of the decade, video games were novelties that sat next to pinball machines in bowling alleys, bars, and roller-skating rinks. With the arrival of *Asteroids* and *Space Invaders* in 1978, arcade video games came into their own. *Space Invaders*, a game in which the player shot row after row of advancing aliens, triggered a nationwide coin shortage in Japan so severe the Japanese government had to more than double yen production. Namco introduced the first color game in 1979 with the arrival of *Galaxian*, and then in 1980 the company released *Pac-Man*. The original name of the game was *Puckman*, derived from the Japanese *pakupaku*, which means "flapping open and closed" (e.g., the character's mouth). Despite the game's simple concept of guiding a yellow, dot-eating ball around a maze, more than 100,000 arcade units were sold in the United States. The game inspired an entire line of merchandise from lunch boxes to stuffed toys. Between 1980 and 1983 many colorful, engaging video games were released, including *Centipede*, *Defender*, *Donkey Kong*, *Frogger*, and *Ms. Pac-Man*, which still holds the record for the most arcade games sold at 115,000, according to William Hunter in "Player 2 Stage 4: Two Superstars" (2014, http://www.emuunlim.com/doteaters/play2sta4.htm). Video arcades sprang up in every mall and town in the United States. On January 18, 1982, the cover of *Time* magazine read: GRONK! FLASH! ZAP! VIDEO GAMES ARE BLITZING THE WORLD. In the cover story, "Games That Play People," John Skow reported that in 1981 nearly $5 billion in quarters (about $13 billion in 2014 dollars) was spent playing arcade games. By comparison, the U.S. film industry took in $2.8 billion that year (about $7.3 billion in 2014 dollars).

At the same time, game consoles were gaining popularity in living rooms across the United States. In 1977 Atari launched the Atari VCS (later named the Atari 2600) for $250 (about $975 in 2014 dollars). By Christmas 1979 sales were brisk as people realized that the system could support more than just *Pong*. With the release of *Space Invaders* on the system the following year, units flew off the shelves at $150 a piece (roughly $430 in 2014 dollars). Tekla E. Perry and Paul Wallich explain in "Design Case History: The Atari Video Computer System" (*IEEE Spectrum*, March 1983) that Atari sold more than 12 million consoles between 1977 and 1983. More than 200 games were made for the system. Other video systems such as Intellivision and Colecovision gained huge followings as well. Skow noted that 600,000 Intellivision units were sold in 1981. Overall, 1981 sales for home video games exceeded $1 billion (approximately $2.6 billion in 2014 dollars).

Video Game Industry Stumbles

By 1984 the Commodore 64 home computer had debuted at $1,000 (about $2,275 in 2014 dollars), and the Apple IIc was introduced at the comparatively affordable price of $1,300 ($2,955 in 2014 dollars). Such computers not only offered better graphics than the contemporary video game consoles but also they were useful for practical applications such as spreadsheets and word processors. Consequently, people began to lose interest in video games and buy home computers instead. In 1983, faced with a collapsing video game market, losses of hundreds of millions of dollars, and far too much inventory, Atari loaded 14 tractor-trailer trucks with thousands of unsold cartridges and pieces of hardware. It drove the surplus out to a landfill site in Alamogordo, New Mexico, and buried the inventory in a concrete bunker under the desert. The following year Warner Communications, the owner of Atari, sold the game and computer divisions of Atari to Jack Tramiel (1928–2012), the founder of Commodore. Mattel, the maker of Intellivision, also shed its electronics division, and hundreds of arcades closed as well.

For several years gaming was relegated to the computer. Before 1983 computer games were low on graphics and heavy on text, but by 1984 a number of colorful and entertaining games became available for home computers, including the *Ultima* and *King's Quest* series. However, toy and electronics manufacturers in the United States were wary of investing in video game consoles after the Atari disaster.

Japanese companies were not nearly as pessimistic and continued to invest money into video console development. Nintendo, a company that originally manufactured Japanese playing cards, surprised the entire gaming market in 1986 when it released the Nintendo Entertainment System (NES). The games looked better than most arcade games from the early 1980s and took as long to play through as computer games. After two years on the market, the NES found its way into almost as many homes as the Atari 2600. As Pat Davies reported in "The Hottest Game in Town" (*Globe and Mail*, May 19, 1989), the sales of NES video games in 1988 reached $1.7 billion ($3.4 billion in 2014 dollars) in the United States alone. Arcades at the time also enjoyed a brief revival with the advent of complex fighting games such as *Mortal Kombat* and *Street Fighter II*. *Mortal Kombat*, which eventually made it onto the NES, inspired a congressional investigation into violence in video games and led to the establishment in 1994 of the Entertainment Software Rating Board, an industry self-regulatory organization that monitors the content of video games for depictions of violence, nudity, profanity, and other material that parents might find objectionable for young children.

Current and Future Gaming

Since the late 1980s the U.S. electronic gaming market has continued its rise, with the majority of the gaming industry's revenues coming from console systems and games. After the NES ran its course with estimated sales of 60 million units worldwide, the Sega Genesis video game system enjoyed a period of popularity. The electronics giant Sony entered the fray in 1995 when it released PlayStation in the United States. Nintendo answered Sony's challenge with Nintendo 64 in 1996, which sold 1.7 million units in the United States in the first three months, according to Michael Miller in "A History of Home Video Game Consoles" (April 1, 2005, http://www.informit.com/articles/article.aspx?p=378141). In 2000 Sony PlayStation launched the PlayStation2. Taking note of the profits brought in by successful gaming systems, Microsoft, the largest software firm in the United States, launched the Xbox in 2001. Both Sony and Microsoft funded enormous advertising campaigns to promote their systems, and Microsoft sold its system at a loss to introduce it into more homes. Peter Lewis stated in "Should You Wait for the PS3?" (Money.CNN.com, November 22, 2005) that over 96 million PlayStation 2 consoles and 25 million Xbox systems had sold worldwide by the end of 2005. With the release of the Xbox 360 in 2005 and the PlayStation 3 and Nintendo Wii in 2006, the video game market enjoyed double-digit year-over-year growth.

By decade's end, however, overall sales began to slip. The marketing research firm NPD Group reports in the press release "2009 U.S. Video Game Industry and PC Game Software Retail Sales Reach $20.2 Billion" (January 14, 2010, http://www.npd.com/press/releases/press_100114.html) that retail video games produced roughly $19.7 billion in sales in 2009, an 8% drop from 2008 revenues of $21.4 billion. Sales of console hardware saw the biggest decline (13%), while console and portable software also saw sales decrease by approximately 10%. Sales continued to slump over the next three years. As the NPD Group reports in "Research Shows $15.39 Billion Spent on Video Game Content in the U.S. in 2013, a 1 Percent Increase over 2012" (February 11, 2014, https://www.npd.com/wps/portal/npd/us/news/press-releases/research-shows-15.39-billion-dollars-spent-on-video-game-content-in-the-us-in-2013-a-1-percent-increase-over-2012), by 2013 annual revenues in the retail video game market fell to $15.4 billion by 2013, a 28% decline since 2008.

Overall, the computer game market has grown at a slower pace than the video game market. During the 1990s with the advent of Microsoft's Windows operating system, the computer game market split in two. Solitaire and countless other card and puzzle games found their way onto the desktops of every personal computer and provided a brief escape from work or schoolwork. At the same time, computers also became the platform for cutting-edge strategy and shooting games, which are generally played by a relatively small, devoted computer-gaming audience. Graphics-intensive games such as *Quake* and *Half Life 2* led to increased sales in computer components as gamers bought extra memory and bigger hard drives to boost computer performance to handle advanced graphic engines.

In the mid-1990s computer games began to go online. Hardcore fans of card games and battle and quest adventures found competitors on the Internet. The next generation of console systems also enabled gamers to go online and play against one another. In "The Future of Online Gaming" (PCMag.com, March 27, 2003), Cade Metz noted that by 2002 online gaming traffic made up nearly 9% of the overall traffic along the Internet backbone in the United States. The fastest growing segment of online gaming appeared to be in the console game market. Xbox Live, an online service for the Xbox, gained 350,000 subscriptions at the beginning of 2003. In 2005 Microsoft launched a more advanced version of the console, the Xbox 360, and in 2013 it launched yet another version, the Xbox One. As Michael Archambault reports in "Xbox One Sales Numbers Crush the Xbox 360—Combined Consoles Hold 43% of the Market" (March 14, 2014, http://www.wpcentral.com/xbox-one-sales-numbers-february-2014), by February 2014 the Xbox 360 and Xbox One combined accounted for 43% of the U.S. game console market, and nearly half (47%) of the domestic video game software market. According to *Essential Facts about the Video Gaming Industry*, the biggest selling video games of 2013 (in order of popularity) were *Grand Theft Auto V*, *Call of Duty: Ghosts*, and *Madden NFL 25*.

Gaming Violence and Addiction

Over the years games have grown exceedingly more complex and engaging. The *Sims* series by Electronic Arts Inc. has provided gamers with a "real-life" fantasy world where they can simulate alternate lives. Game series such as *Doom* and *Grand Theft Auto* allow people to take out their aggressions on virtual demons or rival gang members. Massively multiplayer online role-playing games (MMORPGs; in which a large number of players interact with each other in a virtual world that continues even when a player is offline), such as *World of Warcraft*, open up entire fantasy worlds where players are free to roam and embark on quests with other gamers.

As the complexity of games has grown, so, too, has the temptation for many to play video games in excess to escape their problems. Although still a relatively unstudied phenomenon, gaming addiction appears to be more and more commonplace. In "Video Games: Are They Really a Source of Addiction?" (2013, http://psychcentral.com/blog/archives/2013/07/

21/video-games-are-they-really-a-source-of-addiction), Kristi A. DeName cites an American Medical Association (AMA) report claiming that, of the 90% of children and young adults who played video games in 2013, 15% showed signs of video game addiction. Among these signs are foregoing sleeping or eating to continue playing, having reduced social contacts, losing a sense of time while playing the game, and allowing school, work, or other responsibilities to lapse.

Furthermore, video game addiction appears to be a greater risk for children suffering from developmental disorders. As Serena Gordon writes in "Video Game 'Addiction' More Likely with Autism, ADHD" (Health .USNews.com, July 29, 2013), children who struggle in social situations, in particular those with autism or attention deficit disorders, are more likely to view video games as a form of escape.

Many psychologists believe games provide a means of escape for people with stressful lives or mental problems in much the same way as drugs and alcohol. A number of symptoms that accompany gaming addiction are similar to those of other impulse control disorders, including alcoholism and drug abuse. These include preoccupation with gaming life over real-life events, failed attempts to stem gaming behavior, having a sense of well-being while playing games, craving more game time as well as feeling irritable when not playing, neglecting family and friends, lying about the amount of time spent gaming, and denying the adverse effects of too much gaming. In June 2007 the Council on Science and Public Health urged the AMA to classify excessive gaming an addiction. In response to mounting concerns about gaming and other forms of online addiction, in 2012 the American Psychiatric Association decided to list "Internet use disorder" as a subject "recommended for further study" in the fifth edition of the *Diagnostic and Statistical Manual for Mental Disorders*, published in May 2013.

Another problem people have with video games is violence. Parents and teachers have always been concerned that violent games may lead to violent aggressive behavior. Fears were fueled in 1999 by the shootings at Columbine High School in Littleton, Colorado, where two teenage students killed 15 people. In their suicide note, the murderers said they drew inspiration from the video game *Doom*. In *Grand Theft of Innocence? Teens and Video Games* (September 16, 2003, http://www.gallup.com/poll/ 9253/Grand-Theft-Innocence-Teens-Video-Games.aspx), Steve Crabtree indicates that many parents and educators are concerned about the violence in video games such as *Grand Theft Auto*. Crabtree states that the concern is perhaps justified. Nearly three-quarters (74%) of teens played video games at least one hour per week in 2003, and 60% of teens had at some point played a game in the *Grand Theft Auto* series. Not only do such violent games give teens a false impression of adult life, but also studies show that the games may hinder social development in some teens. According to Crabtree, a 2001 study at Tokyo University indicated that violent games stunt the development of the brain's frontal lobe, which is the part of the brain that controls antisocial behavior. However, other studies have found that there is no proven connection between violent video game content and aggression. In "Aggression from Video Games 'Linked to Incompetence'" (BBC.com, April 7, 2014), Dave Lee cites a study conducted by researchers at Oxford University and the University of Rochester, which indicated that feelings of aggression were related to a player's inability to succeed at video games, rather than the game's violent content.

The ease with which young teens were able to obtain violent video games was also a cause for concern. To confront this trend, some state governments began to craft legislation aimed at keeping violent video games out of the hands of children. In 2005 the state of California passed a law making it illegal to sell violent video games to minors. The ESA challenged the legislation in federal court, and in 2009 the U.S. Ninth Court of Appeals declared the law unconstitutional. As Bill Mears reports in "California Ban on Sale of 'Violent' Video Games to Children Rejected" (CNN.com, June 27, 2011), in June 2011 the Supreme Court of the United States ruled the California law unconstitutional by a 7 to 2 vote.

In spite of the negative consequences sometimes associated with video games, several studies examining the positive effects of gaming have emerged over the years. In *Video Games and Your Family* (2014, http:// mediasmarts.ca/sites/default/files/pdfs/tipsheet/VideoGame TipSheet_Final_EN.pdf), the Media Awareness Network outlined numerous benefits that video games offered children. According to the report, video games had the potential to teach reading and other learning skills, promote socialization with other game players, and help young people feel more comfortable with technology. At the same time, the report cautions that the violent images found in some video games can have a negative impact on a young child's development, and that parents should play a role in steering their children away from potentially traumatizing games. Other researchers have questioned the link between violent video games and aggressive behavior altogether. In "The Hitman Study: Violent Video Game Exposure Effects on Aggressive Behavior, Hostile Feelings, and Depression" (*European Psychologist*, 2010), Christopher J. Ferguson and Stephanie M. Rueda of Texas A&M International University find that there is no proven connection between violent games and aggression, while suggesting that in some cases violent games can actually help individuals suffering from depression or other mood disorders. In "Video Games May Provide Learning, Health, Social Benefits, Review Finds" (November 25, 2013, http://www.apa.org/news/press/releases/2013/11/video-games.aspx), the American Psychological Association asserts that video games have the potential to improve a child's memory, to teach them problem-solving techniques, and to foster values such as teamwork and cooperation, notably in collaborative game environments.

Online Gambling

There is no doubt inside or outside the scientific community that gambling can be addictive. One troubling development on the Internet in the early 2000s was the continued rise in online gambling. According to a congressional statement by U.S. Deputy Assistant Attorney General John G. Malcolm (March 18, 2003, http://banking.senate.gov/03_03hrg/031803/malcolm.htm), 700 Internet gambling sites existed in 1999. By 2003 the U.S. Department of Justice estimated that 1,800 gambling sites were in place, bringing in roughly $4.2 billion. As Enjoli Francis reports in "Online Gambling, Casinos to 'Sweep' U.S. in 2012" (ABCNews.go.com, December 28, 2011), by 2011 online gambling was generating between $60 and $70 billion in revenues worldwide.

Many of these sites allow gamblers to transfer money from their checking accounts into a gambling account run by the casino. When the player wishes to gamble, he or she simply goes online and begins a session. Because most of these big online gambling operations are based in foreign nations in the Caribbean or South America, the U.S. government cannot regulate them. Malcolm pointed to instances in which the online houses manipulated the software so that the odds of games such as blackjack are skewed heavily in the house's favor. Other fly-by-night gambling operations had simply run off with people's money. Even when these gambling houses are honest, they are still perceived as a threat to society by many lawmakers. People addicted to gambling, for example, might log in and gamble unfettered for hours at a time from work or home. They might lose hundreds or thousands of dollars with a few clicks of the mouse.

Malcolm also addressed the issue of money laundering through online casinos. Criminals who make their money from illegal activities such as drugs are known to use online casino accounts to stash their profits. Once the money is in the casino, the crooks use the games themselves to transfer money to their associates. Some criminals set up private tables at online casino sites and then intentionally lose their money to business associates at the table. In other instances, the casino is part of the crime organization. All the criminal has to do in these cases is to lose money to the casino.

In October 2006 Congress approved the Unlawful Internet Gambling Enforcement Act (Title VIII of the Security and Accountability for Every Port Act of 2006), which made it illegal for banks and credit card companies in the United States to make payments to Internet gambling sites, effectively ending online gambling nationwide. The prohibition was rooted in the Federal Wire Act of 1961, which outlawed the use of wire communication to transmit bets or wagers. As Michael McCarthy and Jon Swartz report in "New Legislation May Pull the Plug on Online Gambling" (USAToday.com, October 3, 2006), PartyGaming, the world's largest online gambling company, generated 80% of its $1 billion revenue in 2005 from 920,000 active customers in the United States. At the time of the ban, the U.S. market accounted for an estimated 50% to 60% of online gambling worldwide. After the passage of the act, several bills came under consideration to review and revise the regulation of online gaming. Among the items introduced were the Skill Game Protection Act, a bill sponsored by U.S. Representative Robert Wexler (1961–; D-FL) in 2007, which set out to exempt such games as poker, backgammon, and other games requiring skill from regulation under the Unlawful Internet Gambling Enforcement Act; the Internet Gambling Regulation, Consumer Protection, and Enforcement Act, sponsored by Barney Frank (1940–; D-MA) in 2009, which proposed legalizing online gambling under a new system of federal oversight and regulation; and the Internet Gambling Regulation and Tax Enforcement Act, a bill sponsored by Jim McDermott (1936–; D-WA) in 2010, which proposed licensing operators of Internet gambling sites and imposing taxes and fees on both gamers and site operators. A turning point in the legal struggle over online gambling came in December 2011, when the U.S. Justice Department declared that the 1961 Wire Act applied solely to sports-related gambling. As Nathan Vardi reports in "Department of Justice Flip-Flops on Internet Gambling" (Forbes.com, December 23, 2011), the decision enabled states to begin selling lottery tickets online, while also creating a legal opening for Internet poker and other forms of casino gambling sites.

By 2013 three states (Nevada, New Jersey, and Delaware) had legalized Internet gambling. In "U.S. Should Go All in with Online Gambling" (BloombergView.com, November 25, 2013), BloombergView projected that tax revenues on Internet gambling had the potential to generate up to $41 billion between 2013 and 2023. However, as Brad Tuttle notes in "So Far, Online Gambling Revenues Have Been Pathetic" (Time.com, April 3, 2014), online gambling in New Jersey generated only $4.2 million in tax revenues between November 2013 and February 2014, a far cry from the $160 million in annual tax revenues originally projected by proponents of legalization. Meanwhile, as Nicholas Confessore and Eric Lipton report in "Seeking to Ban Online Betting, G.O.P. Donor Tests Influence" (NYTimes.com, March 27, 2014), in

2014 many in the gambling industry, led by billionaire casino owner Sheldon G. Adelson (1933–), were still actively lobbying the U.S. Congress to pass legislation that banned online gaming.

RECORDED MUSIC

The conversion from analog recordings to digital music during the 1980s changed the way Americans listened to music. Humans talk and listen in analog. When people speak, they create vibrations in their throats that then travel through the air around them like ripples in a pond. A membrane in the ear, known as an eardrum, picks up these vibrations, allowing people to hear. Patterns in these vibrations enable people to differentiate sounds from one another. Before compact discs (CDs) and MP3 files, all music was recorded in analog form. On a record player, the vibrations that create music are impressed into grooves on a vinyl disc. A needle passing over this impression vibrates in the same way, turning those vibrations into electrical waveforms that travel along a wire to an amplifier and into a speaker. With tape players, the analog waveforms are recorded in electronic form nearly verbatim on a magnetic tape.

The biggest problem with analog recordings is that each time the music is recorded or copied, the waveform degrades in quality, much like a photocopy of an image. Digitizing the music resolves this problem of fidelity. To record and play music digitally, an analog-to-digital converter (ADC) and a digital-to-analog converter (DAC) are needed. In the recording process, the analog music is fed through the ADC, which samples the analog waveforms and then breaks them down into a series of binary numbers represented by zeros and ones. The numbers are then stored on a disc or a memory chip like any other type of digital information. To play the music back, these numbers are fed through a DAC. The DAC reads the numbers and reproduces the original analog waveform that then travels to the headphones or speakers. Because the numbers always reproduce a high-quality version of the original recording, no quality (fidelity) is lost, regardless of how many times the song is transferred or recorded.

Compact Discs

Digital music was first introduced into the U.S. mainstream in 1983 in the form of CDs. Klaas Compaan, a Dutch physicist, originally came up with the idea for the CD in 1969 and developed a glass prototype a year later at Philips Corporation. Over the next nine years both Philips and Sony worked on various prototypes of a CD player. In 1979 the two companies came together to create a final version and set the standards for the CD. The first CD players were sold in Japan and Europe in 1982 and then in the United States in 1983.

With a standard CD, music is recorded digitally on the surface of a polycarbonate plastic disc in a long spiral track 0.00002 inches (0.00005 cm) wide that winds from the center of the disk to the outer edges. A space 0.00006 inches (0.00015 cm) wide separates each ring of the spiral track from the one next to it. Tiny divots, or pits, a minimum of 0.00003 inches (0.00008 cm) long, are engraved into the surface of the track. The polycarbonate disc is then covered by a layer of aluminum, followed by a layer of clear acrylic. As the disc spins in the disc drive, a laser follows this tiny track counterclockwise, and a light sensor, sitting next to the laser, tracks the changes in the laser light as it reflects off the CD. The laser strikes a nondivoted section of track, which causes the laser light to bounce off the aluminum and then back to the light sensor uninterrupted. However, each time the laser hits one of the divots along the CD track, the light is scattered. These flashes of light represent the binary code that makes up the music. Electronics in the disc player read this code. The ones and zeros are then fed into a digital signal processor, which acts as a DAC, and the analog waveform for the music moves to the headphones or speakers.

When CD players were first released in the United States by both Sony and Philips in 1983, they were priced close to $900 a piece ($2,150 in 2014 dollars). The CDs themselves, which occupied a small section of the music store at the time, went for close to $20 a piece ($48 in 2014 dollars). Despite the high costs, the Census Bureau indicated in *Statistical Abstract of the United States: 2003* (2004, http://www.census.gov/prod/2004pubs/03statab/inforcomm.pdf) that 22.6 million CDs were sold in 1985. By 1990, 286.5 million CDs were sold. As reported in the *Proquest Statistical Abstract of the United States: 2014*, by 2000 this number peaked at 942.5 million, before plummeting to 210.9 million by 2012 due to competition from MP3 players and other digital and online music formats. Over the years CD players have become much more compact and have been equipped with many more features, often designed to increase sound quality. By 2014 personal CD players and portable CD stereo units were widely available for less than $50.

Rise of the MP3 Format

In 1985 the first CD read-only memory (CD-ROM) players were released for computers, again by Sony and Philips. CD-ROM players can read computer data from CD-ROMs as well as music from CDs. Even though people with early CD-ROMs were able to listen to CD music, downloading it onto a computer was difficult. A three-minute song on a CD consisted roughly of 32 megabytes. (Each byte consists of a string of eight ones and zeros that can be used to represent binary numbers from 0 to 255. In binary, which is a base-two number system, 1 is 00000001, 2 is 00000010, 3 is 00000011, and so on up to 255, which is represented as 11111111.) During the late 1980s and early 1990s most computer hard drives were only big enough to hold a few songs straight from an audio CD. In 1987 researchers at the Fraunhofer Institute for Integrated Circuits in Germany began to look into ways to compress digital video and sound data into smaller sizes for broadcasting purposes. Out of this work, the MP2 (MPEG-1 Audio Layer II) and then the MP3 (MPEG-1 Audio Layer III) audio file formats emerged. Other compression formats, such as Windows Media Audio and Advanced Audio Coding, have come onto the market since then but are not nearly as well known.

Using such compression formats and encoding software, digital songs can be compressed from 32 megabytes per song to as little as 3 megabytes per song. CD recordings pick up any and every sound in a studio or concert. Compression systems, such as MP3, work by cutting out sounds in CD recordings that people do not pay attention to or do not hear. This may include sounds drowned out by louder instruments. In classical music, an MP3 encoder might cut out a nearly indiscernible note from a flautist or the sound of a faint cough in the audience. It then condenses the recording to one-tenth its previous size. When played back, the encoder reconstructs the song. The compressed files sound nearly as good as CD tracks and much better than audiotapes.

At first, these compression formats and encoding software existed only on home computers. In February 1999 Diamond Multimedia released the first hard drive–based music player. Because early players mainly played MP3 formats, all hard drive–based music players, such as the Apple iPod, became known as MP3 players. All MP3 players consist of a hard drive (many were available in 60 to 500 gigabyte range in 2014) and all the electronic circuitry necessary to transform MP3 and other compressed music files into analog music. Using a cable, these players can be hooked up directly to a home computer. Once the device is connected, the user can download thousands of songs onto the hard drive of the MP3 device. When the user selects a song, a microprocessor in the player pulls the song from the hard drive. A built-in signal processor decompresses the MP3 file (or other type of compressed music file) into a digital CD format, converts the digital signal to an analog signal, and then sends the analog waveform to the headphones. Although compressed music files do not sound quite as good as CD tracks, people can place their entire music collection on a player smaller than the palm of their hand. Since 1999 significant advances in technology have led to major improvements in iPods and other MP3 players. In 2014 most new players had color screens and the ability to play video files, which typically were compressed using an MPEG-4 video compression format. At the same time, by

TABLE 5.3

Percentage of cell owners who listen to music on their phones, by select characteristics, 2013

All cell phone owners	48%
a Men	51
b Women	45
Race/ethnicity	
a White, non-Hispanic	42
b Black, non-Hispanic	61
c Hispanic	64
Age	
a 18–29	80
b 30–49	59
c 50–64	26
d 65+	8
Education attainment	
a No high school diploma	45
b High school grad	41
c Some college	53
d College+	52
Household income	
a Less than $30,000/yr	46
b $30,000–$49,999	47
c $50,000–$74,999	49
d $75,000+	58
Urbanity	
a Urban	52
b Suburban	49
c Rural	37

SOURCE: Maeve Duggan, "Listening to Music," in *Cell Phone Activities 2013*, Pew Research Center, September 16, 2013, http://www.pewinternet.org/files/old-media/Files/Reports/2013/PIP_Cell%20Phone%20Activities%20May%202013.pdf (accessed June 4, 2014)

2013 nearly half (48%) of all cell phone owners were listening to music on their phones. (See Table 5.3.)

MP3 and Peer-to-Peer File Sharing

The widespread use of MP3 files and the increased size of hard drives in the late 1990s caused a transformation in the music industry almost as big as the advent of digital music. People suddenly had the ability to store entire music libraries on their computers and swap music for free using peer-to-peer file-sharing networks. According to Michael Gowan in "Requiem for Napster" (PCWorld.com, May 17, 2002), the Napster file-sharing service had approximately 80 million subscribers at its peak. However, the availability of free music cut deeply into the recording industry's sales, and the Recording Industry Association of America (RIAA) sued Napster and the users of other peer-to-peer networks who shared music files (see Chapter 4). Some high-profile bands at the time, such as Metallica and Creed, joined the RIAA in its attempt to close down Napster. Other musicians, however, did not seem fazed by Internet file sharing. Radiohead released its 2000 album *Kid A* on the Internet three weeks before it was released in stores. The buzz generated by the Internet prerelease catapulted the album to number one in the United States after it hit record stores. Before *Kid A*, Radiohead had never had a number-one album in the United States.

The lawsuits brought on by the RIAA succeeded in putting an end to much of the free file-swapping on the Internet. The free Napster website shut down in July 2001 and reopened later as a pay music service where users could buy songs. After the RIAA began going after private citizens, traffic on many of the remaining peer-to-peer sites diminished greatly. The number of people using noncentralized peer-to-peer networks such as Kazaa dropped precipitously after the RIAA became litigious with file swappers in 2003. Lee Rainie et al. reported in the Pew data memo *The Impact of Music Industry Suits against Music File Swappers* (January 2004, http://www.pewinternet.org/~/media//Files/Reports/2004/PIP_File_Swapping_Memo_0104.pdf.pdf) that only 14% of American adults downloaded music from the Internet in the last two months of 2003, compared with 29% only six months earlier. However, even after the demise of Napster, revenues in the recording industry decreased. The *Proquest Statistical Abstract of the United States: 2014* reports that the recording industry had revenues of $15.2 billion in 2007. Sales then fell steadily over the next five years, eventually dropping to $12.1 billion by 2011. As Joshua P. Friedlander of the RIAA reports in *News and Notes on 2013 RIAA Music Industry Shipment and Revenue Statistics* (2014, http://76.74.24.142/2463566A-FF96-E0CA-2766-72779A364D01.pdf), the industry's domestic sales fell from $8.8 billion in 2008 to $7 billion in 2010, although revenues stabilized over the next three years. (See Figure 5.2.)

After the RIAA took legal steps to combat free music-sharing sites, sales of digital music downloads increased. According to the *Proquest Statistical Abstract of the United States: 2014*, Americans purchased 363.3 million digital singles in 2005, along with 135.7 million digital albums. By 2012 Americans purchased more than 1.6 billion singles online, and more than 1.2 million digital albums. According to Apple (2014, http://www.apple.com/pr/products/ipodhistory), by June 2008 the company had sold 5 billion songs through its iTunes service. By February 2010 the total number of songs sold on iTunes had climbed to 10 billion. During this time, more and more Americans were also turning to online music streaming services, such as Pandora and Spotify, to gain personalized access to extensive digital music libraries. As John Paul Titlow reports in "6 Million People Pay for Spotify—Is That Good Enough?" (Readwrite.com, March 13, 2013), by 2013 Spotify had 24 million registered users, 6 million of whom were paid subscribers. As Figure 5.3 shows, streaming services accounted for more than one-fifth (21%) of music industry revenues in 2013. That year, digital downloads and streaming services accounted for more than three-fifths (61%) of all music industry revenues. (See Figure 5.4.)

TELEVISION

Although inventors had been trying to create a television as early as 1877, many people consider Philo Farnsworth (1906–1971) to be the father of the first modern, electronic television. He demonstrated his device for the first time in San Francisco in 1927, when he transmitted an image of a dollar sign. Using Farnsworth's design, Radio Corporation of America (RCA; then the owner of the National Broadcasting Company [NBC] network) began work on the first commercial

FIGURE 5.2

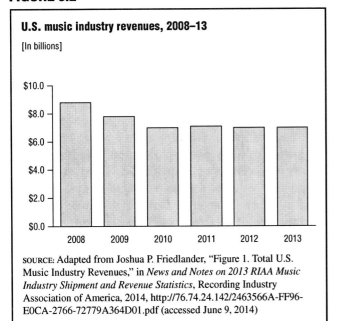

U.S. music industry revenues, 2008–13

[In billions]

SOURCE: Adapted from Joshua P. Friedlander, "Figure 1. Total U.S. Music Industry Revenues," in *News and Notes on 2013 RIAA Music Industry Shipment and Revenue Statistics*, Recording Industry Association of America, 2014, http://76.74.24.142/2463566A-FF96-E0CA-2766-72779A364D01.pdf (accessed June 9, 2014)

FIGURE 5.3

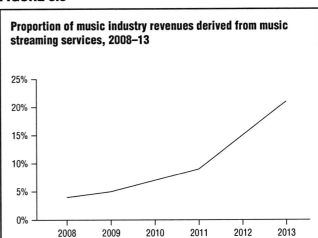

Proportion of music industry revenues derived from music streaming services, 2008–13

SOURCE: Adapted from Joshua P. Friedlander, "Figure 3. Proportion of Total Music Industry Revenues from Streaming," in *News and Notes on 2013 RIAA Music Industry Shipment and Revenue Statistics*, Recording Industry Association of America, 2014, http://76.74.24.142/2463566A-FF96-E0CA-2766-72779A364D01.pdf (accessed June 9, 2014)

FIGURE 5.4

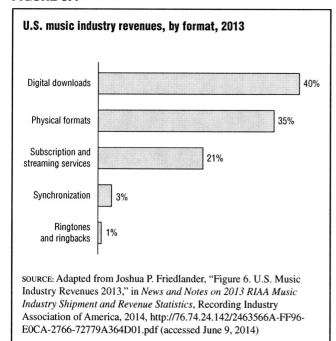

U.S. music industry revenues, by format, 2013

- Digital downloads — 40%
- Physical formats — 35%
- Subscription and streaming services — 21%
- Synchronization — 3%
- Ringtones and ringbacks — 1%

SOURCE: Adapted from Joshua P. Friedlander, "Figure 6. U.S. Music Industry Revenues 2013," in *News and Notes on 2013 RIAA Music Industry Shipment and Revenue Statistics*, Recording Industry Association of America, 2014, http://76.74.24.142/2463566A-FF96-E0CA-2766-72779A364D01.pdf (accessed June 9, 2014)

television system during the late 1930s. In 1939 the first commercial televisions were introduced. Early televisions had tiny screens and were as big as small dressers. The pictures were in black and white, and at first the major networks broadcast only in the largest cities. Full-scale broadcasting began nationwide in 1947.

Since the early 1960s television has been the most popular medium of entertainment for Americans. In *There's No Place Like Home to Spend an Evening, Say Most Americans* (January 10, 2002, http://www.gallup.com/poll/5164/theres-place-like-home-spend-evening-say-most-americans.aspx), Lydia Saad reported that 27% of Americans in a December 1960 poll said their favorite way of spending their evening was in front of a television. Resting, reading, and entertaining and visiting friends were ranked second, third, and fourth, respectively. Television appeared to hit its peak between the mid-1960s and early 1970s. A full 46% of people polled in February 1974 rated watching television as their favorite evening activity, followed by reading (14%), dining out (12%), and the somewhat ambiguous response of "staying at home with the family" (10%).

A survey reported in the *Proquest Statistical Abstract of the United States: 2014* finds that in 2012 approximately 232.7 million adults, or 91.7%, had watched television within the week prior to participating in the survey. Of those, 81.6% had viewed cable television during that period. Among age groups, seniors watched more prime-time television than any other demographic, with 89.7% of those 65 and older watching TV during prime viewing hours over the course of the previous week. By comparison, 68.6% of those aged 18 to 24 had watched

prime-time television over that same span. Indeed, by 2014 many younger media users had begun turning to the Internet and mobile technology as their preferred source for video content. In "Ownership of TV Sets Falls in U.S." (NYTimes.com May 3, 2011), Brian Stelter reports that U.S. television ownership fell to 96.7% in 2011, down from 98.9% the previous year; according to the Nielsen Company, it marked the first time in 20 years that TV ownership fell in the United States. As Stelter notes, one key reason for the decline was the increasing popularity of alternative video-viewing platforms.

Cable Television

Since the 1970s steady advances in cable, satellite, and digital technology have changed the way Americans watch television. According to *Proquest Statistical Abstract of the United States: 2014*, the number of cable television subscribers peaked in 2001, when 66.7 million adults subscribed to cable TV. By 2010 this figure had fallen to just under 61 million subscribers. By comparison, 84.5 million Americans had fixed broadband Internet in their homes in 2010; by 2011 this number had risen to 88.3 million. The number of mobile broadband subscribers grew even more dramatically during this period. In 2008, 26.5 million adults subscribed to mobile broadband service; over the next year this figure more than doubled, to 56.3 million. By 2011, 142.1 million Americans subscribed to mobile broadband.

Cable television began in 1948 in Mahanoy City, Pennsylvania. John Walson (1915–1993), the owner of an electronics shop, began selling televisions in 1947. However, few customers in the local area wanted to buy a television because of the bad reception caused by the surrounding mountains. To increase sales potential, Walson erected an antenna on a nearby mountaintop, ran a cable from the antenna to his store, and connected it to his television. He then agreed to attach cables from his antenna to the houses of those who bought televisions from him. From then until the early 1970s, cable networks were generally used only in rural or mountainous areas. At most, early cable television programming included local broadcasts and a broadcast or two from a nearby region.

As early as 1965 the U.S. government and various contractors began putting up a communications satellite network. A satellite network remedied the biggest obstacle faced by broadcasters during the 1960s, which was the curvature of the earth. If the earth was flat, televisions could receive broadcast signals from thousands of miles away. However, because of the curvature of the earth, these broadcast signals escape into space after traveling about 100 miles (161 km). With a satellite system in place, a transmitter on the East Coast can beam a signal to a satellite above Kansas. The satellite then relays the signal to the West Coast without interruption.

Home Box Office (HBO) became the first pay cable station in 1972 and was the first television broadcaster to take advantage of a satellite communications network. HBO began in Wilkes-Barre, Pennsylvania, and broadcast its movies and shows to a limited number of cable networks in and around the state. In 1975, to expand the subscription television market, HBO leased the right to use one of the uplinks on RCA's *Satcom I* communications satellite. Once HBO was on the satellite network, any cable network provider in the United States could buy a 9.8-foot (3-m) satellite dish and provide HBO for any house on the network. By 1978 HBO had 1 million customers. Ted Turner (1938–), who put his Atlanta-based station, WTBS, on the satellite network in 1976, created the Cable News Network (CNN) in 1980. The Music Television Network (MTV) and a number of other stations followed in 1981 and launched an era of exponential growth for the cable industry.

The early 1980s also saw the emergence of VCRs. As the Nielsen Company reports in *Television Audience 2010 & 2011* (2011, http://www.nielsen.com/content/dam/corporate/us/en/reports-downloads/2011-Reports/2010-2011-nielsen-television-audience-report.pdf), the percentage of television households with VCRs rose from 14% in 1985 to 66% in 1990, eventually climbing to 90% by 2005. As the market turned from videotape to digital video discs (DVDs), however, the percentage of homes with a VCR began to fall steadily; according to Nielsen, VCR ownership declined to 65% in 2010, and was projected to drop to 57% by 2012.

Advances in Broadcasting Technology

In 1994 a new way of broadcasting movies and television shows became available when RCA released its Direct Satellite System (DSS). The DSS was the first affordable satellite receiver available to the American public. By installing an 18-inch (46-cm) satellite dish on their houses, Americans could receive nearly 200 channels in their living rooms. To squeeze so many channels into a stream of data small enough to travel through space and back, the direct broadcasting satellite provider had to use a form of digital compression known as MPEG-1. The MPEG-1 compression format works much like an MP3 format. (The MP3 format in fact was developed from the audio portion of the MPEG-1 format.) To employ the MPEG-1 format, all television shows recorded in analog must first be transformed by ADCs into a digital format. MPEG-1 encoders, owned by the direct broadcasting satellite provider, then compress the digital data largely by removing redundant scenery between frames. For example, if a character's face movement is the only discernible change between two frames in a movie, then the background from the first frame is applied to both frames, cutting out the redundant information in the second frame. The compressed signal is then beamed to the satellite network. On receiving the signal, the satellite network broadcasts the signal to homes all across the country. A DSS box in the home decompresses the signal and delivers it to the viewer.

Several years after the first direct broadcast satellites were released, cable companies introduced digital cable. Digital cable works in much the same way as direct broadcast satellites but uses a slightly more advanced MPEG-2 format for compression. By digitally compressing their programming, cable providers found they could transmit 10 times more television stations than before along their cables. Many cable providers added music stations, pay-per-view movies, and multiple movie channels to their services. The only drawback with both the digital cable and satellite systems is that the decoder can work only on one television at a time, and it is usually bulky.

In terms of television accessories, the big development during the late 1990s was the DVD. DVDs work almost exactly in the same way as CDs, but the standard DVD can hold up to seven times more information per disc, which allows the DVD to carry the data needed for much larger video files. After its release in 1997, the DVD quickly rose to become the preferred format for watching recorded movies. In *Television Audience 2010 & 2011* the Nielsen Company reports that 76% of TV households owned a DVD player in 2006, compared with 89% that owned a VCR. By 2010 the percentage of TV households with a DVD player climbed to 88%, whereas VCR ownership dropped to 65%.

The design and quality of TV sets also experienced a radical evolution beginning in the 1990s. Among the most significant innovations was the development of flat-screen (or flat-panel) televisions. Flat-screen televisions offered numerous advantages over traditional television sets. For one, flat screens were more streamlined and energy efficient than traditional televisions, which used bulky cathode-ray tubes to generate images. At the same time, flat screens offered the potential for a higher-resolution picture quality. The two principal technologies behind the emergence of flat screens were liquid crystal display (LCD) and plasma. Already widely used in calculators and laptop computers, LCD screens are composed of two polarized panels containing millions of liquid crystals, each of which controls a particular aspect of the light being projected through the screen. Plasma screens, on the other hand, contain tubes of gases that emit light when charged with electricity. By manipulating light in this way, LCD and plasma technologies are able to project images onto a television screen. The first flat-screen plasma televisions became widely available to consumers in 1997, and cost more than $7,000 ($10,300 in 2014 dollars). While LCD technology developed more gradually, by the early part of the new century LCD TVs began to compete with plasma models. Many higher-quality LCD televisions also began to use Light Emitting Diode (LED) backlighting technology, which produced a sharper picture quality while requiring less energy.

THE DEVELOPMENT OF 3-D TELEVISION. By 2014 a number of television manufacturers had introduced three-dimensional (3-D) television sets. Most of the new models projected 3-D images to viewers wearing special glasses, but in late 2010 Toshiba debuted the Regza GL1, a flat-panel 3-D television that required no glasses. Instead, as Dan Reisinger reports in "Digital Home" (October 4, 2010, http://news.cnet.com/8301-13506_3-20018421-17.html), the Regza presented multiple images of each two-dimensional frame that viewers' brains "superimposed... to create a three-dimensional impression of the image." At the time of the product release, the sets were available only in 12- and 20-inch (30.5- and 50.8-cm) models, and the 3-D effect was viewable only within a limited area two to three feet (0.61 to 0.91 m) from the screen.

Two years later, Toshiba released the 55ZL2 3-D television. As John Archer reports (TechRadar.com, May 17, 2012), the 55ZL2 boasted a 55-inch (139.7 cm), ultra high-definition (HD) screen. Meanwhile, as Larry Frum writes in "4K TV Promises to Be Four Times Clearer than High-Def" (CNN.com, May 2, 2013), a new television technology, dubbed 4K, was launched in 2013, promising resolution quality four times greater than HD technology. As Jim Boulden and Ivana Kottasova report in "Watching the World Cup? Forget 3D, It's All about 4K Now" (CNN.com, June 18, 2014), the Fédération International de Football Association (FIFA), soccer's global governing body, intended to broadcast three matches from the 2014 World Cup in Brazil using the new 4K format. Meanwhile, Boulden and Kottasova note, many networks, including ESPN and BBC, had reduced their 3-D broadcasts due to lack of consumer interest.

Television and the Internet

As higher connection speeds and faster computers became more widespread, the Internet became a popular source of video entertainment. By the early 21st century, several video-sharing websites had been established, enabling Internet users from around the world to post videos and other recorded content online. Of these sites, You-Tube quickly emerged as one of the most popular. Created in February 2005, YouTube allowed visitors to view and upload videos free of charge, while also enabling users to create their own accounts and video libraries. In "Video Websites Pop Up, Invite Postings" (USA Today.com, November 22, 2005), Jefferson Graham reports that the site had more than 200,000 registered users by late 2005. Traditional media outlets quickly recognized the marketing potential of YouTube, and soon clips from television programs, movie trailers, news features, and other mainstream content became available on the video site. YouTube's rapidly increasing popularity soon attracted the attention of major media and technology corporations, who regarded the site as a means of reaching new audiences of younger consumers. Indeed, the site's growth was staggering; as Andrew Ross Sorkin reports (NYTimes.com, October 10, 2006), by October 2006 YouTube visitors were watching more than 100 million videos per day, a 4,900% increase in less than a year. A month later, Google acquired YouTube for $1.7 billion.

The success of YouTube inspired a wide range of other online outlets for video content. Prominent among these was Hulu, a streaming video site that airs shows and movies produced by major studios and TV networks, and Netflix, which began offering streaming services to its subscribers in 2007. The spread of streaming video channels was accompanied by a rise in the popularity of the Roku player, a device that enabled users to stream Internet content directly into their TV sets. A number of other websites, particularly news and sports outlets, began to use video as a way of augmenting or supplementing their written content. At the same time, sites like YouTube enabled anyone to post videos online, making a broader and more diverse range of content available for viewing. As Kristen Purcell reports in "Online Video 2013" (October 10, 2013, http://www.pewinternet.org/2013/10/10/online-video-2013), 78% of adult Internet users watched or downloaded videos online in 2013, up from 69% in 2009. This practice was most common among online adults between the ages of 18 and 29 (95%). Meanwhile, the percentage of online adults who posted videos to the Internet more than doubled between 2009 and 2013, from 14% to 31%.

Digital Television

Many confuse the concept of digital cable with digital television. Digital cable simply uses digital technology to compress the size of broadcasts so the customer has more channels. The digital signal also does not degrade as it travels across miles of coaxial cable. Most of the programming fed through the digital cable systems is not digitally recorded. Digital television, however, is digital from start to finish. Digital cameras are used to record the broadcast; cables, satellite systems, and broadcast towers send a digital signal; and digital televisions play the broadcast. The result is a television picture that more closely resembles an image on a computer monitor than an image on a television set.

The Federal Communications Commission (FCC) established a number of standards for digital television, which became mandatory for full-power stations on June 12, 2009. Standard-definition television (SDTV) has the resolution of an analog television, which is roughly 480 x 440 dots per inch (dpi) or 210,000 pixels in total. The next step up in visual quality is enhanced-definition television (EDTV), which generally has the same overall resolution as SDTV but features a wider screen. Finally, high-definition television (HDTV) is the highest-quality television format with resolutions up to 1,920 dpi horizontally and 1,080 dpi vertically. Overall, HDTV has more than 2 million pixels to display each image, which provides the viewer with 10 times the detail of SDTV. For a television to meet HDTV standards, it also has to have the ability to play the latest versions of Dolby stereo.

As HDTV became more widespread, electronics manufacturers began to develop a higher-quality DVD format known as Blu-ray. Capable of storing between 25 and 50 gigabytes of data, Blu-ray discs produced a picture definition that was far sharper than that offered by conventional DVDs. The first Blu-ray player was released by Sony in 2006. According to data compiled by the Digital Entertainment Group (January 7, 2014, http://degonline.org/wp-content/uploads/2014/01/DEG-Year-End-2013-Home-Entertainment-Report.pdf), by January 2014 more than 72 million American households owned Blu-ray players.

The digital television standards were adopted by the FCC after Congress passed the 1996 Telecommunications Act. The act called for a full conversion to digital television across the United States within 10 years. By 2006 every television station serving every market in the United States would be required to air digital programming. In addition, broadcasters would no longer have to air analog content. Americans with an analog television set would be required to buy either a digital television or a $50 to $100 ADC device to watch television. In 2005, however, only a small percentage of Americans had HDTV or even EDTV. Consequently, in 2005 Congress pushed the deadline for the digitization of television to February 17, 2009. This deadline, too, was later extended to June 2009.

On January 1, 2008, the National Telecommunications and Information Administration of the U.S. Department of Commerce began issuing $40 coupons that defrayed the cost of converter boxes, allowing consumers to continue using older, analog television sets after the conversion to digital broadcasting. Households were eligible to receive two coupons and were required to redeem them toward the purchase of converter boxes within 90 days. In December 2009 the TV Converter Box Coupon Program (December 9, 2009, http://www.ntia.doc.gov/legacy/dtvcoupon/reports/NTIA_DTVWeekly_120909.pdf) released the final number of coupon requests that had been received, processed, and redeemed. As of December 9, 2009, the program had received 64.1 million requests, and had approved coupons for 34.8 million households.

JOURNALISM AND NEW MEDIA

The many advances in new media have fundamentally changed the manner in which Americans get their news. As the Pew Research Center reports in "In Changing News Landscape, Even Television Is Vulnerable" (September 27, 2012, http://www.people-press.org/2012/09/27/in-changing-news-landscape-even-television-is-vulnerable), during the early 1990s more than 70% of Americans said they had watched television news the day before; by 2012 this number had fallen to 55%. Over this same span, daily newspaper readership dropped from 56% to 29%, while the proportion of Americans who received news regularly over the radio fell from 54% to 33%. By contrast, the percentage of Americans who claimed to have regularly gotten news either online or on a mobile device climbed from 24% in 2004 to 39% in 2012; when including e-mail, podcast, social networking sites, and other electronic formats, this number rose to half (50%) of Americans. This trend coincided with a steady erosion of consumer confidence toward mainstream news outlets between the 1990s and 2013. (See Figure 5.5.)

High technology has not only changed how news and information are sold but also how reporters and writers do their jobs. Advanced communications and video technology have allowed reporters with established organizations to report from anywhere in the world in real time, something that most modern viewers take for granted. With the Internet, anyone can report on current events or start a publication or web log (blog) and begin writing commentary. No longer do reporters and writers have to work for a large publishing house or magazine to build a reputation. Some blogs have grown so popular that they have a readership bigger than some major newspapers and magazines. For example, Matt Drudge (1967–) began the Drudge Report website in 1997 to report on current events. He was largely responsible for breaking the story of President Bill Clinton's (1946–) relationship with the former White House intern Monica Lewinsky (1973–) in 1998. By June 2014 the website (June 19, 2014, http://www.drudgereport.com) reported more than 10.3 billion visits in the previous 12 months and a daily tally of over 28 million readers.

FIGURE 5.5

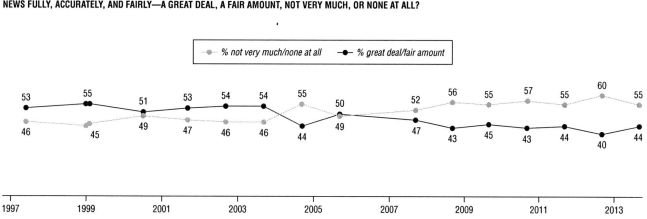

Public trust in mass media news reporting, 1997–2013

IN GENERAL, HOW MUCH TRUST AND CONFIDENCE DO YOU HAVE IN THE MASS MEDIA—SUCH AS NEWSPAPERS, TV, AND RADIO—WHEN IT COMES TO REPORTING THE NEWS FULLY, ACCURATELY, AND FAIRLY—A GREAT DEAL, A FAIR AMOUNT, NOT VERY MUCH, OR NONE AT ALL?

SOURCE: Elizabeth Mendes, "Americans' Trust in the Mass Media," in *In U.S., Trust in Media Recovers Slightly from All-Time Low*, The Gallup Organization, September 19, 2013, http://www.gallup.com/poll/164459/trust-media-recovers-slightly-time-low.aspx (accessed June 4, 2014). Copyright © 2013 Gallup, Inc. All rights reserved. The content is used with permission; however, Gallup retains all rights of republication.

CHAPTER 6
HIGH TECHNOLOGY AND EDUCATION

Knowing how to use a computer or Internet browser has become as important a skill in modern life as knowing multiplication tables. Not having exposure to information technology restricts a person's access to job listings, e-mail communication, and dozens of convenient, efficient computer applications that make work and life easier. Aware of this, high schools and colleges in the late 1990s increased efforts to expose students to computers and the Internet before graduation. Most elementary and secondary schools installed computers with Internet access in classrooms and libraries. Many schools set up programs wherein their students could borrow laptops and handheld computers for extended periods. College administrations provided widespread broadband access to students on campus, and many professors required the use of the Internet and computer programs in college courses.

Providing students with access to high technology, however, has not been without problems. The Internet, computers, and cell phones have introduced a great deal of distraction into the life of many young people. They allow teenagers access to illicit material, such as pornography, that they normally could not obtain so easily. In addition, these technologies open up avenues for cheating and plagiarism. Largely because of the Internet, academic cheating and plagiarism skyrocketed around the start of the 21st century. Students appeared to have no qualms about copying text from the Internet and pasting it verbatim into reports and papers.

In spite of these potential drawbacks, by 2014 technology was becoming increasingly interwoven into the educational experience of most U.S. students. As Chris Riedel writes in "10 Major Technology Trends in Education" (Journal.com, February 3, 2014), 89% of all high school students had access to smartphones in 2013. Sixty percent of all high school students were using mobile devices to conduct research, and 40% were using their phones as a

means of collaborating on school projects with their peers. At the same time, technology also offered educators a wide range of innovative instructional tools. As Kelsey Sheehy reports in "Technology Trends for Teachers to Try in 2014" (USNews.com, December 23, 2013), in 2014 many teachers were using educational networking platforms, such as Share My Lesson and NROC Math, to share curricula and lesson plans with other teachers.

TECHNOLOGY AT SCHOOL

In February 1996 President Bill Clinton (1946–) signed the Telecommunications Act into law. This legislation ushered in the E-Rate Program, which provided elementary and secondary public schools with discounts of between 20% and 90% when purchasing computers for classrooms and libraries. The program had a tremendous impact on computer and Internet accessibility in public schools. By the 2011–12 school year, 96% of Advanced Placement (AP) and National Writing Project (NWP) public school students had access to computers in their classrooms. (See Figure 6.1.)

Technology and Instruction

Figure 6.1 presents a breakdown of the diverse types of technology used by AP and NWP public school teachers during the 2011–12 school year. Among the AP and NWP teachers surveyed, 97% used some type of digital projector in the classroom, the highest percentage of all the technologies listed. At the same time, nearly three-quarters (73%) of teachers surveyed used cell phones or smartphones for instructional purposes in 2011–12, and more than two-thirds (67%) used digital cameras. Other popular forms of technology used in classroom instruction that year included digital video recorders (55%) and interactive whiteboards (52%). Fewer than half of the AP and NWP teachers surveyed made e-readers (45%) or tablets (43%) available for use by their students in 2011–12.

FIGURE 6.1

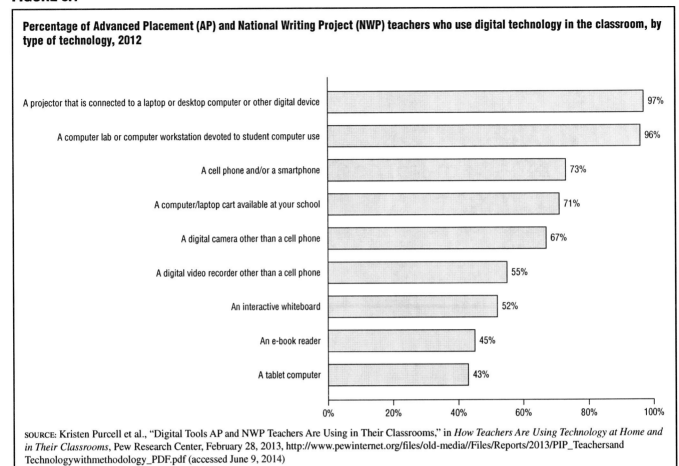

Percentage of Advanced Placement (AP) and National Writing Project (NWP) teachers who use digital technology in the classroom, by type of technology, 2012

SOURCE: Kristen Purcell et al., "Digital Tools AP and NWP Teachers Are Using in Their Classrooms," in *How Teachers Are Using Technology at Home and in Their Classrooms*, Pew Research Center, February 28, 2013, http://www.pewinternet.org/files/old-media//Files/Reports/2013/PIP_Teachersand Technologywithmethodology_PDF.pdf (accessed June 9, 2014)

As Figure 6.2 shows, in 2013 public school teachers and principals held similar views concerning the value of using technology in the classroom. In general, school principals were more likely to support the notion that various technologies enhanced the educational experience of their students; the one exception was in the category of digital games, which public school teachers were more likely than principals to find useful as educational tools. Students were more likely than teachers, principals, or their parents to see the value of mobile devices, digital games, text messaging, social networking, and online modes of instruction in their educational experience; students were also more likely than any other group to support the idea of making laptops available for every student. By comparison, parents were more likely than any other group to support the use of digital textbooks in the education of their children.

While public school teachers have generally embraced the use of classroom technologies, managing students' use of these technologies still presents a challenge. During the 2011–12 school year, nearly three-quarters (71%) of AP and NWP teachers believed that managing the use of cell phones and other technologies in the classroom presented either a major issue (28%) or a minor issue (43%); another

11% thought that cell phones and other technologies presented no issue at all, and nearly one in five (19%) had implemented rules banning the use of phones in the classroom altogether. (See Figure 6.3.) At the same time, nearly two-thirds (64%) of AP and NWP teachers surveyed believed that their school's policies had either a major impact (21%) or minor impact (43%) on cell phone use among students; roughly one-third (34%) believed the school policies had no impact on student cell phone use at all. (See Figure 6.4.)

The Internet has also provided teachers with a valuable educational tool in the 21st century. Table 6.1 offers a glimpse into the various ways that AP and NWP teachers used the Internet for classroom instruction during the 2011–12 school year. As Table 6.1 shows, 59% of all AP and NWP teachers created their own website that year, and slightly more than half (51%) used online content to create instructional materials. Science teachers (66%) were the most likely to create their own website in 2011–12, followed by math teachers (61%), history and social studies teachers (58%), and English and language arts teachers (55%). By comparison, English and language arts teachers (46%) were the group most likely to create an online blog or journal for their

FIGURE 6.2

Attitudes among teachers, administrators, students, and parents concerning use of various technologies in school, by type of technology, 2013

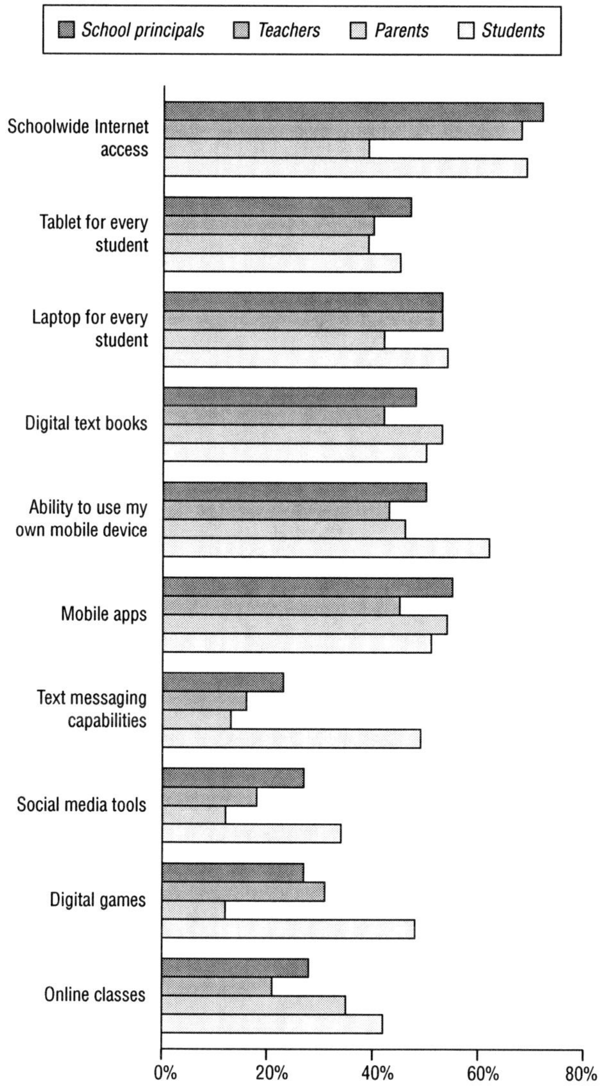
School principals
Teachers
Parents
Students
Schoolwide Internet access
Tablet for every student
Laptop for every student
Digital text books
Ability to use my own mobile device
Mobile apps
Text messaging capabilities
Social media tools
Digital games
Online classes
0%
20%
40%
60%
80%

SOURCE: "Chart 6. Do We Have a Shared Vision of Digital Learning?" in *The New Digital Learning Playbook: Understanding the Spectrum of Students' Activities and Aspirations*, Project Tomorrow, Speak Up, 2014, http://www.tomorrow.org/speakup/pdfs/SU13StudentsReport.pdf (accessed June 9, 2014)

FIGURE 6.3

Attitudes of Advanced Placement (AP) and National Writing Project (NWP) teachers toward managing students' use of cell phones and other digital technologies in the classroom, 2012

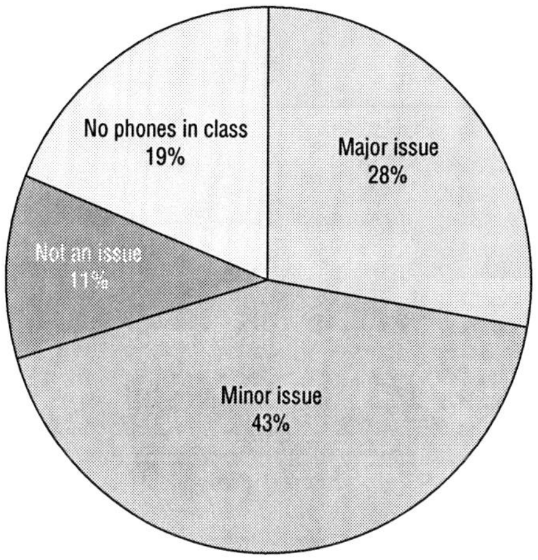
No phones in class
19%
Major issue
28%
Not an issue
11%
Minor issue
43%

SOURCE: Kristen Purcell et al., "71% of Teachers Say Managing Student Use of Cell Phones and Other Digital Tools in Class Is an Issue," in *How Teachers Are Using Technology at Home and in Their Classrooms*, Pew Research Center, February 28, 2013, http://www.pewinternet.org/files/old-media//Files/Reports/2013/PIP_TeachersandTechnologywithmethodology_PDF.pdf (accessed June 9, 2014)

students. When creating online assignments for their students, 95% of AP and NWP teachers asked their students to conduct research over the Internet; 79% had their students download content from a class website, and 76% asked students to submit their work over the Internet. (See Figure 6.5.)

The use of the Internet for school purposes becomes more prevalent as students become older. In 2013 less than one-third (31%) of elementary school students in grades three through five accessed school assignments through an online portal; by comparison, 68% of middle school students and 75% of high school students accessed their assignments over the Internet that year. (See Table 6.2.) At the same time, high school students (37%) and middle school students (32%) were more than twice as likely as elementary school students (14%) to use online textbooks. On the other hand, the proportion of elementary school students (44%) who took tests online was roughly comparable to the proportion of middle school (47%) and high school (52%) students who took tests over the Internet.

On the whole, AP and NWP teachers expressed positive views concerning the use of the Internet and digital technologies in the classroom in 2012. As Figure 6.6 shows, 99% of all teachers surveyed either strongly agreed (76%) or agreed (23%) that the Internet provided their students with access to research they would not have been able to find otherwise; at the same time, a majority (65%) either strongly agreed (18%) or agreed (47%) that the Internet helped teach their students how to approach their research tasks with greater independence. Nearly three-quarters (72%) of AP and NWP teachers either strongly agreed (23%) or agreed (49%) that digital content had played a role in expanding their students perspective on the world. (See Figure 6.7.) On the other hand, 83% of teachers surveyed either strongly agreed (35%) or agreed (48%) that the amount of information

FIGURE 6.4

Ways that Advanced Placement (AP) and National Writing Project (NWP) teachers believe that their school's policies impact their ability to use technology in the classroom, by type of school policy, 2012

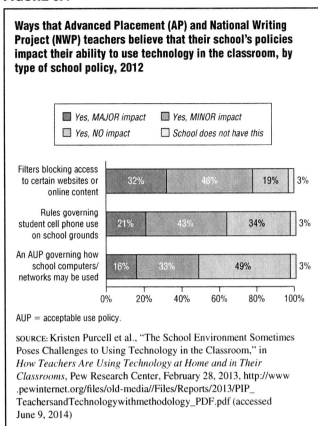

AUP = acceptable use policy.

SOURCE: Kristen Purcell et al., "The School Environment Sometimes Poses Challenges to Using Technology in the Classroom," in *How Teachers Are Using Technology at Home and in Their Classrooms*, Pew Research Center, February 28, 2013, http://www.pewinternet.org/files/old-media//Files/Reports/2013/PIP_TeachersandTechnologywithmethodology_PDF.pdf (accessed June 9, 2014)

TABLE 6.1

Ways that Advanced Placement (AP) and National Writing Project (NWP) teachers use the Internet for instruction, by subject matter taught, 2012

% of each group who use the Internet to...	Create your own webpage	Take material you find online and remix it into your own creation	Create your own online journal or blog
All teachers	59	51	39
All adult Internet users	14	17	14
All adults	11	12	11
Teacher age			
22–34	62	48	46
35–54	60	52	41
55+	51	50	30
Years teaching			
15 or fewer	62	50	44
16 or more	56	52	34
Teacher sex			
Male	65	56	40
Female	57	49	39
Subject matter taught			
English/Language Arts	55	48	46
History/Social Studies	58	50	40
Math	61	44	26
Science	66	55	30

SOURCE: Kristen Purcell et al., "Science teachers are most likely to create their own website and remix online material; English teachers are most likely to blog," in *How Teachers Are Using Technology at Home and in Their Classrooms*, Pew Research Center, February 28, 2013, http://www.pewinternet.org/files/old-media//Files/Reports/2013/PIP_TeachersandTechnologywithmethodology_PDF.pdf (accessed June 9, 2014)

available online was overwhelming for most of their students. (See Figure 6.6.)

PREVENTING ACCESS TO INAPPROPRIATE MATERIAL

In 2000 Congress passed the Children's Internet Protection Act (CIPA). Under CIPA, public schools and libraries that could not prove they use filtering or blocking technology to keep children from viewing pornographic or sexually explicit websites were no longer eligible for the E-Rate Program. Signed into law in April 2001, CIPA promptly became the target of a legal challenge launched by the American Library Association (ALA) and the American Civil Liberties Union (ACLU). In the lawsuit, the ALA and the ACLU argued that CIPA violated free speech rights guaranteed in the First Amendment. In June 2003 the U.S. Supreme Court upheld the legality of CIPA in *United States v. American Library Association* (539 U.S. 194). By 2005, 100% of U.S. public schools were in compliance with the law. In spite of this widespread acceptance of CIPA, some educators have raised questions about the law's potential to prevent students from engaging in legitimate research. Paul T. Jaeger and Zheng Yan suggest in "One Law with Two Outcomes: Comparing the Implementation of CIPA in Public Libraries and Schools" (*Information Technology & Libraries*, vol. 28, no. 1, March 2009) that even

though opposition to CIPA in schools has been "very small," there are still some concerns that "filters in schools may create two classes of students—ones with only filtered access at school and ones who also can get unfiltered access at home." In "Minors' First Amendment Rights: CIPA and School Libraries" (*Knowledge Quest*, vol. 31, no. 1, September–October 2010), Theresa Chmara raises questions concerning the impact of CIPA on the first amendment rights of children, suggesting that the scope of the law has the potential to restrict students' access to legitimate educational material.

COLLEGES AND UNIVERSITIES

College students are among the most wired Americans and are typically the first to embrace new technologies. The marketing research firm Student Monitor (June 2014, http://www.studentmonitor.com/computing.php) reports that in 2014, 86% of full-time undergraduate college students owned their own computers before starting college and 17% planned to buy a new computer within the next year. The firm also reports that 88% of college students accessed the Internet at least once per day. With a weekly average of 19 hours, students spent twice as much time online in 2014 as those interviewed in 2000. Student Monitor also notes that nearly nine out of 10 (88%) full-time undergraduate students had a cell phone.

FIGURE 6.5

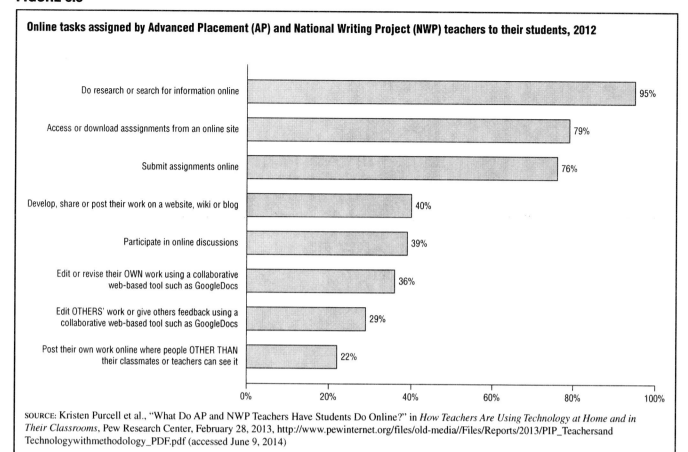

Online tasks assigned by Advanced Placement (AP) and National Writing Project (NWP) teachers to their students, 2012

Task	Percentage
Do research or search for information online	95%
Access or download assignments from an online site	79%
Submit assignments online	76%
Develop, share or post their work on a website, wiki or blog	40%
Participate in online discussions	39%
Edit or revise their OWN work using a collaborative web-based tool such as GoogleDocs	36%
Edit OTHERS' work or give others feedback using a collaborative web-based tool such as GoogleDocs	29%
Post their own work online where people OTHER THAN their classmates or teachers can see it	22%

SOURCE: Kristen Purcell et al., "What Do AP and NWP Teachers Have Students Do Online?" in *How Teachers Are Using Technology at Home and in Their Classrooms*, Pew Research Center, February 28, 2013, http://www.pewinternet.org/files/old-media//Files/Reports/2013/PIP_Teachersand Technologywithmethodology_PDF.pdf (accessed June 9, 2014)

TABLE 6.2

Student use of technology in the classroom, by grade and type of technology, 2013

Digital activity	Elementary school grades 3–5	Middle school grades 6–8	High school grades 9–12
Access class information through online portal	31%	68%	75%
Take tests online	44%	47%	52%
Use online textbooks	14%	32%	37%
Use a mobile device provided by school	25%	30%	32%
Watch teacher created videos	14%	22%	22%

SOURCE: "Table 1. Students' Use of Teacher-Facilitated Technology in the Classroom," in *The New Digital Learning Playbook: Understanding the Spectrum of Students' Activities and Aspirations*, Project Tomorrow, Speak Up, 2014, http://www.tomorrow.org/speakup/pdfs/SU13StudentsReport.pdf (accessed June 9, 2014)

By 2014 Internet use had become a dominant feature of college life. As Scott A. Peterson, Tun Aye, and Padao Yang Wheeler observe in "Internet Use and Romantic Relationships among College Students" (*North American Journal of Psychology*, vol. 16, no. 1, March 2014), the average college student spent a little over 19.5 hours per week online in 2014. Peterson, Aye, and Wheeler note that most of this time was dedicated to activities unrelated to academic work. According to the study, nearly one-third (6.3 hours per week) of all time spent online by college students in 2014 was devoted to social networking; this figure was more than double the 2.9 hours per week devoted to school work.

For male college students, relationship status appeared to have an influence on their Internet activities, according to Peterson, Aye, and Wheeler. Male students involved in a romantic relationship spent a little under four hours per week on social media sites; among male students who were not romantically involved, this figure rose to 7.2 hours a week. By comparison, female students involved in romantic relationships (6.5 hours per week) devoted roughly the same amount of time as female students who were not romantically involved (6.7 hours per week) to social networking on the Internet.

Technology and College Academics

The Internet has transformed college life from beginning to end, from the selection process undertaken by high school students considering different institutions to the employment and career services offered online to recent college graduates. In the 21st century, high school students research prospective colleges and universities online, take virtual campus and dormitory tours, and download recruitment materials and application forms. College students enroll in classes, pay fees, order books and course materials, and may even take classes and tests online. For some

FIGURE 6.6

Attitudes of Advanced Placement (AP) and National Writing Project (NWP) teachers concerning influence of the Internet on their students, 2012

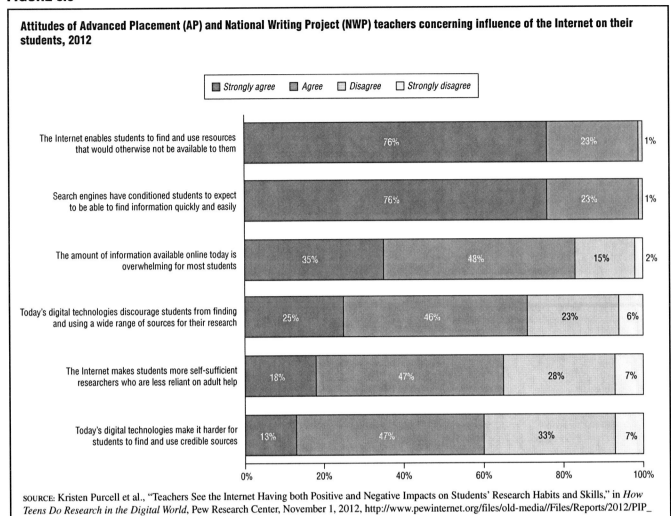

SOURCE: Kristen Purcell et al., "Teachers See the Internet Having both Positive and Negative Impacts on Students' Research Habits and Skills," in *How Teens Do Research in the Digital World*, Pew Research Center, November 1, 2012, http://www.pewinternet.org/files/old-media//Files/Reports/2012/PIP_ TeacherSurveyReportWithMethodology110112.pdf (accessed June 9, 2014)

professors, electronic textbooks (e-textbooks) have supplanted traditional textbooks as a means of assigning reading to their students. The Internet has also become a vital mode of communication between students and faculty. I. Elaine Allen and Jeff Seaman note in *Digital Faculty: Professors, Teaching and Technology, 2012* (August 2012, http://www.insidehighered.com/ sites/default/server_files/DigitalFaculty.htm) that just over three-quarters (75.1%) of professors reported that digital communication had increased their overall level of communication with their students. Allen and Seaman also find that female faculty members were somewhat more likely than male faculty to report increased digital communication with their students.

The Internet has also radically transformed the ways that university libraries allocate their financial resources. As the Publishers Communication Group reports in *Library Budget Predictions for 2013* (2013, http://www .pcgplus.com/wp-content/uploads/2013/03/Library-Budget-Predictions-for-2013_public1.pdf), in 2005 North American university and research libraries devoted just under

one-third (31.4%) of their annual budgets to electronic resources. By 2011 this figure exceeded 60%, before slipping to 59.3% in 2012. At the same time, in 2012 more than two-thirds (69%) of all journal subscriptions in North American university and research libraries were available only in electronic formats; by contrast, 16% of all journal subscriptions at North American university and research libraries were available in print-only editions. Another 15% of journals at North American university and research libraries in 2012 were available in both print and electronic versions.

The Internet and College Social Life

Since the 1990s technology has had a profound impact on everyday campus life. E-mail, the Internet, and mobile phones have transformed the way that college students communicate with each other, whether they are discussing academic coursework or simply making plans for the weekend. In particular, social networking sites such as Facebook have played an important role in shaping the social relationships of college students in the 21st

FIGURE 6.7

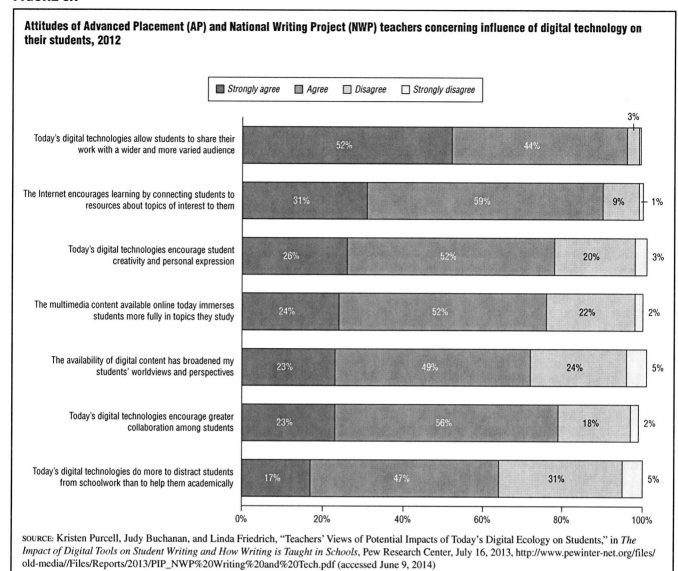

Attitudes of Advanced Placement (AP) and National Writing Project (NWP) teachers concerning influence of digital technology on their students, 2012

■ Strongly agree ▨ Agree ▨ Disagree □ Strongly disagree

Today's digital technologies allow students to share their work with a wider and more varied audience — 52% | 44% | 3%

The Internet encourages learning by connecting students to resources about topics of interest to them — 31% | 59% | 9% | 1%

Today's digital technologies encourage student creativity and personal expression — 26% | 52% | 20% | 3%

The multimedia content available online today immerses students more fully in topics they study — 24% | 52% | 22% | 2%

The availability of digital content has broadened my students' worldviews and perspectives — 23% | 49% | 24% | 5%

Today's digital technologies encourage greater collaboration among students — 23% | 56% | 18% | 2%

Today's digital technologies do more to distract students from schoolwork than to help them academically — 17% | 47% | 31% | 5%

0%   20%   40%   60%   80%   100%

SOURCE: Kristen Purcell, Judy Buchanan, and Linda Friedrich, "Teachers' Views of Potential Impacts of Today's Digital Ecology on Students," in *The Impact of Digital Tools on Student Writing and How Writing is Taught in Schools*, Pew Research Center, July 16, 2013, http://www.pewinter-net.org/files/old-media//Files/Reports/2013/PIP_NWP%20Writing%20and%20Tech.pdf (accessed June 9, 2014)

century. College students create social networking profiles for a variety of reasons. Many students view social networking sites as a way to maintain contact with old friends and meet new people. Reynol Junco of Lock Haven University finds in "In-Class Multitasking and Academic Performance" (*Computers in Human Behavior*, vol. 28, no. 6, November 2012) that in 2012 between 87% and 92% of college undergraduates used Facebook every day, compared with 73% who sent or received text messages daily. On average, students who used Facebook spent more than an hour and 40 minutes on the site each day. Whereas 34% of college students reported texting during class at least sometimes, only 13% reported using Facebook 50% or more of the time they were in class.

At times, social media can also provide college advisers with crucial insights into potential problems confronted by their student residents. As Lauren E. Kacvinsky and Megan A. Moreno report in "Facebook Use

between College Resident Advisors and Their Residents: A Mixed Method Approach" (*College Student Journal*, vol. 8, no. 1, Spring 2014), 40% of college freshmen surveyed had become friends with their resident advisers (RAs) on Facebook; according to Kacvinsky and Moreno, these students were nearly 50% more likely than their RAs to have initiated the friend request. Among the RAs interviewed by Kacvinsky and Moreno, many believed that the images and status updates posted by their residents offered important indications of potential struggles students might be facing, particularly with alcohol abuse. At the same time, RAs generally agreed that following up on potential issues in person was vital to building trusting relationships with their students.

Still, for most college students social media is primarily a means of making connections with their peers. Indeed, the desire to escape the scrutiny of parents and other adults on social media pages has led many young people to abandon Facebook and other popular social media platforms altogether. As Eilene Zimmerman writes in "A Social Network That's Just for College Students" (NYTimes.com, February 6, 2014), between 2011 and 2014 the number of teenagers using Facebook declined by 25%; during this same span, the number of Facebook users 55 years of age and older grew by 80%. According to Zimmerman, the desire to engage in social media outside the view of adults has driven many college students to new social networking platforms. One site aimed specifically at college students is Blend. First launched in 2013, Blend is a mobile app that invites college students to post photographs relating to a particular subject or theme; if a student's post attracts a certain number of "snaps" (the equivalent of "likes" on Facebook), then they earn credit toward free gift cards for certain sponsored products. As Zimmerman reports, by February 2014 Blend had attracted 50,000 users.

Another popular mobile social networking platform among college students in 2014 was Snapchat. Snapchat is an app that allows users to send timed photographs to other people in their account; once a predetermined time allotment elapses, the photograph disappears from the recipient's inbox. As Kurt Wagner notes in "Study Finds 77% of College Students Use Snapchat Daily" (Mashable.com, February 24, 2014), more than three-quarters (77%) of all college students used Snapchat at least once a day during the 2013–14 school year. According to Wagner, more than one-third (37%) of students reported that they used Snapchat as a way of expressing themselves creatively to their fellow students; 27% said that they used the social media platform primarily as a way of staying in touch, and 23% reported that they primarily used Snapchat because it was easier than texting.

DISTANCE LEARNING

Besides providing students with a host of valuable new research tools, the Internet has also made education more widely available to a greater portion of the population. In the past, people who lived in remote areas of the country, had limited access to transportation, suffered from illness or other disabilities, or were constrained by work or other obligations struggled to pursue educational opportunities. With the emergence of distance learning programs, however, students were able to take classes online from their own home. As Table 6.3 shows, during the 2009–10 academic year 55% of all public school districts in the United States offered distance learning programs for their students. Larger school districts were the most likely to offer online classes, with nearly three-quarters (74%) of districts with 10,000 students or more providing distance learning opportunities in 2009–10, compared with 51% of districts with fewer than 2,500 students.

Thomas A. Snyder and Sally A. Dillow report in *Digest of Education Statistics 2012* (December 2013, http://nces.ed.gov/pubs2014/2014015.pdf) that in 2002–03 a total of 317,070 students in kindergarten to 12th grade were enrolled in distance learning courses nationwide; by 2009–10 this number had risen to 1.8 million, an increase of 473%. High school students (1.3 million) accounted for the large majority of distance learning enrollments in 2009–10, followed by combined elementary and high school students (234,460), middle school students (154,970), and elementary school students (78,040). By region, the highest proportion of school districts offering distance learning in 2009–10 was in the Southeast, where 78% of all schools offered distance education courses; by comparison, only 39% of school districts in the Northeast offered distance learning opportunities to their students.

Distance learning programs also became widespread at colleges and universities in the early 21st century. Indeed, for some students taking online courses was a more attractive option than attending classes in person. There are many reasons students prefer distance learning to traditional college course offerings. For some, geographical distance or scheduling conflicts make it difficult to attend traditional classes, and online courses offer far greater flexibility and convenience. Figure 6.8 provides a breakdown of college students enrolled exclusively in distance learning courses in fall 2012. As Figure 6.8 shows, more than half (58%) of all students enrolled in private, four-year, for-profit institutions took only online classes in the fall of 2012. By comparison, 10% of students enrolled in either private, four-year, nonprofit institutions or two-year public institutions were enrolled exclusively in distance learning classes that term. Only 2% of students enrolled in two-year, private, nonprofit colleges were enrolled exclusively in distance learning courses in fall 2012.

Figure 6.9 offers an overview of distance learning participation among postbaccalaureate students in fall 2012. Postbaccalaureate students are those who continue taking courses at the undergraduate level even after completing their college degrees. As Figure 6.9 shows, 70% of all postbaccalaureate students enrolled at degree-granting postsecondary institutions took no online classes in the fall of 2012. These percentages were highest for students enrolled at private nonprofit (77%) and public (76%) institutions. Among postbaccalaureate students enrolled at private, for-profit institutions, on the other hand, only 18% took no distance learning classes in the fall of 2012. Among postbaccalaureate students enrolled exclusively in distance learning classes that term, the highest proportion were enrolled at private, for-profit postsecondary institutions, where 77% of all postbaccalaureate students were taking online courses exclusively.

TABLE 6.3

Percentage of public school districts with students enrolled in distance-learning courses, with enrollment numbers, by instruction level and select district characteristics, 2002–03, 2004–05, 2009–10

District characteristic	Percent of districts enrolling distance education students	Number of enrollments in technology-based distance education courses,[a] by instructional level				
		All instructional levels	Elementary schools	Middle or junior high schools	High schools	Combined or ungraded schools[b]
1	2	3	4	5	6	7
2002–03						
Total	36	317,070	2,780!	6,390	214,140	93,760
District enrollment size						
Less than 2,500	37	116,300	‡	1,250!	72,730	42,240!
2,500 to 9,999	32	82,370	230!	1,870!	44,170	36,110
10,000 or more	50	118,390	2,480!	3,270	97,240	‡
Region						
Northeast	21	41,950!	100!	‡	17,300	‡
Southeast	45	59,240	‡	2,530	50,640	4,680
Central	46	106,690	940!	1,050!	59,110	45,590
West	32	109,190	350!	2,620	87,090	19,130!
Poverty concentration						
Less than 10 percent	33	75,740	‡	2,020	55,670	17,470!
10 to 19 percent	42	95,510	‡	1,830	78,680	13,560
20 percent or more	42	86,110	760!	2,540!	75,930	6,880
2004–05						
Total	37	506,950	12,540!	15,150	309,630	169,630!
District enrollment size						
Less than 2,500	37	210,200	610!	‡	103,190	‡
2,500 to 9,999	35	102,730	‡	2,570	48,420	45,080
10,000 or more	50	193,440	5,280!	6,520	157,440	24,210
Region						
Northeast	22	108,300!	570!	‡	16,860	‡
Southeast	46	112,830	‡	5,030	89,800	16,090
Central	45	128,650	‡	2,130!	70,450	46,190!
West	35	157,180	200!	4,110!	132,520	20,350!
Poverty concentration						
Less than 10 percent	35	112,320	‡	4,070	80,150	‡
10 to 19 percent	42	151,050	‡	4,800	124,540	19,700
20 percent or more	43	106,610	‡	6,280!	78,590	21,340
2009–10						
Total	55	1,816,390	78,040!	154,970	1,348,920	‡
District enrollment size						
Less than 2,500	51	509,030!	‡	‡	408,030!	6,570!
2,500 to 9,999	66	579,250!	‡	23,960!	312,130	‡
10,000 or more	74	728,110	11,540	77,750	628,760	10,060
Metropolitan status						
City	37	653,660!	‡	40,400!	405,740	‡
Suburban	47	527,250	22,900!	62,210	434,260	7,880
Town	67	306,840!	‡	‡	246,850!	9,310!
Rural	59	328,640	‡	15,360	262,070	‡
Region						
Northeast	39	77,670	‡	4,970	71,330	‡
Southeast	78	518,770	12,070!	57,500	443,770	5,440!
Central	62	697,140!	37,920!	‡	416,550	‡
West	51	522,810	‡	41,620	417,270	36,510!
Poverty concentration						
Less than 10 percent	54	287,680	‡	12,620	231,890	‡
10 to 19 percent	56	1,009,290	23,540!	97,220	682,380	‡
20 percent or more	56	519,420	‡	‡	434,640	5,750!

Allen and Seaman explain in *Digital Faculty* that faculty and administrators at colleges and universities identified numerous positive benefits that are associated with online education. According to the report, roughly 90% of administrators and nearly 75% of faculty reported feeling more excitement than fear about the potential of online courses to increase the amount of data related to teaching and learning. A majority of both administrators and faculty also felt more excitement than fear about the expansion of hybrid models of education that incorporate both in-class and online coursework (92.9% and 71.1%, respectively), about the prospect of libraries focusing on

TABLE 6.3

Percentage of public school districts with students enrolled in distance-learning courses, with enrollment numbers, by instruction level and select district characteristics, 2002–03, 2004–05, 2009–10 [CONTINUED]

!Interpret data with caution.
‡Reporting standards not met.
aBased on students regularly enrolled in the districts. Enrollments may include duplicated counts of students, since districts were instructed to count a student enrolled in multiple courses for each course in which he or she was enrolled.
bCombined or ungraded schools are those in which the grades offered in the school span both elementary and secondary grades or that are not divided into grade levels.
Note: Percentages are based on unrounded numbers. For the 2002–03 FRSS study sample, there were 3 cases for which district enrollment size was missing and 112 cases for which poverty concentration was missing. For the 2004–05 FRSS study sample, there were 7 cases for which district enrollment size was missing and 103 cases for which poverty concentration was missing. Detail may not sum to totals because of rounding or missing data.

SOURCE: Thomas D. Snyder and Sally A. Dillow, "Table 121. Percentage of Public School Districts with Students Enrolled in Technology-Based Distance Education Courses and Number of Enrollments in Such Courses, by Instructional Level and District Characteristics: 2002–03, 2004–05, and 2009–10," in *Digest of Education Statistics 2012*, U.S. Department of Education, Institute of Education Statistics, National Center for Education Statistics, December 2013, http://nces.ed.gov/pubs2014/2014015.pdf (accessed June 9, 2014)

FIGURE 6.8

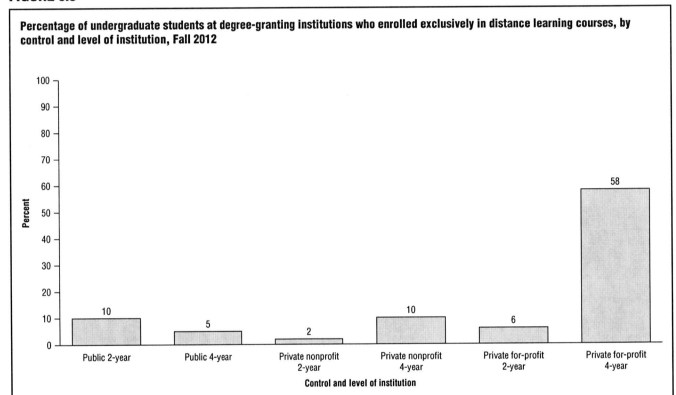

Percentage of undergraduate students at degree-granting institutions who enrolled exclusively in distance learning courses, by control and level of institution, Fall 2012

SOURCE: Grace Kena et al., "Figure 5. Percentage of Undergraduate Students at Degree-Granting Postsecondary Institutions Who Participated Exclusively in Distance Education Courses, by Control and Level of Institution: Fall 2012," in *The Condition of Education 2014*, U.S. Department of Education, National Center for Education Statistics, May 2014, http://nces.ed.gov/pubs2014/2014083.pdf (accessed June 9, 2014)

digital rather than on print collections (87.7% and 70.6%), and about the potential of online instruction to allow faculty to devote more time to coaching students individually (89% and 68.7%). A small minority of administrators and faculty members (19.3% and 12%, respectively) also expressed excitement about the prospect of expanding for-profit education through online course offerings.

Still, Allen and Seaman report in *Conflicted: Faculty and Online Education, 2012* (June 2012, http://www.insidehighered.com/sites/default/server_files/files/ IHE-BSRG-Conflict.pdf) that faculty at institutions of higher learning also experienced anxiety at the prospect of the continued growth of online education in the 21st century. In the report, Allen and Seaman examine attitudes of higher education faculty toward the expansion of online education, separated according to academic discipline, tenure status, part-time or full-time status, and experience. Among academic disciplines, only the professions and applied sciences (e.g., medicine, law, accounting, and engineering) contained a majority (55.5%) of faculty members who expressed more excitement than fear about

FIGURE 6.9

Percentage of postbaccalaureate students at degree-granting institutions who enrolled in distance learning courses, by number of courses and control of institution, Fall 2012

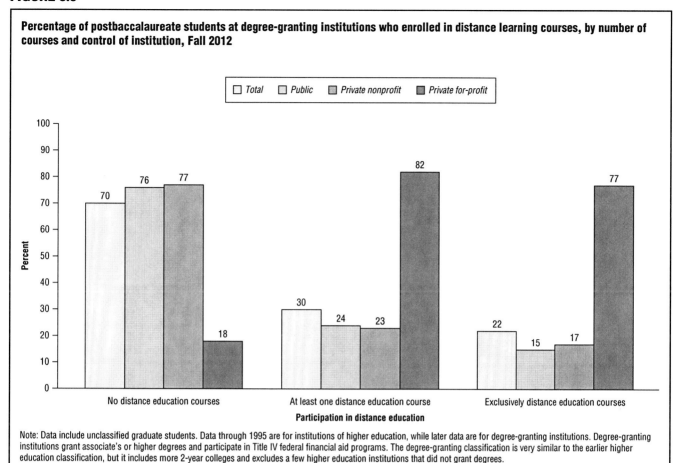

Note: Data include unclassified graduate students. Data through 1995 are for institutions of higher education, while later data are for degree-granting institutions. Degree-granting institutions grant associate's or higher degrees and participate in Title IV federal financial aid programs. The degree-granting classification is very similar to the earlier higher education classification, but it includes more 2-year colleges and excludes a few higher education institutions that did not grant degrees.

SOURCE: Grace Kena et al., "Figure 4. Percentage of Postbaccalaureate Students Enrolled in Degree-Granting Postsecondary Institutions Who Took Distance Education Courses, by Control of Institution: Fall 2012," in *The Condition of Education 2014*, U.S. Department of Education, National Center for Education Statistics, May 2014, http://nces.ed.gov/pubs2014/2014083.pdf (accessed June 9, 2014)

the growth of online learning in the 21st century. According to Allen and Seaman, instructors in the social sciences (36.2%) and humanities and arts (34.5%) were the least likely to feel more excitement than fear about online education's future growth. A slim majority (50.7%) of nontenure track professors expressed more excitement than fear about the expansion of online education, compared with 35.4% of faculty who were tenure-tracked but not yet tenured and 34.8% of tenured faculty members.

Support for online courses among faculty varied between academic disciplines in 2012 as reported by Allen and Seaman in *Conflicted: Faculty and Online Education, 2012*. Nearly 74% of faculty who taught courses in the professions and applied sciences had recommended online classes to their students, compared with roughly 60% of faculty in mathematics, computer science, and the social sciences and just over half of faculty teaching courses in arts, humanities, and the natural sciences.

Table 6.4 offers a breakdown of online course enrollment among all adults in October 2013, by select demographic characteristics. As Table 6.4 shows, young adults

between the ages of 18 and 29 years (8%) were the most likely age group to be enrolled in an online class in 2013. Adults living in the West (8%) and the South (5%) were more likely than those living in the Midwest (3%) and East (3%) to be taking an online course that year.

Enrollment in distance learning remained relatively small in comparison to the overall adult population, but many people still saw clear advantages to online educational opportunities in 2013. For example, more adults believed that a student could take advantage of a broader selection of courses through distance learning (33%) than through classroom-based courses (23%); 39% believed that distance learning and traditional classrooms provided the same breadth of course offerings in 2013. (See Table 6.5.) More adults also thought a student could get better value for their money through distance learning (33%) than classroom-based education (27%).

CHEATING AND HIGH TECHNOLOGY

Cheating is one of the biggest problems facing academia and includes any instance in which a student

TABLE 6.4

Percentage of adults currently enrolled in an online class, by sex, age, race, and geographical region, October 2013

ARE YOU CURRENTLY TAKING AN ONLINE COURSE, OR NOT?

	Yes	No
	%	%
U.S. adults	5	95
Men	6	94
Women	4	96
18 to 29 years	8	92
30 to 49 years	5	95
50 to 64 years	4	96
65 and older	2	98
White	4	96
Nonwhite	6	94
East	3	97
Midwest	3	97
South	5	95
West	8	92

SOURCE: Lydia Saad, Brandon Busteed, and Mitchell Ogisi, "Are You Currently Enrolled in an Online Course, Or Not?" in *In U.S., Online Education Rated Best for Value and Options*, The Gallup Organization, October 15, 2013, http://www.gallup.com/poll/165425/online-education-rated-best-value-options.aspx (accessed June 9, 2014). Copyright © 2014 Gallup, Inc. All rights reserved. The content is used with permission; however, Gallup retains all rights of republication.

TABLE 6.5

Attitudes toward online education, by select characteristics, 2013

[Americans' views of online education vs. traditional classroom-based education]

	Online better	The same	Online worse	Net better
	%	%	%	
Providing a wide range of options for curriculum	33	39	23	+10
Providing good value for the money	33	34	27	+6
Providing a format most students can succeed in	23	42	30	−7
Providing instruction tailored to each individual	23	31	41	−18
Providing high-quality instruction from well-qualified instructors	15	37	43	−28
Providing rigorous testing and grading that can be trusted	11	39	45	−34
Providing a degree that will be viewed positively by employers	13	33	49	−36

SOURCE: Lydia Saad, Brandon Busteed, and Mitchell Ogisi, "Americans' Views of Online Education vs. Traditional Classroom-Based Education," in *In U.S., Online Education Rated Best for Value and Options*, The Gallup Organization, October 15, 2013, http://www.gallup.com/poll/165425/online-education-rated-best-value-options.aspx (accessed June 9, 2014). Copyright © 2014 Gallup, Inc. All rights reserved. The content is used with permission; however, Gallup retains all rights of republication.

breaks the rules for an assignment or test to gain an advantage over fellow classmates. A specific type of cheating known as plagiarism occurs when a student submits someone else's work as his or her own. Plagiarism itself has several forms, including purchasing a previously written paper, copying sentences or ideas from an original source document without proper attribution, or paying someone else to complete the work. In June 2005 Donald L. McCabe of Rutgers University, the founder of the International Center for Academic Integrity (http://www.academicintegrity.org), published the results of a three-year survey of 50,000 college students at 60 campuses across the country. Of those who admitted cheating in 2005, a quarter said they had cheated seriously on a test and half said they had cheated seriously on a written assignment. The Josephson Institute of Ethics states in *2012 Report Card on the Ethics of American Youth, Installment 1: Honesty and Integrity* (November 20, 2012, http://charactercounts.org/pdf/reportcard/2012/ReportCard-2012-DataTables-HonestyIntegrityCheating.pdf) that nearly one-third (32%) of high school students had copied a document from the Internet for a class assignment in 2012. The institute shows that male students (37%) were more likely to have plagiarized from the Internet than female students (27%). Of those surveyed, 52% admitted to having cheated on a test at least once.

The Internet and other types of information technology have only served to fuel the cheating epidemic in the United States. Phones with text messaging allow students the opportunity to communicate with outsiders or others in class during a test. Companies that specialize in writing papers for students, commonly known as "paper mills," can deliver papers discreetly to students via e-mail. In general, the Internet provides an endless source of documents and papers from which students might copy material. Catching plagiarism on the Internet, however, involves combing through countless articles and websites. The issue of plagiarism from web sources is further complicated by the fact that the Internet has obscured the distinction between what information requires attribution and what is public knowledge.

To catch plagiarizers, some schools are using high-technology online services such as Turnitin.com. This online service receives papers from students and teachers and scans them into a database. The papers are then checked against more than 9 billion web pages, previously submitted student papers, and a number of books and encyclopedias. Turnitin.com (2014, http://turnitin.com/en_us/about-us/our-company) indicates that it handled more than 100 million papers in 2013; on certain peak days that year the service processed 600,000 papers.

As of 2014, Princeton University and many other leading schools were still not using antiplagiarism services, holding to the belief that their campuses did not foster a culture in which cheating is acceptable. Paul Craft writes in "Some Schools Resist Anti-cheating Software" (*Washington Monthly College Guide*, July 13, 2010) that Emily Aronson, a spokesperson for Princeton, asserted that even though the university had considered implementing Turnitin software, it ultimately decided that "adopting this kind of software sends a message to our students that is not one that we want to send. We don't want to presume that they aren't approaching their work honestly. We want to presume that they're behaving with integrity." Regardless, cheating remains a serious problem even at the nation's most elite institutions.

This adherence to principles suffered a serious challenge in 2012, after details emerged concerning a major plagiarism scandal at Harvard University. According to Hana N. Rouse and Justin C. Worland in "Faust Addresses Cheating Scandal" (*Harvard Crimson*, October 4, 2012), 125 students enrolled in a government course were accused of plagiarizing or illegally collaborating on a take-home exam. Citing the university president Drew Faust's response to the incident, Rouse and Worland report that the scandal "sparked an important discussion about cheating in higher education" during the fall of 2012, both at Harvard and other Ivy League institutions. As Richard Pérez-Peña reports in "Students Disciplined in Harvard Scandal" (NYTimes.com, February 1, 2013), in early 2013 Harvard forced 70 students involved in the scandal to withdraw from school. Pérez-Peña notes that in an average year 17 Harvard students are dismissed from the university for academic dishonesty.

CHAPTER 7
INFORMATION TECHNOLOGY AND GOVERNMENT

Since the 1990s government bodies in the United States at the local, state, and federal levels have made a concerted effort to use the Internet and other types of information technology (IT) to streamline their operations and dealings with the public. Much of this effort has been focused on making information available via the Internet. Local and municipal governments post meeting minutes and agendas online. States have erected websites that allow citizens to renew registrations, obtain licenses, and track legislation online. The federal government has brought myriad services and information to the Internet, allowing Americans to do everything from applying for a patent online to reviewing the holdings of the Smithsonian Institution. The American public has taken advantage of these services in large numbers. Aaron Smith of the Pew Research Center reports in *Government Online* (April 27, 2010, http://pewinternet.org/~/media//Files/Reports/2010/PIP_Government_Online_2010_with_topline.pdf) that in 2010, 82% of all Internet users had visited a government website in the previous 12 months; 48% had looked for information about a specific policy or issue, and 46% had visited government websites to learn what sort of services a particular agency provides.

Various government entities have employed other forms of IT to streamline services outside of cyberspace. After the hotly contested 2000 presidential race between Governor George W. Bush (1946–; R-TX) and Vice President Albert Gore Jr. (1948–; D-TN), state election commissions replaced many of the aging mechanical voting systems with electronic touch screen and optical scanning systems. These systems made the voting booth accessible for many disabled people and presumably led to more accurate ballot totals in elections. Advances in communications and detection systems have also given rise to networks along U.S. highways that monitor traffic and weather conditions on a real-time basis. For example, in 1999 the federal government designated 511 as the universal phone number by which people can access these systems to obtain details on traffic and weather in their area. In addition, technology has enabled the federal government to undertake ambitious and far-reaching improvements to the nation's infrastructure. For example, the Energy Independence and Security Act of 2007 included a provision calling for the creation of a smart grid, with the aim of streamlining the transmission and distribution of electricity throughout the United States.

American citizens are constantly interacting with their government online. According to the government IT firm MeriTalk in *Uncle Sam at Your Service: The 2011 Federal Customer Experience Study* (August 29, 2011, http://www.meritalk.com/pdfs/MeriTalk_2011_Federal_Customer_Experience_Report_082911_Final.pdf), 44% of Americans surveyed had visited a federal government website to find information about government programs or benefits between 2010 and 2011, and 41% had gone online to download a government form. By comparison, 34% of respondents had contacted a federal agency by phone, and 24% had visited a federal office in person. Of those Americans who interacted with the federal government via a website in 2011, approximately two-thirds (67%) described the experience as either "good" or "excellent." Meanwhile, roughly half of Americans who interacted with federal agencies in person (52%), via e-mail (51%), or over the phone (51%) reported their experience as being "good" or "excellent." At the same time, improvements in information technology have also had a profound impact on the work lives of government employees. As MeriTalk reports in *Feds on the Go: Network Needs for Maximum Mobility* (August 19, 2013, http://www.meritalk.com/fedsonthego), in 2013, 70% of federal employees reported that mobile technology had transformed the way that they approached their jobs. Of these, 45% stated that remote connectivity had made them more efficient, and 28% noted that remote access had led to more frequent collaboration with their colleagues.

FEDERAL GOVERNMENT AND INTERNET TECHNOLOGIES

Since the early 1990s hundreds of federal government websites have been established on the Internet. In the beginning each agency or division developed its website in a unique way, offering varying levels of accessibility to the user. Some were useful and informative. For example, in 1994 the U.S. Census Bureau launched the first U.S. government World Wide Web portal. From the start, hundreds of U.S. census records from decades past could be easily viewed on the website.

The Internal Revenue Service (IRS) also maintained a useful site. In 1997 the IRS began allowing people to download tax forms and file their taxes electronically. Nearly a million tax returns were filed from home computers that first year. Filing taxes online quickly became one of the most popular forms of Internet contact with the federal government. The IRS (May 22, 2014, http://www.irs.gov/uac/Newsroom/Filing-Season-Statistics-for-Week-Ending-May-16,-2014) reports that during the 2013 filing year, as of May 16, 2014, it had received 117.8 million individual tax returns online. This was a 3% increase over the number of e-filings during the same period in the previous year (114.4 million) and represented 86% of the total number of individual returns received in 2014.

However, many other government websites, such as the National Oceanic and Atmospheric Administration website, offered citizens little in the way of practical information or accessibility. By the late 1990s profit-driven commercial websites far outshone most government websites in both appearance and functionality. Seeing the untapped potential of many government websites, Congress and the White House put through a series of initiatives and laws to make federal government websites and services more accessible to the American people.

Government Paperwork Elimination Act

One of the first major congressional acts designed to improve the functionality of government websites was the Government Paperwork Elimination Act (GPEA) of 1998. The GPEA required that by October 2003 each government agency should provide people, wherever possible, with the option of submitting information or transacting business electronically. The act mandated that forms and documents involved in government transactions be placed online and that electronic signature systems be put in place to replace paper signatures. For example, companies that made electronic components for the National Aeronautics and Space Administration (NASA) were required to have the option to bid for contracts, complete all paperwork with regard to sale of the merchandise, and receive payment without having to use paper. Similarly, individuals were to have the option

to apply for a patent online or to fill out a U.S. census survey on the Internet. FedForms.gov was created as a portal to all electronic forms that are available from the federal government, and by 2014 it cataloged thousands of forms for more than 170 agencies.

E-Government Act

In 2001 President Bush initiated the President's Management Agenda, which contained a number of initiatives that were intended to expand the role of the Internet in the federal government beyond the scope of the GPEA. Many of these initiatives were made law in 2002, when Congress passed the E-Government Act. The E-Government Act was a broad-reaching piece of legislation that was designed to streamline government websites and provide a wide range of services to the American people via the Internet. The act established the E-Government Fund to provide money for agencies that could not afford IT and website development. In *FY 2013 Annual Report to Congress: E-Government Act Implementation* (March 1, 2014, http://www.whitehouse.gov/sites/default/files/omb/assets/egov_docs/fy_2013_e-government_act_implementation_report_final_03_01_2014_0.pdf), the Office of Management and Budget (OMB) notes that in 2013, $6.2 million of the fund was dedicated to promoting greater transparency, in large part through the implementation of the Federal Funding Accountability and Transparency Act (FFATA) of 2006. Among the online services funded by this initiative are USASpending.gov, which provides citizens with information concerning federal spending and contracts, and Performance.gov, a site dedicated to promoting federal initiatives that are aimed at improving government accountability and efficiency. In addition, nearly $3.8 million of the fund was devoted to improving cloud computing and security protections within the federal IT system.

Many of these goals established standards for government websites that were already in operation. Existing government websites were required to provide links to organization policy and hierarchy on the front page and to present their information in a way that was easily searchable. Many agencies with multiple websites, such as NASA or the U.S. Environmental Protection Agency, were asked to consolidate their sites so that all the information for the public could be reached within a few clicks of the agency's main page. The E-Government Act also supported new websites that were designed to provide basic services for American citizens. The site FirstGov.gov was deemed the official portal for all federal government websites. FirstGov.gov, which began operating in February 2000, provided links to more than 22,000 federal and state websites as well as a hierarchical index of all government organizations. In January 2007 FirstGov.gov was renamed USA.gov; three years later the administration of President Barack Obama (1961–)

launched an updated version of USA.gov that featured a new design and a wider range of applications, including portals offering services for both citizens (http://www.usa.gov/Citizen/Services.shtml) and federal employees (http://www.usa.gov/Federal-Employees/Online-Services.shtml).

Another website that the E-Government Act officially authorized was Regulations.gov, which was launched in January 2003. Regulations.gov lists pending regulations that are proposed by government agencies and allows citizens and nongovernmental agencies to comment on the regulations. The government agencies are then required to review the comments on Regulations.gov before putting a regulation into effect. This process provides the American people with the ability to influence government regulation, a privilege that was previously available primarily to organized lobbyists.

As a result of these White House initiatives and congressional acts supporting e-government, federal agencies have come to offer many valuable online services to Americans. For example, the Environmental Protection Agency oversees the web portal My Environment (http://www.epa.gov/myenvironment) that enables citizens to search for information about environmental issues such as air quality and water conditions, report violations, and find ways to communicate and collaborate with other environmental activists in their area. In December 2008 the Social Security Administration launched an online application system for retirees aimed at streamlining the benefits process for the nation's seniors.

In January 2011 President Obama signed the GPRA Modernization Act. The law effectively updated the 1993 Government Performance and Results Act, which attempted to make the management of government programs more efficient. Overseen by the director of the OMB, the GPRA Modernization Act requires government agencies to make information about programs, strategic objectives, and other aspects of their work more accessible to Congress and the public, both by improving their websites and by publishing all plans and reports in "searchable, machine-readable" formats.

In April 2011, in recognition of the increasing importance of the Internet as a means for American citizens to interact with the federal government, President Obama issued Executive Order 13571, "Streamlining Service Delivery and Improving Customer Service" (April 27, 2011, http://www.whitehouse.gov/the-press-office/2011/04/27/executive-order-streamlining-service-delivery-and-improving-customer-ser), in which he called on government agencies to focus on developing "lower-cost, self-service options accessed by the Internet or mobile phone and improved processes that deliver services faster and more responsively." In order to create greater overall transparency and access in the sharing of government

information, on May 9, 2013, President Obama issued an executive order entitled *Making Open and Machine Readable the New Default for Government Information* (May 9, 2013, http://www.whitehouse.gov/sites/default/files/omb/memoranda/2013/m-13-13.pdf), which intended to "institutionalize the principles of effective information management at each stage of the information's life cycle to promote interoperability and openness."

SATISFACTION WITH GOVERNMENT WEBSITES. Even though some dissatisfaction exists with federal government websites, the American people seem to be happy with the improvements in e-government. Since 2003 the U.S. government has tracked websites in its annual American Customer Service Index. This index measures how satisfied the American people are with various aspects of the federal government. Table 7.1 shows that, out of the websites on the survey that facilitated transactions or e-commerce with the government during the fourth quarter of 2013, users were happiest with two Social Security Administration sites: iClaim (http://www.socialsecurity.gov/applyonline), which helps facilitate the Social Security application process, and the Retirement Estimator (http://www.ssa.gov/estimator), a site that is designed to help retirees calculate their potential benefits. The lowest score in the survey (56 out of a possible 100 points) was received by FEMA.gov, the home page of the Federal Emergency Management Agency (FEMA).

Overall, satisfaction with government websites rose considerably between 2003 and 2013, from a low of 69 points (out of a possible 100 points) during the fourth quarter in 2003 to 74.6 points during the fourth quarter in 2013. (See Figure 7.1.) Among departmental portals or main sites, the National Cancer Institute website (Cancer.gov) scored highest, with a satisfaction rating of 84 points out of 100, followed by the Centers for Disease Control and Prevention (CDC.gov) and the U.S. Citizenship and Immigration Services Resource Center Español (http://www.uscis.gov/portal/site/uscis-es), each with satisfaction ratings of 83 out of a possible 100 points. (See Table 7.2.) Among government employment portals, the Central Intelligence Agency recruitment page (CIA.gov/careers) scored highest, with a score of 84 points out of 100. (See Table 7.3.)

One notable government IT failure occurred in October 2013, when the Obama administration unveiled HealthCare.gov, the enrollment portal for Americans seeking health insurance through the Patient Protection and Affordable Care Act of 2010 (often informally referred to as "Obamacare"). As Andrew Couts writes in "We Paid over $500 Million for the Obamacare Sites and All We Got Was This Lousy 404" (DigitalTrends.com, October 8, 2013), the government devoted roughly $363 million over a three-year period to make the website

TABLE 7.1

American Consumer Satisfaction Index (ACSI) scores for e-government websites, fourth quarter 2013

[Out of 100 points]

Department	Website	Satisfaction
Average		74.6
SSA	SSA iClaim—socialsecurity.gov/applyonline	90
SSA	SSA Retirement Estimator—ssa.gov/estimator	90
SSA	Extra Help with Medicare Prescription Drug Plan Costs—socialsecurity.gov/i1020	89
HHS	MedlinePlus—medlineplus.gov	88
HHS	MedlinePlus en español—medlineplus.gov/esp	87
SSA	SSA-my Social Security	87
HHS	National Women's Health Information Center (NWHIC) main website—womenshealth.gov	86
SSA	Social Security Business Services Online—ssa.gov/bso/bsowelcome.htm	86
SEC	U.S. Securities and Exchange Commission—investor.gov	85
HHS	National Cancer Institute main website—cancer.gov	84
HHS	National Library of Medicine AIDS information—aidsinfo.nih.gov	84
CIA	Recruitment website—cia.gov/careers	84
SSA	Social Security Internet Disability Report—ssa.gov/applyfordisability	84
Boards, Commissions, and Committees	American Battle Monuments Commission—abmc.gov	83
HHS	CDC main website—cdc.gov	83
HHS	HHS Healthy People—Healthypeople.gov	83
HHS	National Cancer Institute Site en Español—cancer.gov/espanol	83
HHS	NIDDK—www2.niddk.nih.gov	83
HHS	NIH-Senior Health—nihseniorhealth.gov	83
DHS	U.S. Citizenship and Immigration Services Español—uscis.gov/portal/site/uscis-es	83
DHS	U.S. Citizenship and Immigration Services Resource Center—uscis.gov/portal/site/uscis/citizenship	83
NASA	NASA main website—nasa.gov	82
DOS	U.S. Department of State Bureau of Educational and Cultural Affairs alumni website—https://alumni.state.gov	82
Treasury	U.S. Mint Online Catalog and main website—usmint.gov	82
DOD	DoD Navy—navy.mil	81
DOJ	National Institute of Justice—nij.gov	81
HHS	National Institutes of Health, National Institute on Aging—nia.nih.gov/health	81
HHS	SAMHSA Store—store.samhsa.gov	81
DOJ	FBI main website—fbi.gov	80
HHS	National Institute of Dental and Craniofacial Research—nidcr.nih.gov	80
HHS	NIAMS public website—niams.nih.gov	80
DOS	Recruitment website—careers.state.gov	80
DHS	Federal Emergency Management Agency Ready Campaign—ready.gov	79
FTC	FTC OnGuardOnline—onguardonline.gov	79
HHS	Girls Health—girlshealth.gov	79
PBGC	MyPAA—https://egov.pbgc.gov/mypaa	79
DOS	Bureau of Consular Affairs—travel.state.gov	78
PBGC	MyPBA—https://egov.pbgc.gov/mypba	78
DOC	National Geodetic Society, National Oceanic and Atmospheric Administration website—ngs.noaa.gov	78
HHS	National Library of Medicine main website—nlm.nih.gov	78
DOI	National Park Service main website—nps.gov	78
HHS	U.S. Food and Drug Administration main website—fda.gov	78
DOL	Bureau of Labor Statistics—bls.gov	77
DOL	Department of Labor Job Listings—doors.dol.gov	77
HHS	National Institute of Allergy and Infectious Diseases—www3.niaid.nih.gov	77
SSA	SSA iAppeals - Diability Appeal—ssa.gov	77
NIH	The National Center for Complementary and Alternative Medicine (NCCAM)—nccam.nih.gov	77
NRC	U.S. Nuclear Regulatory Commission website—nrc.gov	77
HHS	Agency for Healthcare Research and Quality—ahrq.gov	76
DOD	DOD Pentagon Channel—pentagonchannel.mil	76
DOJ	National Criminal Justice Reference Service—ncjrs.gov	76
SBA	SBA main website—sba.gov	76
DOI	U.S. Geological Survey—usgs.gov	76
HHS	U.S. Preventative Services Task Force—uspreventiveservicestaskforce.org	76
DOS	Department of State blog website—blogs.state.gov	75
DOD	DoD Air Force—af.mil	75
USDA	ERS main website—ers.usda.gov	75
GAO	GAO main public website—gao.gov	75
PBGC	U.S. PBGC main website—pbgc.gov	75
NIST	National Institute for Standards and Technology main website—nist.gov	74
USDA	Recreation One-Stop—recreation.gov	74
DOT	U.S. Department of Transportation—fhwa.dot.gov	74
DOD	Department of Defense portal—defense.gov	73

Agencies scoring 80+

operational by its official launch date of October 1, 2013. In spite of this considerable investment, the portal's launch was marred by numerous technical problems experienced by users, including repeated system shutdowns. According to Couts, the website's problems were primarily related to "poorly written code," which left the site unprepared to process the massive volume of applications filed following its launch. At the same time, as Tom Cohen notes in

TABLE 7.1

American Consumer Satisfaction Index (ACSI) scores for e-government websites, fourth quarter 2013 [CONTINUED]

[Out of 100 points]

Department	Website	Satisfaction
DOD	DoD Marines—marines.mil	73
DOT	Federal Aviation Administration—faa.gov	73
GSA	GSA main website—gsa.gov	73
Treasury	Making Home Affordable—makinghomeaffordable.gov	73
HHS	National Library of Medicine Clinical Trials website—clinicaltrials.gov	73
DHS	U.S. Citizenship and Immigration Services—uscis.gov/portal/site/uscis	73
SEC	U.S. Securities and Exchange Commission—sec.gov	73
FDIC	FDIC main website—fdic.gov	72
Treasury	Financial Stability—financialstability.gov	72
FTC	FTC main website—ftc.gov	72
OPM	Recruitment website—usajobs.gov	72
DHS	Department of Homeland Security main website—dhs.gov	71
HHS	SAMHSA website—samhsa.gov	71
FTC	FTC Complaint Assistant website—ftccomplaintassistant.gov	70
GSA	GSA Auctions—gsaauctions.gov	70
SSA	Social Security Online: Frequently Asked Questions—ssa-custhelp.ssa.gov	70
ITC	U.S. International Trade Commission main website—usitc.gov	70
FDIC	FDIC Applications—www2.fdic.gov	69
EPA	U.S. Environmental Protection Agency—epa.gov	69
DOC	BEA main website—bea.gov	68
HHS	HHS National Health Information Center—Healthfinder.gov	67
NARA	NARA main public website—archives.gov	67
Treasury	Treasury main website—treasury.gov	67
DOC	U.S. Census Bureau main website—census.gov	67
DOC	U.S. Patent and Trade Office—uspto.gov	67
DOS	Department of State main website—state.gov	66
DHS	U.S. Citizenship and Immigration Services—uscis.gov/e-verify	66
DOT	Federal Railroad Administration main website—fra.dot.gov	65
USDA	FSIS main website—fsis.usda.gov	65
Treasury	IRS main website—irs.gov	65
SSA	Social Security Online (Main Website)—socialsecurity.gov	65
VA	VA Main website—va.gov and myhealthva.gov	65
DOT	DOT Research and Innovative Technology Administration website—rita.dot.gov	64
USDA	Forest Service main website—fs.usda.gov	64
Treasury	USTTB website—ttb.gov	64
HHS	Health Resources and Services Administration main website—hrsa.gov	63
USDA	NRCS website—nrcs.usda.gov	63
GSA	Official Site to Buy U.S. Government Property—govsales.gov	62
DOD	TRICARE—tricare.mil	62
DOT	Federal Motor Carrier Safety Administration main website—fmcsa.dot.gov	60
HHS	HHS—grants.gov	60
DOE	U.S. Department of Education—ed.gov	60
DOL	Disability—Disability.gov	59
Treasury	TreasuryDirect—treasurydirect.gov	57
DHS	Federal Emergency Management Agency main website—fema.gov	56

SOURCE: "Figure 2. Q4 2013 E-Government Satisfaction Scores," in *The ForeSee E-Government Satisfaction Index (Q4 2013)*, copyright ForeSee, February 2014, http://www.foresee.com/research-white-papers/_downloads/e-gov-q4-2013-foresee.pdf (accessed June 5, 2014)

"Contractors Blame Government for Obamacare Website Woes" (CNN.com, October 25, 2013), contractors hired to build the portal cited a lack of adequate testing in the weeks leading up to the launch for the website's failure.

Government Regulation

The federal government has passed few laws that are designed to control Internet commerce or content compared with other broadcasting media. The Federal Communications Commission (FCC), which regulates all television and radio content, treats the Internet more like print media than like broadcast media. Unless a major law is being violated, people can publish all manner of pornography, illicit writing, and misleading information on the Internet without fear of repercussion. Activities that are illegal in many states or the United States as a whole, such as purchasing Cuban cigars, can be done online with little fear of prosecution. In addition, most purchases made on the Internet were not subject to local sales tax as of 2014, and states and municipalities were forbidden by the Internet Tax Freedom Act of 1998 to tax Internet use.

For the most part, Congress has been reluctant to place restrictions or taxes on the Internet. In 2005 a bill to make spyware illegal was rejected in the U.S. Senate, and in November 2007 Congress extended the tax ban on both interstate Internet commerce and Internet service to 2014. As for content, Congress is wary of potential public backlash that it would encounter if it regulates activities such as Internet pornography. Furthermore, enforcing strict regulations would be difficult. Unlike radio or television, publishing content on the web is exceedingly

FIGURE 7.1

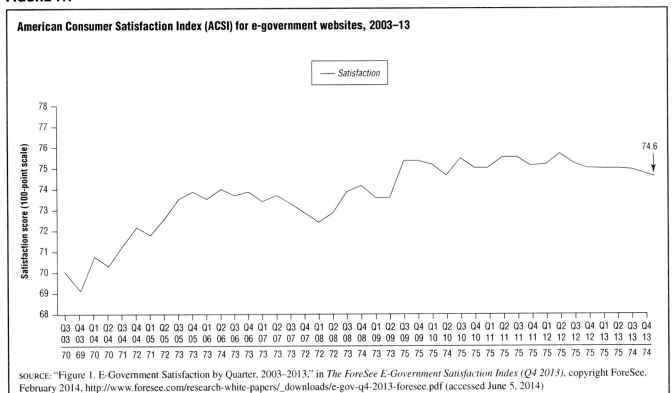

American Consumer Satisfaction Index (ACSI) for e-government websites, 2003–13

SOURCE: "Figure 1. E-Government Satisfaction by Quarter, 2003–2013," in *The ForeSee E-Government Satisfaction Index (Q4 2013)*, copyright ForeSee, February 2014, http://www.foresee.com/research-white-papers/_downloads/e-gov-q4-2013-foresee.pdf (accessed June 5, 2014)

easy. Anyone, provided he or she has willing participants, can set up a web server for several thousand dollars, take pornographic pictures, and post them on the Internet. If the U.S. government did make Internet pornography illegal altogether, such sites could easily be moved offshore, where U.S. laws would not apply. Another option the government has is to place restrictions and controls on all computers and web browsers in the United States. Such a plan may have been feasible back in the early 1990s, when Internet backbones and browsers were still in the development phase. However, placing such controls on the tens of millions of current computers and web browsers now in use would neither be well received nor easily implemented.

NETWORK NEUTRALITY. During the first decade of the 21st century the issue of network neutrality became the subject of fierce debate among policymakers, private corporations, and consumer advocates. Network neutrality, or net neutrality, is a legal principle aimed at guaranteeing open and unlimited access to all legal content, applications, and other products and services on the Internet, without regulation or other forms of interference from Internet Service Providers (ISPs) or the government.

The concept of net neutrality first became widespread in 2003, with the publication of Tim Wu's "Network Neutrality, Broadband Discrimination" (*Journal of Telecommunications and High Technology Law*, vol. 2, 2003). In this influential paper, Wu, a law professor at the University of Virginia, argues that legislation guaranteeing net neutrality is the best way to ensure that all online content and applications remain equally available to Internet users. Wu's position arose partly in response to an emerging tendency among some telecommunications companies to privilege some online content or applications over others. Specifically, some cable providers had begun blocking certain applications or content or transmitting some data faster than other data, typically by establishing unique contracts with individual companies. In doing so, cable providers granted companies that were willing to pay additional charges a clear advantage over their competitors, while simultaneously denying consumers equal access to rival information or products.

Two years after Wu's paper appeared, the FCC released its "Broadband Policy Statement" (September 23, 2005, http://www.publicknowledge.org/pdf/FCC-05-151A1.pdf), in which it outlined four basic principles that were intended to guarantee the right to unlimited Internet access for all U.S. citizens: "*To encourage broadband deployment and preserve and promote the open and interconnected nature of the public Internet,* consumers are entitled to access the lawful Internet content of their choice . . . . [To] run applications and use services of their choice, subject to the needs of law enforcement . . . . [To] connect their choice of legal devices that do not harm the network . . . . [To] competi-

TABLE 7.2

American Consumer Satisfaction Index (ACSI) for e-government portals and main websites, fourth quarter 2013

[Out of 100 points]

Department	Website	Satisfaction
Portal and department aggregate		72
HHS	National Cancer Institute main website—cancer.gov	84
HHS	CDC main website—cdc.gov	83
DHS	U.S. Citizenship and Immigration Services Español—uscis.gov/portal/site/uscis-es	83
NASA	NASA main website—nasa.gov	82
DOJ	FBI main website—fbi.gov	80
HHS	National Institute of Dental and Craniofacial Research—nidcr.nih.gov	80
HHS	NIAMS public website—niams.nih.gov	80
HHS	National Library of Medicine main website—nlm.nih.gov	78
DOI	National Park Service main website—nps.gov	78
HHS	U.S. Food and Drug Administration main website—fda.gov	78
SBA	SBA main website—sba.gov	76
GAO	GAO main public website—gao.gov	75
PBGC	U.S. PBGC main website—pbgc.gov	75
NIST	National Institute for Standards and Technology main website—nist.gov	74
DOD	Department of Defense portal—defense.gov	73
GSA	GSA main website—gsa.gov	73
DHS	U.S. Citizenship and Immigration Services—uscis.gov/portal/site/uscis	73
FDIC	FDIC main website—fdic.gov	72
FTC	FTC main website—ftc.gov	72
DHS	Department of Homeland Security main website—dhs.gov	71
HHS	SAMHSA website—samhsa.gov	71
ITC	U.S. International Trade Commission main website—usitc.gov	70
EPA	U.S. Environmental Protection Agency—epa.gov	69
NARA	NARA main public website—archives.gov	67
Treasury	Treasury main website—treasury.gov	67
DOS	Department of State main website—state.gov	66
Treasury	IRS main website—irs.gov	65
SSA	Social Security Online (Main Website)—socialsecurity.gov	65
VA	VA Main website—va.gov and myhealthva.gov	65
DOT	Federal Railroad Administration main website—fra.dot.gov	65
DOE	U.S. Department of Education—ed.gov	60
DOL	Disability—Disability.gov	59
DHS	Federal Emergency Management Agency main website—fema.gov	56

SOURCE: "Figure 6. Federal Portals and Department Main Websites," in *The ForeSee E-Government Satisfaction Index (Q4 2013)*, copyright ForeSee, February 2014, http://www.foresee.com/research-white-papers/_downloads/e-gov-q4-2013-foresee.pdf (accessed June 5, 2014).

TABLE 7.3

American Consumer Satisfaction Index (ACSI) for e-government career and recruitment sites, fourth quarter 2013

[Out of 100 points]

Department	Website	Satisfaction
CIA	Recruitment website—cia.gov/careers	84
DOS	Recruitment website—careers.state.gov	80
DOL	Department of Labor Job Listings—doors.dol.gov	77
OPM	Recruitment website—usajobs.gov	72

SOURCE: "Figure 7. Federal Career and Recruitment Websites," in *The ForeSee E-Government Satisfaction Index (Q4 2013)*, copyright ForeSee, February 2014, http://www.foresee.com/research-white-papers/_downloads/e-gov-q4-2013-foresee.pdf (accessed June 5, 2014).

tion among network providers, application and service providers, and content providers."

Also known as the "Internet Policy Statement," the FCC's position was largely aimed at preventing telecommunications companies from unfairly controlling the flow of information online.

Proponents of net neutrality generally believe that free, unregulated access to online information and services is vital to guaranteeing the rights of all citizens to view the Internet content of their choice. Furthermore, supporters of net neutrality have argued that maintaining an open Internet is the best way to ensure continued technological innovation in the digital age. A number of major corporations, notably Microsoft and Google, have been outspoken in their support of net neutrality. Opponents of net neutrality, such as cable providers and network hardware manufacturers, have insisted that the right to offer tiered services (in other words, different levels of service based on different fees) is guaranteed by law. Opponents have also asserted that tiered service plans ultimately promote free market competition on the Internet. The question of net neutrality has also sparked a wide range of opinions among lawmakers. Some members of Congress have attempted to grant the federal government additional powers to oversee and regulate telecommunications companies, with the specific aim of safeguarding net neutrality. Notable among these was the Internet Freedom Preservation Act of 2009, introduced by Representative Edward Markey (1946–: D-MA). That same year the FCC introduced two additional principles to its original "Broadband Policy Statement" that were aimed at preventing ISPs from discriminating against certain Internet content, while also granting consumers the right to total access to all ISP policies.

The battle between the federal government and the telecommunications companies became more intense in 2008. That year the FCC ruled that the telecommunications firm Comcast had illegally blocked its subscribers from using certain Internet software applications. In March 2010 a federal court overturned the FCC's judgment against Comcast, throwing the agency's power to ensure net neutrality into doubt. In response to the ruling, the FCC began exploring other means of guaranteeing the right to neutral broadband use. Joe Nocera reports in "The Struggle for What We Already Have" (NYTimes .com, September 3, 2010) that the commission hoped to use a broader interpretation of the Telecommunications Act of 1996 to impose tighter controls over ISPs.

The FCC attempted to reach a compromise in December 2010, when it voted 3–2 to prohibit telecommunications companies from controlling Internet traffic in ways that favored certain subscribers over others; however, the new restriction did not apply to smartphones or tablets. According to David Lieberman in "Net Neutrality Vote Irks Many" (USAToday.com, December 21, 2010), the FCC ruling provoked harsh criticism from supporters on both sides of the issue. Net neutrality advocates complained that the regulation contained loopholes that would enable telecommunications companies to continue manipulating certain forms of web traffic. On the contrary, John Boehner (1949–; R-OH), the Speaker of the U.S. House of Representatives, asserted that the ruling represented a "power grab" on the part of the federal government and promised to fight it in Congress. Indeed, the FCC decision remained the subject of intense debate over the next two years. In "No Neutrality on Net" (*Daily Variety*, October 13, 2012), Ted Johnson reports that opposition to the government's net neutrality rules prompted a legal challenge from the telecommunications giant Verizon, while also forming a key component of the Republican Party's presidential election platform in 2012.

Opponents of net neutrality appeared to achieve a victory in January 2014, when the U.S. Court of Appeals for Washington, D.C., ruled that the FCC did not have the authority to force telecommunications companies to treat all of their customers equally. Nevertheless, as the FCC reports in "Open Internet" (2014, http://www.fcc.gov/openinternet), the judges also reiterated that the agency retained the authority to impose regulations on Internet access. In the press release "FCC Launches Broad Rulemaking on How Best to Protect and Promote the Open Internet" (May 15, 2014, http://transition.fcc.gov/Daily _Releases/Daily_Business/2014/db0515/DOC-327104 A1.pdf), the FCC announced that it would seek public opinion on how best to ensure fair and equal use of the Internet. As Leticia Miranda writes in "The FCC's Net Neutrality Proposal Explained" (Nation.com, May 21, 2014), many advocates of net neutrality wanted the FCC to reclassify broadband as a public utility, thus empowering the agency to impose tighter restrictions on the telecommunications industry. The deadline for members of the public to submit their proposals was September 10, 2014.

CONTROLLING THE ASSAULT OF NON-SOLICITED PORNOGRAPHY AND MARKETING ACT. What little Internet regulation the federal government has enacted has been met with mixed results. On January 1, 2004, the Controlling the Assault of Non-Solicited Pornography and Marketing (CAN-SPAM) Act went into effect. The act required that all unsolicited commercial e-mail contain a legitimate return address as well as instructions on how to opt out of receiving additional solicitations from the sender. Spam must also state in the subject line if the e-mail is pornographic in nature. Violators of these rules were to be subject to heavy fines. As of 2014, the largest fine ever imposed under the CAN-SPAM Act was an $873 million judgment awarded to the social networking site Facebook in 2008. Jessica Guynn reports in "Facebook Wins $873-Million Judgment against Spammer" (LATimes.com, November 24, 2008) that the Canadian citizen Adam Guerbuez (1976?–) was found guilty of sending more than 4 million spam messages to Facebook users over a two-month period. The judgment was nearly four times greater than the $230 million won by the rival social networking site MySpace in a similar case the previous May.

CHILDREN'S INTERNET PROTECTION ACT. A more successful regulation is the Children's Internet Protection Act (CIPA) of 2000. Under the act, public schools and libraries were required to keep minors from viewing explicitly sexual content on public school and library computers. If these organizations did not comply, they would no longer receive government assistance in buying IT equipment. Public school systems throughout the country were quick to adapt to the new law, and by 2005, 100% of U.S. public schools had complied with CIPA. Regulations involving children's welfare have always been warmly received by the public, so this fact may account for CIPA's success.

ADAM WALSH CHILD PROTECTION AND SAFETY ACT. Another effort using IT and the Internet in an attempt to protect the innocence and safety of children is the Adam Walsh Child Protection and Safety Act of 2006. It established a tiered-system of sexual offenses and required that convicted sexual offenders register and update their whereabouts with local law enforcement agencies for

TABLE 7.4

Required registration information under the Sex Offender Registration and Notification Act

- Criminal history
- Date of birth
- DNA sample
- Driver's license or identification card
- Employer address
- Fingerprints
- Internet identifiers
- Name
- Palm prints
- Passport and immigration documents
- Phone numbers
- Photograph
- Physical description
- Professional licensing information
- Resident address
- School address
- Social Security number(s)
- Temporary lodging information
- Text of registration offense
- Vehicle license plate number and description

SOURCE: Laura L. Rogers, "VI. Required Registration Information: SORNA, §114," in *The Adam Walsh Act: A National Endeavor to Protect Children and Families*, U.S. Department of Justice, Office of Justice Programs, SMART Office, July 2008, http://www.search.org/files/ppt/SMARTOfficeUpdate0708.ppt (accessed June 5, 2014)

TABLE 7.5

Public website information required under the Sex Offender Registration and Notification Act

- Name
- Photograph
- Physical description
- Current offense & prior sex offenses
- Employer address
- Resident address
- School address
- Vehicle(s) license plate number and description

SOURCE: Laura L. Rogers, "VII. Disclosure and Sharing of Information: Public Website Required Information," in *The Adam Walsh Act: A National Endeavor to Protect Children and Families*, U.S. Department of Justice, Office of Justice Programs, SMART Office, July 2008, http://www.search.org/files/ppt/SMARTOfficeUpdate0708.ppt (accessed June 5, 2014)

designated periods based on the seriousness of their offenses. Named after Adam John Walsh (1974–1981), a Florida boy who was abducted from a shopping mall and murdered, the act established the National Sex Offender Public Registry Website (http://www.nsopr .gov; the site was renamed the Dru Sjodin National Sex Offender Public Website in 2006), a national database of registered sex offenders that is searchable by name, state, county, town, or zip code. Table 7.4 shows the information that convicted offenders are required to provide to law enforcement agencies under the Adam Walsh Child Protection and Safety Act, Title I, which is known as the Sex Offender Registration and Notification Act. Nonetheless, the public website discloses only the personal data that are presented in Table 7.5. In "Department of Justice Releases First National Strategy for Child Exploitation Prevention and Interdiction" (August 2, 2010, http://www.justice.gov/opa/pr/2010/August/10-opa-887.html), the U.S. Department of Justice announced that it was launching a nationwide law enforcement operation aimed at apprehending the 500 most dangerous sex offenders who were not in compliance with registry requirements. According to the National Center for Missing and Exploited Children (June 3, 2014, http://www.missing kids.com/en_US/documents/Sex_Offenders_Map.pdf), by 2014 there were 774,600 registered sex offenders in the United States.

TECHNOLOGY AND NATIONAL SECURITY

The use of IT has become central to issues of national security in the 21st century. The speed at which information in the modern age can be retrieved has played a key role in the War on Terror that began in the aftermath of the attacks on the United States on September 11, 2001 (9/11). Identifying the terrorists who were responsible for the attacks would have been an arduous if not impossible task were it not for electronic records of the terrorists' credit card and rental car use. The Federal Bureau of Investigation (FBI) was able to post a full list of the suspected terrorists within three days of the attacks, giving the White House the necessary information it needed to plan retaliatory measures.

In the aftermath of 9/11, many new technologies have been designed to catch terrorists before they strike. Data mining is by far the most controversial and perhaps the most powerful of the new technologies that are being developed. Since 2001 the U.S. Department of Homeland Security has spent a tremendous amount of time and money trying to create a database and database-searching techniques that enable authorities to view records of millions of citizens within seconds and determine if they have a link to terrorism. According to John Borland in "A Global Assault on Anonymity" (CNET.com, October 20, 2004), one attempt at such a system was called the Multistate Anti-Terrorism Information Exchange (MATRIX). The system contained the data from five state law enforcement centers as well as nationwide financial and commercial data of millions of Americans. Before its termination, the system was reportedly able to match criminal records with financial records to assess whether or not a person was a terrorist threat. The database held much more information than a typical criminal database and could be used, for instance, to do a background check on someone applying for a license to drive hazardous materials across the country. The project was canceled in April 2005 after many complaints from concerned citizens and civil rights organizations such as the American Civil Liberties Union (ACLU).

Many believed that other data mining systems were still being developed by the federal government following the cancellation of MATRIX. In "Pentagon Sets Its Sights on Social Networking Websites" (*New Scientist*, June 9, 2006), Paul Marks explains that the National Security Agency (NSA) was funding a program called the Disruptive Technology Office (DTO) in 2006. The reported role of the DTO was to combine data on people from many different sources, including phone records and online social networks such as MySpace. The existence of the program was not beyond the realm of reason. Leslie Cauley reports in "NSA Has Massive Database of Americans' Phone Calls" (USAToday.com, May 11, 2006) that in 2006 the NSA was already secretly analyzing billions of phone records in an effort to find potential terrorists in the United States. The NSA did not obtain a court's approval before searching the phone records, which many considered to be an illegal act. In August 2006 Judge Anna Diggs-Taylor (1932–) of the U.S. District Court declared the program unconstitutional and ordered it to stop. However, the program continued while the case was appealed and Congress worked to develop a modified system of surveillance.

In July 2008 President Bush signed into law the Foreign Intelligence Surveillance Act of 1978 Amendments Act of 2008. Besides broadening the ability of the federal government to conduct high-tech investigations that are aimed at identifying foreign terrorist activity, the act shields U.S. telecommunications firms from lawsuits that stem from their cooperation in government wiretap investigations of their customers. On the day the new law was passed, the ACLU filed a lawsuit in federal court contending that the new law violated the U.S. Constitution on numerous grounds, including the right to privacy. Although the case was dismissed by a district court judge in August 2009, a federal appeals court reversed the district judge's decision in March 2011, reinstating the ACLU's lawsuit against the government. In May 2012 the U.S. Supreme Court agreed to hear the case, and oral arguments were heard that October. In February 2013 the Supreme Court voted 5–4 to dismiss the case.

Even as IT serves as a vital tool in the War on Terror, it can also pose a serious challenge to the government's control of classified information. The extent to which government secrets were vulnerable in the information age was exposed in April 2010, when WikiLeaks, an activist media website, released a classified video that showed a U.S. Apache helicopter killing 11 unarmed civilians in Iraq in 2007. The following month Private First Class Bradley Manning (1987–; later Chelsea Manning), a U.S. Army intelligence analyst, was arrested on charges of illegally copying the video, along with more than 250,000 classified diplomatic cables, and sending them to the website. David Dishneau and Ben Nuckols

report in "Prosecutors to Question Manning in Wiki-Leaks Case" (Yahoo.com, November 30, 2012) that Manning's actions represented "the biggest leak of classified material in U.S. history." Even though many politicians and U.S. officials saw Manning as a traitor, a number of free-speech advocates and political activists considered him to be a hero. Eventually, his supporters established the website BradleyManning.org (later ChelseaManning.org) to help promote his legal defense and to protest reports of his harsh treatment while in prison awaiting trial.

In "WikiLeaks' Julian Assange Suffering from Chronic Lung Condition" (Time.com, November 29, 2012), Sorcha Pollak indicates that Julian Assange (1971–), the Australian founder of WikiLeaks, also faced the possibility of extradition to the United States for his role in making the classified documents public. However, no legal action had proceeded against him in the United States as of August 2014.

One of the most damaging leaks of classified materials in American history occurred in June 2013, when it emerged that the Foreign Intelligence Surveillance Court (FISC) had ordered telecommunications firm Verizon to turn over the private phone data of millions of U.S. citizens to the NSA and the FBI. In "NSA Collecting Phone Records of Millions of Verizon Customers Daily" (Guardian.com, June 5, 2013), Glenn Greenwald reports that the court's secret order, dated April 25, 2013, granted the government unlimited access to the "metadata" of Verizon customers, information that included contact and location data, call durations, and other details relating to individual telephone records. In the ensuing days, other classified information, including the revelation that the NSA had been monitoring the online activities of U.S. citizens through a program called Prism, became public.

Days after the initial story became public, an NSA contractor named Edward Snowden (1983–) disclosed that he had leaked thousands of classified NSA documents to Greenwald. As Noam Schreiber reports in "Why'd He Do It?" (NewRepublic.com, June 10, 2013), Snowden revealed his motivations in an interview conducted in Hong Kong, where he had fled after leaking the documents. "I don't want to live in a world where there's no privacy and therefore no room for intellectual exploration and creativity," Schreiber quotes Snowden as saying. In the face of extradition efforts on the part of the U.S. government, Snowden left Hong Kong for Russia, where he was granted temporary asylum. He remained in exile in Russia as of August 2014.

IT also has the capacity to inflict damage that goes beyond the exchange of classified data. With the emergence in government agencies and private industry of increasingly complex computer systems, terrorists, hackers, and governments soon developed the power to disrupt, and even destroy, real physical targets. The extent of this threat first achieved widespread attention in 2010, when cybersecurity experts became aware of a new form of malware that had the capacity to infiltrate massive industrial control systems and seize control of the systems' functions. Dubbed Stuxnet, this highly sophisticated cyberworm had the potential to trigger a catastrophic chain of events at a high-security site, such as a nuclear power plant. Indeed, Mark Clayton reports in "Stuxnet Malware Is 'Weapon' out to Destroy... Iran's Bushehr Nuclear Plant?" (CSMonitor.com, September 21, 2010) that in 2010 many cybersecurity experts believed Stuxnet had infected the Bushehr nuclear power plant in Iran, which is one of the most sensitive, high-risk nuclear sites in the world. According to Ellen Nakashima and Joby Warrick in "Stuxnet Was Work of U.S. and Israeli Experts, Officials Say" (WashingtonPost.com, June 1, 2012), the operation against the Iranian nuclear program was later discovered to have been launched as a joint mission between the United States and Israel and authorized by President Obama. In the end, the Stuxnet attack destroyed roughly one-sixth of Iran's uranium centrifuges.

By 2012 the potential for other sophisticated forms of cyberwarfare had emerged as a new type of threat to U.S. national security. In *Occupying the Information High Ground: Chinese Capabilities for Computer Network Operations and Cyber Espionage* (March 7, 2012, http://origin.www.uscc.gov/sites/default/files/Research/USCC_Report_Chinese_Capabilities_for_Computer_Network_Operations_and_Cyber_%20Espionage.pdf), a report prepared for the U.S.-China Economic and Security Review Commission by Northrop Grumman Corporation, authors Bryan Krekel, Patton Adams, and George Bakos assert that in 2012 China was in the process of developing a strategy known as "information confrontation," making "the ability to exert control over an adversary's information and information systems" one of its key defense priorities in the early 21st century. The article "How to Survive a Cyberwar" (Bloomberg.com, August 2, 2012) notes that according to General Keith Alexander, the head of the U.S. Cyber Command, electronic breaches of U.S. targets resulted in roughly $1 trillion in intellectual property losses between 2009 and 2011. In the face of these burgeoning threats, President Obama issued in October 2012 "Presidential Policy Directive 20" (http://fas.org/irp/offdocs/ppd/ppd-20.pdf), a classified order that established new guidelines for the "cyber-operations of military and federal agencies."

As Sandra I. Erwin reports in "NSA Chief: Military Not Organized for Cyber Warfare" (NationalDefense Magazine.org, June 12, 2014), U.S. Cyber Command, a Pentagon division formed in 2009, had a $500 million annual budget dedicated to combating cyberattacks against the United States. As Erwin notes, however, in 2014 Cyber Command was still contending with the U.S. military's "hidebound culture and outdated procurement system," which hindered the division's efforts to develop an effective defense against cyberwarfare. "Our greater challenge is not technology but organization," Erwin quotes Navy Admiral Michael S. Rogers, head of both the NSA and Cyber Command, as saying. "Military commanders must 'own' cyber."

ELECTIONS AND POLITICS

The Internet has not only influenced how people interact with the government but also how people engage with politics. As Table 7.6 shows, in October 2012 more people found news relating to the 2012 presidential campaign on the Internet (36%) than in local (23%) or national (13%) newspapers. At the same time, more than one in 10 (11%) adults who watched the 2012 presidential debates on television followed the debates over the Internet or a mobile device simultaneously; 3% watched the debates exclusively online. (See Figure 7.2.)

In 2012, 5% of all Americans discussed politics through e-mail, text messaging, or over the Internet at least once a day; 11% discussed politics using these technologies at least once a week, and another 11% used them to discuss politics at least once a month. (See Figure 7.3.) An individual's educational attainment was a strong indicator of their online political engagement in 2012. As Figure 7.4

TABLE 7.6

Principal sources of campaign news, January–October 2012

	January 2012	October 2012
TV		
Cable news	36%	41%
Local news	32	38
Network news	26	31
Cable news talk shows	15	18
Late night comedy shows	9	12
Internet	**25**	**36**
Print		
Local newspapers	20	23
National newspapers	8	13
Radio		
NPR	12	12
Talk radio shows	16	16
Social media		
Facebook	6	12
Twitter	2	4
YouTube	3	7

Note: Figures do not add up to a 100% because respondents could answer regularly to more than one item.

SOURCE: Aaron Smith, "Where People Turn for Campaign News," in *Digital Politics: Pew Research Findings on Technology and Campaign 2012*, Pew Research Center, February 20, 2013, http://www.pewinternet.org/files/old-media//Files/Presentations/2012/Feb/Social%20Media%20Week%20Feb%202013_v2_PDF.pdf (accessed June 5, 2014)

shows, 51% of all college graduates voiced political opinions online in 2012; by contrast, only 10% of adults with less than a high school diploma shared their political views on the Internet. At the same time, the period between 2008 and 2012 saw an increase in the percentage of political donors who sent campaign contributions over the Internet. In 2008, 15% of all political donors contributed money exclusively online, compared with 69% who contributed funds exclusively offline; another 15% made campaign contributions both online and offline that year. (See Figure 7.5.) In 2012 nearly one-quarter (23%) of political donors made campaign contributions exclusively online, 60% made their donations exclusively offline, and 16% did both.

Online Participation in Politics

During the 2012 presidential campaign, social networking sites played a central role in the way Internet users engaged in politics. Overall, younger social media users were more likely than older social media users to engage in political activities via social networking sites. For example, in 2012, 44% of social media users between the ages of 18 and 29 either "liked" certain political content on Facebook, or else promoted specific political views on their social networking accounts; by comparison, less than one-quarter (24%) of social media users 65 years of age and older either liked or promoted specific political content on their pages. (See Figure 7.6.) Social media users between the ages of 18 and 29 were also more likely than those in any other age group to post their opinions on specific issues (42%), urge other social media users to get involved in a particular political cause (36%), or belong to a political group on social media (26%). At the same time, social networking users between the ages of 18 and 29 were the most likely to encourage other social media users to vote for a particular candidate during the 2012 election season. (See Figure 7.7.)

FIGURE 7.2

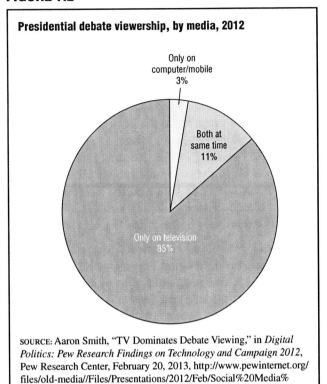

Presidential debate viewership, by media, 2012

Only on computer/mobile 3%

Both at same time 11%

Only on television 85%

SOURCE: Aaron Smith, "TV Dominates Debate Viewing," in *Digital Politics: Pew Research Findings on Technology and Campaign 2012*, Pew Research Center, February 20, 2013, http://www.pewinternet.org/files/old-media//Files/Presentations/2012/Feb/Social%20Media%20Week%20Feb%202013_v2_PDF.pdf (accessed June 5, 2014)

FIGURE 7.3

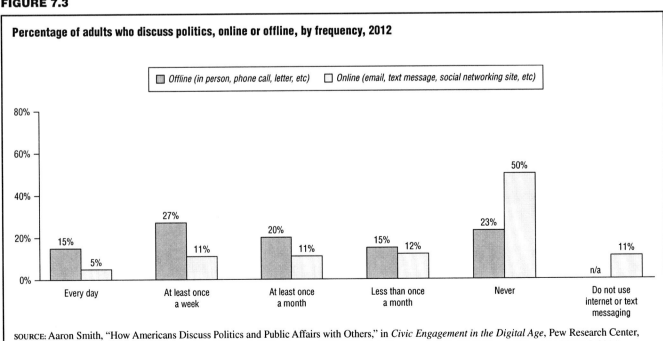

Percentage of adults who discuss politics, online or offline, by frequency, 2012

■ Offline (in person, phone call, letter, etc)   □ Online (email, text message, social networking site, etc)

	Every day	At least once a week	At least once a month	Less than once a month	Never	Do not use internet or text messaging
Offline	15%	27%	20%	15%	23%	n/a
Online	5%	11%	11%	12%	50%	11%

SOURCE: Aaron Smith, "How Americans Discuss Politics and Public Affairs with Others," in *Civic Engagement in the Digital Age*, Pew Research Center, April 25, 2013, http://www.pewinternet.org/files/old-media//Files/Reports/2013/PIP_CivicEngagementintheDigitalAge.pdf (accessed June 5, 2014)

FIGURE 7.4

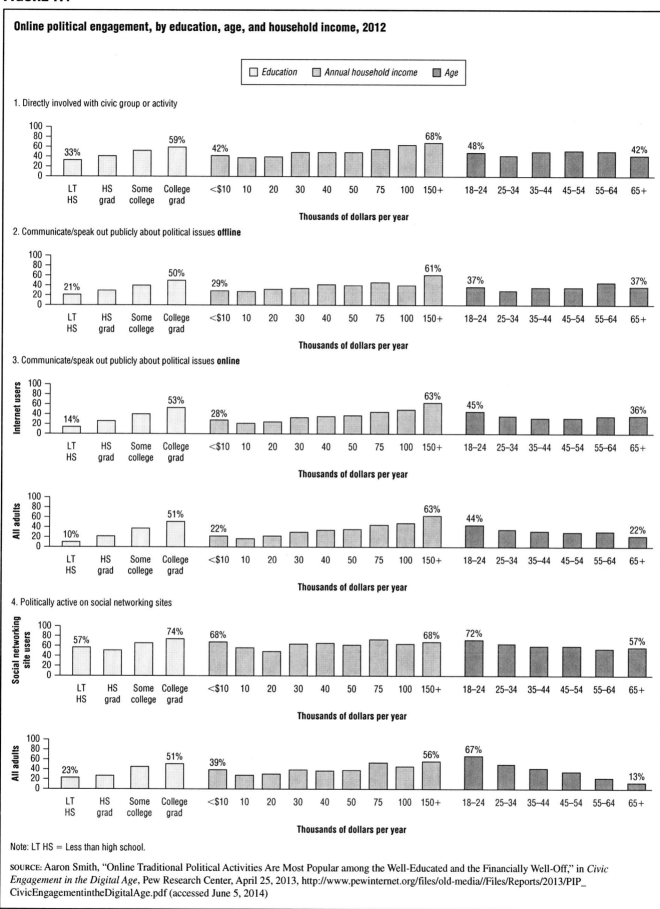

Online political engagement, by education, age, and household income, 2012

Note: LT HS = Less than high school.

SOURCE: Aaron Smith, "Online Traditional Political Activities Are Most Popular among the Well-Educated and the Financially Well-Off," in *Civic Engagement in the Digital Age*, Pew Research Center, April 25, 2013, http://www.pewinternet.org/files/old-media//Files/Reports/2013/PIP_CivicEngagementintheDigitalAge.pdf (accessed June 5, 2014)

FIGURE 7.5

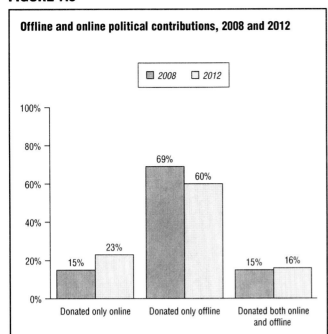

Offline and online political contributions, 2008 and 2012

■ 2008   □ 2012

SOURCE: Aaron Smith, "Online Political Contributions Have Grown More Common since 2008, but Most Donations Still Occur Offline," in *Civic Engagement in the Digital Age*, Pew Research Center, April 25, 2013, http://www.pewinternet.org/files/old-media//Files/Reports/2013/PIP_CivicEngagementintheDigitalAge.pdf (accessed June 5, 2014)

By 2014 mobile devices had become another important tool for finding political news and information. Table 7.7 provides a breakdown of the types of political activities engaged in by mobile phone owners in 2014, by party affiliation. As Table 7.7 shows, Democrats (31%) were more likely than Republicans (23%) or independents (19%) to use their mobile devices to receive communications from political interest groups; Democrats (28%) were also more likely than Republicans (19%) or independents (16%) to receive communications directly from political campaigns on their phones. By contrast, Republicans (20%) were more likely than either Democrats (17%) or independents (14%) to use their phones to share their political views online. (See Table 7.7.)

IT and the Voting Booth

To help bring IT into voting booths, in 2002 Congress passed and President Bush signed the Help America Vote Act (HAVA). The act was a direct response to the hotly contested 2000 presidential campaign in which disputes over punch-card ballots in Florida contributed to a month-long delay of nationwide presidential election results. The punch-card ballots were prone to human error in that people would sometimes punch out the wrong perforated circle or not punch the card all the

FIGURE 7.6

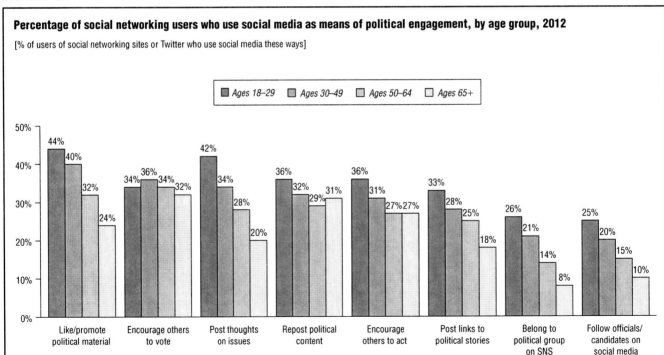

Percentage of social networking users who use social media as means of political engagement, by age group, 2012

[% of users of social networking sites or Twitter who use social media these ways]

■ Ages 18–29   ■ Ages 30–49   ■ Ages 50–64   □ Ages 65+

SNS = social networking site.

SOURCE: Lee Rainie et al., "Younger Social Media Users Are More Likely to Use the Tools for Civic Activities," in *Social Media and Political Engagement*, Pew Research Center, October 19, 2012, http://www.pewinternet.org/files/old-media//Files/Reports/2012/PIP_SocialMediaAndPoliticalEngagement_PDF.pdf (accessed June 5, 2014)

FIGURE 7.7

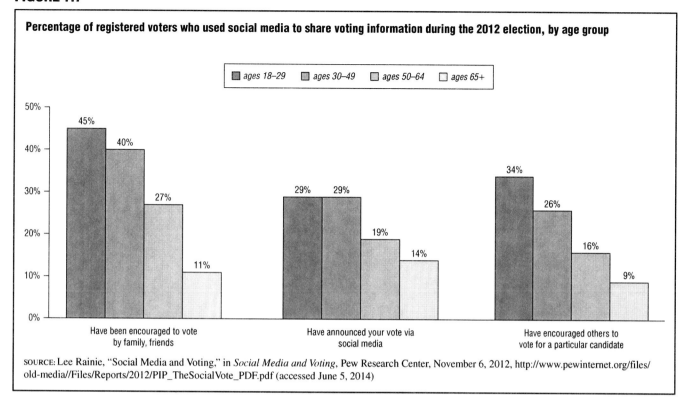

Percentage of registered voters who used social media to share voting information during the 2012 election, by age group

■ ages 18–29   ■ ages 30–49   ■ ages 50–64   □ ages 65+

SOURCE: Lee Rainie, "Social Media and Voting," in *Social Media and Voting*, Pew Research Center, November 6, 2012, http://www.pewinternet.org/files/old-media//Files/Reports/2012/PIP_TheSocialVote_PDF.pdf (accessed June 5, 2014)

TABLE 7.7

Percentage of adults who engage in political activities on their mobile devices, by party affiliation, 2014

	% Yes		
	Republicans	Independents	Democrats
	%	%	%
Received electronic communications from political interest groups through email, social media, or text message	23	19	31
Shared, "liked," or retweeted posts or links that express political opinions similar to your own	28	21	23
Received requests on your smartphone or other electronic device from interest groups asking you to contact your elected representative or take some action on a bill being considered in Congress or the state legislature	25	18	25
Received electronic communications from elected officials or candidates for office through email, social media, or text message	21	18	24
Received electronic communications from political parties through email, social media, or text message	19	16	28
Posted your opinions about politics and political issues, elected officials, elections, or candidates for office on Twitter, Facebook, or other Internet sites	20	14	17
Received instant electronic notification on your smartphone or other electronic device about political rallies or political protests in your area	8	7	15
Made a monetary donation to political candidates or political interest groups using your smartphone or tablet—that is, using PayPal or having the dollar amount charged to your Amazon, Google, phone company, or other account	2	3	8

SOURCE: Frank Newport, "Political Connection via Mobile Devices, by Partisanship," in *Mobile Technology in Politics More Potential Than Reality*, The Gallup Organization, April 29, 2014, http://www.gallup.com/poll/168767/mobile-technology-politics-potential-reality.aspx (accessed June 5, 2014). Copyright © 2014 Gallup, Inc. All rights reserved. The content is used with permission; however, Gallup retains all rights of republication.

way through. HAVA required states to upgrade to electronic voting systems by the 2006 national election. The bill allotted $3.9 billion to help states replace old punch-card and lever systems with new voting machines. Even though HAVA did not specify precisely which voting machines states were required to use, the act did provide a list of features the machines should have. Among other things, the machines should keep an electronic and paper record of the votes, be accessible to those with disabilities, allow voters to review their ballots before they are cast, and notify voters if they misvote (e.g., vote twice for the same office).

The two types of machines that came closest to meeting HAVA's requirements were used heavily in subsequent elections. The first type is the optical scanning (Marksense) voting system. This system operates much like the paper-based standardized tests given in high schools and colleges. Using a dark lead pencil or black ink pen, voters darken ovals next to the names of candidates for whom they wish to vote. With the sheet in front of them, voters can review their ballots before casting them. The sheet is then fed into a scanner. If an error or misvote occurs on the ballot, the scanner spits the ballot out. It is then discarded and the voter votes again. If the ballot is acceptable, the machine scans the ballot using lasers and the votes are registered in the machine. The problem with optical scanning systems, however, is that they are not accessible to disabled people who have trouble seeing or do not have complete control of their fine motor skills.

The second type of machine, known as a direct recording electronic (DRE) voting system, covers all the requirements laid down by HAVA. DRE systems are akin to touch-screen automated teller machines. The voter stands in front of the touch screen and a list of candidates for a given political contest is displayed on the screen. The voter simply touches the candidate's name to vote for that person, and the machine displays the next list of candidates. DRE systems can be equipped with Braille keyboards and headsets for the blind, and voting choices can be made larger on the screen for those who lack fine motor skills. The machine notifies the voter if he or she has misvoted and allows for a review of votes on a final checkout screen before they are cast. The machine prints out a paper record resembling a spreadsheet at the end of the voting day. Proponents claim that the DRE system is better than the optical system because the DRE system eliminates the potential human error involved in coloring in circles and is easier for the disabled.

Even though DRE systems meet HAVA's requirements, controversy still surrounds their use. Many people are concerned that hackers can somehow tap into these systems and change the votes. A second concern is that the complicated computer hardware and software in these systems can malfunction. In "Is E-Voting Safe?" (PCWorld.com, April 28, 2004), Paul Boutin discusses a study on DRE systems that was conducted by computer scientists at the California Institute of Technology and the Massachusetts Institute of Technology (MIT) in 2001. The study concluded that touch-screen machines were slightly more accurate than punch-card machines. The residual margin of error for the DRE machines, which equates to the percentage of votes that are thrown out because of error, was 2.3%. This was only marginally better than the 2.5% error rate generated by punch-card systems. By contrast, optically scanned paper ballots had an error rate of only 1.5%. One possible solution for the DRE systems that some states have implemented is the use of redundant paper ballots. In this instance, receipt printers are attached to the DRE machines. When the person is done voting, the printer prints a version of the person's vote. This paper can then be reviewed and placed into a ballot box for later review if necessary.

The new voting machines did appear to make some difference in the 2004 presidential election. Charles Stewart III of MIT states in "Measuring the Improvement (or Lack of Improvement) in Voting since 2000 in the U.S." (January 14, 2006, http://web.mit.edu/cstewart/www/papers/measuring_2.pdf) that the number of votes that had to be thrown out because of error between the 2000 and 2004 presidential elections dropped from 1.9% to 1.1% among those states and counties where the statistics were available. (It should be noted that the reported/detected error from election officials may have been lower than the actual error.) Even though many factors could have contributed to this reduction, those counties that updated to optical scanning voting machines or DRE systems showed some of the most significant drops in voting error.

In spite of these promising signs, by 2008 a number of states, notably Florida, were compelled to replace many of the voting machines they had installed only six years earlier, amid concerns that the machines were vulnerable to error or security risks. The article "Voting Shouldn't Be a Game of Chance" (WashingtonPost.com, November 2, 2008) reports numerous problems that were related to early electronic voting in the weeks preceding the 2008 presidential election, including instances where voters were unable to select the candidates they wanted on touch-screen voting systems. Even with a record turnout of 132.6 million voters for the November 4 election, incidences of problems with electronic voting machines were relatively minor. Still, the question of the reliability of e-voting remained a subject of debate, particularly as one-third of all states did not require paper records of electronic ballots. In August 2010 a number of lawmakers, led by Representative Rush D. Holt Jr. (1948–; D-NJ), submitted a letter to the U.S. attorney general Eric Holder Jr. (1951–) recommending that the Department of Justice require all states to generate paper voting records during the November 2010 elections.

Even though the reliability of voting machines remained a source of concern during the 2012 presidential campaign, no serious issues emerged that affected the outcome of the election. However, Clayton reports in "Voting-Machine Glitches: How Bad Was It on Election Day around the Country?" (CSMonitor.com, November 7, 2012) that on election day 2012 problems with voting machines resulted in long delays at polling places, as instances of machine breakdowns and "vote flipping" (poorly calibrated machines that mistakenly turn a vote for one candidate into a vote for another candidate) were reported from several states throughout the country.

VOTING AND THE INTERNET. As the normalcy of conducting many personal transactions over the Internet became more widespread during the early 21st century, some observers began anticipating online voting and suggested that the convenience of voting online would increase voter participation in elections. However, Susannah Fox, Janna Quitney Anderson, and Lee Rainie report in *The Future of the Internet* (January 9, 2005, http://www.pewinternet.org/~/media//Files/Reports/2005/PIP_Future_of_Internet.pdf.pdf) that a Pew survey of 1,286 technology experts found only 32% of those interviewed agreed that network security concerns would be solved to the point that more than half of American votes would be cast online by 2014. Among those who disagreed with this prediction, Peter Denning of the Naval Postgraduate School in Monterey, California, wrote, "There's a good chance that . . . [by 2014] we will have learned to design robust, trustworthy voting systems. But voter apathy is related not to the voting system but to the perception that the vote counts." Ted Eytan of Group Health Cooperative in Maryland maintained, "Voting security is likely unobtainable, regardless of the technology. There is too much at stake, and there are too many incentives to corrupt the process. There will need to be a physical representation of a vote in the future."

A turning point in the evolution of online voting came in October 2009, with the passage of the Military and Overseas Voter Empowerment Act. Under the new law, states were empowered to send electronic voter registration forms, election information, and even blank ballots to Americans living overseas, thereby saving the time and money associated with sending materials through conventional mail. Perhaps more significantly, the new system made it possible for the votes of military personnel and other overseas Americans to be counted in a timely manner, eliminating the lag time that was traditionally associated with counting absentee voting ballots. A month after the law passed, Massachusetts became the first state to adopt the new procedures. In "States Move to Allow Overseas and Military Voters to Cast Ballots by Internet" (NYTimes.com, May 8, 2010), Ian Urbina notes that by May 2010, 33 states had instituted laws allowing Americans abroad to vote via e-mail or fax. The shift to Internet voting caused a great deal of concern among Internet security experts and other voting advocates. Urbina quotes John Bonifaz of the voting rights organization Voter Action as saying that the move toward online voting "basically takes the hazards we've seen with electronic voting and puts them on steroids."

GOVERNMENT IMPROVEMENTS IN DAILY LIFE

511 Travel Information System

Using advanced technology, the federal and state governments have begun to put into place a nationwide travel information system known as 511. The 511 system is an attempt to unify the many automated information systems that were already operated by state and local governments. Dozens of cities and states set up these systems during the 1990s, when cell phones and advanced communications became affordable. Callers and Internet users could retrieve information on traffic jams and road conditions over the phone or on the Internet. For example, the Advanced Regional Traffic Interactive Management and Information System (ARTIMIS) was set up in 1995 to monitor traffic and alert people to traffic problems on 88 miles (142 km) of freeway in the Cincinnati, Ohio, metropolitan area. ARTIMIS used cameras and hundreds of detectors to monitor the flow of traffic along these freeways. People could dial into the system at any time to retrieve the information.

However, most of these systems had one big flaw. To access them by phone, drivers typically had to remember an unfamiliar, seven-digit number. Consequently, these services were rarely used. Noticing this problem, the U.S. Department of Transportation (DOT) approached the FCC and asked that a three-digit number be established to connect users to local travel information anywhere in the country. The FCC chose 511. The number was short and would automatically be associated with the more widely used 411 and 911. Ultimately, the DOT wanted all driver information systems to adopt the 511 number so that any driver in the country could receive information by simply dialing 511.

With the support of the DOT, the 511 Deployment Coalition was formed in 2001 by a number of federal and state agencies to establish guidelines and procedures for implementing local 511 travel information systems. The coalition explains in *America's Travel Information Number: Implementation and Operational Guidelines for 511 Services* (September 2005, http://www.ops.fhwa.dot.gov/511/resources/publications/511guide_ver3/511guide3.htm) that 511 services should allow a driver to access automated recordings on travel conditions through a series of voice commands or touch-tone commands on the phone. At bare minimum, the system should provide conditions for major arteries in the designated region.

Many previously developed systems such as the TravInfo service in San Francisco, California, quickly adopted the number for their travel services. The DOT also awarded $100,000 grants to states or cities without traffic advisory systems to fund implementation plans. Figure 7.8 displays the states that used the 511 number and those that received funding to implement a system as of February 2014.

National Do Not Call Registry

Another attempt by the federal government to respond to the everyday concerns of the American public is the National Do Not Call Registry (https://www.donotcall.gov/default.aspx), which is managed by the Federal Trade Commission (FTC). Launched in June 2003, the registry was established with the simple goal of reducing

FIGURE 7.8

Area in which 511, the traveler information number, is available, as of February 18, 2014

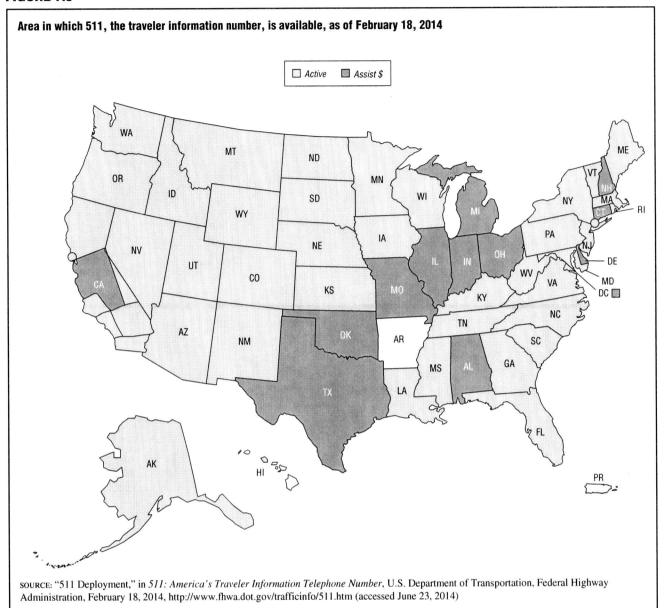

□ *Active* ■ *Assist $*

SOURCE: "511 Deployment," in *511: America's Traveler Information Telephone Number*, U.S. Department of Transportation, Federal Highway Administration, February 18, 2014, http://www.fhwa.dot.gov/trafficinfo/511.htm (accessed June 23, 2014)

the number of unwanted telemarketing calls received by consumers. Under the Telemarketing Sales Rule that outlined the program, commercial telemarketers were allowed to access the list for a fee to continue making unsolicited calls to numbers in their area that were not registered. In addition, telemarketers could continue to call those on the list with whom they had an established business relationship within the preceding 18 months. The Do Not Call Registry contained more than 142 million phone numbers within its first four years of operation, according to the FTC in *The FTC in 2007: A Champion for Consumers and Competition* (April 2007, http://www.ftc.gov/sites/default/files/documents/reports

_annual/annual-report-2007/chairmansreport2007_0.pdf). The FTC indicates in *National Do Not Call Registry Data Book FY 2013* (December 2013, http://www .ftc.gov/sites/default/files/documents/reports/national-do-not-call-registry-data-book-fiscal-year-2013/131204dnc databook.pdf) that in 2013, 223.4 million phone numbers had been submitted to the service, which covered all U.S. states and territories. (See Figure 7.9.) As Table 7.8 shows, California led the nation in both active Do Not Call registrations (25.1 million) and complaints (511,815) in 2013. New Hampshire had the highest proportion of active registrations among the states in 2013, with 89,154 out of every 100,000 residents registered that year. (See Figure 7.10.)

FIGURE 7.9

Do Not Call registrations and complaints, 2003–13

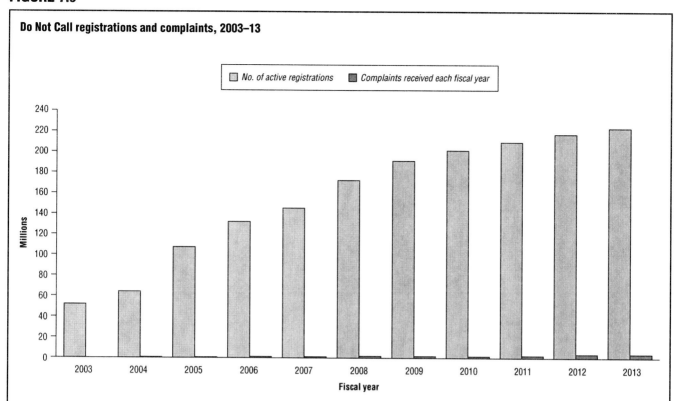

Note: Active registration and complaint figures reflect the total number of phone numbers registered and the total number of National Do Not Call Registry complaints submitted to the Federal Trade Commission (FTC) as of September 30, 2013.

SOURCE: "National Do Not Call Registry Active Registration and Complaint Figures," in *National Do Not Call Registry Data Book: FY 2013*, Federal Trade Commission, December 2013, http://www.ftc.gov/sites/default/files/documents/reports/national-do-not-call-registry-data-book-fiscal-year-2013/131204dncdatabook.pdf (accessed June 5, 2014)

Fiscal year	No. of active registrations	Increase in active registrations	No. of cumulative complaints	Complaints received each fiscal year
2003	51,968,777	51,968,777	0	0
2004	64,288,175	12,319,398	579,838	579,838
2005	107,440,316	43,152,141	1,249,312	669,474
2006	132,219,163	24,778,847	2,399,130	1,149,818
2007	145,498,656	13,279,493	3,696,995	1,297,865
2008	172,523,449	27,024,793	5,464,793	1,767,798
2009	191,453,726	18,930,277	7,273,144	1,808,351
2010	201,542,746	10,089,020	8,906,959	1,633,815
2011	209,723,135	8,180,389	11,180,475	2,273,516
2012	217,568,284	7,845,149	15,021,044	3,840,569
2013	223,429,112	5,860,828	18,769,699	3,748,655

TABLE 7.8

Do Not Call registrations and complaints, by state, 2013

Consumer state	Active registrations		Fiscal year 2013 complaints	
	Active registrations[a]	Active registrations per 100,000 population[b]	Fiscal year 2013 complaints[c]	Fiscal year 2013 complaints per 100,000 population[b]
Alabama	3,312,149	68,688	81,843	1,697
Alaska	342,120	46,773	2,197	300
Arizona	4,606,921	70,300	117,011	1,786
Arkansas	1,975,625	66,990	28,758	975
California	25,096,003	65,970	511,815	1,345
Colorado	4,431,872	85,432	78,294	1,509
Connecticut	3,077,015	85,702	56,135	1,563
Delaware	736,387	80,296	12,786	1,394
District of Columbia	595,115	94,116	9,866	1,560
Florida	14,373,073	74,404	246,479	1,276
Georgia	6,979,434	70,358	111,257	1,122
Hawaii	744,542	53,475	6,775	487
Idaho	1,119,074	70,129	16,527	1,036
Illinois	9,666,740	75,080	205,407	1,595
Indiana	3,889,428	59,496	28,756	440
Iowa	2,420,078	78,723	23,971	780
Kansas	2,321,057	80,427	25,848	896
Kentucky	3,238,446	73,930	39,579	904
Louisiana	2,769,982	60,192	42,350	920
Maine	1,034,223	77,808	10,344	778
Maryland	4,639,403	78,840	86,771	1,475
Massachusetts	5,673,246	85,361	76,659	1,153
Michigan	7,767,241	78,589	119,150	1,206
Minnesota	4,265,442	79,296	52,110	969
Mississippi	1,594,789	53,428	20,013	670
Missouri	3,958,716	65,738	41,838	695
Montana	763,807	75,990	7,988	795
Nebraska	1,466,246	79,021	17,598	948
Nevada	1,869,787	67,772	37,330	1,353
New Hampshire	1,177,469	89,154	19,246	1,457
New Jersey	7,116,422	80,279	163,747	1,847
New Mexico	1,384,297	66,376	18,558	890
New York	13,648,616	69,742	249,798	1,276
North Carolina	6,658,033	68,273	90,973	933
North Dakota	500,921	71,598	4,906	701
Ohio	8,826,553	76,459	169,651	1,470
Oklahoma	2,608,853	68,387	31,014	813
Oregon	2,860,963	73,370	56,469	1,448
Pennsylvania	9,959,314	78,029	146,865	1,151
Rhode Island	815,228	77,619	12,720	1,211
South Carolina	3,001,471	63,540	46,282	980
South Dakota	614,564	73,746	6,280	754
Tennessee	4,473,926	69,296	79,992	1,239
Texas	15,175,079	58,233	221,666	851
Utah	1,868,589	65,443	26,473	927
Vermont	470,898	75,222	7,010	1,120
Virginia	6,158,498	75,233	99,251	1,212
Washington	5,052,477	73,256	98,511	1,428
West Virginia	1,174,929	63,324	15,512	836
Wisconsin	3,992,895	69,728	32,218	563
Wyoming	440,679	76,452	6,705	1,163

[a]"Active registrations" reflect the total number of phone numbers registered on the National Do Not Call Registry as of September 30, 2013.
[b]Population estimates are based on the 2012 U.S. Census population estimates.
[c]"FY 2013 complaints" reflect National Do Not Call Registry complaints received by the Commission during fiscal year 2013.

SOURCE: "Fiscal Year 2013 National Do Not Call Registry Registration and Complaint Figures by State Population," in *National Do Not Call Registry Data Book: FY 2013*, Federal Trade Commission, December 2013, http://www.ftc.gov/sites/default/files/documents/reports/national-do-not-call-registry-data-book-fiscal-year-2013/131204dncdatabook.pdf (accessed June 5, 2014)

FIGURE 7.10

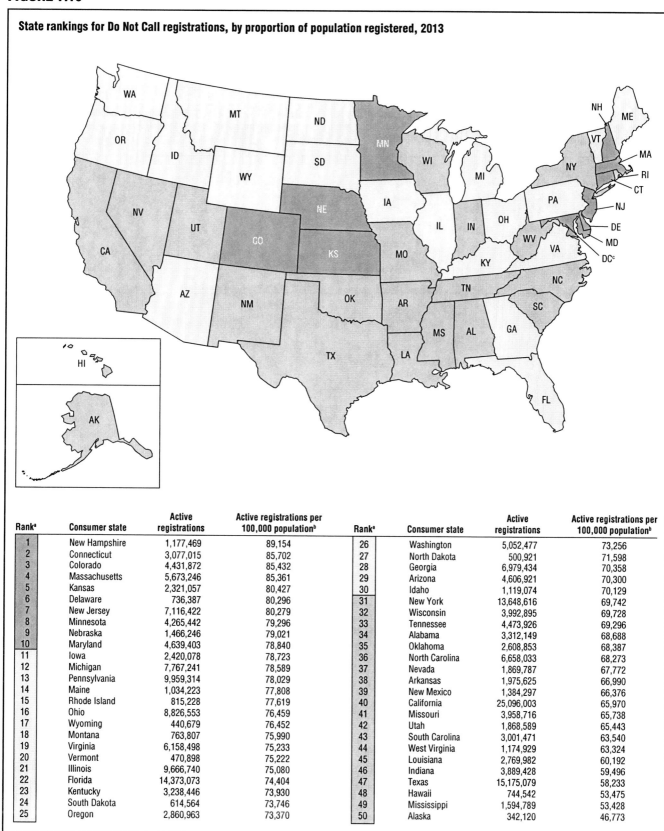

State rankings for Do Not Call registrations, by proportion of population registered, 2013

Rank[a]	Consumer state	Active registrations	Active registrations per 100,000 population[b]	Rank[a]	Consumer state	Active registrations	Active registrations per 100,000 population[b]
1	New Hampshire	1,177,469	89,154	26	Washington	5,052,477	73,256
2	Connecticut	3,077,015	85,702	27	North Dakota	500,921	71,598
3	Colorado	4,431,872	85,432	28	Georgia	6,979,434	70,358
4	Massachusetts	5,673,246	85,361	29	Arizona	4,606,921	70,300
5	Kansas	2,321,057	80,427	30	Idaho	1,119,074	70,129
6	Delaware	736,387	80,296	31	New York	13,648,616	69,742
7	New Jersey	7,116,422	80,279	32	Wisconsin	3,992,895	69,728
8	Minnesota	4,265,442	79,296	33	Tennessee	4,473,926	69,296
9	Nebraska	1,466,246	79,021	34	Alabama	3,312,149	68,688
10	Maryland	4,639,403	78,840	35	Oklahoma	2,608,853	68,387
11	Iowa	2,420,078	78,723	36	North Carolina	6,658,033	68,273
12	Michigan	7,767,241	78,589	37	Nevada	1,869,787	67,772
13	Pennsylvania	9,959,314	78,029	38	Arkansas	1,975,625	66,990
14	Maine	1,034,223	77,808	39	New Mexico	1,384,297	66,376
15	Rhode Island	815,228	77,619	40	California	25,096,003	65,970
16	Ohio	8,826,553	76,459	41	Missouri	3,958,716	65,738
17	Wyoming	440,679	76,452	42	Utah	1,868,589	65,443
18	Montana	763,807	75,990	43	South Carolina	3,001,471	63,540
19	Virginia	6,158,498	75,233	44	West Virginia	1,174,929	63,324
20	Vermont	470,898	75,222	45	Louisiana	2,769,982	60,192
21	Illinois	9,666,740	75,080	46	Indiana	3,889,428	59,496
22	Florida	14,373,073	74,404	47	Texas	15,175,079	58,233
23	Kentucky	3,238,446	73,930	48	Hawaii	744,542	53,475
24	South Dakota	614,564	73,746	49	Mississippi	1,594,789	53,428
25	Oregon	2,860,963	73,370	50	Alaska	342,120	46,773

FIGURE 7.10

State rankings for Do Not Call registrations, by proportion of population registered, 2013 [CONTINUED]

[a]Rankings are based on the "Active registrations per 100,000 population." "Active registrations" reflect the total number of phone numbers registered on the National Do Not Call Registry as of September 30, 2013.
[b]Population estimates are based on the 2012 U.S. Census population estimates.
[c]Numbers for the District of Columbia are as follows: Active registrations = 595,115; and Active registrations per 100,000 population = 94,116.

SOURCE: "State Rankings for National Do Not Call Registry Registrations by State Population," in *National Do Not Call Registry Data Book: FY 2013*, Federal Trade Commission, December 2013, http://www.ftc.gov/sites/default/files/documents/reports/national-do-not-call-registry-data-book-fiscal-year-2013/131204dncdatabook.pdf (accessed June 5, 2014)

CHAPTER 8
HEALTH RESOURCES IN THE INFORMATION AGE

Before the Internet, finding the latest information on a health issue typically required access to a university or medical library. Most medical studies and information existed in expensive books and journals, which were generally written for those with formal training. The Internet gave rise to a plethora of accessible, informative websites that average consumers could comprehend. The rise of online pharmacies also allowed people the convenience of ordering and receiving prescription drugs and medical supplies at home. Despite some problems such as the online sale of counterfeit medications and the existence of faulty medical information on the web, a majority of Americans used the Internet to research health-related matters in 2014. Susannah Fox, Maeve Duggan, and Kristen Purcell of the Pew Research Center report in *Family Caregivers Are Wired for Health* (June 20, 2013, http://www.pewinternet.org/files/old-media//Files/Reports/2013/PewResearch_FamilyCaregivers.pdf) that in 2012, 84% of caregivers who used the Internet went online to research medical or health issues; among other adult Internet users, this figure was 64%. (See Table 8.1.) At the same time, an increasing number of Americans were using their cell phones to seek information on health-related topics. In *Mobile Health 2012* (November 8, 2012, http://www.pewinternet.org/files/old-media//Files/Reports/2012/PIP_MobileHealth2012_FINAL.pdf), Fox and Duggan note that nearly one in five (19%) smartphone owners downloaded health-related software applications (apps) to their mobile devices in 2012. (See Table 8.2.) Women (23%) were more likely than men (16%) to have downloaded a health app that year. Among smartphone owners who downloaded a health app in 2012, more than one-third (38%) downloaded an exercise or fitness app, the highest percentage for any category of health app. (See Table 8.3.) Slightly less than one-third (31%) of smartphone owners downloaded diet-related apps in 2012.

The Internet has also benefited those who work in the health care fields. The Internet allows medical researchers to share information as never before. Enormous databases accessible on the Internet contain references to nearly all published medical papers, sparing researchers the tedium of hunting through print indexes. The Internet also provides the perfect medium for posting health care research data, such as statistics on disease prevalence, and research organizations can post data from thousands of disease studies. The availability of research data has fostered a new era of scientific cooperation wherein medical results from laboratories halfway around the world can be brought together with a click of a mouse.

HEALTH CARE ON THE INTERNET

Overall, a majority of adults, regardless of their health status, monitored specific indicators relating to their health in 2012. For example, 59% of adults not suffering from a chronic condition kept track of their weight, diet, or exercise routine, compared with 61% of adults with one chronic condition and 64% of adults with two or more chronic conditions. (See Table 8.4.) That year, fewer than one in five (19%) adults with no chronic conditions monitored their blood pressure, blood sugar, sleep patterns, or other health indicators or symptoms; by contrast, 40% of adults with one chronic condition, and 62% of adults with two or more chronic conditions, monitored their blood pressure, blood sugar, sleep patterns, or other health indicators or symptoms that year. Among adults without a chronic condition, 40% reported that monitoring certain health indicators had changed their approach to either their own health or the health of someone else in 2012; among adults with one or more chronic conditions, this figure was 51%. (See Figure 8.1.)

Table 8.5 offers a glimpse into the types of topics Internet users research online. Overall, 71% of all online adults not suffering from a chronic condition researched a specific health topic on the Internet in 2012; by comparison,

TABLE 8.1

Percentage of online caregivers and other Internet users who search the web for health information, by topic, 2012

Have you ever looked online for information about...	Online caregivers (sample size = 1,003)	Other internet users (sample size = 1,389)
A specific disease or medical problem	71	44
A certain medical treatment or procedure	57	34
How to lose weight or how to control your weight	31	23
Health insurance (private, Medicare or Medicaid)	31	21
Food safety or recalls	25	15
Drug safety or recalls	25	10
Caring for an aging relative or friend	25	7
A drug you saw advertised	23	11
Medical test results	22	10
How to reduce your health care costs	15	8
Pregnancy and childbirth	14	10
Any other health issue	28	15
Yes to any of the above topics	84	64

SOURCE: Susannah Fox, Maeve Duggan, and Kristen Purcell, "Health Topics," in *Family Caregivers Are Wired for Health*, Pew Research Center, June 20, 2013, http://www.pewinternet.org/files/old-media//Files/Reports/2013/PewResearch_FamilyCaregivers.pdf (accessed June 6, 2014)

TABLE 8.2

Percentage of smartphone owners who use health apps, by select characteristics, 2012

All smartphone owners	19%
a Men	16
b Women	23[a]
Age	
a 18–29	24[c, d]
b 30–49	19[d]
c 50–64	16
d 65+	10
Race/ethnicity	
a White, non-Hispanic	19
b Black, non-Hispanic	21
c Hispanic	15
Annual household income	
a Less than $30,000/yr	14
b $30,000–$49,999	21
c $50,000–$74,999	21
d $75,000+	23[a]
Education level	
a High school grad	11
b Some college	24[a]
c College+	22[a]

Note: Columns marked with a superscript letter (a) or another letter indicate a statistically significant difference between that row and the row designated by that superscript letter. Statistical significance is determined inside the specific section covering each demographic trait.

SOURCE: Susannah Fox and Maeve Duggan, "Who Uses Health Apps?" in *Mobile Health 2012*, Pew Research Center, November 8, 2012, http://www.pewinternet.org/files/old-media//Files/Reports/2012/PIP_MobileHealth2012_FINAL.pdf (accessed June 6, 2014)

TABLE 8.3

Health app usage, by type of app, 2012

All health app users	
Exercise, fitness, pedometer or heart rate monitoring	38%
Diet, food, calorie counter	31
Weight	12
Period or menstrual cycle	7
Blood pressure	5
WebMD	4
Pregnancy	3
Blood sugar or diabetes	2
Medication management (tracking, alerts, etc)	2
Mood	*
Sleep	*
Other	14

*Less than 1% of respondents.

SOURCE: Susannah Fox and Maeve Duggan, "Types of Health Apps," in *Mobile Health 2012*, Pew Research Center, November 8, 2012, http://www.pewinternet.org/files/old-media//Files/Reports/2012/PIP_MobileHealth2012_FINAL.pdf (accessed June 6, 2014)

shows, nearly two-thirds (62%) of online adults with two or more chronic conditions researched a specific disease or health problem in 2012, whereas a little more than half (52%) of adult Internet users not suffering from a chronic condition conducted the same type of research. That year, online adults with no chronic health problems (13%) were slightly more likely than those with one chronic condition (12%) or those with two or more chronic conditions (6%) to search for information about pregnancy online.

Adults who are responsible for caring for a child, parent, friend, or other loved one also take advantage of the Internet as a health information resource. Overall, 72% of all adult caregivers searched for health information online, compared with 50% of all adult non-caregivers. (See Figure 8.2.) As Table 8.1 shows, 71% of caregivers who used the Internet went online to research a specific medical condition in 2012; more than half (57%) went online to research specific medical treatments or procedures.

Roughly one-quarter (24%) of online caregivers read reviews of particular medications or medical treatments on the Internet in 2012; 22% consulted online rankings or reviews of physicians or providers, and 19% went online to find rankings of hospitals or medical facilities. (See Figure 8.3.) In 2012 adult caregivers who used the Internet were more likely than other online adults to have read online commentary concerning another person's health issues (34% compared with 20%, respectively), searched online to find other people with health concerns similar to their own (22% compared with 11%, respectively), and downloaded insurance forms from the Internet (15% and 9%, respectively). (See Table 8.6.)

As more and more adults go online for health information, many health care officials have begun to worry

73% of online adults with one chronic condition researched a specific health topic on the Internet that year, and 76% of adult Internet users with two or more chronic conditions searched for health-related information online. As Table 8.5

TABLE 8.4

Percentage of adults who track health indicators, by health status and indicator, 2012

Do you happen to track...	No chronic conditions (sample size = 1,516)	1 chronic condition (sample size = 809)	2+ chronic conditions (sample size = 689)
Your own weight, diet or exercise routine?	59	61	64
Any other health indicators or symptoms like blood pressure, blood sugar, sleep patterns, headaches, or anything else?	19	40	62
Any health indicators or symptoms for anyone besides yourself?	10	13	16
Any of the above	61	70	80

SOURCE: Susannah Fox and Maeve Duggan, "Tracking Health Indicators," in *The Diagnosis Difference: A Portrait of the 45% of U.S. Adults Living with Chronic Health Conditions*, Pew Research Center, November 26, 2013, http://www.pewinternet.org/files/old-media//Files/Reports/2013/PewResearch_DiagnosisDifference.pdf (accessed June 6, 2014)

FIGURE 8.1

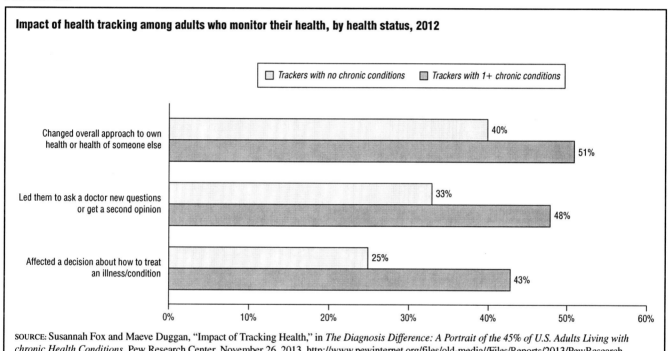

Impact of health tracking among adults who monitor their health, by health status, 2012

SOURCE: Susannah Fox and Maeve Duggan, "Impact of Tracking Health," in *The Diagnosis Difference: A Portrait of the 45% of U.S. Adults Living with chronic Health Conditions*, Pew Research Center, November 26, 2013, http://www.pewinternet.org/files/old-media//Files/Reports/2013/PewResearch_DiagnosisDifference.pdf (accessed June 6, 2014)

TABLE 8.5

Percentage of Internet users who search for health information online, by health status and topic, 2012

Have you looked online for information about...	No chronic conditions (sample size = 1,325)	1 chronic condition (sample size = 630)	2+ chronic conditions (sample size = 437)
A specific disease or medical problem	52	59	62
A certain medical treatment or procedure	41	42	53
How to lose weight or how to control your weight	27	25	27
Health insurance (private, Medicare or Medicaid)	24	25	29
Food safety or recalls	18	22	21
Drug safety or recalls	15	17	21
Caring for an aging relative or friend	14	15	14
A drug you saw advertised	13	19	20
Medical test results	13	17	18
Pregnancy and childbirth	13	12	6
How to reduce your health care costs	10	13	12
Any other health issue	18	23	26
Yes to any of the above topics	71	73	76

SOURCE: Susannah Fox and Maeve Duggan, "Health Topics," in *The Diagnosis Difference: A Portrait of the 45% of U.S. Adults Living with Chronic Health Conditions*, Pew Research Center, November 26, 2013, http://www.pewinternet.org/files/old-media//Files/Reports/2013/PewResearch_DiagnosisDifference.pdf (accessed June 6, 2014)

FIGURE 8.2

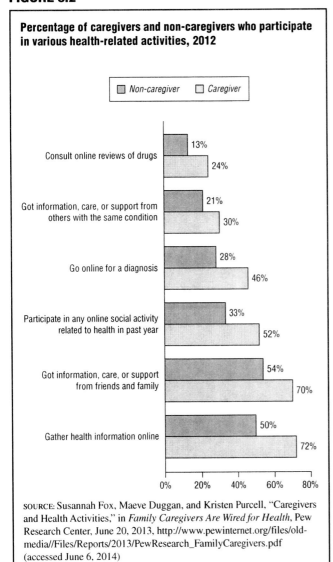

Percentage of caregivers and non-caregivers who participate in various health-related activities, 2012

Legend: Non-caregiver / Caregiver

Consult online reviews of drugs — 13% / 24%

Got information, care, or support from others with the same condition — 21% / 30%

Go online for a diagnosis — 28% / 46%

Participate in any online social activity related to health in past year — 33% / 52%

Got information, care, or support from friends and family — 54% / 70%

Gather health information online — 50% / 72%

(0% 20% 40% 60% 80%)

SOURCE: Susannah Fox, Maeve Duggan, and Kristen Purcell, "Caregivers and Health Activities," in *Family Caregivers Are Wired for Health*, Pew Research Center, June 20, 2013, http://www.pewinternet.org/files/old-media//Files/Reports/2013/PewResearch_FamilyCaregivers.pdf (accessed June 6, 2014)

that Americans are using the Internet to diagnose their own ailments in the hope of avoiding time-consuming but necessary visits to the doctor's office. The biggest problem with self-diagnosis is that it is rarely objective. Using advice from online websites is especially problematic in that it is often incomplete. In "Find and Evaluate Health Information on the Web" (2014, http://www.mlanet.org/resources/userguide.html), the Medical Library Association (MLA) provides a list of recommendations that those seeking health information on the Internet should follow. These recommendations include identifying each site's sponsor, checking the date of information on the site, and verifying that the material is rooted in fact, as opposed to opinion.

Top Websites for Health Information

According to the MLA in "MLA Top Health Web Sites" (2014, https://www.mlanet.org/resources/medspeak/topten.html), the most useful medical websites in 2014 were:

- Cancer.gov, National Cancer Institute (http://www.cancer.gov)
- Centers for Disease Control and Prevention (CDC; http://www.cdc.gov)
- Familydoctor.org, American Academy of Family Physicians (http://familydoctor.org)
- Healthfinder, National Health Information Center (http://www.healthfinder.gov)
- HIV InSite, University of California, San Francisco Center for HIV Information (http://hivinsite.ucsf.edu)
- KidsHealth, Nemours Foundation (http://www.kidshealth.org)
- Mayo Clinic (http://www.mayoclinic.com)
- MedlinePlus, U.S. National Library of Medicine (http://www.medlineplus.gov)
- NetWellness, Universities of Cincinnati, Ohio State, and Case Western Reserve (http://www.netwellness.org)
- NIHSeniorHealth, National Institutes of Health (NIH) health and wellness information for older adults (http://nihseniorhealth.gov)

These websites were evaluated in part on their credibility, content, sponsorship/authorship, purpose, and design. The general medicine websites noted by the MLA (Healthfinder.gov, Familydoctor.org, MedlinePlus.gov, and Mayoclinic.com) contain information on many medical diseases and conditions. The nonprofit Kidshealth.org focuses on health care for children from prenatal care through adolescence. Facts on the human immunodeficiency virus (HIV) are available at HIVInsite.com, and Cancer.gov presents information on cancer types, causes, and treatments. Cancer.gov also maintains a database of clinical trials that are being conducted all over the country for those who seek information on alternative treatments. Finally, CDC.gov contains information on communicable diseases, immunization, and disease prevention.

MedlinePlus, the most comprehensive general medicine site, made its debut on the Internet in October 1998 with 22 health topics in its library. The site received more than 682,000 page hits during its first three months. By 2014 the site held information on more than 900 diseases and conditions. A search on MedlinePlus for a disease typically yields definitions, fact sheets, drug information, the latest news on the disease, and links to places where further information can be found. During the second quarter of fiscal year (FY) 2007 the site recorded 245 million page views, an all-time high. (See Figure 8.4.) Traffic dropped considerably over the next year and a half, however, falling to 161 million views during the fourth quarter of FY 2008. Traffic to MedlinePlus began

FIGURE 8.3

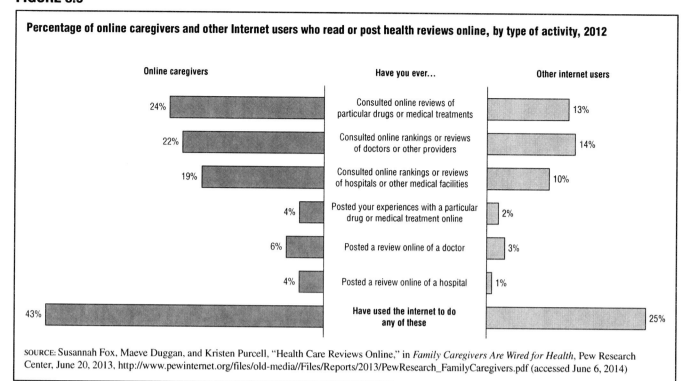

Percentage of online caregivers and other Internet users who read or post health reviews online, by type of activity, 2012

SOURCE: Susannah Fox, Maeve Duggan, and Kristen Purcell, "Health Care Reviews Online," in *Family Caregivers Are Wired for Health*, Pew Research Center, June 20, 2013, http://www.pewinternet.org/files/old-media//Files/Reports/2013/PewResearch_FamilyCaregivers.pdf (accessed June 6, 2014)

TABLE 8.6

Percentage of online caregivers and other Internet users who interact online about health-related issues, by type of activity, 2012

In the past 12 months, have you...	Caregivers (sample size = 1,003)	Non-caregivers (sample size = 1,389)
Read or watched someone else's commentary or experience about health or medical issues online?	34	20
Gone online to find others who might have health concerns similar to yours?	22	11
Downloaded forms online or applied for health insurance online, including private insurance, Medicare, or Medicaid?	15	9
Signed up to receive email updates or alerts about health or medical issues?	15	7
Posted a health-related question online or shared your own personal health experience online in any way?	11	6
Used the internet to do any of these	52	33

SOURCE: Susannah Fox, Maeve Duggan, and Kristen Purcell, "The Social Life of Health Information," in *Family Caregivers Are Wired for Health*, Pew Research Center, June 20, 2013, http://www.pewinternet.org/files/old-media//Files/Reports/2013/PewResearch_FamilyCaregivers.pdf (accessed June 6, 2014)

an upward trend again, reaching 221 million page views and a record 83.6 million unique visitors during the second quarter of 2013.

MEDICATION ONLINE

The Internet also contains a wealth of information about prescription and nonprescription drugs. Since the late 1990s the online pharmacy business has been growing at a steady rate. Most major online pharmacies, such as Drugstore.com and Walgreen's online pharmacy, are legitimate. They carry the Verified Internet Pharmacy Practice Sites (VIPPS) seal of approval issued by the National Association of Boards of Pharmacy (NABP), meaning that they comply with all state and federal laws. Much like traditional pharmacies, these online drugstores require that a prescription be sent or called in by a doctor. Such pharmacies also send the drug to the patient complete with dosage and warning information on the bottle. According to the NABP in "Buying Medicine Online" (June 2014, http://www.nabp.net/programs/consumer-protection/buying-medicine-online), as of June 2014 there were 57 VIPPS-certified pharmaceutical websites, working in collaboration with more than 12,000 online pharmacies, operating in the United States.

However, unlawful virtual pharmacies, which do not follow U.S. state and federal regulations, have begun operating on the Internet as well. In some cases, online pharmacies are operating illegally simply because they are based in other countries. For example, even though many Canadian pharmacies follow strict standards that are comparable to those imposed on legitimate U.S. pharmacies, as of 2014 it was still illegal for individuals in the United States to buy pharmaceuticals from Canadian pharmacies. Of greater concern to health and law enforcement officials, however, is the rise of illegitimate online pharmacies. Although many online pharmacies that cater to the U.S. market claim to be located in Canada, research shows that

FIGURE 8.4

Use of MedlinePlus, fiscal years 1999–2013

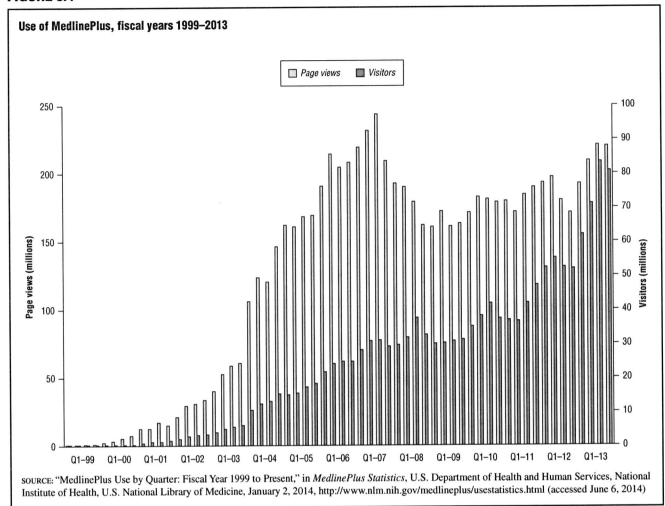

SOURCE: "MedlinePlus Use by Quarter: Fiscal Year 1999 to Present," in *MedlinePlus Statistics*, U.S. Department of Health and Human Services, National Institute of Health, U.S. National Library of Medicine, January 2, 2014, http://www.nlm.nih.gov/medlineplus/usestatistics.html (accessed June 6, 2014)

many of them are actually located in other countries, including the United States. Many of these pharmacies will sell patients prescription drugs without a prescription, provide counterfeit or contaminated drugs, or send medications in the wrong dosages.

For many patients in the United States, the lure of online pharmacies is their convenience and low cost. In 2014 millions of Americans were without health insurance, and millions more had limited prescription drug benefits. In some cases, cheaper online pharmacies represented the difference between obtaining much-needed medications and going without them. As Paul Jablow notes in "Ins, Outs of Getting Meds from Overseas" (Philly.com, January 12, 2014), brand-name medications purchased from foreign-based online pharmacies cost 75% less than those acquired in the United States.

Online Pharmacies, Safety, and the Law

Regardless, purchasing drugs online carries substantial risks. Illegitimate online pharmacies have generated a great deal of concern among health care professionals and government regulators in the United States. One

problem is that state medical boards, which typically oversee brick-and-mortar operations, have difficulty monitoring pharmaceutical websites. Even though some of these pharmacies follow many of the same standards as legitimate operations, others disregard them altogether. Besides providing drugs without a prescription, many send patients drugs without warning labels or dosage information. In an investigation of approximately 10,000 online pharmacies marketing to patients in the United States, the NABP (June 2014, http://www.nabp .net/programs/consumer-protection/buying-medicine-online) finds that only 3% adhered to standard pharmacy regulations and practices. Of the online pharmacies labeled "not recommended" by the NAPB, 23% were operating outside of the United States, and 49% sold drugs that were either foreign or had not received official approval from the U.S. Food and Drug Administration (FDA). Furthermore, 88% of online pharmacies that failed to comply with U.S. law offered to sell drugs without a prescription.

In response to this trend, Congress crafted legislation aimed at controlling the rapidly expanding trade in illegal online drugs. In 2008 President George W. Bush (1946–)

signed the Ryan Haight Online Pharmacy Consumer Protection Act, a law that imposed several new restrictions on the sale of online pharmaceuticals. The law was named for Ryan Haight (1982–2001), a California teenager who died after overdosing on painkillers he had purchased illegally over the Internet. Among the law's key provisions is the requirement that all prescriptions be accompanied by a physical consultation between a doctor and a patient. Furthermore, the law imposed a ban on all online advertisements for illegal prescription medications.

When federal and state agencies become aware of illegitimate pharmacies in the United States, they attempt to shut them down. In a speech delivered to the Opiate Abuse Conference in September 2010, the U.S. attorney general Eric Holder Jr. (1951–; http://www.justice.gov/ ag/speeches/2010/ag-speech-100910.html) asserted that, during the first nine months of 2010, the Drug Enforcement Agency (DEA) had seized "more than $62 million in proceeds and assets and...helped to shut down 'pill mill' pain clinics, prescription forgery rings, and illegal online pharmacies." Holder also claimed that the Ryan Haight Act had already played a major role in reducing the number of illegal online pharmacies selling prescription drugs in the United States. In "Two Indicted in Phila. in Illegal Online Drug Sales" (Philly.com, May 13, 2010), Nathan Gorenstein reports that the first prosecution under the Ryan Haight Act was initiated in May 2010, when federal prosecutors indicted two individuals, one American and one from the Bahamas, in association with an illegal online diet pill ring.

As Amy Pavuk reports in "DEA Targets FedEx, UPS in Online-Pharmacy Probe" (OrlandoSentinel.com, March 26, 2013), by 2013 the DEA had also begun investigating the role of major shipping companies in the transport of prescription drugs into the United States by illegal online pharmacies. However, government regulators can do little about controlling pharmacies that are outside of U.S. borders.

In the view of law enforcement officials, global cooperation is critical to controlling traffic in illegal online drugs. As Dina Fine Maron writes in "Pill of Goods: International Counterfeit Drug Ring Hit in Massive Sting" (ScientificAmerican.com, July 3, 2013), in July 2013 the FDA closed down 1,677 illegal online pharmacies, the largest Internet-based operation of its kind. Although all of the websites claimed to be operating in Canada, Maron writes, none of the illegal prescription medications actually originated there.

In "Thousands of Illicit Online Pharmacies Shut Down in the Largest-Ever Global Operation Targeting Fake Medicines" (May 22, 2014, http://www.interpol .int/News-and-media/News/2014/N2014-089), the International Criminal Police Organization (Interpol) reports that in May 2014 approximately 200 law enforcement organizations in more than 110 countries participated in a worldwide raid aimed at disrupting global traffic in fake and illicit pharmaceuticals. Dubbed Operation Pangea VII, the raid resulted in a total of 237 arrests, as well as the confiscation of 9.4 million counterfeit and illegal prescription drugs worth an estimated $36 billion. In the course of the operation, officials deleted over 19,000 advertisements for illegal pharmaceuticals from social networking sites, while also shutting down more than 10,500 websites selling illicit medications. According to Interpol, Operation Pangea VII was the largest single enforcement action targeting counterfeit medications in history. A number of international agencies and entities participated in the operation, including the Center for Safe Internet Pharmacies (CSIP), the Permanent Forum of International Pharmaceutical Crime (PFIPC), and the World Customs Organization (WCO). In addition, several global corporations, among them MasterCard, Microsoft, and Visa cooperated with Interpol in the effort.

Because of the many unethical and illegal practices that are encountered by consumers making pharmaceutical purchases online, the FDA provides the guide "Buying Prescription Medicine Online: A Consumer Safety Guide" (October 4, 2012, http://www.fda.gov/Drugs/ ResourcesForYou/ucm080588.htm) to reduce or eliminate many issues surrounding Internet pharmacies. The FDA recommends that patients use only sites that require a prescription, have pharmacists available to answer questions, and adequately protect the privacy of customers. It also suggests that online consumers use only state-licensed U.S. pharmacies. In 2012 the FDA launched the BeSafeRx initiative (http://www.fda.gov/drugs/resources foryou/consumers/buyingusingmedicinesafely/buyingmed icinesovertheinternet/besaferxknowyouronlinepharmacy/ default.htm), which is aimed at providing the public with vital information concerning the dangers that are involved with purchasing drugs over the Internet.

MEDICAL DATA REVOLUTION

Since the 1980s information technology (IT) and the Internet have transformed the field of medical research. Before launching a medical research project, a scientist must first know what has been done in the area he or she plans to study. For example, the initial step for a researcher who wants to find a cure for Alzheimer's would be to analyze previous data on the subject. Only then could the researcher formulate new theories and design experiments that advance the field. Before the Internet and the widespread use of computer databases, researchers seeking such information were required to spend days at medical libraries, sifting through thick journal indexes that cataloged thousands upon thousands of past journal articles by subject. The advent of computer databases changed all that. Huge medical indexes were put in digital form, which allowed researchers to compile a full list of research articles in minutes instead of days. MEDLINE/PubMed, which is maintained by the National Library of Medicine, is one of the most comprehensive and widely used of these databases. The National Library of Medicine (May 7, 2014, http://www.nlm.nih.gov/pubs/factsheets/dif_med_pub.html) states that in 2014 MEDLINE contained 21 million citations and abstracts summarizing papers that were published in nearly 5,600 biomedical journals in the United States and throughout the world. By simply going online to MEDLINE and typing a query, a researcher can track down every published paper on most medical topics.

The ability of computers and the Internet to store and transmit scientific data has also transformed the way medical research is conducted. The Internet allows scientists from all over the world to share data on diseases and patient attributes. Computers can then perform statistical analyses on disease data in relation to various aspects of patient histories, such as age, geographic location, and even the presence of other diseases.

The CDC's National Center for Health Statistics (NCHS, http://www.cdc.gov/nchs) database contains statistics on a variety of diseases including arthritis, heart disease, HIV, and even tooth decay. All this information is freely available for scientists to use in their research. The NCHS also provides valuable data to other government agencies. For example, in 2013 the NCHS collaborated with the Federal Interagency Forum on Child and Family Statistics, a group of government agencies that is dedicated to collecting and sharing data on children and families, to produce *America's Children in Brief: Key National Indicators of Well-Being, 2013* (July 2013, http://www.childstats.gov/pdf/ac2013/ac_13.pdf). Among the contributions provided by the NCHS to the report were data measuring premature births and low birthrates, blood-lead levels in children between the ages of one and five years, and statistics evaluating the link between poverty and dental care in school-age children.

Computer databases and the Internet have also become invaluable resources for organ and tissue donor programs. For example, treatments for leukemia (a type of cancer) sometimes destroy the bone marrow, which produces red and white blood cells and platelets. To replace the bone marrow, a transplant from another person is needed. However, finding compatible bone marrow is difficult. Typically, a match may not even exist within the same family. The National Bone Marrow Donor Registry (http://bethematch.org) is a computer database of people who have agreed to donate their bone marrow to those in need. A doctor with a patient in need of a transplant can simply log onto the registry via the Internet and pull up all possible matches in the country. The Organ Procurement and Transplantation Network

TABLE 8.7

Number of organ-transplant candidates registered with the Organ Procurement and Transplantation Network, June 2014

All*	123,024
Kidney	100,781
Pancreas	1,192
Kidney/pancreas	2,047
Liver	15,740
Intestine	261
Heart	4,017
Lung	1,650
Heart/lung	55

*All candidates will be less than the sum due to candidates waiting for multiple organs.

SOURCE: Adapted from "Waiting List Candidates," U.S. Department of Health and Human Services, Health Resources and Services Administration, Organ Procurement and Transplantation Network, June 6, 2014, http://optn.transplant.hrsa.gov/data/ (accessed June 6, 2014)

(OPTN; http://optn.transplant.hrsa.gov) maintains a similar database for internal organ transplants, including kidney, pancreas, heart, lung, and intestine. The OPTN's secure transplant information database keeps track of exactly which patients are in need of a transplant. Table 8.7 displays the number of candidates who were waiting on the OPTN in June 2014. All necessary forms and patient histories are also included in the database. Should a donor's heart become available in a medical facility anywhere in the United States, the attending physician can access the database to find patients who are waiting for a new heart.

HEALTH IT

IT is changing the way patients interact with their health care providers and the way health care providers interact with one another to ensure prompt, safe, and effective treatments. Electronic health records are expected to improve health care by keeping all information about a patient's health history, including medications, immunizations, laboratory and test results, allergies, and family history in one accessible online location. As U.S. health care systems become networked, information about a patient will be immediately available regardless of the treatment location.

Even though electronic medical records provide enormous benefits to both patients and health care professionals, they also pose a number of new challenges. Alicia Gallegos indicates in "Legal Risks of Going Paperless" (AMedNews.com, March 5, 2012) that the potential for data breaches, system errors, and other problems relating to the transmission of data online leave health care professionals vulnerable to new forms of legal action. In "Benefits and Drawbacks of Electronic Health Record Systems" (*Journal of Risk Management and Healthcare Policy*, vol. 4, May 11, 2012), Nir Menachemi and Taleah H. Collum cite a number of financial disadvantages involved with implementing electronic health records, including the high costs that are related to launching and maintaining medical information online and the problems of lost productivity that are involved with the transition from paper to electronic data-keeping systems.

Despite all of these concerns, by 2014 adoption of health IT had become widespread across the medical profession. As Chun-Ju Hsiao and Esther Hing of the CDC report in "Use and Characteristics of Electronic Health Records Systems among Office-Based Physician Practices: United States, 2001–2013" *NCHS Data Brief*, no. 143, January 2014), between 2001 and 2013 the use of electronic health record (EHR) systems among office-based doctors rose from 18% to 78%. In 2013 Minnesota (94%) had the highest proportion of office-based physicians who had adopted some form of EHR system, and New Jersey (66%) had the lowest percentage of office-based doctors who had implemented an EHR system.

The Agency for Healthcare Research and Quality (AHRQ) of the U.S. Department of Health and Human Services (HHS) maintains a website (http://www.ahrq.gov/qual/patientsafetyix.htm#online) that provides information and resources aimed at reducing incidences of medical error. The AHRQ believes that by using IT to integrate health history with medication information many deaths and injuries stemming from medical errors can be prevented. Computerized health record systems would provide attending doctors with dosage information about medications already prescribed for each patient, check for potential interactions with other medications, and alert physicians to patient allergies. Anticipated benefits of integrated health IT include electronic health records for patients that can be easily shared by health care providers; electronic transmittal of medical test results; and electronic prescription messaging, which will improve efficiency and reduce human errors in reading paper prescriptions.

To facilitate the development of a nationwide electronic health system, President Bush established in April 2004 the Office of the National Coordinator for Health Information Technology (ONC) within the HHS. This office provides leadership in developing standards, policies, and the necessary infrastructure that will allow the flow of health information nationwide. *Healthcare IT News* (http://www.healthcareitnews.com), an online journal examining the role of IT in the medical profession, maintains a website that is dedicated to providing regular updates on the development of the Nationwide Health Information Network (NHIN). Known as HIEWatch (http://www.hiewatch.com), the site reports on various federal, state, and local health care IT initiatives, analyzes critical surveys and studies, and provides other news relating to the NHIN project.

The Health Information Technology for Economic and Clinical Health (HITECH) Act, which was part of the Economic Recovery and Reinvestment Act of 2009, was designed to improve and expand IT systems across the U.S. health care industry. HITECH provided the HHS with approximately $2 billion to help fund regional health care IT networks, with the aim of helping medical professionals coordinate patient care more quickly and efficiently, while reducing cases of medical errors. Supervised by the ONC, HITECH was also dedicated to maintaining online security to safeguard patient privacy. In June 2013 the ONC presented the status report *Update on the Adoption of Health Information Technology and Related Efforts to Facilitate the Electronic Use and Exchange of Health Information* (http://www.healthit.gov/sites/default/files/rtc_adoption_of_healthit_and_relatedefforts.pdf) to Congress. As Figure 8.5 shows, 72% of nonhospital-based primary physicians had adopted electronic health record systems in 2012, up from 42% in 2008. Among physicians who had not adopted EHR systems by 2011, 73% cited cost as the principal barrier to implementation, and 59% cited a loss of work productivity. (See Table 8.8.)

FIGURE 8.5

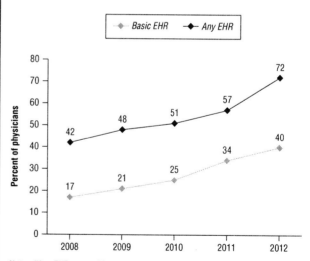

Adoption of electronic health records (EHR) among nonhospital-based physicians, by type of EHR, 2008–12

Notes: "Any EHR system" is a medical or health record system that is all or partially electronic (excluding billing systems). A basic EHR includes: patient history and demographics, patient problem lists, physician clinical notes, comprehensive list of patients' medications and allergies, computerized orders for prescriptions, and view laboratory and imaging results electronically.

SOURCE: "Figure 1. Percentage of Office-Based Physicians with EHRs: United States, 2008–2012," in *Update on the Adoption of Health Information Technology and Related Efforts to Facilitate the Electronic Use and Exchange of Health Information: A Report to Congress*, U.S. Department of Health and Human Services, Office of the National Coordinator for Health Information Technology (ONC), June 2013, http://www.healthit.gov/sites/default/files/rtc_adoption_of_healthit_and_relatedefforts.pdf (accessed June 6, 2014)

TABLE 8.8

Barriers to adoption of electronic health records (EHR), by adoption status, 2011

	Adopters	Nonadopters	Difference
Cost of purchasing a system	52	73	21*
Loss of productivity	37	59	22*
Effort needed to select a system	28	38	11*
Adequacy of training	27	41	14*
Annual maintenance cost	26	46	20*
Finding an EHR that meets practice needs	26	45	20*
Adequacy of technical support	25	40	15*
Resistance of practice to change work habits	22	40	19*
Reliability of the system	15	40	25*
Ability to secure financing	14	29	15*
Reaching consensus within the practice	10	18	8*
Access to high speed Internet	9	7	(1)

*Significant difference between adopter and nonadopter (p < 0.01). Numbers may not add up due to rounding.

SOURCE: "Table 8. Barriers to EHR Adoption by Adoption Status," in *Update on the Adoption of Health Information Technology and Related Efforts to Facilitate the Electronic Use and Exchange of Health Information: A Report to Congress*, U.S. Department of Health and Human Services, Office of the National Coordinator for Health Information Technology (ONC), June 2013, http://www.healthit.gov/sites/default/files/rtc_adoption_of_healthit_and_relatedefforts.pdf (accessed June 6, 2014)

The ONC notes an even more dramatic rise in the use of electronic prescription technology by physicians. Whereas only one state (Massachusetts) had an online prescription rate of more than 20% in 2008, by 2012 only Nevada had an online prescription rate of under 40%; 16 states had online prescription adoption rates of between 60% and 79% in 2012, and Massachusetts saw online prescription rates surpass 80% that year. (See Figure 8.6.) Nationwide, nearly half (47%) of all new prescriptions and prescription renewals were sent by physicians to pharmacies electronically in 2012, up from only 4% in 2008. (See Table 8.9.)

Information technology also played a key role in the implementation of the Patient Protection and Affordable Care Act of 2010 (PPACA; often informally referred to as "Obamacare"). The law called for the establishment of a federal web portal, HealthCare.gov, as well as online marketplaces for coverage provided within individual states. As Fredric Blavin, Stephen Zuckerman, and Michael Karpman of the Urban Institute's Health Policy Center observe in *Who Has Been Looking for Information in the ACA Marketplaces? Why? And How?* (March 5, 2014, http://hrms.urban.org/briefs/early-market-experiences .html), while the initial October 2013 launch of HealthCare.gov and the state marketplaces was marred by technical problems, by the fourth quarter of 2013 more than one-quarter (28.8%) of all adults had either searched for information about health coverage under the PPACA (11.8%) or intended to seek information about coverage (17%). (See Figure 8.7.) As Figure 8.8 shows, among adults who searched for information about coverage, 85.1% looked for it on an PPACA website. Overall, more than half (51.2%) of adults who went online in search of coverage information during the fourth quarter of 2013 found the process "very or somewhat easy"; slightly less than half (48.8%) found the search to be "very or somewhat hard." (See Figure 8.9.) As the U.S. Department of Health and Human Services reports (May 1, 2014, http://www.hhs.gov/news/press/2014pres/05/ 20140501a.html), more than 8 million people had enrolled in health insurance programs through the online marketplaces by the end of the initial enrollment period, which extended from October 2013 to March 2014.

FIGURE 8.6

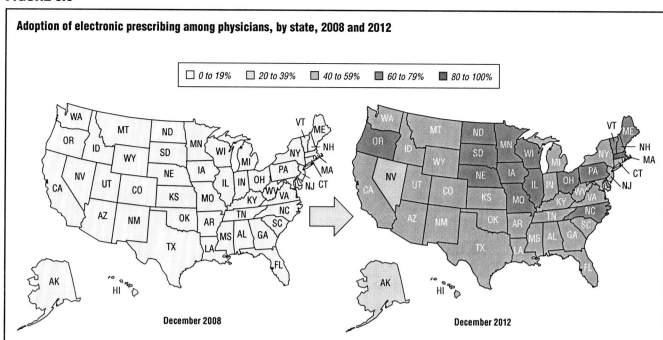

Adoption of electronic prescribing among physicians, by state, 2008 and 2012

☐ 0 to 19%　☐ 20 to 39%　▨ 40 to 59%　▨ 60 to 79%　▨ 80 to 100%

December 2008

December 2012

SOURCE: "Figure 8. Percent of Physicians E-Prescribing Using an EHR in 2008 and 2012," in *Update on the Adoption of Health Information Technology and Related Efforts to Facilitate the Electronic Use and Exchange of Health Information: A Report to Congress*, U.S. Department of Health and Human Services, Office of the National Coordinator for Health Information Technology (ONC), June 2013, http://www.healthit.gov/sites/default/files/rtc_adoption_of_healthit_and_relatedefforts.pdf (accessed June 6, 2014)

TABLE 8.9

Percentage of prescriptions and prescription renewals sent electronically, by state, 2008 and 2012

State	New and renewals 2008	New and renewals 2012	Percentage point increase	State	New and renewals 2008	New and renewals 2012	Percentage point increase
United States	4%	47%	43%	Missouri	4%	72%	68%
Alabama	2%	39%	37%	Montana	1%	45%	44%
Alaska	2%	33%	31%	Nebraska	2%	48%	46%
Arizona	6%	60%	54%	Nevada	9%	37%	28%
Arkansas	2%	43%	41%	New Hampshire	3%	64%	61%
California	3%	38%	35%	New Jersey	5%	34%	29%
Colorado	4%	39%	35%	New Mexico	2%	45%	43%
Connecticut	6%	46%	40%	New York	3%	43%	40%
Delaware	7%	53%	46%	North Carolina	6%	52%	46%
District of Columbia	3%	31%	28%	North Dakota	0%	57%	57%
Florida	4%	40%	36%	Ohio	4%	80%	76%
Georgia	2%	40%	38%	Oklahoma	2%	44%	42%
Hawaii	1%	45%	44%	Oregon	4%	58%	54%
Idaho	4%	44%	40%	Pennsylvania	6%	47%	41%
Illinois	4%	48%	44%	Rhode Island	17%	57%	40%
Indiana	3%	48%	45%	South Carolina	1%	42%	41%
Iowa	2%	60%	58%	South Dakota	1%	60%	59%
Kansas	3%	49%	46%	Tennessee	4%	39%	35%
Kentucky	3%	44%	41%	Texas	3%	44%	41%
Louisiana	3%	32%	29%	Utah	1%	41%	40%
Maine	6%	60%	54%	Vermont	4%	61%	57%
Maryland	5%	42%	37%	Virginia	3%	46%	43%
Massachusetts	20%	67%	47%	Washington	4%	54%	50%
Michigan	8%	49%	41%	West Virginia	3%	35%	32%
Minnesota	4%	80%	76%	Wisconsin	2%	65%	63%
Mississippi	1%	39%	38%	Wyoming	2%	39%	37%

SOURCE: "Table 2. New and Renewal Prescriptions Sent Electronically in 2008 and 2012, by State," in *Update on the Adoption of Health Information Technology and Related Efforts to Facilitate the Electronic Use and Exchange of Health Information: A Report to Congress*, U.S. Department of Health and Human Services, Office of the National Coordinator for Health Information Technology (ONC), June 2013, http://www.healthit.gov/sites/default/files/rtc_adoption_of_healthit_and_relatedefforts.pdf (accessed June 6, 2014)

FIGURE 8.7

Adults who had searched for information about health insurance plans available through the Affordable Care Act (ACA), by insurance status, age, and income, December 2013

Sample = 7,873

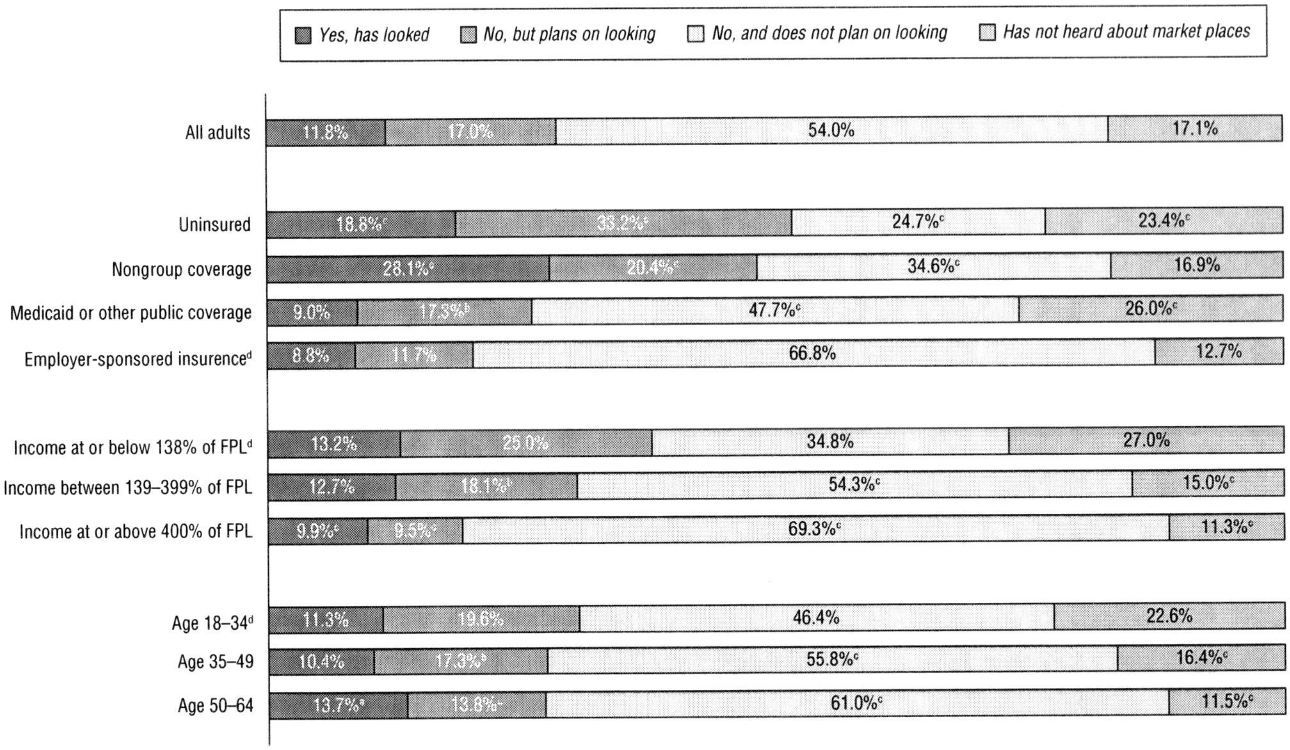

Legend: ■ Yes, has looked ▦ No, but plans on looking ▢ No, and does not plan on looking ▢ Has not heard about market places

Category	Yes, has looked	No, but plans on looking	No, and does not plan on looking	Has not heard about market places
All adults	11.8%	17.0%	54.0%	17.1%
Uninsured	18.8%ᶜ	33.2%ᵇ	24.7%ᶜ	23.4%ᶜ
Nongroup coverage	28.1%ᶜ	20.4%ᶜ	34.6%ᶜ	16.9%
Medicaid or other public coverage	9.0%	17.3%ᵇ	47.7%ᶜ	26.0%ᶜ
Employer-sponsored insurenceᵈ	8.8%	11.7%	66.8%	12.7%
Income at or below 138% of FPLᵈ	13.2%	25.0%	34.8%	27.0%
Income between 139–399% of FPL	12.7%	18.1%ᵇ	54.3%ᶜ	15.0%ᶜ
Income at or above 400% of FPL	9.9%ᶜ	9.5%ᶜ	69.3%ᶜ	11.3%ᶜ
Age 18–34ᵈ	11.3%	19.6%	46.4%	22.6%
Age 35–49	10.4%	17.3%ᵃ	55.8%ᶜ	16.4%ᶜ
Age 50–64	13.7%ᵃ	13.8%ᶜ	61.0%ᶜ	11.5%ᶜ

ᵃ/ᵇ/ᶜ Estimate differs significantly from those in the reference group, denoted by ᵈ, at the 0.10 / 0.05 / 0.01 level, using two-tailed tests.

Notes: FPL is federal poverty level. Estimates are reported based on complete cases. Among the respondents who had heard about health insurance marketplaces, 0.5% did not report whether they looked for or planned on looking for information on health plans in the marketplace, and this group is excluded from the calculations above. We do not report subgroup estimates for the 191 respondents with nonspecified coverage. Percentages may not total 100 due to rounding.

SOURCE: Fredric Blavin, Stephen Zuckerman, and Michael Karpman, "Figure 1. Looked for Information on Health Plans in Marketplace among Adults Age 18–64, Overall and by Insurance Coverage Status, Income, and Age," in *Who Has Been Looking for Information in the ACA Marketplaces? Why? And How?* Urban Institute Health Policy Center, Health Reform Monitoring Survey, March 5, 2014, http://hrms.urban.org/briefs/early-market-experiences.html (accessed June 6, 2014). Copyright © 2014 The Urban Institute.

FIGURE 8.8

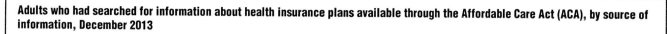

Adults who had searched for information about health insurance plans available through the Affordable Care Act (ACA), by source of information, December 2013

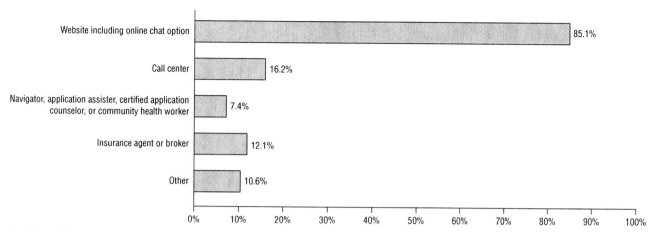

Population = 1,020.
Note: We report based on complete cases; 2.2% of respondents who looked for information on health plans in the marketplace did not report the source they used to obtain information. These estimates total more than 100 percent because respondents could identify more than one source of information.

SOURCE: Fredric Blavin, Stephen Zuckerman, and Michael Karpman, "Figure 2. Sources Used to Obtain Information on Health Plans in Marketplace among Adults Age 18–64 Who Have Looked for Information on Health Plans in Marketplace," in *Who Has Been Looking for Information in the ACA Marketplaces? Why? And How?* Urban Institute Health Policy Center, Health Reform Monitoring Survey, March 5, 2014, http://hrms.urban.org/briefs/early-market-experiences.html (accessed June 6, 2014). Copyright © 2014 The Urban Institute.

FIGURE 8.9

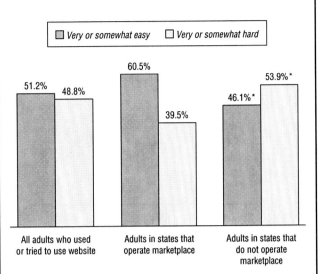

Experience of adults who had searched for information about health insurance plans available through the Affordable Care Act (ACA), December 2013

Legend: ▨ Very or somewhat easy   ☐ Very or somewhat hard

	Very or somewhat easy	Very or somewhat hard
All adults who used or tried to use website	51.2%	48.8%
Adults in states that operate marketplace	60.5%	39.5%
Adults in states that do not operate marketplace	46.1%*	53.9%*

*Estimate differs significantly from adults in states that operate marketplace at the 0.01 level, using two-tailed tests.

Notes: Statuses of state marketplace decisions are based on data compiled by the Kaiser Family Foundatoin and are current as of December 11, 2013. However, we place Idaho and New Mexico in the category of "states that do not operate marketplace" because the federal government is temporarily operating their information technology (IT) systems. We report based on complete cases; we exclude from these calculations the 1.0% of respondents who initially reported using or trying to use the website but did not report whether the website was easy or hard to use, as well as the 3.3% of respondents who initially reported that they used or tried to use the website, but then reported that they did not try to use the website in this follow-up question.

SOURCE: Fredric Blavin, Stephen Zuckerman, and Michael Karpman, "Figure 3. Experience Using Website to Obtain Information on Health Plans in Marketplace among Adults Age 18–64 Who Used or Tried to Use Website, Overall and by State Marketplace Structure," in *Who Has Been Looking for Information in the ACA Marketplaces? Why? And How?* Urban Institute Health Policy Center, Health Reform Monitoring Survey, March 5, 2014, http://hrms.urban.org/briefs/early-market-experiences.html (accessed June 6, 2014). Copyright © 2014 The Urban Institute.

CHAPTER 9

HIGH TECHNOLOGY AND DAILY LIFE

Since the early 1980s high technology (high tech) has crept into every aspect of American life and has become in some instances as mundane as running water or refrigeration. Many Americans think nothing of going online to check the weather, purchase movie tickets, watch videos, or read up on their favorite hobbies. The Internet also contains an endless list of resources that most people would never have room for on their bookshelf but now take for granted nonetheless, including maps, dictionaries, phone books, and even manuals on most products. The Internet has become a great way to communicate with others as well, and millions have used it to make a date, schedule appointments, or find old friends.

Over time, innovations in computing have also allowed Americans to become more mobile. This mobility has transformed the way that people conduct their daily lives. As Table 9.1 shows, mobile technology has helped people communicate with each other more frequently. Among working adults between the ages of 18 and 29, more than three-quarters (76%) said that mobile technology had significantly increased their communication with family and friends; 71% of working adults between the ages of 30 and 49 reported that mobile technology had led to more frequent communication with family and friends, and sizable proportions of working adults between the ages of 50 and 64 (55%) and 65 years of age and older (37%) also reported significant increases in their personal communication. At the same time, more than one-third of employed adults between the ages of 18 and 29 (37%) and between the ages of 30 and 49 (37%) reported that mobile technology had led to a substantial increase in the amount of work they performed outside of normal working hours. (See Table 9.1.)

The Internet and mobile devices are not the only new technology to have become ubiquitous in everyday American life. Microchips, sensors, and display screens can be found on or in just about every appliance in the home. They allow people to do everything from control the home thermostat from a remote computer to heat water with microwave radiation. Most American automobiles have dozens of complex sensors that monitor engine performance, regulate gas flow, sense obstacles, and pinpoint the vehicle's location. As of 2014, robots were making their way into U.S. homes to complete time-consuming tasks such as mowing the lawn and vacuuming the living room.

In 2014 most people believed that continued technological advances would bring significant improvements to everyday life. In a survey of U.S. adults by the Pew Research Center in 2014, 59% of respondents believed that technology would lead to a future in which their lives were "mostly better" than in the present; by contrast, 30% thought that their future lives would be "mostly worse" due to technological advances. (See Table 9.2.) Men (67%) were considerably more optimistic than women (51%) about technology's impact on the future, and more college graduates (66%) were positive about technology's impact than adults who either had attended college without earning a degree (56%) or who had earned a high school diploma or less (56%). Survey respondents with annual incomes of $75,000 or more (67%) were significantly more likely to believe that technology would make future everyday life better than those earning less than $30,000 a year (52%).

Although most Americans felt optimistic about the future of technology in general, many viewed specific technological advances with skepticism or even anxiety. Figure 9.1 provides a glimpse into American attitudes toward potential near-term technological changes. As shown in Figure 9.1, more than half (53%) of survey respondents felt that the use of devices or implants to augment an individual's ability to receive information would represent a change for the worse; 37% believed such technology would represent an improvement in

TABLE 9.1

Increases in various activities among mobile technology users, by age, 2014

	18 to 29 years	30 to 49 years	50 to 64 years	65+ years
	%	%	%	%
Communication with friends and family	76	71	55	37
Amount of work you do outside out of regular working hours*	37	37	25	15
Involvement in election campaigns and other political activities	21	19	14	12

*Based on adults employed full or part time.

SOURCE: Jeffrey M. Jones, "Increase in Activities as a Result of Mobile Technology, by Age," in *In U.S., Mobile Tech Aids Interpersonal Communication Most*, The Gallup Organization, April 28, 2014, http://www.gallup.com/poll/168734/mobile-tech-aids-interpersonal-communication.aspx (accessed June 6, 2014). Copyright © 2014 Gallup, Inc. All rights reserved. The content is used with permission; however, Gallup retains all rights of republication.

TABLE 9.2

Attitudes concerning impact of technological change on the future, by sex, age, education attained, and household income, 2014

[% who feel that technological changes will lead to a future where people's lives are...]

	Mostly better	Mostly worse
Total	59%	30%
Gender		
Male	67	25
Female	51	36
Age		
18–29	59	29
30–49	60	32
50–64	59	30
65+	56	28
Education		
High school grad or less	56	35
Some college	56	33
College graduate	66	21
Household income		
Less than $30,000	52	38
$30,000–$49,999	63	27
$50,000–$74,999	63	28
$75,000 or more	67	22

SOURCE: Aaron Smith, "Technological Change and the Future," in *U.S. Views of Technology and the Future*, Pew Research Center, April 17, 2014, http://www.pewinternet.org/files/2014/04/US-Views-of-Technology-and-the-Future.pdf (accessed June 7, 2014)

people's lives. Two-thirds (66%) of all respondents believed that using technology to alter the DNA (deoxyribonucleic acid) of unborn children would represent a change for the worse, compared with only 26% who thought it would represent a change for the better. Nearly two-thirds (63%) of those surveyed felt that opening U.S. airspace to personal drones would make their lives worse, whereas only 22% viewed personal drones as a change for the better. (See Figure 9.1.)

Americans also differ in their views concerning what types of technological changes the future has in store for the world. Figure 9.2 outlines some of the emerging technological advances Americans in 2014 believed might happen within the next 50 years. As Figure 9.2 shows, more than four out of five (81%) of adults believed that medical scientists would have the capability to produce customized transplant organs in a laboratory by 2064. Slightly over half (51%) of American adults believed that computers would have the ability to produce art as well as humans within 50 years, whereas more than one-third (39%) of adults believed that humans would be able to use teleportation technology by 2064. In addition, one-third (33%) of adults surveyed believed the human race would establish colonies in outer space by 2064, whereas nearly one in five (19%) believed humans would have the power to control the weather by that year. (See Figure 9.2.)

EVERYDAY ACTIVITIES AND THE INTERNET
Mobile Connectivity

Mobile technology has played an increasingly important role in people's everyday Internet experiences. E-mail, instant messaging, social networking, and other software applications (or apps) have allowed individuals to maintain contact with family, friends, and associates

from their mobile devices. Other popular phone apps offer games, music, entertainment, health and fitness monitoring, shopping, navigation, photo sharing, video editing, and much more. As Table 9.3 shows, by 2013 half (50%) of all cell phone owners were downloading apps to their phones. Among younger cell phone owners, this figure was even higher. In 2013 more than three-quarters (77%) of cell owners between the ages of 18 and 29 downloaded apps to their mobile devices; by contrast, only 14% of cell phone owners 65 years of age and older downloaded an app that year. African American cell phone owners (60%) were considerably more likely than Hispanic cell phone owners (52%) and white cell owners (48%) to have downloaded an app in 2013. At the same time, cell owners living in urban (52%) and suburban (52%) areas were more likely than those living in rural areas (39%) to have downloaded apps that year. (See Table 9.3.)

Wireless connectivity has also enabled people to work remotely, establish contact with organizations, become acquainted with others who share similar interests, or simply meet new people. Indeed, by 2014 many American workers were checking their work e-mail outside of normal work hours. As Table 9.4 shows, nearly half (48%) of all college-educated adults checked work-related e-mails remotely with some frequency in 2014. At the same time, there appeared to be a direct correlation

FIGURE 9.1

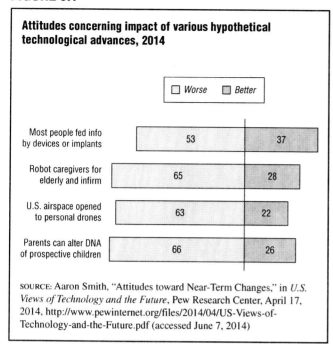

Attitudes concerning impact of various hypothetical technological advances, 2014

SOURCE: Aaron Smith, "Attitudes toward Near-Term Changes," in *U.S. Views of Technology and the Future*, Pew Research Center, April 17, 2014, http://www.pewinternet.org/files/2014/04/US-Views-of-Technology-and-the-Future.pdf (accessed June 7, 2014)

FIGURE 9.2

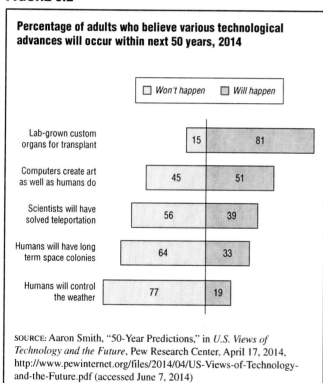

Percentage of adults who believe various technological advances will occur within next 50 years, 2014

SOURCE: Aaron Smith, "50-Year Predictions," in *U.S. Views of Technology and the Future*, Pew Research Center, April 17, 2014, http://www.pewinternet.org/files/2014/04/US-Views-of-Technology-and-the-Future.pdf (accessed June 7, 2014)

between annual salary and the likelihood that a person checked work e-mails remotely that year. For example, more than half (53%) of individuals who earned $120,000 or more checked work e-mails remotely with some frequency in 2014; by contrast, only one-quarter (25%) of workers earning between $24,000 and $36,000 a year frequently checked their work e-mails outside of normal working hours that year. (See Table 9.4.)

TABLE 9.3

Percentage of cell owners who download apps to their phones, by select characteristics, 2013

All cell phone owners	50%
a Men	52
b Women	48
Race/ethnicity	
a White, non-Hispanic	48
b Black, non-Hispanic	60
c Hispanic	52
Age	
a 18–29	77
b 30–49	59
c 50–64	33
d 65+ (n = 478)	14
Education attainment	
a No high school diploma	36
b High school grad	42
c Some college	53
d College+	62
Household income	
a Less than $30,000/yr	41
b $30,000–$49,999	48
c $50,000–$74,999	50
d $75,000+	66
Urbanity	
a Urban	52
b Suburban	52
c Rural	39

SOURCE: Maeve Duggan, "Downloading Apps," in *Cell Phone Activities 2013*, Pew Research Center, September 16, 2013, http://www.pewinternet.org/files/old-media/Files/Reports/2013/PIP_Cell%20Phone%20Activities%20May%202013.pdf (accessed June 4, 2014)

Technology and Human Relationships

As communication, banking, and other forms of personal business have moved online, the private lives of individuals have become increasingly intertwined. This change has been particularly true for people involved in committed relationships. Indeed, by 2013 more than two-thirds (67%) of adults involved in serious relationships shared their online passwords with their significant others. (See Figure 9.3.) More than one-quarter (27%) of couples shared an e-mail account that year, and just over one in 10 either used the same online calendar (11%) or shared an account on a social media site (11%).

In many respects, adults involved in committed relationships believed that technology had affected their interactions with their significant others in a positive way. For example, in 2013 more than one in five (21%) of online adults involved in a serious relationship felt that texting or other forms of electronic communication had brought them closer to their spouse or partner. (See Figure 9.4.) The duration of a relationship seemed to be a factor in determining a person's feelings about the benefits of technology on their marriage or partnership. Nearly one-third (32%) of adults involved in a committed relationship for 10 years or less thought that texting or online messaging had made them feel closer to their

TABLE 9.4

Percentage of full-time employees who check work e-mail remotely, by frequency and select demographic characteristics, 2014

[U.S. Full-Time Employees' Remote Working Habits]

HOW OFTEN DO YOU NORMALLY CHECK YOUR WORK EMAIL OUTSIDE OF NORMAL WORKING HOURS—FREQUENTLY, OCCASIONALLY, RARELY, OR NEVER?

	Frequently	Occasionally, rarely or never
Male	40%	60%
Female	31%	70%
Millennials (1980–1996)	38%	62%
Generation X (1965–1979)	37%	63%
Baby boomers (1946–1964)	33%	67%
Less than a college degree	23%	77%
Some college	41%	59%
College degree or higher	48%	52%
$24,000–>$36,000	25%	75%
$36,000–>$48,000	30%	70%
$48,000–>$60,000	31%	69%
$60,000–>$90,000	38%	62%
$90,000–>$120,000	43%	57%
$120,000 or more	53%	47%

SOURCE: Jim Harter, Sangeeta Agrawal, and Susan Sorenson, "U.S. Full-Time Employees' Remote Working Habits," in *Most U.S. Workers See Upside to Staying Connected to Work*, The Gallup Organization, April 30, 2014, http://www.gallup.com/poll/168794/workers-upside-staying-connected-work .aspx (accessed June 6, 2014). Copyright © 2014 Gallup, Inc. All rights reserved. The content is used with permission; however, Gallup retains all rights of republication.

FIGURE 9.3

Percentage of Internet users involved in a committed relationship who share online account information with their partners, 2013

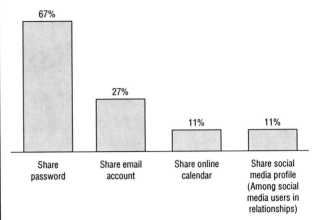

Note: Sharing social media profiles was measured among all social media users in committed relationships (sample size = 889).

SOURCE: Amanda Lenhart and Maeve Duggan, "Sharing Online Accounts with a Partner," in *Couples, the Internet, and Social Media*, Pew Research Center, February 11, 2014, http://www.pewinternet.org/ files/2014/02/PIP_Couples_and_Technology-FIN_021114.pdf (accessed June 7, 2014)

significant other, but only 12% of those involved in a relationship for 10 years or longer felt the same way. In addition, whereas 17% of adults involved in a relationship for 10 years or less felt that texting or online communication helped them resolve an argument with their spouse or partner in 2013, only 3% of those in a relationship for 10 years or more reported the same thing. (See Figure 9.4.)

At the same time, adults involved in committed relationships also reported several negative effects of technology on their marriage or partnership in 2013. One-quarter (25%) of all adults involved in a marriage or partnership felt that their partner became distracted by their cell phone when they were together. This feeling was considerably more pronounced among people who had been involved with their significant other for 10 years or less (36%) than among those who had been involved for 10 years or more (17%). (See Figure 9.5.) At the same time, online adults who had been married or partnered for 10 years or less were more likely to argue with their partner (11%) than adults who had been involved in their relationships for 10 years or more (5%) about the amount of time their spouse or partner spent online (11%). Those in shorter relationships also reported becoming upset about something their partner was doing online at a higher rate (6%) than those who had been in longer relationships (2%).

Social Networking

Arguably the most important development in online communication has been the rise of social networking during the early 21st century. Websites such as Facebook, LinkedIn, and Google+ allow members to create virtual profiles on the Internet, where they can upload pictures, share personal and professional information, post messages, and forge connections with other social network users (a process commonly known as "friending"). Of the major social networking sites, Facebook has emerged as the most popular. According to Internet Live Stats (August 2014, http://www.internetlivestats.com), by August 2014 there were nearly 1.3 billion Facebook users worldwide.

"Top 15 Most Popular Social Networking Sites" (eBizMBA, June 2014, http://www.ebizmba.com/articles/ social-networking-websites), offers a breakdown of the busiest social media sites in 2014. As the rankings indicate, Facebook was the most visited social media site in August 2014, with approximately 900 million monthly users; this figure was nearly three times the 310 million unique monthly visitors to Twitter, the second-most popular site during that period. Other leading social media sites in August 2014 were LinkedIn, with 255 million monthly users, followed by Pinterest (250 million), Google+ (120 million), Tumblr (110 million), and Instagram (100 million).

FIGURE 9.4

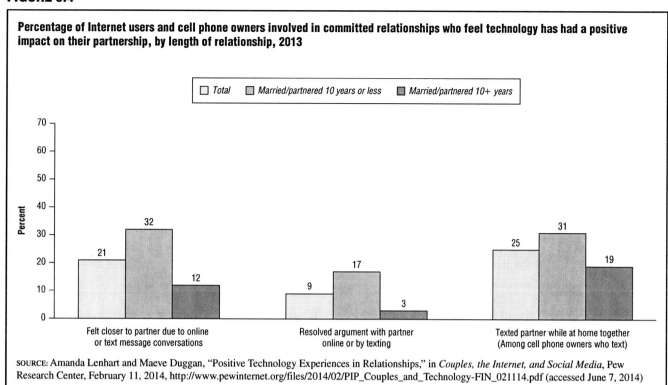

Percentage of Internet users and cell phone owners involved in committed relationships who feel technology has had a positive impact on their partnership, by length of relationship, 2013

☐ Total　☐ Married/partnered 10 years or less　■ Married/partnered 10+ years

SOURCE: Amanda Lenhart and Maeve Duggan, "Positive Technology Experiences in Relationships," in *Couples, the Internet, and Social Media*, Pew Research Center, February 11, 2014, http://www.pewinternet.org/files/2014/02/PIP_Couples_and_Technology-FIN_021114.pdf (accessed June 7, 2014)

FIGURE 9.5

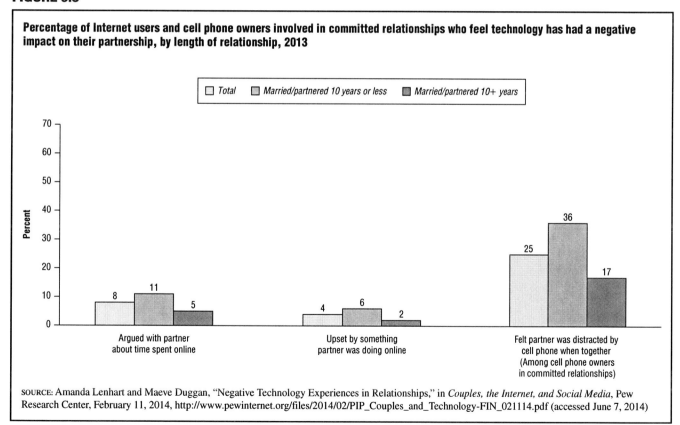

Percentage of Internet users and cell phone owners involved in committed relationships who feel technology has had a negative impact on their partnership, by length of relationship, 2013

☐ Total　☐ Married/partnered 10 years or less　■ Married/partnered 10+ years

SOURCE: Amanda Lenhart and Maeve Duggan, "Negative Technology Experiences in Relationships," in *Couples, the Internet, and Social Media*, Pew Research Center, February 11, 2014, http://www.pewinternet.org/files/2014/02/PIP_Couples_and_Technology-FIN_021114.pdf (accessed June 7, 2014)

Cyberbullying

Advances in communication have also led to new forms of negative online behavior, particularly among children and adolescents. One form of abuse that became a concern during the early part of the 21st century was cyberbullying. Cyberbullying refers to situations in which a child or teenager is harassed, humiliated, or intimidated by other children, teens, or adults through the use of the Internet or other forms of interactive communication, notably cell phones. Cyberbullies torment their victims by sending them malicious, sometimes threatening e-mails or text messages, or by posting pernicious rumors about the victims on the Internet, typically on blogs or social networking sites. In the Pew report *Teens, Kindness and Cruelty on Social Network Sites* (November 9, 2011, http://www.pewinternet.org/files/old-media//Files/Reports/2011/PIP_Teens_Kindness_Cruelty_SNS_Report_Nov_2011_FINAL_110711.pdf), Amanda Lenhart and Mary Madden report that 8% of American teens had experienced some form of online bullying in 2011, and 9% had been bullied via text messages. Cyberbullying is particularly damaging to the emotional health of children because of its potential to spread to wide audiences, as well as the relative ease with which it eludes the detection of parents and teachers. In addition, the physical distance separating the cyberbullies from the victims can desensitize antagonists to the harm they are inflicting, leading to behavior that is far more hateful and cruel than it would be if the perpetrators and victims were face to face. Because it uses technologies that have become omnipresent in the lives of most young people, cyberbullying also has the power to reach far beyond the schoolyard, following victims wherever they go, at any hour of the day.

Sometimes, cyberbullying can inflict fatal consequences. In one notorious case, Megan Meier (1992–2006), a 13-year-old girl from Missouri, committed suicide after receiving malicious communications from a teenage boy over MySpace. As it later turned out, the teenage boy was a fictitious character created by the mother of one of Megan's friends. The case prompted several states to pass anti-cyberbullying legislation the following year. In 2008 the state of Missouri passed its own statute, commonly known as Megan's Law, prohibiting malicious online communications between adults and children.

Cyberbullying once again received national attention in September 2010, when Tyler Clementi (1992–2010), a freshman at Rutgers University, jumped to his death from New York's George Washington Bridge. The ensuing investigation revealed that Clementi's roommate, Dharun Ravi (1992–), had secretly used a webcam controlled from another dorm room to view Clementi engaged in sexual activity with another male; another resident of Clementi's dorm, Molly Wei, was also implicated in the incident. In a bitter irony, Clementi used his cell phone to post a brief suicide message on his Facebook page minutes before jumping off the bridge, writing simply: "Jumping off the gw bridge sorry." In February 2012 Wei entered into a plea agreement with prosecutors. As part of the deal, she was sentenced to 300 hours of community service and ordered to undergo counseling, in exchange for testifying against Ravi in court. The following May, Ravi was convicted on multiple charges relating to Clementi's death, including bias intimidation and invasion of privacy. He was sentenced to 30 days in jail, three years of probation, and 300 hours of community service; in addition he was fined $10,000 and ordered to complete counseling related to cyberbullying and alternative lifestyles.

By 2014 legislation appeared to have some positive effect on curbing instances of cyberbullying. According to Sameer Hinduja and Justin W. Patchin of the Cyberbullying Research Center in *State Cyberbullying Laws: A Brief Review of State Cyberbullying Laws and Policies* (April 2014, http://www.cyberbullying.us/Bullying_and_Cyberbullying_Laws.pdf), as of April 2014 every state in the country except Montana had passed some form of antibullying statute. Of these state laws, 48 included provisions outlawing electronic harassment; 20 states specifically prohibited cyberbullying.

Work

Information technology has touched nearly every industry in the U.S. economy, and for many Americans communications technologies have provided the opportunity to work at home either in a home-based business or after hours for their primary employer. As Peter J. Mateyka, Melanie A. Rapino, and Liana Christin Landivar report in *Home-Based Workers in the United States: 2010* (October 2012, http://www.census.gov/prod/2012pubs/p70-132.pdf), the number of U.S. workers who did their jobs from home at least one day per week rose from 9.2 million in 1997 to 13.4 million in 2010. Over this same span, the proportion of employed Americans who worked at home one day a week increased to 9.5% from 7%. Meanwhile, the percentage of Americans who worked exclusively at home rose from 4.8% in 1997 to 6.6% in 2010. Among Americans who worked solely from home most were native born (89.4%), white (87%), and married (68%). A similar distribution existed among men (51.3%) and women (48.7%) who worked exclusively at home in 2010, and just over half (50.5%) had college degrees.

One development with the potential to revolutionize how Americans work was the rapid evolution of cloud computing technologies. Cloud computing refers to the use of software, tools, and other applications that are available on online servers, as opposed to being stored on the hard drive of a personal computer. For example, Google Docs enables users to create and save documents online, thereby allowing another user (such as a co-worker) to access the information directly through his or her own Internet connection. Many popular forms of cloud computing had already gained widespread popularity by 2014, notably the file sharing site Dropbox, web-based e-mail services such as Hotmail and Gmail, social networking sites such as Facebook, and the status updating service Twitter. Furthermore, cloud computing has made it possible for businesses to form virtual offices, allowing workers at various remote locations to link up and collaborate with each other through a common web-based platform. For example, Microsoft SharePoint enables partners in a business enterprise to exchange documents and other files, share tools and applications, and communicate with each other all within a common Internet platform. According to Janna Quitney Anderson and Lee Rainie in *The Future of Cloud Computing* (June 11, 2010, http://www.pewinternet.org/~/media//Files/Reports/2010/PIP_Future_of_the_Internet_cloud_computing.pdf), a Pew survey of technology experts indicates that 71% believe the majority of Americans who use computers for their jobs will work primarily via cloud computing by 2020.

Romance

Besides hosting a wide range of online dating sites such as eHarmony and Match.com, the Internet also plays a role in the way that Americans experience their romantic relationships. In "Online Dating Statistics" (July 7, 2014, http://www.statisticbrain.com/online-dating-statistics), Statistic Brain reports that 41.3 million American adults had tried an online dating service by 2014. That same year Match.com had nearly 21.6 million members and eHarmony had 15.5 million members. Overall, 20% of all committed relationships in 2014 originated on the Internet; likewise, 17% of marriages that had taken place in the previous year began as an online relationship. On average, married couples who met online dated for 18.5 months before marrying; by comparison, couples who did not meet online dated for an average of 42 months before marrying. By 2014 the online dating industry was generating revenues of more than $1.2 billion annually.

Figure 9.6 compares general attitudes toward online dating between 2005 and 2013. In 2005 fewer than half (44%) of online adults believed that Internet dating was a good way to meet people; by 2013 this figure had risen to 59%. Whereas 29% of adult Internet users in 2005 thought that people who used online dating sites were "desperate," by 2013 only 21% felt this way. In 2013 a majority (53%) of online adults believed that Internet dating offered users a better chance to find a compatible partner, compared with 47% who believed that Internet dating could help users find a more compatible partner in 2005.

Social networking has also had a profound influence on the way people form and maintain romantic relationships in the digital age. As Figure 9.7 shows, in 2013 nearly one-third (30%) of social media users with recent

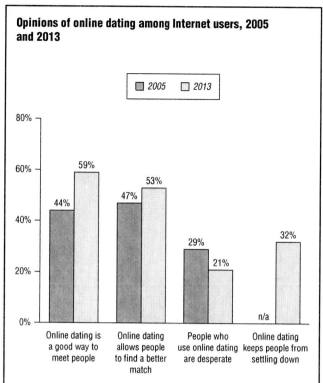

FIGURE 9.6

Opinions of online dating among Internet users, 2005 and 2013

Legend: 2005, 2013

- Online dating is a good way to meet people: 44% (2005), 59% (2013)
- Online dating allows people to find a better match: 47% (2005), 53% (2013)
- People who use online dating are desperate: 29% (2005), 21% (2013)
- Online dating keeps people from settling down: n/a (2005), 32% (2013)

SOURCE: Amanda Lenhart, "Opinions of Online Dating, 2005–2013," in *Dating & Mating in the Digital Age: Relationships and Technology in the Modern Era*, Pew Research Center, April 26, 2014, http://www.pewinternet.org/files/2014/05/Dating-Mating-Digitally_CCF_April_26_2014_pdf-.pdf (accessed June 6, 2014)

dating experience used a social networking site to learn more about someone they wanted to date. This figure was considerably higher among social media users between the ages of 18 and 29 (41%) than among those between the ages of 30 and 49 (24%). In addition, 17% of social media users between the ages of 18 and 29, along with 14% social media users between the ages of 30 and 49, asked someone out on a date through a social networking site in 2013. At the same time, in 2013 nearly half (48%) of all social media users used social networking as a way to check on someone they had dated in the past. (See Figure 9.8.)

Shopping

Use of the Internet for making retail purchases has been rising steadily for several years. The U.S. Census Bureau states in *Quarterly Retail E-Commerce Sales: 2nd Quarter 2014* (August 15, 2014, http://www.census.gov/retail/mrts/www/data/pdf/ec_current.pdf) that retail e-commerce sales for the second quarter of 2014 amounted to $70.1 billion, or 5.9% of the $1.2 trillion total retail sales in the United States. The $70.1 billion figure represented an increase of 15.9% over e-commerce retail sales for the second quarter of 2013.

In "Number of Digital Shoppers in the United States from 2010 to 2018" (2014, http://www.statista.com/statis

FIGURE 9.7

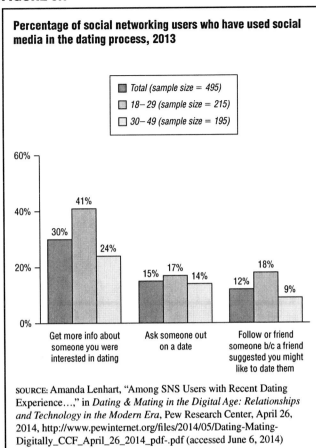

Percentage of social networking users who have used social media in the dating process, 2013

Legend:
- Total (sample size = 495)
- 18–29 (sample size = 215)
- 30–49 (sample size = 195)

SOURCE: Amanda Lenhart, "Among SNS Users with Recent Dating Experience…," in *Dating & Mating in the Digital Age: Relationships and Technology in the Modern Era*, Pew Research Center, April 26, 2014, http://www.pewinternet.org/files/2014/05/Dating-Mating-Digitally_CCF_April_26_2014_pdf-.pdf (accessed June 6, 2014)

FIGURE 9.8

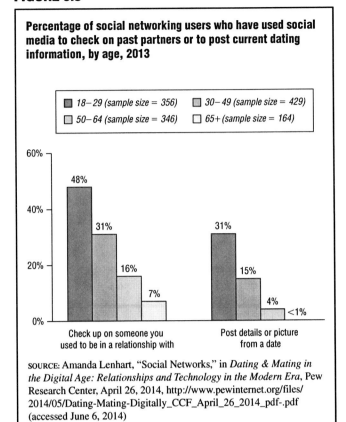

Percentage of social networking users who have used social media to check on past partners or to post current dating information, by age, 2013

Legend:
- 18–29 (sample size = 356)
- 30–49 (sample size = 429)
- 50–64 (sample size = 346)
- 65+ (sample size = 164)

SOURCE: Amanda Lenhart, "Social Networks," in *Dating & Mating in the Digital Age: Relationships and Technology in the Modern Era*, Pew Research Center, April 26, 2014, http://www.pewinternet.org/files/2014/05/Dating-Mating-Digitally_CCF_April_26_2014_pdf-.pdf (accessed June 6, 2014)

tics/183755/number-of-us-internet-shoppers-since-2009), the statistical data company Statista reports that 172.3 million Americans purchased something online in 2010; by 2013 this figure had risen to 191.1 million, an increase of nearly 11%. As the Internet analysis firm comScore reports in "Final Online Shopping Week Falls Short of Expectations as Shortened Holiday Calendar Weighs on Season-to-Date Growth Rates" (December 26, 2013, https://www.comscore.com/Insights/Press_Re leases/2013/12/Final_Online_Shopping_Week_Falls_Short _of_Expectations_as_Shortened_Holiday_Calendar_Weighs _on_Season-to-Date_Growth_Rates), Americans spent nearly $42.8 million in online holiday shopping through December 22, 2013. This figure represented an increase of 10% over the $38.9 million spent by holiday shoppers online during the same period in 2012.

In addition, cell phones are becoming an important tool for consumers who still prefer to do their shopping in person. Aaron Smith notes in *In-Store Mobile Commerce during the 2012 Holiday Shopping Season* (January 31, 2013, http://www.pewinternet.org/files/old-media//Files/ Reports/2013/PIP_In_store_mobile_commerce_PDF.pdf) that 27% of all cell phone owners used their mobile device to conduct price comparisons while shopping at a retail store during the 2012 holiday season. Forty-six percent of cell phone owners called a friend for advice

TABLE 9.5

Impact of mobile technology on in-person retail shopping habits, by age, 2014

	Increased	Decreased	Not affected
18–29 years	29%	15%	56%
30–49 years	24%	23%	52%
50–64 years	17%	20%	62%
65+ years	16%	16%	67%

SOURCE: Jeffrey M. Jones, "Effect of Mobile Technology on In-Person Retail Shopping, by Age," in *For Many, Mobile Technology Increasing Retail Shopping*, The Gallup Organization, May 1, 2014, http://www.gallup.com/poll/168800/mobile-technology-increasing-retail-shopping.aspx (accessed June 6, 2014). Copyright © 2014 Gallup, Inc. All rights reserved. The content is used with permission; however, Gallup retains all rights of republication.

while shopping, and 28% used their phone to search for product reviews online. For many Americans, mobile technology has actually made them more likely to spend time in retail stores. As Table 9.5 shows, in 2014, 29% of adults between the ages of 18 and 29 reported that their time spent in retail stores had increased as a result of mobile technology; 15% of 18-to-29-year-olds reported that they spent less time in retail stores because of mobile technology, and 56% in this age group claimed that mobile technology had no impact on their in-store shopping habits.

Alternate Realities

As time passed, many Internet users met, developed social relationships, or spent long periods online in virtual worlds such as Second Life (http://secondlife.com), Ultima Online (http://uo.com), and other massively multiplayer online role-playing games. Even children took care of virtual pets online in WebKinz World (http://www.webkinz.com), where among many other activities players could send their pets to school; earn money by working, growing crops, or playing games; and shop for virtual groceries, vacations, and home furnishings. According to Amanda Lenhart et al. in *Social Media & Mobile Internet Use among Teens and Young Adults* (February 3, 2010, http://www.pewinternet.org/~/media//Files/Reports/2010/PIP_Social_Media_and_Young_Adults_Report_Final_with_toplines.pdf), involvement with virtual worlds becomes increasingly less common as Internet users become older. Among online teens aged 12 to 13 years, 11% were engaged with virtual worlds in 2010, whereas among teens aged 14 to 17 years this proportion fell to 7%. Among online adults, only 4% used virtual worlds.

Nevertheless, in 2014 many in the technology industry were beginning to observe ways in which virtual and alternative realities were becoming incorporated into everyday life. One trend that was garnering some attention within tech circles was the concept of "gamification." Gamification describes a process through which aspects of game-playing (including the pleasure involved with confronting certain challenges, participating in interactive competitions, and receiving rewards for performing particular tasks) becomes incorporated into an increasing number of everyday activities. In *Gamification: Experts Expect Game Layers to Expand in the Future, with Positive and Negative Results* (May 18, 2012, http://www.pewinternet.org/~/media//Files/Reports/2012/PIP_Future_of_Internet_2012_Gamification.pdf), Janna Quitney Anderson and Lee Rainie asked 1,021 technology experts and stakeholders their views on the extent to which gamification will impact American life in the coming decade. A majority (53%) of those surveyed said gamification will play a key role in transforming numerous facets of everyday life, including work, health, and education. Cathy Cavanagh, an associate professor of educational technology at the University of Florida, told Anderson and Rainie, "People will increasingly expect game elements in a wide range of activities. Game-development tools will enable most people to gamify many aspects of life and work, in digital, physical, and blended environments." However, for some experts the prospect of increased gamification of society also carries certain risks. Danah Boyd, a researcher for Microsoft, reported in the survey, "It's a modern-day form of manipulation. And like all cognitive manipulation, it can help people and it can hurt people. And we will see both." David Kirschner, a research assistant at the Nanyang Technological University in Singapore, expressed particular concern about the power of corporations to use gamification to exert greater control over individuals. "Companies should take responsibility for the tremendous power they wield in society. I fear they won't, but I hope they do," Kirschner argued. "We've all got to be very critical when fun can mask trouble."

Another major technological development during these years was in the field of augmented reality. Augmented reality is a form of digital technology that enables users to supplement their experience of the world with additional graphics, data, or other computer-generated content. For example, with augmented reality smartphone owners can view a shopping plaza through the lens of their mobile device and immediately learn which stores and businesses the plaza contains, what their hours of operation are, or what menu specials the restaurants are offering that day. As Brandon Widder writes in "Best Augmented Reality Apps" (DigitalTrends.com, March 14, 2014), some of the most popular augmented reality apps in 2014 included Wikitude World Browser, a travel app that enables smartphone owners to access information about historical sites, hotel and restaurant recommendations, and other useful data, and SpecTrek, a game that populates the surrounding landscape with virtual ghosts, which the user must hunt down and destroy.

One of the most high-profile developments in augmented reality during this time was Google Glass. Developed by Google X, the company's research and development division, Google Glass consists of a pair of eyeglasses with a small Internet-enabled computer embedded into one of the lenses, thereby allowing the user to access data about their surroundings while performing normal tasks. As Amy Hubbard writes in "Sergey Brin Wears Project Glass; Google Specs Spur Fear, Punch Lines" (LATimes.com, April 6, 2012), Google Glass made its public debut in April 2012, when Google cofounder Sergey Brin (1973–) wore a prototype of the augmented reality glasses to a charity event in San Francisco. Within a year, Claire Cain Miller notes in "New Apps Arrive on Google Glass" (NYTimes.com, May 16, 2013), Google had introduced several apps, known as Glassware, for use with Google Glass. As of 2014, Google Glass was still not widely available, although a limited number of prototypes had been released to the public for testing and feedback purposes.

HOME ELECTRONICS REVOLUTION

During the 1970s and early 1980s advances in circuit manufacturing lowered the price of integrated electronic components from hundreds of dollars to less than $10 in some instances. Since then, electronic chips, displays, and sensors have worked their way into everything from washing machines to hairdryers to coffeemakers. Overall, these electronics have given people more control over the settings on their appliances, lighting, and heating and cooling systems.

High-Tech Home Features

Many home appliances and systems have become fully programmable and even Internet accessible. For example, interactive, online thermostats come installed in many new homes. These thermostats, which can be connected to the Internet, give the homeowner the option of remotely setting and monitoring the temperature of the house from any computer or cell phone with Internet access. The thermostat also alerts the user of a malfunction or a gas leak in the system. Zone lighting systems contain electronics that enable homeowners to program lighting configurations for multiple areas of the same room. With the touch of a button, one side of a room can be illuminated for reading while the other side remains dark for watching television.

Another programmable fixture that is available in many newer homes is the electronic keypad locking system. The advantage of the keypad over the normal lock is that it can be easily reprogrammed. If a homeowner wants to keep someone out, this can be done by simply changing the lock code. The lock can also be set to let in certain people, such as a painter, only during certain times of the day. Some keypad locks contain circuit boards that can be plugged into a broadband connection, which gives the homeowner the option of remotely changing the lock codes or keeping a record of who comes and goes. By 2014 some companies offered automated home systems that tied the lights, door locks, thermostat, and home security system into one control center that could be accessed via the Internet. These systems can be placed in different modes for when the homeowner is awake, asleep, or away. For example, when the homeowner goes out of town, all he or she has to do is press a button and the lights are turned off, the alarm is set, and the thermostat is turned down. In addition, in the event a security alarm is activated, systems automatically send prerecorded messages to phone numbers that have been programmed into the system, including emergency services or the homeowner's work or cell phone.

Smart Appliances

As technology progresses and electronics become even more affordable, makers of appliances will likely continue to add additional electronic features. By 2014 many of these advances were aimed at making appliances more energy efficient. As part of the American Recovery and Reinvestment Act of 2009, the federal government offered cash rebates to consumers who traded in older appliances for new, more eco-friendly models. The law also provided $4 billion in funding to the U.S. Department of Energy toward improvements to the nation's smart grid, a system that will allow power suppliers to "communicate" with home appliances, through a system of sensors and other digital technologies, to regulate and reduce overall electricity usage. Richard Babyak notes in "Searching for Smart Standards" (ApplianceDesign.com, January

2010) that many advances in the manufacturing of environmentally friendly appliances are being undertaken to streamline interaction with the smart grid. Babyak also raises several of the key issues surrounding this process, including safety standards and the degree of control that consumers will maintain over their home appliances.

ROBOTS

Around the turn of the 21st century the first practical, automated robots went on sale for the consumer market. Far from the convenient marvels depicted in futuristic television shows, these robots performed only simple tasks. As of 2014, a number of models of robotic vacuum cleaners could be found on the market, and people were buying them. According to the iRobot Corporation (2014, http://www.irobot.com/en/us/Company/About/Our_History .aspx), the maker of Roomba robotic vacuums and Scooba floor washers, the company had sold more than 10 million home robots worldwide by 2014. Most robotic vacuum cleaners used various sensors to feel their way around the room, picking up dirt as they went. For example, the Neato Botvac (http://www.neatorobotics.com) uses a laser scan to map the cleaning area, allowing it to detect and avoid obstacles in its way as it goes back and forth across the room, sucking up dirt and recording where it has been.

Other devices available in 2014 included robotic mowers, pool cleaners, and gutter cleaners. The Robomow (http://www.robomow.com/en-USA) automatically zigzags back and forth over a lawn, cutting the grass as it goes. Sensors are embedded in bumpers that surround the entire mower, and if it bangs into something bigger than a large piece of bark, it backs off. A low-voltage guide wire set up by the user around the perimeter of the yard lets the mower know if it is crossing the boundaries of the lawn, in which case it turns around. In addition, the mower can be programmed to leave its base station and mow the lawn at preset days and times, and then return to the base station to be recharged. Robotic lawn mower models were available from several well-known manufacturers, including Husqvarna and John Deere in 2014 and were priced at $1,100 and up.

Programmable Robots

Another type of robot, which made its debut in 2005, was the PC-BOT by White Box Robotics. In "Plug-and-Play Robots" (ScientificAmerican.com, March 22, 2004), W. Wayt Gibbs remarks that the knee-high robots "look like R2-D2 droids that have been redesigned by Cadillac." PC-BOTs are built from everyday computer components and accessories. Each one has a digital camera, speakers, slots for peripheral components such as a disc drive, and sensors mounted on the outside. A standard hard drive, microprocessor, drive motor, and stabilizer are contained within the chassis. The whole unit is mounted on wheels. The innovation behind the PC-BOTs, however, does not lie in its components, but in the fact that the machine is fully programmable. According to Gibbs, face and object recognition software can be installed on a PC-BOT, which allow it to recognize various people and objects in its environment and then act on that information. One useful application allows the robot to roam around the owner's house when the owner is out of town. If the robot spots a strange figure or detects a loud noise, it can e-mail or send a page to the owner.

Humanoid Robots

Several large companies and many academic laboratories have been experimenting with complex humanoid robots. The most famous of these is probably Honda's Advanced Step in Innovation Mobility (ASIMO) robot (http://world.honda.com/ASIMO). Researchers at Honda have been working on the ASIMO design since 1986. As of 2014, the robot could recognize faces programmed into its memory, walk over uneven surfaces, hop on one leg, climb stairs, and run at a speed of 5.6 miles (9 km) per hour. Honda's goal is to create a robot that can be remotely controlled by a handicapped person to complete basic chores around the house such as retrieving the mail, doing the dishes, or moving items from one place to another. In November 2007 the Vietnamese robotics company TOSY introduced the TOSY Ping Pong Playing Robot (TOPIO) at the International Robot Exhibition in Tokyo, Japan. Capable of playing table tennis against a human opponent, the TOPIO used cameras and image recognition software to detect the precise location and movement of a ping pong ball. Within two years, the company introduced a lighter, more agile version of its robot, the TOPIO 3.0.

During the first decade of the 21st century the National Aeronautics and Space Administration (NASA) developed a humanoid robot that was designed to perform repairs and other basic operations on the outside of the *International Space Station*. A robotic torso modeled after the upper half of the human body, the Robonaut simulated the actions of an astronaut inside the space station using virtual reality technology. Whereas astronauts required several hours of preparation before entering the deadly vacuum outside the space station, the Robonaut could make the transition within a matter of minutes. By 2010 NASA, working together with engineers from General Motors (GM), had developed a faster, more dexterous version of its humanoid robot, the Robonaut 2 (R2), which employed a "touch sensitivity" technology to perform more complex tasks. The R2 successfully joined the crew of the *International Space Station* in February 2011. According to "Robonaut 2 Getting Its Space Legs" (RedOrbit.com, April 24, 2014), in April 2014 a NASA space capsule arrived at the *International Space Station* with a pair of legs for the R2. The legs were designed to increase the R2's mobility, enabling it to perform a greater range of tasks on its own.

Many scientists and engineers worldwide have been working on ways to make robots even more anthropomorphic (having human characteristics) than ASIMO and other humanoid robots. In late 2009 researchers at the Campus Bio-Medico in Rome successfully tested a biomechanical hand. In the experiment, the robotic hand was linked with electrodes to the arm of an amputee, who was able to make the hand move and perform basic actions with his thoughts. In October 2010 researchers working at the National Institute of Advanced Industrial Science and Technology in Japan unveiled the HRP-4C, a "female" robot that used voice and motion-capture software to simulate human singing, breathing patterns, facial expressions, and gestures.

HIGH-TECH AUTOMOBILES

Technological innovations for everyday life are not just occurring in the home. Many types of advanced information technology have made it into automobiles as well. Vehicle buyers in 2014 had the option to choose certain models of sedans and minivans that were equipped with night-vision cameras and proximity sensors in their bumpers. Night-vision cameras enable drivers to see obstacles in the road at night, and proximity sensors help prevent accidents by alerting the driver if something, such as a parked vehicle or a small child, is too close to the bumper. Global positioning systems (GPS) have been incorporated into many new vehicles. GPS continuously picks up signals that are broadcast from a network of stationary (nonorbiting) satellites positioned above the earth. By analyzing its proximity in relation to three of the satellites in the network, GPS can pinpoint its location on the earth's surface. Most systems that use GPS then combine this information with an up-to-date map of the local roads to display the vehicle's position on a street map.

Advances in Safety

In "Intelligence: Behold the All-Seeing, Self-Parking, Safety-Enforcing, Networked Automobile" (PopularScience.com, September 25, 2004), Paul Horrell suggests that vehicles will not only continue to become more fuel efficient but also more intelligent. Companies are employing external sensors to inform the driver and systems within the vehicle of impending danger. For example, the French automobile maker Peugeot Citroën installed a system of infrared sensors that scan painted road markings on each side of the vehicle and alert the driver if he or she strays out of the lane. If the blinker is not on and the driver strays to the left, the sensors perceive the vehicle crossing the line in the road and the left side of the driver's seat vibrates. If the driver strays to the right, the right side of the seat vibrates. In 2009 Peugeot Citroën introduced Snow Motion, an antiskid system that was designed for extreme road conditions. Automobile makers have also developed systems that allow vehicles to communicate with one another to warn drivers of delays or of dangerous road conditions ahead. Sensor-equipped cars employing the wireless local area network (WLAN) send information via the WLAN to warn other cars in close proximity when they encounter a traffic jam or black ice. These cars then relay the information to other cars and so on until every car and driver in the area is made aware of the traffic jam or the black ice.

Among the most promising new safety technologies are frontal radar and driver-state monitoring. Frontal radar is a collision-avoidance technology that works by informing drivers of obstacles in their path up to 660 feet (200 m) ahead. The technology is integrated into adaptive cruise control to automatically slow the vehicle to keep a safe distance behind other vehicles. Driver-state monitoring incorporates infrared cameras to assess the driver's fatigue level, issuing a warning if the driver seems too tired to drive safely. Another important advancement in automobile safety has been the development of the electronic stability control (ESC) system. Using smart-braking technology, ESC helps prevent collisions and rollovers in situations where the driver is losing control of the vehicle. According to the article "Electronic Stability Control 101" (ConsumerReports.org, April 15, 2010), ESC represents the "single most important safety advance since the development of the safety belt." In "The Effect of ESC on Passenger Vehicle Rollover Fatality Trends" (*Traffic Safety Facts*, June 2014, http://www-nrd.nhtsa.dot.gov/Pubs/812031.pdf), the National Highway Traffic Safety Administration indicates that ESC technology likely played a role in a 91% decline in newer passenger vehicle (vehicles five years old or newer) rollover fatalities between 2001 and 2012.

In-Vehicle Communications Systems

By combining GPS, cell phone, and sensor technology, several companies have developed in-vehicle communications systems. GM's OnStar (2014, https://www.onstar.com/web/portal/onstartechnology) is one of the most widely used of these in-vehicle systems, with more than 6 million subscribers. The OnStar Corporation, which is a subsidiary of GM, first offered the OnStar system on GM vehicles in 1996. The system is activated when the user presses either a blue button or a red button in the vehicle or when the vehicle's air bags are deployed. Pressing the blue button instructs the OnStar cellular unit to dial the main OnStar switchboard. A GPS then relays the vehicle's coordinates through the built-in mobile phone to the operator, telling him or her exactly where the vehicle is. Sensors planted on the vehicle's major systems let the operator know how it is functioning. The vehicle owner can then request roadside assistance, directions, or information on the status of the vehicle. In the event of a life-threatening emergency, the red button contacts an OnStar emergency service operator,

who calls the nearest emergency service provider. The system is also triggered if the air bags are deployed. In this event, the OnStar emergency operator is called, and he or she notifies the nearest emergency service provider, telling it where the accident took place as well as the make and model of the vehicle. Furthermore, the user can call the OnStar operator from a phone outside the vehicle to open the door locks or to report a stolen vehicle. Finally, once each month owners of OnStar-equipped vehicles receive an e-mail containing a diagnostic analysis of their vehicle that covers everything from the condition of the engine and braking systems to the pressure in their tires and when they need to change their oil.

Automated Vehicles

In October 2010 the technology company Google announced that it had developed automated vehicles that had driven more than 140,000 miles (225,000 km) without human control during testing events on U.S. roads. To navigate the streets without human control, the vehicles used a combination of video cameras, radar sensors, laser range finders, and maps. The only reported accident that occurred during road testing was when a Google automated vehicle was hit from behind by a human-operated car that failed to stop at a traffic light.

Cy Ryan reports in "Nevada Issues Google First License for Self-Driving Car" (LasVegasSun.com, May 7, 2012) that in November 2011 Nevada became the first U.S. state to allow driverless cars on public roads. In May 2012 the Nevada Department of Motor Vehicles issued the first official self-driving car license to Google, enabling the company to begin testing the vehicles on the state's streets and highways. In September 2012 Governor Jerry Brown (1938–) of California signed a similar law that allowed self-driving cars to travel on public roadways. In an interview with Miguel Helft (Fortune.com, December 11, 2012), Larry Page, the cofounder and chief executive officer of Google, described the motivation behind the company's ambitious self-driving car project. "We want to do things that will motivate the most amazing people in the world to want to work on them," Page said. "You look at self-driving cars. You know a lot of people die, and there's a lot of wasted labor. The better transportation you have, the more choice in jobs. And that's social good. That's probably an economic good. I like it when we're picking problems like that: big things where technology can have a really big impact. And we're pretty sure we can do it." As John Markoff writes in "Google's Next Phase in Driverless Cars: No Steering Wheel or Brake Pedals" (NYTimes.com, May 27, 2014), in May 2014 Google announced a plan to manufacture 100 electric driverless cars that would contain no manual control mechanisms in the vehicle. According to Markoff, the new automated car would be controlled exclusively with a smartphone app.

IMPORTANT NAMES
AND ADDRESSES

American Customer Satisfaction Index LLC
625 Avis Dr.
Ann Arbor, MI 48108
(734) 913-0788
FAX: (734) 913-0790
E-mail: info@theacsi.org
URL: http://www.theacsi.org/

Apple Inc.
1 Infinite Loop
Cupertino, CA 95014
(408) 996-1010
URL: https://www.apple.com/

Association of Public and Land-Grant Universities
1307 New York Ave. NW, Ste. 400
Washington, DC 20005-4722
(202) 478-6040
FAX: (202) 478-6046
URL: http://www.aplu.org/

Centers for Disease Control and Prevention
1600 Clifton Rd.
Atlanta, GA 30333
1-800-232-4636
URL: http://www.cdc.gov/

CERT Program
4500 Fifth Ave.
Pittsburgh, PA 15213-2612
(412) 268-7090
FAX: (412) 268-6989
E-mail: cert@cert.org
URL: http://www.cert.org/

Economics and Statistics Administration
U.S. Department of Commerce
1401 Constitution Ave. NW, Rm. 4848
Washington, DC 20230
(202) 482-6607
E-mail: ESAwebmaster@doc.gov
URL: http://www.esa.doc.gov/

Facebook, Inc.
1601 Willow Rd.
Menlo Park, CA 94025
(650) 543-4800
URL: http://www.facebook.com/

Federal Bureau of Investigation
935 Pennsylvania Ave. NW
Washington, DC 20535-0001
(202) 324-3000
URL: http://www.fbi.gov/

Federal Communications Commission
445 12th St. SW
Washington, DC 20554
1-888-225-5322
FAX: 1-866-418-0232
URL: http://www.fcc.gov/

Federal Deposit Insurance Corporation
550 17th St. NW
Washington, DC 20429
1-877-275-3342
E-mail: publicinfo@fdic.gov
URL: http://www.fdic.gov/

Federal Election Commission
999 E St. NW
Washington, DC 20463
(202) 694-1000
1-800-424-9530
E-mail: info@fec.gov
URL: http://www.fec.gov/

Federal Trade Commission
600 Pennsylvania Ave. NW
Washington, DC 20580
(202) 326-2222
URL: http://www.ftc.gov/

Google Inc.
1600 Amphitheatre Pkwy.
Mountain View, CA 94043
(650) 253-0000
FAX: (650) 253-0001

URL: http://www.google.com/about/company/

Governors Highway Safety Association
444 N. Capitol St. NW, Ste. 722
Washington, DC 20001
(202) 789-0942
FAX: (202) 789-0946
E-mail: headquarters@ghsa.org
URL: http://www.statehighwaysafety.org/

Intelligent Transportation Society of America
1100 New Jersey Ave. SE, Ste. 850
Washington, DC 20003
(202) 484-4847
1-800-374-8472
E-mail: info@itsa.org
URL: http://www.itsa.org/

Intelligent Transportation Systems Joint Program Office
Research and Innovative Technology Administration
U.S. Department of Transportation
1200 New Jersey Ave. SE, HOIT
Washington, DC 20590
1-866-367-7487
E-mail: ITSHelp@dot.gov
URL: http://www.its.dot.gov/

International Center for Academic Integrity
126 Hardin Hall
Clemson University
Clemson, SC 29634-5138
(864) 656-1293
FAX: (864) 656-2858
E-mail: CAI-L@clemson.edu
URL: http://www.academicintegrity.org/

Internet Society
1775 Wiehle Ave., Ste. 201
Reston, VA 20190-5108
(703) 439-2120
FAX: (703) 326-9881

E-mail: isoc@isoc.org
URL: http://www.internetsociety.org/

Internet2
1000 Oakbrook Dr., Ste. 300
Ann Arbor, MI 48104
(734) 913-4250
FAX: (734) 913-4255
URL: http://www.internet2.edu/

iRobot Corporation
8 Crosby Dr.
Bedford, MA 01730
(781) 430-3000
FAX: (781) 430-3001
URL: http://www.irobot.com/

Kaspersky Lab US
500 Unicorn Park, Third Fl.
Woburn, MA 01801
(781) 503-1800
1-866-328-5700
FAX: (781) 503-1818
URL: http://usa.kaspersky.com/

Medical Library Association
65 E. Wacker Pl., Ste. 1900
Chicago, IL 60601-7246
(312) 419-9094
FAX: (312) 419-8950
E-mail: info@mlahq.org
URL: http://www.mlanet.org/

Microsoft Corporation
1 Microsoft Way
Redmond, WA 98052-6399
(425) 882-8080
FAX: (425) 706-7329
URL: http://www.microsoft.com/

Motion Picture Association of America
1600 Eye St. NW
Washington, DC 20006
(202) 293-1966
FAX: (202) 296-7410
E-mail: contactus@mpaa.org
URL: http://www.mpaa.org/

National Aeronautics and Space Administration
NASA Headquarters, Ste. 2R40
Washington, DC 20546
(202) 358-0001

FAX: (202) 358-4338
E-mail: public-inquiries@hq.nasa.gov
URL: http://www.nasa.gov/

National Association of Boards of Pharmacy
1600 Feehanville Dr.
Mount Prospect, IL 60056
(847) 391-4406
FAX: (847) 391-4502
E-mail: custserv@nabp.net
URL: http://www.nabp.net/

National Center for Education Statistics Institute of Education Sciences
1990 K St. NW, Eighth and Ninth Fls.
Washington, DC 20006
(202) 502-7300
FAX: (202) 502-7466
URL: http://nces.ed.gov/

National Science Foundation
4201 Wilson Blvd.
Arlington, VA 22230
(703) 292-5111
1-800-877-8339
E-mail: info@nsf.gov
URL: http://www.nsf.gov/

The Nielsen Company
85 Broad St.
New York, NY 10004
1-800-684-1224
URL: http://www.nielsen.com/

Office of Management and Budget
725 17th St. NW
Washington, DC 20503
(202) 395-3080
FAX: (202) 395-3888
URL: http://www.whitehouse.gov/omb/

On-Line Gamers Anonymous World Services Inc.
104 Miller Ln.
Harrisburg, PA 17110
(612) 245-1115
URL: http://www.olganon.org/

Pew Research Center
1615 L St. NW, Ste. 700
Washington, DC 20036
(202) 419-4300

FAX: (202) 419-4349
E-mail: data@pewinternet.org
URL: http://www.pewinternet.org/

Recording Industry Association of America
1025 F St. NW, 10th Fl.
Washington, DC 20004
(202) 775-0101
URL: http://www.riaa.com/

The Spamhaus Project
18 Ave. Louis Casai
Geneva, Switzerland CH-1209
E-mail: admin-sec-ch@spamhaus.org
URL: http://www.spamhaus.org/

United Network for Organ Sharing
700 N. Fourth St.
Richmond, VA 23219
(804) 782-4800
FAX: (804) 782-4817
URL: http://www.unos.org/

U.S. Census Bureau
4600 Silver Hill Rd.
Washington, DC 20233
(301) 763-4636
1-800-923-8282
URL: http://www.census.gov/

US-CERT Security Operations Center
U.S. Department of Homeland Security
245 Murray Ln. SW, Bldg. 410
Washington, DC 20598
1-888-282-0870
E-mail: info@us-cert.gov
URL: http://www.us-cert.gov/

U.S. Department of Justice—Computer Crime and Intellectual Property Section
950 Pennsylvania Ave. NW
Washington, DC 20530-0001
(202) 514-2000
E-mail: AskDOJ@usdoj.gov
URL: http://www.justice.gov/

U.S. Department of Labor
200 Constitution Ave. NW
Washington, DC 20210
1-866-487-2365
URL: http://www.dol.gov/

RESOURCES

Since 1999 the Pew Research Center has conducted dozens of surveys on the impact of technology on American life, including who uses the Internet and how they use it. *Cell Phone Activities 2013* (Maeve Duggan, September 16, 2013), *Older Adults and Technology Use* (Aaron Smith, April 4, 2014), *Teens and Technology 2013* (Mary Madden et al., March 13, 2013), and *The Web at 25 in the U.S.* (Susannah Fox and Lee Rainie, February 27, 2014) report Pew's findings on the adoption of Internet and mobile technology in the United States. *African Americans and Technology Use* (Aaron Smith, January 6, 2014) and *Teens, Social Media, and Privacy* (Mary Madden et al., May 21, 2013) report on specific demographic groups. *Civic Engagement in the Digital Age* (Aaron Smith, April 25, 2013), *Digital Politics: Pew Research Findings on Technology and Campaign 2012* (Aaron Smith, February 20, 2013), *Social Media and Political Engagement* (Lee Rainie et al., October 19, 2012), and *Social Media and Voting* (Lee Rainie, November 6, 2012) illustrate how much the Internet influences the various ways that Americans engage with politics and the government. *Couples, the Internet, and Social Media* (Amanda Lenhart and Maeve Duggan, February 11, 2014), *Dating & Mating in the Digital Age: Relationships and Technology in the Modern Era* (Amanda Lenhart, April 26, 2014), and *Social Media Update 2013* (Maeve Duggan and Aaron Smith, December 30, 2013) examine social networking trends among online adults. Pew publications that examine health care and the Internet include *The Diagnosis Difference: A Portrait of the 45% of U.S. Adults Living with Chronic Health Conditions* (Susannah Fox and Maeve Duggan, November 26, 2013), *Family Caregivers Are Wired for Health* (Susannah Fox, Maeve Duggan, and Kristen Purcell, June 20, 2013), and *Mobile Health 2012* (Susannah Fox and Maeve Duggan, November 8, 2012). *U.S. Views of Technology and the Future* (Aaron Smith, April 17, 2014) offers a glimpse into American attitudes concerning the impact of technological advances on everyday life.

Other publications by Pew that were useful in preparing this volume include *How Teachers Are Using Technology at Home and in Their Classrooms* (Kristen Purcell et al., February 8, 2013), *How Teens Do Research in the Digital World* (Kristen Purcell et al., November 1, 2012), and *The Impact of Digital Tools on Student Writing and How Writing Is Taught in Schools* (Kristen Purcell, Judy Buchanan, and Linda Friedrich, July 16, 2013), among others.

The Gallup Organization provides valuable results from polls on topics such as Internet and cell phone use, e-crime, e-commerce, and entertainment, among others. Reports consulted for this book include *Americans' Tech Tastes Change with Times* (2014), *For Many, Mobile Technology Increasing Retail Shopping* (2014), *In U.S., Mobile Tech Aids Interpersonal Communication Most* (2014), *In U.S., Online Education Rated Best for Value and Options* (2013), *In U.S., Trust in Media Recovers Slightly from All-Time Low* (2013), *Mobile Technology in Politics More Potential than Reality* (2014), and *Most U.S. Workers See Upside to Staying Connected to Work* (2014).

A number of excellent accounts of Internet history can be found online, including Robert H. Zakon's *Hobbes' Internet Timeline 10.2* (January 30, 2014, http://www.zakon.org/robert/internet/timeline/). Most of these histories are listed in the Internet Society's *Histories of the Internet* (2014, http://www.isoc.org/internet/history/). *A Brief History of the Internet* (December 2003, http://www.internetsociety.org/internet/what-internet/history-internet/brief-history-internet) was written by some of the people who gave rise to the Internet, including Vinton G. Cerf, the creator of TCP/IP. *An Atlas of Cyberspaces* (February 2007, http://personalpages.manchester.ac.uk/staff/m.dodge/cybergeography/atlas/atlas.html) by Martin Dodge and Rob Kitchin displays map after map of the Internet networks that developed in the

United States after the creation of ARPANET. The Internet2 website (http://www.internet2.edu/) contains a great deal of information on the Internet2 consortium as well as on the future of the Internet.

A number of magazines and websites report on the latest developments in technology. In print, *New Scientist*, *PC World*, *Popular Science*, *Scientific American*, and *Wired* contain articles on the most recent trends in electronics and software. On the Internet, CNET.com, eWeek.com, TechWeb.com, Wired.com, and ZDNet.com post the latest news in high tech daily.

The Federal Communications Commission (FCC) is the government agency responsible for regulating which devices can use the various portions of the electromagnetic spectrum. The agency also regulates television and radio programming. The FCC website (http://www.fcc.gov/) provides information on the Children's Internet Protection Act, closed captioning, high-definition television, radio spectrum allocation, and the transition to digital television.

The *Proquest Statistical Abstract of the United States* contains a number of statistics illustrating the effects of technology on American life. These include the percentage of households with computer and Internet access, the amount of time and money Americans spend on various media and media systems (e.g., television and radio), and the number of Americans with credit and debit card accounts. The Census Bureau's *E-Stats* provides financial statistics on e-commerce in the United States.

The U.S. Department of Commerce compiles reports on Internet usage and on the effects of high tech on the economy. Its landmark study *Digital Economy 2003* (December 2003) reports on how high tech transformed the U.S. economy at the turn of the 21st century. The Department of Commerce also publishes the serial publications *Industry Economic Accounts* and *Quarterly Retail E-Commerce Sales*, which provide information on the economic impact of the Internet and information technology. In addition, the U.S. Department of Labor tracks employment statistics and trends in publications such as *Mass Layoff Statistics* (2013) and *Labor Productivity and Costs* (May 2014).

The Federal Trade Commission (FTC) hosts a website (http://www.ftc.gov/bcp/edu/microsites/idtheft) that houses a number of reports and informational brochures on identity theft and Internet fraud. The FTC publications consulted for this book include the *Consumer Sentinel Network Data Book for January–December 2013* (February 2014). The U.S. Department of Justice maintains a website on cybercrime (http://www.justice.gov/criminal/cybercrime/) that contains reports on identity theft and Internet fraud.

The Internet Crime Complaint Center (IC3), a division of the Federal Bureau of Investigation, monitors and responds to major threats to the Internet such as large-scale hacking incidents and virus attacks. Each year, IC3, in conjunction with the Department of Justice, the Bureau of Justice Assistance, and the National White Collar Crime Center, publishes the *Internet Crime Report*, which outlines e-crime incidents reported by U.S. businesses. These crimes include anything from Internet fraud to hacking incidents to viruses. The U.S. Department of Homeland Security website (http://www.dhs.gov/) and the U.S. Computer Emergency Readiness Team website (http://www.us-cert.gov/) contain reports on how the government is using high tech to combat threats to national security.

To get more information on optical scan and digital recording electronic voting machines and about how national elections are conducted, visit the Federal Election Commission website (http://www.fec.gov/). The Intelligent Transportation Systems Joint Program Office, which is located within the U.S. Department of Transportation, contains reports on 511 deployment and operations. The American Customer Satisfaction Index scores for many of the federal government's most popular sites can be found at http://www.theacsi.org/. The Office of Management and Budget website (http://www.whitehouse.gov/omb/) provides information on President Barack Obama's e-government initiatives as well as on the E-Government Act of 2002.

The Centers for Disease Control and Prevention website (http://www.cdc.gov/) reports on how researchers are employing the Internet, global positioning systems, and other high-tech equipment to analyze the risks that are associated with major diseases. Information on the development of a nationwide health information network is presented by the U.S. Department of Health and Human Services in *Update on the Adoption of Health Information Technology and Related Efforts to Facilitate the Electronic Use and Exchange of Health Information: A Report to Congress* (June 2013).

The National Center for Education Statistics provides a number of reports that detail the use of computers and the Internet in the classroom. The reports discussed in this book are the *Condition of Education 2014* (Grace Kena et al., 2014) and *Digest of Education Statistics 2012* (Thomas A. Snyder and Sally A. Dillow, December 2013).

INDEX

"The Hitman Study: Violent Video Game Exposure Effects on Aggressive Behavior, Hostile Feelings, and Depression" (Ferguson & Rueda), 72–73

HIV InSite website, 122

Hobbes' Internet Timeline 10.2 (Zakon), 7

Holder, Eric, Jr., 112, 125

Holt, Rush D., Jr., 112

Home Box Office (HBO), 78

Home computers
  at birth of Internet, 5
  video game industry and, 70

Home electronics, 133, 141–142

Home-Based Workers in the United States: 2010 (Mateyka, Rapino, & Landivar), 138

Honda, ASIMO robot, 143

Horrell, Paul, 143

"The Hottest Game in Town" (Davies), 70

How Americans Use Instant Messaging (Shiu & Lenhart), 17

"How the Heartbleed Bug Slipped under the Radar More than Two Years Ago" (Eadicicco), 59

"How to Deposit Checks with Your Smartphone" (Johnston), 46

"How to Preserve the Web's Past for the Future" (Kuchler), 12

"How to Survive a Cyberwar" (Bloomberg.com), 107

HRP-4C robot, 143

Hsiao, Chun-Ju, 127

HTML (hypertext markup language), 6, 7

HTTP (hypertext transfer protocol), 6–7

Hubbard, Amy, 141

Hulu, 79

Human relationships
  dating, social networking users who have used social media to check on past partners or post current dating information, 140(*f*9.8)
  dating process, social networking users who have used social media in, 140(*f*9.7)
  Internet users involved in committed relationship who share online account information with their partners, 136*f*
  Internet users/cell phone owners in committed relationships who feel technology has had negative impact on their partnership, 137(*f*9.5)
  Internet users/cell phone owners in committed relationships who feel technology has had positive impact on their partnership, 137(*f*9.4)
  mobile technology's impact on, 133
  online dating, 139
  online dating, opinions of among Internet users, 139*f*
  technology and, 135–136

Humanoid robots, 143

Hunter, William, 70

Hypertext markup language (HTML), 6, 7

Hypertext transfer protocol (HTTP), 6–7

I

"IBM Hits Back at 'Mainframe Monopoly' Accusations" (Shane), 47

IC3. *See* Internet Crime Complaint Center

"ICANN Urges IPv6 Adoption as Global Address Shortage Looms" (Spencer), 12

iClaim website (SSA), 99

Identity theft
  efforts to combat, 56–57
  on the Internet, 52, 55–56
  overview of, 49–52
  rise in with Internet, 1–2
  victim's information, method of misuse, 56*t*

IM (instant messaging), 13, 17

The Impact of Music Industry Suits against Music File Swappers (Rainie et al.), 76

"In Changing News Landscape, Even Television Is Vulnerable" (Pew Research Center), 80

"In-Class Multitasking and Academic Performance" (Junco), 89

Income
  broadband use and, 8
  digital divide by, 7
  online political engagement by, 109*f*
  public opinion on technological advances by, 133, 134(*t*9.2)
  wireless Internet access and, 9

Indian Council for Research on International Economic Relations, 47

"Information confrontation" strategy, 107

Information Sciences Institute, 5

Information technology (IT)
  attitudes about impact of technological change on future, by sex, age, education attained, income, 134(*t*9.2)
  attitudes concerning impact of hypothetical technological advances, 135(*f*9.1)
  government's use of, 97
  health IT, 126–128
  medical data revolution, 125–126
  national security and, 105–107
  technological advances, adults who believe various advances will occur within next 50 years, 135(*f*9.2)
  See also Daily life, high technology and; Government

Information technology (IT) industry
  currency and, 44–46
  effects of on U.S. business, 34–37
  gross output by industry, 35*t*
  IT boom, end of, 33–34
  lost jobs in, 34
  mass layoffs in, 36*t*
  maturing of, 34

overview of, 31–33

types of, listed, 33*t*

See also Business, U.S.

"Ins, Outs of Getting Meds from Overseas" (Jablow), 124

Instagram
  monthly visitors to, 136
  use, frequency of, 19

Instant messaging (IM), 13, 17

Instant Messaging Market (Radicati Group), 17

In-Store Mobile Commerce during the 2012 Holiday Shopping Season (Smith), 140

Intellectual property crimes
  Bittorrent portals, numbers of global visitors to, 63*f*
  copyright violators, creative industries fight against, 60–61
  DOJ prosecution of, 61–62
  Internet users seeking copyright infringing content online, numbers of, 62*f*
  investigated/prosecuted by DOJ, 62*t*
  overview of, 59–60

"Intelligence: Behold the All-Seeing, Self-Parking, Safety-Enforcing, Networked Automobile" (Horrell), 143

Intellivision, 70

Internal Revenue Service (IRS)
  use of ACH system, 46
  website of, online tax returns with, 98

International Criminal Police Organization (Interpol), 125

International Space Station, 143

International Telecommunications Union (ITU), 11

International Trade Administration, 42

Internet
  alternate realities with, 141
  at colleges, social life and, 88–90
  at colleges, use of, 86–88
  computer games on, 71
  computer network hierarchy, 6*f*
  conception of, 13
  cyberbullying via, 137–138
  elections/politics engagement via, 107–108
  fraud, 57
  future incarnations of, 12
  health app usage, 120(*t*8.3)
  health care on, 119–120, 122–123
  health information online, percentage of Internet users who search for, 121(*t*8.5)
  health resources, impact on, 119
  home electronics linked to, 142
  identity theft on, 52, 55–56
  medication online, 123–125
  music file sharing on, 75–76
  as news outlet, 80

R